The Biology of Streams and Rivers

Biology of Habitats
Series editors: M. J. Crawley, C. Little, T.R.E. Southwood, and S. Ulfstrand.

The intention is to publish attractive texts giving an integrated overview of the design, physiology, ecology, and behaviour of the organisms in given habitats. Each book will provide information about the habitat and the types of organisms present, on practical aspects of working within the habitats and the sorts of studies which are possible, and will include a discussion of biodiversity and conservation needs. The series is intended for naturalists, students studying biological or environmental sciences, those beginning independent research, and biologists embarking on research in a new habitat.

The Biology of Rocky Shores
Colin Little and J. A. Kitching

The Biology of Polar Habitats
G. E. Fogg

The Biology of Ponds and Lakes
Christer Brönmark and Lars-Anders Hansson

The Biology of Streams and Rivers
Paul S. Giller and Björn Malmqvist

The Biology of Streams and Rivers

Paul S. Giller and Björn Malmqvist

OXFORD
UNIVERSITY PRESS

OXFORD

UNIVERSITY PRESS

Great Clarendon Street, Oxford OX2 6DP

Oxford University Press is a department of the University of Oxford.
It furthers the University's objective of excellence in research, scholarship,
and education by publishing worldwide in

Oxford New York

Athens Auckland Bangkok Bogotá Buenos Aires Calcutta
Cape Town Chennai Dar es Salaam Delhi Florence Hong Kong Istanbul
Karachi Kuala Lumpur Madrid Melbourne Mexico City Mumbai
Nairobi Paris São Paulo Shanghai Singapore Taipei Tokyo Toronto Warsaw
with associated companies in Berlin Ibadan

Published in the United States
by Oxford University Press Inc., New York

First published 1998
Reprinted 1999, 2000

A catalogue record for this book is available from the British Library

Library of Congress Cataloging in Publication Data
Giller, Paul S.
The biology of streams and rivers / Paul S. Giller and Björn
Malmqvist.
(Biology of habitats)
Includes bibliographical references and index.
1. Stream ecology. I. Malmqvist Björn. II. Title.
III. Series.
QH541.5.S7G55 1998 577.6'4—dc21 98-8281
ISBN 0 19 854977 6 (Pbk)

Printed in Great Britain
on acid-free paper by
Bookcraft Ltd., Midsomer Norton, Avon

Preface

Although they make up less than 1% of the world's water, freshwaters play a vital role in life on planet Earth. Running water or lotic habitats comprise a tiny proportion of these freshwaters, yet they offer important resources to mankind and are rich and complex environments in their own right. Running water, like fire, holds a fascination to the human eye, and to the freshwater biologist this fascination extends below the water surface. From the earliest descriptive investigations, it became clear how morphological and behavioural adaptations of the organisms related to the major environmental conditions of the habitat, particularly flow, substrate and water chemistry, as well as species interactions. The boundaries of research later expanded along the length of the river channels and out onto the banks and beyond, emphazising the important links between the surrounding landscape and the stream and river channels. The consideration of short-term and seasonal changes and flood and drought disturbances also changed our view of these habitats and historical and biogeographic factors added a longer-term perspective to the study of streams and rivers. Much of the progress in our understanding of these systems has been based on the purely scientific quest for knowledge, but without such knowledge we will be unable to conserve and manage the most valuable freshwater resources for humankind.

Rarely has the breadth and complexity of all these aspects of the biology of streams and rivers been dealt with in a single volume. The aim of this book is thus to delve into the rich and growing literature and to provide an up-to-date introduction to stream and river biology. We have done this by building on a foundation of the factors that make running water habitats unique, describing the different kinds of watercourses, and exploring the great heterogeneity of these systems in space and time that help to explain the variation we see and the often high biodiversity. We then outline the range of living organisms and how they are adapted to the habitat templet set by the physical, chemical, and biotic factors. We discuss the most important population, community, and ecosystem patterns and processes such as energy flow, decomposition and nutrient cycling, movement and colonization, species interactions, food webs and community structure and species diversity, and expand the scale to historical and biogeographic perspectives. The book finishes with a discussion of applied issues. This includes the use of water resources and pollution and the threats that exist to biodiversity in running waters around the world and the conservation and management of these habitats. A short section outlining a range of practical biological and ecological studies and a second providing further reading have been included to encourage the reader to delve further into the biology of streams and rivers.

The majority of scientific work on the biology of streams and rivers has been conducted in Northern Hemisphere, temperate, small to medium-sized systems, and while this bias naturally holds for this book, we have tried to provide examples from many different kinds of lotic habitats from all around the world. Similarly, as much of our own research has focused on freshwater invertebrates we have tended to concentrate more on these groups than others. We make no apology for this bias because the invertebrates have been the subject of so much of the work on streams and rivers and because they are so important in all aspects of life in running waters. But again, we have included much on vertebrates and plants and give examples of further readings on them.

This is a sister book to *The biology of lakes and ponds*, also in this series. It is written primarily as an undergraduate text for students in biological, ecological, and environmental sciences, but also provides an overview of the subject for those embarking on a career in freshwater biology and the water industry or with interests in other areas of science and technology associated with freshwater environments. *The biology of streams and rivers* should also appeal to those with a genuine interest in life below the water surface.

As well as being a unique habitat full of interesting organisms and intriguing patterns and processes, the river is also a powerful force in nature. A quote from Mark Twain following the creation of the Mississippi River Commission in 1879 sums this up well; '... ten thousand River Commissions, with the mines of the world at their back, cannot tame that lawless stream, cannot curb or confine it, cannot say to it "Go here" or "Go there" and make it obey, cannot save a shore which it has sentenced, cannot bar its path with obstruction which it will not tear down, dance over and laugh at.' It is in the face of this kind of power that life has evolved in running waters and we hope this book will ignite the same sparks of interest that have kept us and fellow freshwater biologists world-wide so intrigued by streams and rivers.

We have benefited greatly from discussions with friends, colleagues, and students during the preparation of this book. We are grateful to Scott Cooper, Sebastian Diehl, Chuck Hawkins, Steve Kohler, Gary Lamberti, John Morse, Christer Nilsson, Mark Vinson, and Bruce Wallace for providing unpublished data and helpful advice. We are especially grateful to John Gee, Colin Little, Staffan Ulfstrand, and Roger Wotton for patiently reading and critically commenting on earlier drafts of the book. Görel Marklund's wonderful artistic skills have contributed the many original drawings. The art work was generously sponsored by the foundation Längmanska Kulturfonden. Fidelma Burnell helped tremendously with the typescript. The support and confidence of Cathy Kennedy of Oxford University Press was instrumental in seeing the project to a successful conclusion. Finally, we dedicate the book to Janet and Anita, without whose support and forbearance we would never have managed.

Cork and Umeå
December 1997

Paul Giller
Björn Malmqvist

Contents

1   Running waters: a unique habitat

Uisce Beatha is Irish for whiskey but it actually translates as 'Water of Life'. While some may see this as the *raison d'être* for water, this phrase has a rather different connotation to the aquatic biologist, as water provides the very habitat in which aquatic life exists. Aquatic ecosystems range from the open oceans and intertidal marine systems, to freshwater lakes and streams and rivers. There will obviously be some overlap in the patterns and processes among these systems and trying to identify these similarities can only further our understanding of the natural world. However, there is sufficient that is unique about streams and rivers, the subject of this volume, to make their study an intriguing and rewarding experience.

For a start, the evolutionary origins of many members of the running water biota are quite different from those of marine systems and a substantial number of the marine groups are missing. Running water, or 'lotic', systems were probably the primary pathway for the evolutionary movement of many animals from the sea to land (Thorp and Covich, 1991), but the dominant freshwater groups (notably the insects) invaded from the land rather than the sea. Lotic systems are more permanent on both ecological and evolutionary timescales than most lake habitats. This persistence provided ample opportunity for evolution and the development of a unique flora and fauna. Many taxa of freshwater invertebrates are virtually confined to running waters, largely as a result of the unique environmental characteristics of these systems. Streams and rivers are thus likely to have been the ancestral habitat for many organisms. Chironomidae (midges), Odonata (dragonflies and damselflies), Ephemeroptera (mayflies), and Plecoptera (stoneflies) are all believed to have evolved in cool running waters. In fact, one can find a fair degree of world-wide uniformity in freshwater lotic insects, often with the same families and genera occurring in widely separated geographical localities. For example, the torpedo-shaped larvae of the baetid mayflies are a dominant group in Europe, North America, and Australasia.

Running waters range in size from a small trickle a few tens of centimetres wide emerging from a spring to a massive river the size of the Amazon, flowing over 6400 km in length and reaching over 3 km wide in places. The nature of these systems as habitats is characterized by this flow of water within the channel. This can range from swift or torrential and cascading in headwaters that arise in upland areas to the slow-flowing, downstream backwaters of large rivers and canals where, in many respects, conditions begin to resemble those of still waters. Running water habitats are conspicuously rich and complex environments for biological study.

Apart from their important fish stocks and their scenic beauty, they are teeming with other kinds of life forms. Running waters also provide a range of consumer processes for man, from provision of drinking water to their use as an important conduit for effluents from industrial, domestic, and agricultural sources. The variation in water quality requirements for these processes and the requirements for the maintenance of biodiversity of natural communities have led to the well-publicized conflicts in the management and conservation of streams and rivers. A full understanding of how these unique ecosystems function requires a true interdisciplinary approach, incorporating hydrology, water chemistry, and some environmental engineering in addition to, of course, biology. We will be concentrating on the biology of streams and rivers, but to understand this fully we must briefly explore these other disciplines as well.

Water resources, stores, and fluxes

World-wide, rivers and streams drain an area of land of approximately 150 million km^2, and the average water volume carried in the world's river channels at any one time is just over 2000 km^3. While this may seem a lot, it represents only a tiny fraction of freshwater resources on earth, most of which is stored in the polar ice caps (the majority in Antarctica) with the rest held in groundwater and soil stores, the atmosphere, lakes, and marshes. Freshwater in turn represents only a small proportion of the total global water resources, the vast majority of which (>97%) are salty (Table 1.1). There is, however, a rapid turnover of water in river and stream channels, with a mean residence time in the system (time taken for complete replacement of the water) of around 7–14 days. It is estimated that 30 000 km^3 of water is discharged by rivers to the worlds oceans every year (Milliman, 1990), with the ten largest rivers accounting for 40% of this total. Greatest inputs are from tropical and subtropical areas where the highest rainfall occurs.

The rapid turnover of water in rivers and stream channels is driven by the hydrological cycle, which involves the continuous recycling of water among the various storage compartments in the biosphere (Fig. 1.1). Replenishment of

Table 1.1 Distribution of freshwater resources. (From Keller, 1984.)

	Proportion of freshwater resources (%)	Contribution to total global water budget (%)
Polar ice caps, glaciers, snow, permafrost	69.56	1.761
Groundwaters and soil store	30.1	0.76
Atmosphere	0.04	0.001
Freshwater lakes	0.26	0.007
Marshland	0.03	0.0008
Running waters	0.006	0.0002
Biological waters	0.003	0.0001

Fig. 1.1 The global hydrological cycle showing the various storages (boxes; $km^3 \times 10^6$) and fluxes (arrows; $km^3 \times 10^6$ per year) of water on earth. (Modified from Newson, 1994, with data from UNESCO, 1978.)

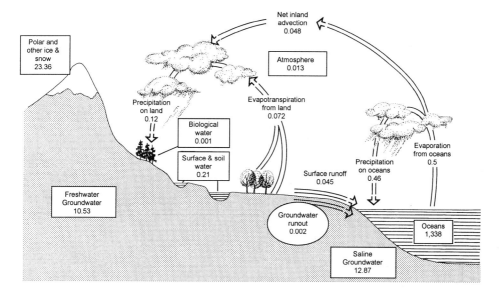

surface water relies on precipitation. Simplistically we can start with evaporation of water from the oceans and the land and evapotranspiration from terrestrial vegetation into the atmosphere, driven by solar energy. Winds then transport moisture-laden air over the landscape. Clouds form when air becomes saturated and water vapour condenses into droplets or ice crystals around nuclei of dust, smoke particles, or salt. This accumulated burden of water then falls to earth as precipitation, particularly when clouds are forced to rise when passing over high ground. The average global rainfall is about 1030 mm per annum. At any one time, the atmosphere only holds enough water to satisfy the annual rainfall of the Amazon (Keller, 1984), but there is a rapid turnover of water in the atmosphere of approximately every nine days.

The proportion of precipitation that ends up as streamflow depends on the weather, soil type and development, vegetation, slope of the land, properties of aquifers (groundwaters), and other local factors. Leopold (1962) calculated that of the 760 mm average annual rainfall in the United States, only 230 mm (35%) ends up in river channels. Very little rain falls directly into streams and rivers. Some precipitation is intercepted by vegetation before reaching the ground and evaporates. Some water passes through the vegetation and into the soil, where it is taken up by plants, and again returns to the atmosphere via evapotranspiration. Drying out of soils by evaporation also returns water to the atmosphere. Still more water percolates down through the soil into the water table where it recharges groundwaters. Alternatively, precipitation may be held over winter as snow or ice. The remainder finds its way downhill to streams and rivers (Fig. 1.2). If soils have

Fig. 1.2 The river catchment, illustrating the general features of the local hydrological processes above and below the surface and the importance of the riparian vegetation to the lotic habitat. (Based partly on Newson, 1994.)

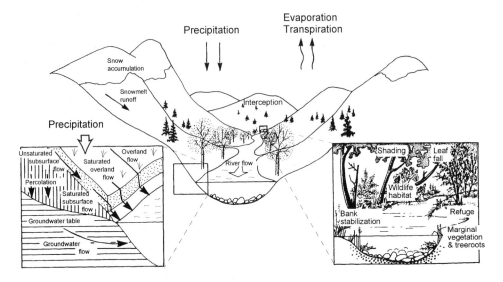

low permeability because they are arid, frozen, compacted, or waterlogged and if precipitation exceeds the infiltration capacity of soil, rainfall can travel as surface runoff directly into stream and river channels but this overland flow is relatively rare. Rainfall percolating into soil can flow just below the surface (subsurface flow) if there is a relatively impermeable layer between the surface and the water table. Alternatively, rainfall that has infiltrated deeper into the soil can be released more slowly from groundwater stores by displacement to enter stream channels from below the surface. There is a tendency to forget, however, that many headwater systems are derived from springs where groundwaters emerge directly onto the surface of the land. The hydrological cycle is completed by the downstream flow of water, which eventually discharges into the sea.

What is important to glean from this simplified description of the hydrological cycle is not just the fact that streams and rivers get their water from a number of sources, but that the water itself has had intimate contact with the atmosphere, vegetation, soil, and rocks before entering the freshwater habitat.

The catchment

Until relatively recently, freshwater biologists considered that the boundaries of rivers extended only from the air–water interface to the bed of the river or stream, but we now know that there are dynamic interactions between the channel and the surrounding landscape (Fig. 1.2). This link was emphasized in H.B.N. Hynes's (1975) famous essay 'The stream and its valley'. The river 'catchment' or drainage basin is the natural unit of landscape, combining the linked terrestrial and aquatic ecosystems, and it encompasses the entire area of land drained by the various tributaries and the main river. Movements of water and elements through the catchment link various components of the system; biotic and abiotic, terrestrial and aquatic, plants and soils, atmosphere and vegetation, and soils and water (Hornung and Reynolds, 1995). Landscape features also tend to govern water movements within catchments and land forms (known as watersheds) such as ridges and hills delimit the extent of the catchment and separate one catchment from another.

Many types of streams derive a considerable portion of their energy from organic matter produced in other ecosystems ('allochthonous' material)—either from further upstream or in the form of detritus (dead organic matter like leaf litter, twigs, etc.) from the surrounding terrestrial ecosystem. As one moves from the stream channel to the land, one crosses the 'riparian zone', an important boundary between aquatic and terrestrial systems. The riparian zone (which includes all the bankside and closely surrounding vegetation) not only supplies organic matter like leaf litter but also influences temperature and light levels through shading, thus affecting instream ('autochthonous') plant production. This zone also controls bank erosion and sediment input (Fig. 1.2). As streams grow into larger rivers, the influence of the riparian zone gradually decreases, hence the relative importance of allochthonous versus autochthonous energy sources changes downstream (Chapter 6).

As most of the water entering streams has been in contact with the soil of the catchment, the soil and ultimately the geology of the catchment have a great impact on the water chemistry. For example, streams flowing through catchments based on igneous rocks (e.g. granites) usually have low levels of dissolved salts and can be acidic, while those flowing over sedimentary rocks (sandstones, limestones) have relatively high levels of dissolved salts, and are either circumneutral or alkaline. Calcium and pH levels in particular have a direct influence on animal and plant communities. Vegetation in the catchment influences the concentration of ions (such as calcium and magnesium) in the soil and the rates at which various ions are delivered to the streams and rivers. Terrestrial vegetation, and in particular coniferous trees, also influences the chemistry of the rainwater falling through the vegetation, often acidifying the throughfall that then reaches the soils (see p. 46).

The pattern of water movement in the stream itself is affected by the slope of the valley, the depth and permeability of the soils, and the local pattern of precipitation. Vegetation in the catchment also plays a role. It does this by increasing the rate of movement of water from the soil to the atmosphere through evapotranspiration and thus creating more storage space in groundwaters so less rainfall eventually reaches the stream channel. Forests, for example, can reduce the amount of water leaving a catchment in the stream by over 30% compared to a non-afforested catchment. Direct links between riparian and aquatic communities tend to be weaker in larger, wider rivers, but the unidirectional flow of water means that the downstream reaches are very much influenced by upstream ecosystems, which in turn are influenced strongly by the surrounding catchment. The interactions between land and water are not always one way, however. Rivers which have extensive floodplains often deliver nutrient rich sediments onto the land. Floodplains themselves, when inundated, can offer highly productive aquatic habitats, especially for fish.

Running waters also provide a link between terrestrial and marine ecosystems. As a result of the erosion and transport of sediment particles from the channel beds and banks, it is estimated that the rivers of the world carry approximately 13.7 billion tonnes of suspended material to the oceans per year, mostly concentrated in the Indian Ocean and China Sea (Milliman and Meade, 1983). Rivers and streams also carry dissolved solids, with an average concentration of 120 mg l^{-1}.

Hynes (1975) concluded that in every respect, the valley rules the stream. The geomorphology of the valley determines the soil (and availability of ions) and slope of the land. Soil and climate determine the vegetation. The vegetation determines the supply of organic matter and, together with the soil, influences water chemistry and water inputs to the stream. Human activity in the catchment too has large effects on streams and rivers, sometimes direct and obvious, sometimes subtle, which has meant that management of lotic ecosystems must be on a landscape scale rather than simply associated with the channel itself. In order to understand the biology of streams and rivers holistically, it is therefore necessary to consider the entire drainage basin, incorporating both the aquatic system and its surrounding catchment.

Catchment area obviously changes with distance from headwaters as more and more tributary streams merge, carrying the influence of their separate catchments with them. The large rivers drain a substantial portion of land surface; the Nile 2 803 000 km^2; the Amazon 6 000 000 km^2, and the Yangtze 1 808 000 km^2 (Cushing et al., 1995). It obviously becomes very difficult to study them on such a large scale. The development of geographical information systems (GIS) and remote sensing such as Landsat has helped, but much of what we know about the function of stream and river ecosystems and the linkages with the catchment has been derived from studies of the much smaller headwater sections, where catchment areas are in the 1–100 km^2 range. How much this has clouded or biased our understanding of running water ecosystems remains to be seen, but at present we are rather limited by techniques, methods, and modelling power to this small-scale approach.

Scale

Scale is important in biology. The way we look at the habitat, from the size of our sampling unit (from the particle to the entire catchment) to the frequency or duration of our observations, will influence how we identify biological responses to the environment, how we perceive the various patterns in biotic and abiotic factors, and what processes we deem to be important in the functioning of lotic systems. Different processes operate on different timescales. In a stream, local surges of flow occur over seconds, while large-scale variation in water levels and temperatures will occur over seasons to decades to hundreds or thousands of years. Most biological samples collected and measurements taken are at the spatial scale of the sampling point, the size of the sampling device, or the transect or stream reach. If the spatial scale is extended further, it rapidly leads one out onto the surrounding landscape and into groundwaters (Fig 1.2). In effect, freshwater biology at the larger spatial scales merges with terrestrial ecology and landscape ecology (Hildrew, *et al.*, 1994).

Different levels of generalization therefore apply, depending on the scale we are working on. Stream biologists face spatial and temporal scales that extend over approximately 16 orders of magnitude (Minshall, 1988) but these can be divided into six general categories, from particle to stream systems (Fig. 1.3). Organic and inorganic particulate matter extends over the lower half of the spatial range, habitat and landscape features over the rest. The larger the scale, the slower the processes and rates of change. Individual organisms, sand grains, rocks and leaf litter, etc. comprise the 'particle' system which together form the 'microhabitat' system, on a scale of centimetres, persisting for weeks to years. The sub-reach scale of the 'pool–riffle' system includes the substrate surface and the hyporheic (below the surface of the substrate) subsystems and regions of exchange between them. The hyporheic subsystem is biologically active, with upwelling and downwelling zones where the water is forced to the surface or infiltrates into the sediments (Grimm, 1994). Riffles are areas of fast turbulent flow and pools are slower and deeper. The 'reach' system includes one to several sub-reaches of upwelling and downwelling zones and pool and riffle sequences, covering metres to tens or hundreds of metres and persisting in their present location for tens to hundreds of years. Broader units of reach and stream section are likely to have existed hundreds to thousands of years, although the exact position may have altered; for example, lowland channels tend to wander across the floodplains over time. Entire drainage basins ('stream' system) covering tens to hundreds of square kilometres have probably a long geological history, and some of the major rivers of the world are several millions of years old.

What is interesting about river systems is that they seem to be hierarchically organized (Frissell *et al.*, 1986; Hildrew and Giller, 1994), where the higher-scale systems described above impose constraints on features of the lower scales. An example will help to illustrate this point. On a single stone, algal distribution is usually controlled by features of flow, turbulence, and hydraulic forces over the stone. At a given stream site, algal biomass and community structure may be controlled by the process of nutrient limitation. Over larger stream reaches, local zones of high nutrient supply may alleviate this limitation, allowing a shift of control of algae to grazing invertebrates or fish where they are important (Fisher, 1994) or, where grazers themselves are limited by water chemistry, to general stream flow and substrate size. Over long periods of time, biomass in large stream reaches may become closely associated with the flood disturbance regime and shading from riparian vegetation. The influence of deforestation in the catchment on channel morphology will act on a spatiotemporal scale vastly different from the effect of grazing insects on algal dynamics. Yet deforestation has implications for

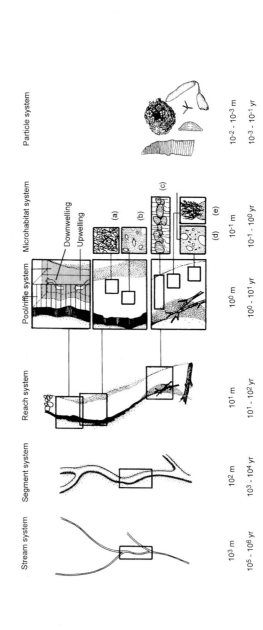

Fig. 1.3 Scale and persistence in stream systems. The figure illustrates the hierarchical classification of stream habitats (after Frissell *et al.*, 1986. Reproduced with permission of Springer-Verlag) showing approximate linear spatial scales and persistence. (Modified from Hildrew and Giller, 1994.) In the microhabitat system, (a) leaf and stick detritus in pool margin; (b) sand-silt over cobbles in the pool; (c) transverse bar over cobbles in riffle; (d) fine gravel patch, and (e) moss on boulder. The particle system contains mineral particles, faecal material, organic fragments, hyphomycete conidia etc.

grazer–algae interactions (through light, sediment levels, etc.), emphasizing the hierarchical relationships (Ward, 1989).

Thus we can see that external physical processes act on different spatiotemporal scales, and each level in the hierarchy has its own characteristic persistence time, disturbance regime, and spatial extent. The biota respond in turn to this set of interlinked physical subsystems—the 'habitat templet' of Southwood (1977). Different organisms perceive this habitat templet in different ways, depending on their size and ecology. To a hippo, a small stream can look like a relatively simple two-dimensional expanse but to an insect larva it is a hugely complicated world, where small-scale variations in the current and substrate provide a highly structured, three-dimensional habitat. Timescales are also perceived very differently by the long-lived hippo and the short-lived insect larva. The size of the organism is also of major importance in determining the nature of the forces experienced by the organism in a given flow rate (see pp. 56, 114). Thus for fish, average stream velocity may be meaningful in influencing their distribution in the stream reach, but to a small insect like the blackfly larva, or to the algal cell, it is the flow and force of water acting on the organism at the very point on which they are resting on the substrate that is of relevance.

The hierarchy of scales involved in the biology of streams and rivers can thus be seen to operate over four dimensions (Fig 1.4).

1. Longitudinal dimension—upstream and downstream—along which there is normally a profound and predictable change in the physicochemical conditions that in turn lead to longitudinal patterns in biotic variables.

2. Lateral dimension, involving the interactions between the stream channel, the riparian zone and the surrounding catchment (i.e. incorporating the land–water interface). There is also some lateral interaction below the substrate surface, where extensive hyporheic systems have been documented, extending up to 2 km from the river channel (Stanford and Ward, 1988).

3. Vertical dimension, primarily involving the interaction between the river waters and contiguous groundwaters through the hyporheic zone. The extent of this zone depends on the permeability of the substrate and subsurface flow of water. In this vertical dimension, one should also consider the air–water interface, which plays a role in stream ecosystem function and on which a number of specialist forms live.

4. Temporal dimension, where predictable changes in physicochemical factors and the biota relate to seasonal aspects and less predictable changes in the structure and function of stream and river ecosystems can be related to flood disturbances, climatic changes and changes in land use or vegetation of the catchment. As the Greek philosopher Heraclitus quite rightly claimed, 'one cannot step into the same river twice'.

Fig. 1.4 The four-dimensional nature of stream and river ecosystems. (Adapted from Ward, 1989.)

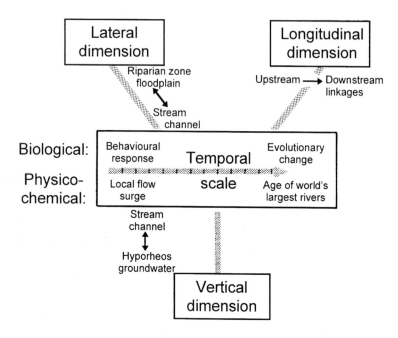

The lotic biota

We have seen that natural running water ecosystems are characterized by dynamic interactions that operate over a range of spatial and temporal scales, within and beyond channel boundaries. This poses a range of adaptive challenges that have been met during the evolution of the biota. There are four useful methods of classifying the running water biota that also impart something of their biology. In this introductory chapter, we outline the various categories and will deal with them in more detail in later chapters.

1. *Microhabitat* (Fig 1.5). The 'pleuston' occurs on the water surface, where organisms make use of the high surface tension. Marginal/shallow water vegetation includes the rooted, larger aquatic plants (macrophytes) found near the banks or rooted in shallower substrates. Biofilm consists of bacteria, fungi, algae, and detrital and silt particles enmeshed in a gelatinous polysaccharide matrix that clothes rocks or wood in the stream channel. Algal mats occur on stones and rocks (periphyton) or on plants (epiphytes). The flowing nature of rivers largely precludes floating/suspended plankton and pelagic forms (other than relatively large swimming vertebrates) except in the larger, deeper downstream reaches or slow-flowing pools in some geographical areas. Most of the animal life exists in, or on the surface layers of, the substrate, an assemblage of organisms known as the *benthos* (Fig. 1.5). However, there are a number of different microhabitats to consider on the stream bed. Some are related to flow (fast turbulent riffles, slow and

Fig. 1.5 A transverse section of a stream showing some of the various microhabitats. Periphyton and biofilm coat the stones, pebbles, and boulders and detritus from the riparian vegetation collects in slow-flowing areas or forms leaf packs in front of obstructions like woody debris. Coarse substrate is found in the riffles where the flow is fast and turbulent and fine substrate settles in the pools and in the lee of large stones and boulders where flow is slow.

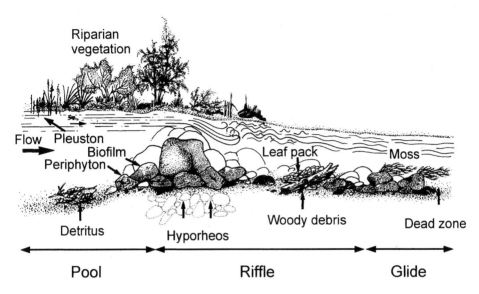

deeper pools, and glides or runs with quite fast but less turbulent flow), some to channel position (such as margins), or others to collections of leaves, twigs, and other woody debris. Many invertebrates can also be found deeper in the substrate (hyporheos) and in groundwaters.

2. *Taxonomy*. This represents the most straightforward basis for classification and it is useful at this point to mention the major groups of organisms found in streams and rivers (see Chapter 4 for more details). Microbes include the fungi and bacteria associated with organic matter and biofilm. Lotic plants include the larger flowering macrophytes that root in the substrate, mosses that cover rocks and boulders, and algae that may form filaments or tufts or are microscopic and form the periphyton or epiphyte layers. Floating algal phytoplankton may be found in slower sections. The dominant invertebrates of most streams are the larvae of insects, particularly the mayflies (Ephemeroptera), stoneflies (Plecoptera), cased and net-spinning caddisflies (Trichoptera), and a varied collection of true flies (Diptera), particularly the midges (Chironomidae) and blackflies (Simuliidae). Dragonflies and damselflies (Odonata), water beetles (Coleoptera) and water bugs (Hemiptera) also occur. Worms (Annelida including oligochaetes and leeches) and various types of snails and bivalves (Mollusca) are found throughout the river system. Among the crustaceans are the larger Malacostraca (including crayfish, crabs, and shrimps), amphipods and isopods, zooplankton which are found in larger rivers, and the diverse group of microcrustaceans, tiny animals (such as Copepoda and Ostracoda) that live within the substrate. The most obvious and

numerous vertebrates are the fish but amphibians, reptiles, birds, and mammals are also important components of the fauna of streams and rivers.

3. *Size*. Microbes represent the smallest forms but freshwater animals and plants also vary over a considerable size range. Plant size varies from unicellular algae, to planktonic forms, to mosses and larger rooted macrophytes. Animal size ranges from microbial protozoa, to microcrustaceans found largely in the hyporheos, to macroinvertebrates (mainly insects, larger crustaceans, annelids, etc.), to vertebrates (from small fish and amphibians to river dolphins, hippos, and large reptiles).

4. *Functional feeding group*. Classification can simply be as 'autotrophs' (the producers including macrophytes, periphyton, epiphytic plants, and phytoplankton) or 'heterotrophs' (from decomposing microorganisms to animals that all rely on ready-made organic matter). However, macroinvertebrate heterotrophs in particular have been further classified into functional feeding groups. *Piercers* and *scrapers* (grazers) feed on biofilm, periphyton, and epiphytes; *shredders* consume larger detrital particles (coarse particulate organic matter like leaves); *collectors* feed on fine particulate organic matter on the substrate; *filterers* feed on similar but suspended particles; and *predators* and *parasites* feed on other animals (see pp. 133–5).

A unique habitat

What is it about running waters that so distinguishes them from other aquatic habitats? There are perhaps eight major factors that readily come to mind.

1. *Unidirectional*, although far from uniform flow. This means that downstream reaches are influenced to a greater or lesser extent by upstream ones.

2. *Linear form*. Rivers and streams are long, thin systems, often divided, poorly integrated with each other and occupying a relatively small area of the landscape, thus resembling islands in a sea of land.

3. *Unstable channel and bed morphology*. The shearing action of flowing water transports and deposits material from the bank and bed and continually changes the physical environment.

4. *Openness of the ecosystem*. Transport of dissolved and particulate organic matter occurs from source to mouth and there is a close linking of the stream with the surrounding terrestrial ecosystem. This link is largely one-way from land to water in the headwaters, but two-way between water and floodplains in the lower reaches.

5. *High degree of spatial and temporal heterogeneity at all scales*. This varies in space from small-scale variations in substrate size, instream vegetation, and more importantly, current velocity, to larger-scale longitudinal gradients in flow rates, bankside vegetation, and water chemistry that influence both biodiversity and nature of the biota. Over time, relatively short-term fluctuations in current velocity and seasonal changes in allochthonous inputs and discharge are common in many systems. Carrying relatively small volumes of

water at any one time, rivers are liable to be disturbed by climatic extremes and changes, thus the occurrence of droughts and/or catastrophic floods are typical of nearly all lotic systems over longer time-frames. Over historical/ geological timescales, the entire drainage patterns may be altered and river flows reversed by geological upheavals. Few other ecosystems possess either the frequency or intensity of such environmental changes over time (Power *et al.*, 1988).

6. *The apparent hierarchical organization of the ecosystem.* The different systems within the stream or river are nested at successively smaller spatiotemporal scales (from the whole stream system to the individual particle), each influenced by the processes operating at the scale above.

7. *Inter-stream variability is high.* Each stream will tend to differ from the next. Basic characteristics are determined by the river's setting within the particular geology, soil type, and geomorphology of the catchment, the latitude and altitude, and, at a more local scale, the nature of the surrounding land use and riparian vegetation, plus the instream use made of the system by man.

8. *The unique biota*, specialized to life in running waters.

Rivers and streams are fascinating ecosystems to study, but as we have seen they are highly variable both within and between systems and in both space and time. At one extreme, all rivers appear to be identical (bearing water down the slope), but at the other extreme, all are different, as no two streams have exactly the same complement of species or physicochemical conditions at the same relative abundance or levels (Cummins *et al.*, 1984). To further our understanding of the biology of streams and rivers, and to begin to be able to successfully manage and rehabilitate them, we must endeavour to make generalizations and predictions and identify the governing processes from among the variability. Over the following chapters we will explore the range of running water habitats and the physicochemical features in more detail, then discuss the variety of organisms and their adaptations to life in running waters. We will then introduce the various patterns and processes that occur in streams and rivers and consider the factors influencing the conservation and biodiversity of these habitats.

2   Running water habitats

The landscape across which rivers and streams flow is formed through geomorphological and geological processes. Landforms are built up through sedimentation and geological activity driven by volcanism and continental drift and are eroded by wind, ice, and water. These complex processes together determine the outlines of the catchments within which precipitation falls, flows downhill, and ultimately forms the physical channels of running waters.

Rivers are dynamic systems that are born and age. Ageing involves continuing erosion of the stream channel back towards the source or out onto the floodplain. Erosion is greatest in certain areas (e.g. China, the south-eastern United States) which is shown in the rivers' particularly heavy silt loads. Typically, river channels have extended lifespans compared to lakes. The world's really large rivers, along with their great age and diversity, also have many unique organisms and a myriad of ecological processes that have a significant influence over the entire catchment system they drain. Unfortunately, these systems have suffered more than any other from man's influence, and few remain in a natural, unaffected state. During periods of large-scale climate change such as glaciations, rivers can be 'consumed' during the formation of ice sheets. Following recession of the ice, rivers can be reformed in old channels or be created in new ones. The development of these new riverine habitats can be readily studied today where glaciers are retreating, as in Glacier Bay, Alaska (Milner, 1994). These cold streams show an interesting rapid succession of primary colonizers piloted by a simple community of hardy chironomid midges that are gradually being replaced by more complex communities including mayflies, stoneflies, caddisflies, and salmonids as the stream temperature increases over time (see p. 199).

Patterns in drainage basins

Despite the immense spatiotemporal heterogeneity of streams and rivers we introduced in Chapter 1, at certain scales of analysis we can see quite distinct patterns in the drainage basins of lotic systems, which give us some insight into their origination and development.

Stream size and stream order

At the landscape scale, running water systems consist of tributary streams that erode the landscape following the weaker strata of bedrock and then gradually coalesce to form the main river as it flows downhill—the drainage pattern (Fig. 2.1). Surprisingly, if one creates imaginary drainage patterns on graph paper by random allocation of direction of flow (N, S, E, or W) towards which each square will drain, the picture shares some of the characteristics of natural systems. If one adds a bias in one direction that mimics the slope of land, then the analogy becomes even closer (Hynes, 1970). While this may give the impression of randomness, there are in fact clear patterns in natural drainage basins. Imagine viewing the drainage system from an aeroplane; you would see a hierarchy of tributary streams which can be classified following the stream order scheme of Strahler (1952). Thus 1st order streams are single, unbranched headwater channels, 2nd order streams are formed when two 1st order streams meet, 3rd order streams are formed when two 2nd order streams meet, and so on. Stream order only increases when two streams of equivalent rank merge (Fig. 2.1). Large rivers, such as the Mississippi and the Nile, are 10th order and the Amazon 12th order. Classifying streams in this way is a useful convenience for organizing information of a spatial nature and helps the biologist when analysing longitudinal changes in stream characteristics within a single catchment, but care should be taken when comparing across catchments.

Fig. 2.1 An example of a river drainage basin (the River Ouse, Sussex, UK) showing the classification of stream orders. (Redrawn from Crosskey, 1990.)

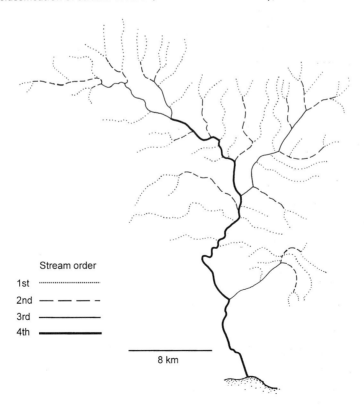

Stream order

1st ·······················

2nd — — — —

3rd ——————

4th ▬▬▬▬

8 km

Clearly, the total number of streams of each order decreases as stream order increases. For Great Britain, for example, there are over 146 000 1st order streams, over 36 000 2nd order streams, but only 66 6th order and 4 7th order rivers (Smith and Lyle, 1978). If one plots the points as log number of streams of each order against stream order, a straight line results. In fact, similar plots of 'log mean length of stream' of each order or 'average drainage area of streams' in each order against stream order also give straight line relationships (Leopold *et al.*, 1964). The river length (L) actually increases with drainage area (A) according to the following relationship:

$$L = 1.4\,A^{0.6}.$$

Bankfull discharge (the amount of water that fills the entire stream channel to the top of the banks) also increases log-linearly with drainage basin area, thus size and depth of channel increase downstream as more water is discharged from the increasing catchment area.

Stream morphometry patterns

Streams do not usually flow far in straight lines, but tend to meander with gentle or sharper bends. Channels may also divide into a series of branches—braiding— especially in middle to lower reaches of rivers, in response to variation in discharge, the nature of the sediment, and the presence of erodable banks, as well as the activity of certain 'animal architects' like beavers. In both straight and meandering segments, water velocity varies longitudinally and sediment on the stream bottom is eroded continuously from some areas and deposited in others. This leads to the alternating sequence of shallower, higher velocity, riffle areas with coarse substrates and deeper, lower velocity, pools with fine substrate. In steep mountain streams, the pool–riffle sequence is replaced by a pool–step sequence where water cascades over short waterfalls, plunging into small scar pools. Due to the hydrodynamic features of running water (see Chapter 3), riffles tend to be spaced 5–7 stream widths apart and so there are typically two riffles per 'wavelength' of a meandering channel reach (Leopold *et al.*, 1964). The distance between meanders is related to several factors, most notably width, and the average meander wavelength is 10–14 times channel width. If you look at an aerial photo of a large river and the meanders of a small stream, the pattern is almost identical.

Runoff and flow patterns

Runoff represents the portion of rainfall that eventually finds its way to streams and leaves the catchment as stream flow. It varies considerably with geography, but is very high in tropical rainforest areas in South-East Asia, West Africa, and tropical South America, and also in some temperate areas including western Canada, southern Alaska, western Norway, southern Iceland, northern Scotland, the Alps, and south-western Chile. Seasonal influences on runoff lead to characteristic patterns of flow in different parts of the world (Fig.2.2).

Fig. 2.2 Discharge patterns over the year vary markedly between different geographical regions. Not only does precipitation matter but also factors such as evapotranspiration and seasonal variation in temperatures. (Redrawn from the *National Atlas of Sweden*, edited by B. Raab and H. Vedin, 1995. Bokförlaget Bra Böcker, Höganäs.)

Dry with no or low discharge most of year

Low winter discharge. Warm and humid

Low summer discharge. Warm and humid

Perennial flow. Warm and humid

Perennial flow. Cold winters, warm summers

Low winter discharge. Montane with snow and glaciers

Low winter discharge. Cold winters, cool summers

Areas with inland ice.

Whereas some rivers show great fluctuations in flow, others remain almost constant throughout the year, especially where they are regulated by damming. Some streams show seasonally predictable flow patterns, others are erratic. This flow variability is an important factor in the biology of streams and rivers to which we will return to later.

Longitudinal patterns

Almost everything about rivers changes longitudinally as one travels from the headwaters downstream. The typical lengthy river is often described as originating in mountainous areas from springs and rivulets, coalescing to fast-flowing, turbulent, and shallow streams. These in turn join with other tributaries to form a large, smoothly flowing, deeper river that meanders through the lowlands to the sea. Associated with the increase in stream size with distance from the source is a decrease in direct influence of the surrounding landscape on the functioning of the running water ecosystem. The boundary between the stream edge and the land is relatively sharp in headwaters but much less so as one progresses downstream, especially where there are seasonal changes in water levels (Naiman *et al.*, 1988). The slope of the channel decreases, discharge increases, variability and nature of flow change, and, in unpolluted systems, so does water chemistry in a quite predictable longitudinal pattern downstream.

These longitudinal changes in physical and chemical characteristics impose significant consequential changes on ecosystem processes (such as decomposition, community respiration, primary production) and patterns (such as standing stock of organic biomass, species richness of invertebrates and fish, and community structure) (Statzner and Borchardt, 1994). Physicochemical changes will be examined in more detail in Chapter 3 and the biological patterns in Chapter 6. Suffice to say at this point that these changes along the lengths of rivers should be visualized more as a complex patchwork of conditions rather than smoothly continuous gradients of conditions often seen on land. In any event, these various and regular patterns in physical characteristics of river systems indicate that there are strong processes at work, which are in turn probably related to hydraulic processes associated with the nature of flowing water.

Below we describe a range of lotic habitats. The selection could have been much larger had space allowed and included, for example, chalk streams (which are well-buffered streams with very constant flow and with few tributaries, as found in parts of southern England), blackwater streams (characterized by high amounts of humic substances), acid streams (low pH systems, often fishless, and with low numbers of most invertebrates), and beaded streams (which are small streams connecting deep pools in subarctic and arctic systems). However, the following sections will give the reader a good idea of the variety of systems and, more importantly, the range of environmental conditions to which running water organisms may be exposed. We also indicate the major or characteristic groups of organisms (with specific families in parentheses) that may be found in these habitats, and readers are referred to Chapter 4 for more detail on these various animals and plants.

Types of lotic habitats

Low- to mid-order temperate streams

By far the largest proportion of studies in stream habitats has been carried out in low- to mid-order streams in temperate areas of Europe and North America. These are typically of coarse substrate, relatively shallow, with riffle–pool sequences and variable flow patterns in space and time. They would typically rise in uplands surrounded by moorland or forested vegetation and flow down through agricultural and/or urban landscapes. Because so much is known about these streams, this bias in the literature is naturally reflected to a considerable extent in this book and hence the nature and functioning of these systems is described in some detail throughout the text. However, the rest of this chapter introduces examples from other biomes or habitat types that are less well studied or of special interest.

Madicolous habitats

Perhaps the simplest lotic habitat is where thin sheets of water constantly seep over rock faces to form a flowing film. Such habitats are called *hygropetric*, or *madicolous* if the water also trickles over other types of substrate (e.g. moss and mud). The nutritional base of these habitats lies in local primary production of algae that typically supports a species-poor assemblage of grazers, including fly larvae and snails, and more rarely predators. Light levels, and thus the aspect of the land, are of importance to algal production.

Although any one site may be species-poor, many species have been found in madicolous habitats, but relatively few of them are restricted to them. Animals found here may also occur in the marginal wetted zone just above the waterline of streams and in the splash zone of torrents and waterfalls (see below). Vaillant (1956) recorded more than 400 species from 74 sites in France but only 83 were confined to madicolous environments. Species that are specialized to these particular conditions are found among the water mites (Acari), beetles (including the suborder Myxophaga and some dytiscids such as *Hydrotarsus*), caddisflies (Trichoptera, especially in the families Philopotamidae and Hydroptilidae), and fly larvae of many families (Tipulidae, Psychodidae, Thaumaleidae, Cerato-pogonidae, Chironomidae, Stratiomyidae, and Dolichopodidae) (Sinclair and Marshall, 1986).

Springs

These occur where groundwaters discharge to the surface of the ground at a more or less restricted point. This can be either at the lowest ground elevation of an aquifer (groundwater store), or where less permeable rocks force the water to the surface (van der Kamp, 1995). In general, flow, water chemistry, and temperature are fairly constant, at least where the springs are fed with water slowly seeping through fine materials. This has led to spring habitats being used as natural laboratories for a variety of ecological studies and experiments. Not only can processes relating to temperature, water flow, or chemistry be conveniently studied along longitudinal gradients (e.g. Crowl and Covich, 1990, in sulphur springs in Oklahoma) but so also can those relating to upstream–downstream linkages of energy (e.g. Odum's 1957 famous Silver Spring study). The status of spring organisms may also be used for assessing groundwater quality (Williams and Danks, 1992).

The species diversity of springs is often low. This may have several explanations. One of the most obvious ones is that each spring is isolated from other springs, which could lead to a dispersal problem for the biota. Alternatively, springs are often quite harsh environments, such as the hot springs (see below), or due to the lack of available food or in some cases intermittent flow of water. Some authors have, however, described springs with quite a varied and unique fauna, such as among the caddis-flies (Erman and Erman, 1995). Springs with permanent flow have stable substrates, which in turn could favour rich growth of aquatic plants.

In areas with geothermal heat flow 'hot' springs may occur. These thermal springs often deviate from non-thermal springs in their chemical properties, but most often temperature itself appears to be the most important factor for their biota (Pritchard, 1992). Warm-adapted species of odonates, bugs, beetles, and dipterans are generally the most important insects. Few of these tolerate temperatures above $40°$ C. Some peracarid and ostracod crustaceans can live at temperatures exceeding $50°$ C (Covich and Thorp, 1991), but the most resistant metazoan is the nematode *Aphelenchoides* sp. which has been recorded at $61.3°$ C (Poinar, 1991). The thermal spring fauna, at least in terms of insect orders present, is quite different from those of non-thermal springs. Therefore, it is believed that thermal spring insects may have originated from water-margin habitats of lakes (Pritchard, 1992).

Torrential habitats and waterfalls

These are associated with steep gradients and high water velocities ranging between 0.5 m s^{-1} near the stream bed and 6 m s^{-1} (the approximate velocity in high water falls) (Murvosh and Hogue, 1991). Such habitats are, of course, most often found in mountainous environments, and their substrate consists of bedrock or large boulders. Where water is cascading or falling, a more or less extended splash zone develops along the margins of the waterbody which has its own characteristic features and biota. This wetted zone is not unlike the madicolous habitat with which it also has organisms in common.

It is not easy to define a torrential lifestyle. Many of the animals dwelling in fast-flowing, torrential conditions are not really directly exposed to the current but forage under rocks; others only come out from such refuges for short feeding bouts. There are very few taxa that more or less permanently use exposed surfaces at fast flow. Specialist adaptations for such an existence are found in their morphology and behaviour, and will be discussed in Chapter 5. Despite the very harsh conditions, torrents may in fact be benign habitats in terms of the low predation risk. Characteristic components of the torrential fauna include beetles of the family Psephenidae, known as water pennies, fly larvae (including members of the families Simuliidae, Blephariceridae, and Chironomidae), mayfly larvae of the family Ephemerellidae, some stoneflies (from the families Taeniopterygidae, Peltoperlidae), and some caddis larvae (from the families Hydropsychidae and Rhyacophilidae). It should be noted that torrential flow often favours the presence of aquatic mosses. This is supposed to be due to an increased availability of carbon dioxide. The mosses, in turn, offer a microhabitat for animals. Supersaturation of gases associated with torrential habitats could also have a negative effect. For instance, this may kill fish below waterfalls and dams.

High latitude and altitude streams

Although streams all over the world may show many similarities, the fact remains that streams at high altitudes and latitudes are quite different. This is due to their harshness as an environment, particularly with respect to low temperatures and food levels. Nevertheless, specific adaptations allow organisms to exist even here, and despite a reduced diversity common to harsh environments, productivity may remain quite high at high latitude, at least during the summer (Howard-Williams *et al.*, 1986).

Antarctic, arctic, and high altitude streams are mainly fed by melting glacial ice. Water deriving from glaciers is often turbid (from the fine inorganic material produced by glacial abrasion) and, of course, cold. While glacier streams are generally species-poor, some taxa, such as chironomid fly larvae, are found at elevations above 5000 m in the Himalayas, feeding on cyanobacteria and bacteria beneath the ice (Sæther and Willasen, 1987). Milner and Petts (1994) characterized glacial rivers as having six attributes: (1) a seasonal ice melt giving rise to one summer peak in discharge; (2) daily fluctuations in flow, peaking in late afternoon; (3) summer water temperatures below 10° C; (4) high turbidity; (5) low levels of dissolved salts (conductivity); and (6) unstable and braided channel morphology close to the glacier, but more stable downstream. The diel variation in flow, temperature, and nutrient content of these streams is due to daytime thawing and freezing at night. Therefore, within-stream rather than catchment physical processes tend to have the greatest influence on the biota. Aspect is also important.

Where animals are scarce, as in Antarctica, microbial biomass can be very high (Howard-Williams *et al.*, 1989) despite the low temperature (mean daily summer temperature: 5° C). Most antarctic streams have microbial mats dominated by cyanobacteria covering the substrate. Such streams can reach rates of nutrient uptake and epilithic production comparable to those of temperate streams. Although biomass is high, turnover is low. Because of the lack of terrestrial vegetation, the surrounding catchment contributes little to the production in these streams. Instead, the production probably relies on wind-borne nutrients trapped in the glacier. This fact leads to gradual nutrient depletion in the stream as one moves further downstream. In addition, biological activity in the streams is sometimes associated with the activities of marine birds and seals. One interesting example is where a particular stream runs through a penguin rookery, where transient but high nutrient levels typically occur at the first flow of the season (Howard-Williams *et al.*, 1986). These systems appear not to be nitrogen-limited.

Although both arctic and antarctic streams are glacier-fed and have marked daily variation in flow, antarctic streams differ in having totally barren catchments and stream beds that completely dry up. Howard-Williams *et al.* (1986) reported that more than 100 streams in southern Victoria Land in Antarctica (latitude about 77° S) flow for only 1–2 months per year. There are also habitats with only seeping water and only a few large rivers, the largest of which, the Onyx river, is less than 40 km long. Despite temperatures dropping to –55° C in winter, the antarctic biota, consisting mainly of algae with associated bacteria, fungi, and microherbivores (protozoa, nematodes, and tardigrades), is apparently able to survive the winters in a freeze-dried condition.

The stream fauna of arctic Alaska is dominated by dipteran larvae followed by plecopterans and ephemeropterans. Many insect groups are scarce compared to temperate regions and net-spinning caddisflies, truly lotic beetles, several families of stoneflies, and burrowing mayflies are extremely scarce or absent. Total invertebrate densities are, suprisingly, not markedly lower than in temperate regions. In the Alaskan Kuparuk river, an arctic tundra river flowing over permafrost, phosphorus is limiting to the growth of microbiota, as it is in many arctic ecosystems (Hullar and Vestal, 1989). We will return later to this river (pp. 163–4), where interesting fertilization experiments have been conducted.

Ice and snow, not surprisingly, influence streams and rivers in colder climates. Since snow limits incoming light, production is negatively related to the thickness of snow cover. Yet ice, being translucent, may play an important role in providing a substrate for benthic algae (cryoperiphyton). For example, in the large Asian River Amur, significant primary production takes place on the lower surface of the ice, especially in those parts of the river that are in the floodplain (Bogatov *et al.*, 1995). Many invertebrates appear to tolerate being frozen into ice or sediment during the winter. Those which do not have adopted other overwintering strategies such as lateral migration away from the freezing-prone littoral zone (Olsson, 1981). Reduced space beneath the ice also drives fish to deeper, ice-free parts of the river.

Intermittent and temporary streams

These streams are common in both arid and Mediterranean climates. In contrast to permanent streams, parts of intermittent streams dry up, often leaving a series of pools which may only be connected through subsurface flow. When the bed dries up completely for periods exceeding three months, these systems are sometimes classified as temporary streams. The fauna of these habitats consists partly of generalist invertebrate taxa common in permanent streams and partly of inhabitants with special adaptations that allow temporary survival in alternative habitats, including the hyporheic zone and disconnected pools, or in drought-resistant stages (Delucchi and Peckarsky, 1989). Some species show life cycle adaptations that are well suited to the intermittent flow regime, but these species may also be present in a permanent stream. Evidence for a specialized intermittent stream fauna is thus scanty.

The duration of flow in intermittent streams sets the level of environmental harshness. While those streams with water present for a large part of the year can have a fauna resembling that of permanent streams, those with short periods of flow only support a restricted set of species. If intermittent streams are also subject to flash floods caused by storms, only a very limited fauna can survive. Species tolerant to intermittency need adaptations in terms of diapause (suspended development) or aestivation (dormancy during the dry season), behaviour to avoid desiccation and increased dispersal capabilities to allow colonization from other habitats. Those tolerant of the unpredictable floods may be small bodied, with accelerated and asynchronous development, and avoid floods through behaviour (see Chapter 5).

During periods of drought many species may be wiped out from reaches or entire streams. In extreme cases species may go through population bottlenecks as in Gran Canaria in the Canary Islands, where the lack of one winter's rains may reduce the number of flowing streams to a fraction of that in normal years. When rain revives the desiccated streams, most of the colonization is from the permanent streams.

Since temporary streams are most commonly found in summer-dry areas, it is not surprising that we construct dams in order to store water for the dry period, especially for irrigation and domestic use. This practice further increases the length of the dry period for downstream habitats as, for example, in the Algarve in Portugal, where rivers essentially cease to exist below dams for most of the year. We will return to this type of conflict where human water usage interferes with requirements of the natural biota in Chapter 9.

Rivers in arid regions

A majority of continental rivers may be classified as dryland rivers, since they flow in arid zones. Despite this fact, they have received far less attention than the streams and rivers of the much wetter temperate zones of the Northern Hemisphere. This is both surprising and unsatisfying, given the value of water in such environments, whether in Africa, Australia, or elsewhere. Naturally, dryland rivers differ in many respects from those in wetter temperate zones. In South African rivers, one especially important factor seems to be the extremely low predictability and high variability in discharge patterns depending on the random nature of rainfall (Davies et al., 1995). This should counteract the evolution of species-rich biota, which instead can be predicted to consist of hardy generalists.

Another major difference to most other types of rivers is the openness of the banks and the limited riparian vegetation of low-order streams leading to relatively low input of leaf litter, high temperature, and potentially high autochthonous primary production by algae and macrophytes. Furthermore, dryland rivers may be considerably saline, partly as a consequence of high evaporation, but also because runoff from the surrounding catchment brings chloride from fossil marine sediments. When humans use arid zone river water for irrigation purposes the situation may deteriorate further. An example of serious concern is the situation in the Aral Sea area, where extensive irrigation programmes have reduced the major tributaries to mere salty trickles (Fig. 2.3).

Fig. 2.3 The river discharge (km³ yr⁻¹) into the Aral Sea decreased considerably during the period 1926–90. (Data from Gleick, 1993.)

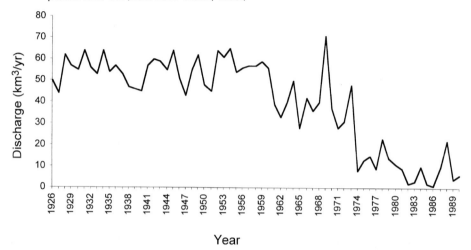

A feature of permanent desert streams, at least in the south-western United States, is that they normally have very low discharges in relation to their drainage areas, a fact that results in very strong effects of the rare rainstorms, which produce flash floods. One example involves a study of an autotrophic stream in the Sonoran Desert, USA, where Fisher *et al.* (1982) found that recurrent flash floods virtually flushed the stream clean of organisms. Yet, recolonization by algae and benthic invertebrates was accomplished within a few weeks and the annual secondary production in this stream is among the highest reported: 135 g dry mass per square metre ($\approx$ 68 g C m⁻²). This is similar in cool desert streams of eastern Washington state although production levels are lower there (Gaines *et al.*, 1989). Apparently, small, short-lived deposit-feeding and filtering collectors (such as mayflies, blackflies, and midges), feeding on an abundance of autochthonous fine detritus, are responsible for the high production in such systems. The river channels are shaped by flash floods and are typically wide relative to the actual wetted stream channel. Primary production in these desert streams is frequently nitrogen-limited and producers chiefly occur in patches dominated by diatoms, filamentous cyanobacteria and green algae, and macrophyte beds (Grimm, 1994).

Lake and reservoir outlets

Where water flows out of lakes extremely productive communities can occur relative to other lotic systems. The fauna found in these lake outlets is partly a specialized one. Typically, many animals filter phyto- and zooplankton of lake origin. It has been suggested than this abundant, high-quality food resource can explain the high productivity, but other factors may also contribute. For example, lake outlets tend to be warmer than downstream habitats. Flow is also more stable, since the lake dampens fluctuations in discharge caused by rainfall, so water levels only rise and fall gently. This reduces the otherwise potential disturbance of flow stress discussed in Chapter 3.

It is clear that this 'lake effect' rapidly declines with distance downstream from the lake outlet, although the rate of decline is related to the magnitude of discharge. In small lake-outlet streams, the lake effect is more restricted than in large rivers, where a visible influence from the lake may occur several kilometres downstream from the lake itself. It appears as if the decline in the lake effect takes place concomitantly with changes in the quality and quantity of the suspended particles transported in the water column. Along with the rapid change in abiotic factors, there is a gradual, downstream transformation in the faunal composition (Fig. 2.4). Near the lake, biomass is greatest and the scene is set for strong biological interactions. Typically there is a dominance of strong competitors such as hydropsychid net-spinning caddis larvae. This may negatively influence diversity in near-lake habitats. The most productive outlet systems show reduced species richness, probably as a consequence of the very high density of hydropsychids (Malmqvist *et al.*, 1991; Malmqvist and Eriksson, 1995).

The number of undisturbed lake outlets is rapidly decreasing on a global scale. Man, for various purposes, including hydroelectric production, flood control, and irrigation, has dammed a large proportion of the rivers, using natural lakes as reservoirs or creating new ones. Dammed rivers often have flow patterns that are strongly altered compared with the natural situation (e.g. in Scandinavia this means high winter flow and low early summer flow, instead of the normally low winter and high early summer flow). This has, of course, led to dramatic changes in the biota (see pp. 223–6). In many other respects, rivers below man-made lakes show many similarities to natural lake outflows.

Fig. 2.4 Downstream succession of five species of net-spinning caddis larvae in a Swedish lake-outlet stream. (Redrawn from Brönmark and Malmqvist, 1984.)

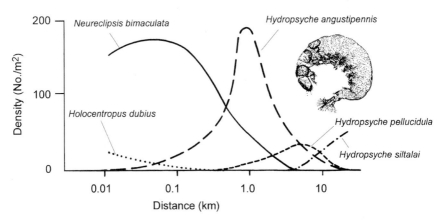

Large and floodplain rivers

Few other lotic ecosystems have been more altered by man than the large rivers of the temperate regions. Unfortunately, little is known of their original conditions. The human impact on some tropical rivers has, however, been less intrusive; the Amazon is still relatively unaffected.

The world's largest rivers are on the largest continents. Large rivers are immensely complex systems in terms of the nature of water flow, riparian zone, catchment, and biota, and it may be difficult to describe them in general terms. To this one must add the fact that they frequently traverse several climatic and geomorphic zones. Many of the large rivers are several million years old and their biota has thus evolved over a considerable period. Typically, many have very high fish species diversity. For instance, in the Amazon basin 2000 species have been found (although many are still undescribed). The complete invertebrate biota and the full nature of ecological processes are virtually unknown in the large rivers of the world (Thorp and Covich, 1991).

Current velocity in the main river channel is generally higher than it at first appears and is usually greater than in upstream reaches (see Chapter 3). Large rivers may therefore not be as lake-like as is often believed—generally no thermoclines form or major oxygen depletions occur within the water column because of currents. Often large rivers are very turbid, a fact that leads to low primary production; for this reason such rivers are often heterotrophic (depending on the import of ready-made organic matter). The benthos may also be depauperate as the substrate is often very unstable. In certain sections of the Amazon river, the substrate consists of fine particles that are formed into eight-metre high unstable sand dunes (Sioli, 1975), which of course provide a harsh environment for animals requiring a firm substrate. In such circumstances submerged wood, roots and trailing branches, and twigs from riparian vegetation can be very important as they provide relatively stable and solid microhabitats for many invertebrates. However, even in the sandy reaches, specialized organisms can be highly productive. This is the case for small chironomid species inhabiting blackwater rivers (so called because they are heavily coloured by humic substances) in the south-eastern United States (Benke et al., 1979). Important macro-invertebrate taxa other than dipterans inhabiting sandy habitats in large rivers include oligochaetes and the larvae of burrowing mayflies and dragonflies.

Floodplain rivers are found where regular floods form lateral plains outside the normal channel which seasonally become inundated, either as a consequence of greatly increased rainfall or snow melt. Some examples of some important floodplain rivers are given in Table 2.1. The surrounding landscape is often forested, and the floodplain river systems are characterized relatively more by lateral than downstream–upstream processes in comparison with rivers with a more constrained channel (Fig. 2.5). Not only does the surrounding land influence the river as described earlier, but the river water at high levels also fertilizes the flooded land. Flow away from the centre of the main channel is typically slow in

Table 2.1 Examples of some large floodplain rivers.

Europe	Danube (now much reclaimed)
Asia	Amur, Euphrates-Tigris, Indus, Ganges, Brahmaputra
North America	Mississippi
South America	Magdalena, Atrato, Catatumbo, Orinoco, Amazon, Paraguay and Paraná
Africa	Senegal, Niger, Zambezi, Nile

Fig. 2.5 Transect of the Amazon floodplain showing its vegetation and structural complexity. (Redrawn from Sioli, 1964. Fig. 19.4(c) 1975. Reproduced with permission of Springer–Verlag).

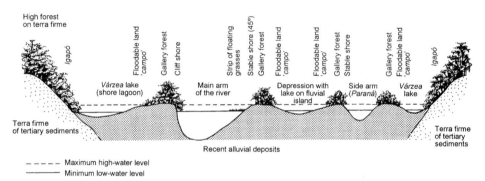

these floodplain rivers and mats of different aquatic vascular plants, such as water hyacinths, are formed in many places.

The scale of the inundated areas ranges from small to enormous. Most tropical and subtropical and many temperate rivers have a fringing floodplain delimited by the walls of the river valley. Typically, their width increases with decreasing slope, which often leads to more elaborate floodplains in the downstream parts of the rivers. Where floods cause economic damage, efforts have been made to contain the river within its channel through construction of levees, retaining walls, etc. Such attempts have a great risk of failing as seen in the 1994 floods of the Mississippi/Missouri rivers. The Danube river had the largest floodplains in Europe, yet today only fragments remain after extensive flood control and damming.

The organisms of floodplain rivers are adapted to changes in discharge and flooding. For many species of fish, this includes migratory behaviours between dry- and wet-season habitats and involves longitudinal and lateral as well as local movements. Some of these have extraordinary capacities to cope with low oxygen concentrations, high temperatures, and desiccation. In South East Asia, floodplains are extensively used for growing deep-water rice, making rice the world's most extensive aquatic macrophyte. Large vertebrates occur in the floodplain rivers, for instance river dolphins enter flooded fields of the Ganges floodplain, and crocodiles are part of such systems in New Guinea (Dudgeon, 1995).

Regional similarities and differences

Many climatic and geomorphological features cause a tremendous variation in landscape patterns and in the flora and fauna between different parts of the world. Obviously, such differences will be reflected to some extent in the representation of different lotic habitats world-wide, as well as in major ecological processes and community structure. Despite this fact, a comparison between streams and rivers of similar gradients and size from around the world clearly shows that there are many striking similarities. This is perhaps not so surprising, given that formation of the lotic habitats is the consequence of basic gravitational and geomorphologic processes following simple natural laws. The greatest differences are seen only when comparing regions with marked differences in climate and geomorphology, which in turn affect temperature and precipitation, and thereby flow patterns, propensity to drought, and riparian vegetation. However, even on a relatively small geographic/regional scale, these factors have an important role for the lotic environment and its biota.

What differences are there? We show some examples below concerning systems where the climate results in more or less extreme amounts of precipitation, and where topography determines important features. This is far from a complete list.

Streams in regions with low summer precipitation may dry up seasonally. This flow intermittency is a characteristic feature of many streams in a Mediterranean climate. Whereas flow at higher latitude may dwindle when the runoff from melting snow cover in the catchment ceases, most higher-latitude and alpine streams rarely dry up. Instead, ice and strongly reduced winter discharge affect the lotic habitats.

In contrast, high precipitation in association with steep gradient and considerable riparian vegetation makes streams in the coastal areas of western North America, and other regions with similar climate and geomorphology, unique through the considerable importance of wood in these streams. Fallen trees contribute to the formation of numerous debris dams which cause major changes concerning in-stream processes and lead to a more step-like profile of the watercourses. High precipitation also contributes to the dilute waters of many streams in tropical rainforests. This fact makes such streams poor habitats with a lower productivity than would be expected at a low latitude.

Large river habitats are very different from those of smaller streams. This is true also within systems, where a gradual change in many of the properties of a running water system is found as the river flows downstream. These changes are partly predictable, at least where the system is in a pristine condition as discussed earlier (see also Chapter 3 and the River Continuum Concept, Chapter 6).

In some lotic systems, such as those on oceanic (especially volcanic) islands like New Zealand, rivers are short and steep. In a sense they reflect incomplete systems, never reaching the higher stream orders. There is also some evidence that rivers in different parts of the world are differently retentive (i.e. they vary in their capacity to retain organic material, such as leaf detritus, which has consequences for the in-stream processing of organic material; see Chapter 6). In short streams with low retentivity, like those in New Zealand, one would expect that much organic material would be lost to the sea.

Low-order streams can be very different across regions. For example, streams originating above the timber line in alpine regions are obviously strikingly different to those emanating from shaded, detritus-loaded forest environments. Low-order streams may often have lower species richness than those of higher orders, although many of those species that do occur are specialized to the small stream environment and do not occur in larger rivers at all.

Biogeographical processes also contribute to the great variations between regions that can sometimes be observed. The long-term dynamic nature of the distribution of organisms often has ecological explanations, and again, the climate may play a role, such as in the case of the dynamics between glaciation and interglaciation periods. Changes in the climate interact with the colonization rates of many plant species, including those forming forests. For instance, in Sweden, the spruce (*Picea abies*) gradually invades areas formerly dominated by deciduous forests in the south of Sweden. Such a shift causes important habitat changes to aquatic ecosystems in, for example, litter fall and the soil and consequently stream pH. Other aspects of biogeography show that the origins of different taxa and their subsequent dispersal within and between regions of the world are extremely important for the understanding of present-day distributions. Perhaps the most important of such historical accounts have been made for lotic midges (Chironomidae). We will discuss such biogeographic patterns again in Chapter 8.

Man causes tremendous changes to the natural lotic habitats by changing the flow pattern of rivers by damming and diverting them, and polluting them. Changes to the lotic habitats are also caused indirectly, for example, via agriculture, acid rain, and clear-cutting of forests. These anthropogenic disturbances are important issues that we will return to later in this book.

3 The habitat templet

Like any other habitat, lotic habitats pose animals and plants distinctive adaptive challenges which are set by the particular and often unique physical, chemical, and biological environment of rivers and streams. To understand how lotic organisms meet these challenges we must first understand the nature of running waters as an environment to live in. Although on the face of it this may seem a reasonably straightforward exercise, things are complicated by the fact that there appears to be a series of interdependent factors that operate in running waters. At the smallest scale, within a pristine stream system, flow patterns, temperature, and substrate seem to be the key physical variables. Oxygen levels are also important to the biota but are largely governed by these three physical factors. The nature of the immediately surrounding catchment influences the flow patterns (through slope) and temperature (through altitude and nature of the riparian vegetation), which are in turn influenced by the local climate. On a larger scale, the geological setting and surrounding land use influence the water chemistry (particularly pH and nutrients) and the riparian vegetation can influence the nature of energy input (through light levels and allochthonous organic matter). The downstream flow of the river from higher to lower altitudes and the associated changes in the rivers' size and form, in turn superimpose a more or less predictable, large-scale, longitudinal variation in physicochemical and biological factors. On a regional basis, flow, temperature and to a lesser extent water chemistry will be influenced by climatic factors (including rainfall, seasonality, etc.). Biogeographical considerations add yet another, even larger scale, layer of factors (which will be dealt with separately on pp. 211–14).

The approach we take in this chapter is to first examine three factors that underpin the basic physiology of organisms, namely temperature, oxygen, and light. The geomorphological setting, encompassing the catchment landscape and substrate are discussed in some detail before concentrating on water chemistry, flow, and hydraulics. Physicochemical factors basically set the environment within which biological interactions are played out. They clearly have a major influence on large-scale distribution patterns of lotic species, but as we will see, some physicochemical features can also influence distribution even at the finest spatial scale. The importance of biological factors, including the riparian zone, energy inputs, and species interactions will be touched on here but will be explored in more detail in later chapters. We also briefly discuss how these various factors influence the biota, but again will refer the reader to later chapters for further details.

Physical factors

Oxygen

Oxygen is required by all aerobic organisms for respiration, yet it is about 30 times less available in water than in air. Oxygen enters water largely via diffusion from the air at the water surface. However, oxygen solubility in water is negatively correlated with water temperature. Pure water in equilibrium with air at standard atmospheric pressure has an oxygen concentration of 12.77 mg l^{-1} at $5°$ C but only 8.26 mg l^{-1} at $25°$ C (Wetzel, 1983). Levels also vary with current speed and turbulence; small fast flowing, turbulent, unpolluted streams are usually saturated with oxygen, whereas pools and stagnant bays, especially with a high organic load of dead leaves, can have relatively low levels. The presence of macrophyte vegetation can also affect oxygen levels. As oxygen is a by-product of photosynthesis, heavy plant growth (especially during summer) can lead to supersaturation during the day. However, concentrations can decrease significantly during the night due to respiration and carbon dioxide levels can increase. In some systems oxygen levels can change from 36 to 164% saturation over 24 hours (Moss, 1998). Longer-term variation can also occur where streams suffer from extended ice cover and due to temperature fluctuations associated with seasons. The amount of groundwaters entering streams can also influence oxygen levels, as groundwaters usually have low concentrations, and similarly, any instream impoundments will tend to reduce oxygen and increase carbon dioxide levels. Dangerously low levels will usually only occur in severely organically polluted sites or through a combination of drought (low flow), high temperature conditions and dense instream vegetation. In addition to these more local variations, as a general rule, oxygen levels decrease downstream, as the upper reaches tend to be more turbulent and cooler and have a greater surface area to volume ratio for diffusion from the atmosphere.

Influence of oxygen on the biota

The current continually replenishes water and hence also oxygen in the immediate vicinity of the respiratory surfaces of the animal or plant and quite low levels can be tolerated in strong currents that renew oxygen at a high rate. In addition, many animals show respiratory movements to further supplement oxygen delivery rates (see p. 124). Generally, metabolic rates and oxygen demand are higher in stream invertebrates than in still water forms at a given temperature. Respiration is temperature-related and rates can increase by 10% or more per $1°$ C temperature rise. Thus not only does increased temperature reduce oxygen availability but it also increases oxygen demand which can add to the physiological stress of organisms.

Species do differ in their respiratory ability and oxygen requirements, as evidenced by different responses to organic pollution that reduces oxygen, and these differences may in turn contribute to differences in species distributions. Many organisms also show clear preference for cold waters which may have as much to do with the effects of temperature on oxygen availability as with the effects of temperature *per se*. For example, stoneflies tend not to occur where temperatures can exceed 25° C largely due to their oxygen requirements (Hynes, 1970).

Temperature

Most freshwater animals and all plants are poikilothermic, such that their temperature varies with that of their surroundings. Physiological processes (such as respiration, digestion, muscle activity, photosynthesis, etc.) are based on bio-chemical reactions and biochemical rates are dependent on ambient temperature. Growth rates, productivity, and length of life cycles are also temperature dependent in poikilotherms. Hence it is clear why temperature should directly influence freshwater biota in addition to the indirect effects on oxygen concentrations mentioned above.

Water is heated by solar radiation and conduction from air or the earth beneath. Heat is lost through radiation at the surface, through evaporation and through conduction at the surface and to the substrate. An outline of the major factors influencing the temperature regime of a stream is given in Fig. 3.1. Water has a very high specific heat—it requires more heat energy to raise the temperature of a unit mass of water by 1° C than most other substances. Practically, this means it takes water longer to heat up and cool down than air. This can be clearly shown in a small stream by monitoring air and water temperature over a 24 hour (diel) period (Fig. 3.2).

In shallow streams, the turbulent water is relatively well mixed and generally isothermal within a single reach at any one time, but diel fluctuations are relatively larger than in deeper waters. Thermal stratification, as found in deep lakes, is rare in running waters, and only deep (>15 m), slow-moving, rivers exhibit a significant

Fig. 3.1 Major factors determining a river's temperature regime. (Modified from Ward, 1985. Reproduced with kind permission of Kluwer Academic Publishers.)

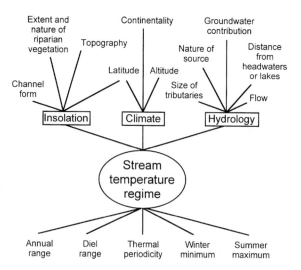

Fig. 3.2 Diurnal temperature fluctuations in a wooded, temperate, shallow stream in March, compared to air temperatures 5 cm and 125 cm above the stream. (Unpublished data, P.Giller.)

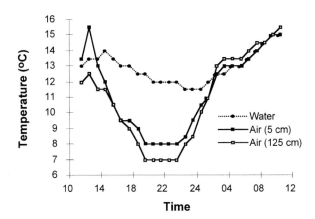

temperature difference between the surface and the bottom waters. Stream temperatures remain fairly constant where there is a large influx of groundwaters or near the source of spring-fed streams, as groundwater temperatures tend to approximate to the mean annual air temperature. For example, water in British chalk springs is constantly close to the annual mean air temperature of 10–11° C. Diel variability tends to increase away from the source and peak in mid-water reaches (Statzner and Higler, 1985) but the large water volumes in lowland rivers tend to reduce diel variability considerably. The lowland Amazon, for example, is always within a few degrees of 29° C (Lewis *et al.*, 1995). There is also a general pattern of increasing temperature with distance from headwaters, especially where the source originates in uplands—in Europe this rise is more or less proportional to the log distance from the source (Hynes, 1970). Tropical streams generally have lower diel variation in middle and low reaches, where air temperatures vary less, but at high elevations, tropical streams are more like temperate systems and show considerable diel and longitudinal temperature variation (Covich, 1988).

The degree of shading by riparian vegetation also influences temperature. Shading tends to lower mean summer temperatures and reduce the daily duration of higher temperatures. For example, in Alaska, streams with substantial riparian vegetation (and no close contact with permafrost) tend to have summer maxima of 12–14° C, whereas streams with no riparian canopy have annual maxima of 21–24° C (Oswood *et al.*, 1995). Similarly, following clearfelling of riparian trees, summer maxima of temperate streams can increase by 6–7° C (Gray and Edington, 1969). Steep canyon or valley walls can have a similar shading effect. Longitudinal temperature patterns can also be influenced by impoundments and dams especially if thermal stratification occurs in the reservoirs upstream of the barrier (see pp. 224–5).

Seasonal variations will be most pronounced in desert, temperate and Arctic systems. In the latter two regions, annual river temperatures can range over 20° C, in intermittent desert streams over 40°C. In contrast the annual amplitude of temperature in equatorial rivers and rainforest streams tends to be only a few degrees (Lewis *et al.*, 1995). Seasonal fluctuations in temperature tend to increase downstream in most boreal, temperate, and Mediterranean systems. For example, in the Spanish River Ter, headwaters vary from 3 to 6°C, whereas middle stretches vary from 4 to 20°C (Sabater *et al.*, 1995).

Extreme maxima can exceed 80°C in hot water springs. Extreme minima in Alaska can lead to complete freezing of streams in winter. Further south, some surface freezing may occur and in very harsh winters this can even happen in large rivers (as in the River Thames in London in the early 1960s), but further cooling is usually prevented by insulation from snow and ice on the surface. Even when river channels freeze solid, there is likely to be free-running interstitial water. What is more serious for the biota is the formation of underwater ice. Frazil or slush is a supercooled layer of water that can reach considerable thickness and scour the substrate. Anchor ice forms in riffles or on upstream faces of large stones in shallow (<50 cm) waterbodies and can spread as a few cm thick layer over much of the stream bed (Hynes, 1970). It can impede flow and scour and carry substrate when dislodged.

Influence of temperature on the biota

Temperature unquestionably sets limits to where species can live and species are generally adapted to certain temperature regimes. As mentioned earlier, the effect of temperature on the biota may be indirect through its influence on metabolic rates and oxygen concentration. For example, coldwater stenothermal fish like salmonids have a high metabolic rate and oxygen demand and an upper incipient lethal temperature of around 24–28°C depending on the species (Elliott, 1994). In Canadian rivers, where weekly maxima exceed 22°C, only marginal trout populations survive (Mackay, 1995). Likewise, the longitudinal distribution of hydropsychid caddis species seems to be related to temperature (Fig. 3.3). The downstream series of species is associated with progressively higher summer temperatures, and species differ in metabolic rates. The temperature at which metabolic rate reaches 1 mg O_2/g dry wt/h increases from 14.5°C for the uppermost *Diplectrona felix* to 21°C for the most downstream *Hydropsyche pellucidula* (Hildrew and Edington, 1979).

Most components in the life history of insects, such as egg development, larval growth rates, emergence time, adult size, and fecundity, are affected significantly by temperature. These will be discussed in more detail in Chapter 5. For brown trout, a curvilinear response is seen, where growth increases from around 6 to 15°C and then declines at 19.5°C (Elliott, 1975). Increased temperatures lead to increased feeding and digestion rates but also increased metabolic rate and respiration; thus there is a balance between energy gains and losses at the threshold temperature. Such influences on growth rates must have consequences for life cycles but rather than considering actual temperatures *per se*, cumulative temperatures seem to be more useful. 'Degree days' are calculated by summing

Fig. 3.3 The distribution of hydropsychid caddis larvae in tributaries and lower reaches of the River Usk in Wales. The values in parentheses give the mean summer temperatures (°C). (Redrawn from Hildrew and Edington, 1979.)

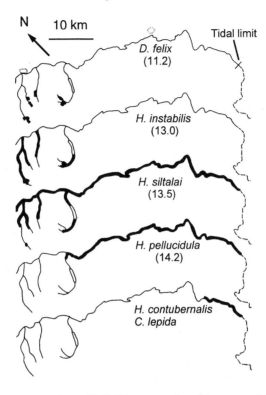

daily mean temperatures above 0° C. There are clear biogeographical patterns in annual degree days, which decrease with increasing altitude and increase with decreasing latitude towards the tropics. In Quebec, eastern Canada, the annual degree days increase from 1702 to 2219 from 1st to 9th order streams (stream order being a surrogate for altitude, Naiman *et al.*, 1987), while in the eastern United States, annual degree days increase from 3000 in northern New York to 7000 further south in Georgia (Webster *et al.*, 1995). These differences lead to variation in the number of generations per year (termed *voltinism*) for individual species of insects. A recent literature survey has also shown that the number of insect orders and families increases linearly with maximum stream temperature and therefore decreases with both altitude and latitude. The relationship is essentially the same in both temperate and tropical streams (Jacobsen *et al.*, 1997).

Light

Solar radiation is a major source of energy in freshwaters and light levels are likely to influence plant populations and primary production rates. The amount of solar radiation reaching stream plants depends on time of year, geography, altitude, state of atmosphere, and local factors including water depth and clarity. Near the equator, for example, solar radiation levels reach $2.16 \text{ kJ cm}^{-2} \text{ d}^{-1}$ with no cloud cover, and vary only $\pm 133 \text{ J cm}^{-2} \text{ d}^{-1}$ over the year. In the arctic however, levels can reach $2.81 \text{KJ cm}^{-2} \text{ d}^{-1}$ in midsummer but zero in midwinter (Maitland, 1990). The amount of radiation received by stream waters also increases with altitude but decreases with increased shading from riparian vegetation (see pp. 37–8).

Significant amounts of light are lost when light strikes the water surface, particularly through reflection. The amount reflected (varying from 20 to 98.5%, Maitland, 1990) depends on the angle of incidence which, in turn, varies with the height of the sun in the sky—the shallower the angle of incidence, the more light is reflected. This will vary with latitude and time of day and can also be influenced by the orientation of the stream valley in relation to movement of the sun through the sky. Once through the water surface, the clarity (or turbidity) and colour of the water affect the transmission of light towards the substrate. In most situations, solar radiation tends to decline logarithmically with depth (Beer's law).

Influence of light on the biota

The role of light as a factor influencing the distribution and abundance of lotic biota is not as simple as one might imagine. While the primary function lies in its effects on photosynthesis of aquatic plants, secondary roles have been identified in the control of animal behaviour and life history patterns. Annual patterns of productivity in temperate lake phytoplankton are associated with seasonal changes in light levels and photoperiod, but suprisingly, under conditions where most variables other than photoperiod and light levels were constant, Sherman and Phinney (1971) found only 9 of 60 stream diatom species were seasonal. Nevertheless, heavily shaded or turbid rivers tend to be devoid of higher plants, and seasonal shading by riparian vegetation can influence periphyton abundance. Likewise, following clearfelling of surrounding shading trees, enhanced periphyton growth has been well documented (O'Halloran et al., 1996). Clear seasonal changes in river macrophytes are associated with a combination of increasing light, daylength and temperature into spring and summer. Some plant species are more abundant in unshaded than shaded stretches and vice versa, such that one can identify shade-adapted and light-adapted plant assemblages. For example, McIntyre (1973) showed a dominance of diatoms over cyanobacteria and green algae in the shade-adapted assemblages (67%, 26%, 7%, respectively) but near equality of diatoms and cyanobacteria (46%, 42%) and more green algae (12%) in the light-adapted assemblages.

There is evidence to suggest that light can influence benthic invertebrate distribution. Some animal taxa, like some plants, show highest abundance in unshaded areas, such as the mayfly *Baetis rhodani*, the cased caddis *Agapetus fuscipes* and *Silo pallipes*, and the beetle *Helodes minuta* (Thorup, 1966). Other taxa prefer shaded areas, such as the larger cased caddis *Limnephilus rhombicus* and *Potamophylax rotundipennis* (Higler, 1975). It is likely, however that this may be partly a response to the effects of light on food sources.

Light may also influence behaviour. For example, it appears to be used as a cue for positional changes related to respiratory regulation, as light is associated with the water–atmosphere interface and hence oxygen/carbon dioxide gradients (Wiley and Kohler, 1984). Many taxa avoid light to keep the organism within the substrate and out of the flow. Light levels also clearly serve as a cue for behavioural drift patterns (see pp. 173–80), where downstream drift dramatically increases at dusk and over night.

Photoperiod is potentially a useful cue for signalling seasonal change, especially in temperate regions, due to its predictability and reliability. However, there is little empirical information on the exact role of photoperiod as a factor influencing life history (Sweeney, 1984). Adult metamorphosis seems to be under the control of photoperiod, especially for Diptera, and daylength may also be important in the phenology of some but not all other groups of aquatic insects (see Chapter 5).

Riparian vegetation

We have already alluded to the importance of riparian vegetation bordering a reach of a stream or river on light and temperature in terms of shading, but it also plays a number of other very important direct and indirect roles that may override the influence of other instream factors (Cummins *et al.*, 1995). The extent of the relationships between the stream and riparian vegetation is related to stream order (Fig. 3.4). Available incident light reaching the stream autotrophs is negatively related to riparian canopy development. From Canadian studies, 1st

Fig. 3.4 Comparison of riparian relationships of pristine streams and rivers of various order. Systems depicted in (a) and (b) show a high influence of riparian vegetation, in (d) intermediate influence, and in (c), (e) and (f) low influence. (Adapted from Cummins *et al.*, 1984.)

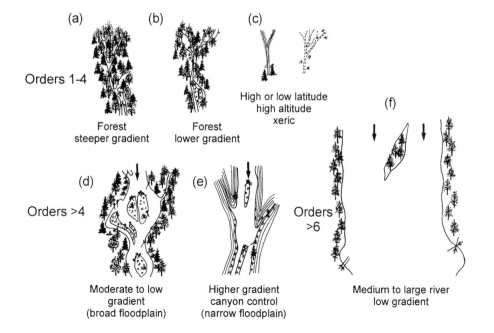

and 2nd order streams may only receive 5–10% of sunlight while in 9th order, relatively shallow rivers, as much as 46% may reach the bottom (Naiman *et al.*, 1987). In tropical moist forests, the canopy reduces irradiance at the forest floor (and stream surface) to 1% of the value at the top of the canopy (Lewis *et al.*, 1995), whereas large rivers are wide enough to be largely unshaded.

The riparian canopy also clearly influences the amount and nature of particulate organic matter (litter) inputs to streams and rivers, which form a very important and often predominant energy base for food webs. Thus the riparian zone influences the relative roles of instream (autochthonous) primary production and inputs of allochthonous organic matter to the stream and river energy budget. We return to this topic in Chapter 6. Macroinvertebrate assemblages in turn can be influenced by the adjacent land use and riparian vegetation, partly associated with the nature of the litter inputs, but also partly associated with the influence on water chemistry.

Vegetation in the catchment influences water chemistry in a number of ways. All vegetation has some capacity to 'scavenge' or intercept chemical ions from the atmosphere onto leaf surfaces and these concentrated ions are subsequently washed off the vegetation by rain and reach the soil and groundwater. Runoff and subsurface flow from the catchment (as described in Chapter 1) thus carries these scavenged ions (following further modification in the soil) to the stream or river. Riparian vegetation also has the capacity to retain nutrients from diffuse sources in the catchment before they reach the river. There is more detail on these aspects on pp. 46–7.

Through evapotranspiration, riparian and catchment vegetation also influences water yield from the catchments to streams and rivers and hence river discharge levels. Models suggest that a 10% decline in stream flow can follow afforestation of 50% of the catchment (Hornung and Reynolds, 1995), and this value can be even higher, as for example in an Irish forest, where stream flows were up to 30% lower than in nearby moorland streams (Giller *et al.*, 1993).

Lastly, riparian vegetation can influence the physical channel morphology of the stream and even the structure of drainage patterns through, for example, bank stabilization by roots and formation of partial or complete large woody debris dams. Riffle–pool–glide sequences can be altered through a tree falling into the stream forming a barrier to water flow, and woody debris and leaves can accumulate in front of obstructions on the stream bed and provide refuges from flow for macroinvertebrates and fish. Indeed, the presence of woody debris has been shown to have positive effects on invertebrate diversity and fish biomass (Bisson and Sedell, 1984; Smock *et al.*, 1992).

Substrate

The overwhelming majority of lotic invertebrates are benthic, hence the nature of the substrate is of prime importance. As Minshall (1984) states 'the substratum is the stage upon which the drama of aquatic insect ecology is acted out'. It provides habitat space for a variety of activities such as resting and movement, reproduction, rooting or fixing to, and for refuge from predators and flow. It also provides food directly (organic particles) or surfaces on which food aggregates (e.g. algae, coarse and fine detrital particles).

Physical properties

The substrate itself comprises a wide variety of inorganic and organic materials. The inorganic material (ranging in size from silt, sand, and gravel to pebbles, cobbles, boulders, and bedrock) is usually eroded from the river basin slopes, river channel and banks, and modified by the current. The organic materials vary from organic fragments and leaves, to fallen trees, derived ultimately from the surrounding catchment and upstream habitats, as well as aquatic plants such as filamentous algae, moss and macrophytes.

Mineral substrate particles can be classified according to size, and the most commonly used scheme is the Wentworth Scale (Table 3.1). This is based on the diameter of each particle size fraction and each category is twice the preceding one. In practice, although it is not easy to categorize a substrate in a stream, one can calculate empirically the relative frequency (or mass or volume) of the different size categories following collection and use of sieves of different mesh sizes or from many point counts of the size of substrate particles within a reach *in*

Table 3.1 Wentworth classification of substrate particle size and current velocity necessary to move particles.

Size Category	Particle Diameter* (range in mm)	Approximate Current Velocity to move Particle (ms^{-1})+
Boulder	>256	
Cobble		
Large	128–256	3.0
Small	64–128	2.0
Pebble		
Large	32–64	1.5
Small	16–32	1.0
Gravel		
Coarse	8–16	0.75
Medium	4–8	0.5
Fine	2-4	
Sand		
Very coarse	1–2	0.25
Coarse	0.500–1	
Medium	0.250–0.500	
Fine	0.125–0.250	0.1
Very fine	0.063–0.125	
Silt	0.0039–0.063	
Clay	<0.0039	

* After Cummins 1962; Tolkamp 1980.
+ After Maitland 1990.

Table 3.2 Nature and size categories of non-living particulate organic matter. (Modified from Cummins, 1974).

Detritus Categories and Subcategories	Approximate Size Ranges
Coarse particulate organic matter (CPOM)	>1 mm
Large woody debris	>64 mm
Terrestrial leaves forming leaf packs	>16 to <64 mm
Leaf, twig & bark fragments, needles, fruits,	
buds and flowers	>4 to <16 mm
Plant and animal detritus, faeces	>1 to < 4 mm
Fine particulate organic matter (FPOM)	>0.5 μm to <1 mm
Ultrafine particulate organic matter	
(includ. microbes)	>0.45 μm to <75 μm
Dissolved organic matter (DOM)	<0.45 μm

situ. Alternatively, one can subjectively describe the substrate visually based on the predominant categories (e.g. boulder, pebbles, and gravel) or state the mean or median substrate size or smallest particle size in a patch or reach. Organic substrate particles can also be classified on the basis of size (Table 3.2). Generally, the smaller particles would function as food and the larger particles as substrate, although some animals do feed on large woody debris. None of these classifications is particularly satisfactory either due to the work involved (frequency distribution), the subjectivity (identifying dominant catagories), or the lack of relevance to the organisms themselves (mean or medium size). Nevertheless, some general patterns in the nature of the substrate are worth describing.

The stronger the current velocity the larger the particle size that can be moved, thus current velocity and substrate type are related (Table 3.1) and mean substrate particle size generally declines downstream. In headwaters, large particles predominate as a result of the proximity of bedrock materials and the erosional ability of the rapid and turbulent flow to move smaller particles. In larger streams on shallow slopes, reduced turbulence and erosional ability (related to reduced shear stress; see p. 58) allows smaller particles to sediment out, thus leading to finer, more uniform substrates. On a smaller, within reach, scale, the flow variation that leads to riffle and pool sequences will also lead to patterns of erosion (and large mean substrate particle size) and deposition (and finer mean substrate particle size). Larger particles can 'protect' smaller ones from being entrained in the current and carried away. Thus in coarser substrates, finer sands and gravels will collect in between or behind the larger particles and increase the heterogeneity of the substrate. '*Embeddedness*' is an index of the degree to which larger particles (boulders and cobbles) are surrounded or covered by finer sediments. A simple index relates to the percentage of surface area of the larger size particles covered by fine sediments (Platts *et al.*, 1983). The higher the embeddedness, the more homogeneous the substrate becomes, and embeddedness will obviously increase in more depositional areas. Such properties also relate to collection of organic matter and detritus on the substrate—so-called '*retentiveness*' of the stream or river. Streams with many obstacles that can act as 'keys' to the accumulation of detritus particles, or with lots of low flow areas of deposition will retain such organic matter for longer than streams with a lower retentiveness. This can have consequences for the diversity and abundance of animal life in the system (see later). Temporal variability in substrate will occur naturally. The 'stability' of the substrate refers to its resistance to movement and is generally proportional to particle size (Table 3.1). Redistribution of substrate and movement of particles will occur during periods of increased discharge following rainstorms, thus the distribution of substrates over the river bed can change over time.

There are a couple of other factors that are also important for macroinvertebrates. Experimental studies by Hart (1978) showed significantly higher numbers of both species and individuals on large than on small rocks as expected but the density was, in fact, lower on the larger rocks—smaller objects have a greater surface area relative to volume than larger ones. However, when the larger rocks were combined into larger patches, they supported higher densities than patches of small rocks. This may be due to the increased microhabitat space for species between rocks as rock size increases. The degree of roughness of individual particles also seems to influence the diversity of colonizing animals; the more complex the surface the greater the species number (Hart, 1978; Thrush, 1979). Single stones present several surfaces to organisms (front, top, sides, back, and underneath) and each surface is under a different flow regime (see later). The actual shape of the particle can thus be influential. The shapes and mixture of particle sizes and the degree of embeddedness will influence the porosity—the size and extent of subsurface pores, tunnels, and spaces within the substrate. Larger and more extensive pores etc. can allow greater subsurface water flow and hence higher oxygen levels and, in fact, a very large portion of the lotic animals live in these microhabitats.

The influence of the substrate on lotic animals

While on the one hand most benthic taxa appear to be substrate generalists, on the other hand, most do show some degree of preference for broad substrate categories, although this may change over the life cycle. Because of this, we can identify characteristic macroinvertebrate assemblages for general substrate types (Ward, 1992a) based largely on a number of factors including:

(1) whether the substrate is living (algae, moss, macrophyte) or dead (leaves, woody debris) organic matter or mineral particles;

(2) the amount of silt on and organic content of the substrate (including moss and algal covering of cobbles, etc.);

(3) particle size and heterogenity of particle size classes and the texture and porosity of the substrate;

(4) stability of the substrate, related to its tendency to move and be retained in the system.

Coarse substrate assemblages: these are ubiquitous and remarkably similar throughout the world. Most prominent types of invertebrates include the small glossosomatid cased caddis larvae, many stonefly families, heptageniid mayflies of the Northern Hemisphere, and the leptophlebiid counterparts of the Southern Hemisphere, Simuliidae, amphipod crustaceans (e.g. *Gammarus*), gastropod snails, and flatworms (platyhelminths).

Gravel assemblages: these overlap a lot with coarse substrate ones. Characteristic fauna include vermiform (long and thin) stoneflies (like the families Leuctridae, Chloroperlidae), elmid riffle beetle larvae, and certain chironomid and tipulid fly larvae, and burrowing mayflies.

Sandy assemblages: these include burrowing midge larvae (e.g. tube-building Chironominae), oligochaetes, mayfly and dragonfly larvae, a few caddis species and sometimes larval lamprey. The burrowing mayfly *Ephemera* is in fact limited to substrates within a particle size range 0.5–3 mm (Hynes, 1970).

Mud assemblages: these occur in a habitat often deficient in oxygen but high in organic matter. A few representatives of mayflies (e.g. *Caenis*), alderflies (e.g. *Sialis*), and stoneflies (e.g. *Leuctra nigra*) often occur along with oligochaetes, chironomids, and some dragonfly species.

Wood (Xylophilous) assemblages: woody debris is quite often densely populated, especially if it offers the only hard substrate in otherwise soft, fine sediments, as in lowland rivers. Most taxa are thus simply facultatively associated with wood, but a considerable number of taxa can be closely associated and some groups, including species of chironomids, caddis and beetles actually consume wood. Characteristic fauna include coleopteran and dipteran larvae, some stoneflies, and caddis (some of which use woody particles to construct cases, e.g. members of the family Limnephilidae).

Assemblages associated with plants: these often hold a diverse and very abundant fauna, especially in association with mosses, that may exceed 15 times the density of bare riffle substrate (Hynes, 1970). Common fauna include chironomids, nemourid stoneflies, the mayflies *Baetis* and *Ephemerella*, and beetles. Rather than acting as a food source itself, moss provides a refuge from flow, attachment sites, and a concentrated indirect food source consisting of attached epiphytes and accumulated detritus. Moss is most common in stony headwater streams, often in forested catchments. Angiosperms on the other hand, like the pond weeds *Elodea*, *Ranunculus*, *Callictriche*, and *Potamogeton*, are more common in less turbulent and deeper middle reaches of rivers. Again, they do not seem to be used directly as a food resource when living (and may contain significant levels of secondary plant defence compounds to deter herbivory). Instead, they offer attachment sites and space for living, as well as holding food sources in the form of epiphytes and accumulated detritus. The numbers of associated animals can again be very high. The primary colonizers are chironomids, simuliids, and caddis larvae and, somewhat surprisingly, there seems to be a general scarcity of predators (Tokeshi, 1994).

The influence of the substrate on diversity

Not only do different substrates harbour different assemblages of animals, but the invertebrate density, diversity, and biomass also vary among them. As a general rule, diversity and abundance tend to increase with substrate stability (which itself increases with mean particle size) and with the presence of organic detritus. Sandy substrates are thus thought to be poorest, due to instability. Within any reach, stony riffles normally have a greater range of invertebrates than pools rich in silt, but if both riffles and pools contain mainly gravels, differences are much reduced (Allan, 1995). Also, as embeddedness increases, biotic productivity of the habitat tends to decrease. The deposition of silt affects inhabitability of the substrate by altering interstitial water movement, clogging interstitial spaces, and reducing oxygen and food availability. Salmonids spawn in gravel beds of a particle size range 0.2–6.3 mm (Christiansen, 1988) called *redds*. If the substrate is too coarse, the redd cannot be created; if it is too fine or silted, egg and fry mortality increases.

These patterns tend to indicate that substrate heterogeneity is also important in controlling abundance and diversity. As median particle size increases, physical complexity increases, up to substrates dominated by large pebbles and cobbles. This should not be surprising, as mixed substrates would provide a greater range of surfaces to colonize and of microflow patterns. In addition, one would also expect both the size range and extent of pores in the substrate to increase within more heterogenous substrates. The more finely divided habitat space becomes, the greater the actual living space that becomes available to ever smaller organisms; thus diversity and abundance will tend to increase. Similar explanations have been applied to explain the very high biodiversity of soils (Giller, 1996b). The increased abundance and diversity of invertebrates on plants which grow in dense clumps, or which have finely divided leaves (see Fig. 4.3b), is a related phenomenon and there is no reason why such considerations should not be applied equally to stream benthos, particularly the hyporheos. In fact, we normally miss much of the small benthic microfauna during normal sampling procedures, but when specifically looked for, this microfauna can be both abundant and diverse.

Because of the above relationships between particle size and heterogeneity, the relationships among particle size and faunal diversity, biomass, and abundance are not linear. All three parameters tend to increase from sand to rubble (pebbles and cobbles), but decrease for large boulders and bedrock (Minshall, 1984).

The influence of the substrate on the fauna is modified by the presence and amount of detritus and vegetation. Leaf packs, collections of leaf litter that form against some obstacle in the stream, generally support a greater abundance and diversity of benthic invertebrates than surrounding substrate. However, because of the finely divided nature of leaf packs, this could be explained simply by the larger available surface area, and actually density per unit area might not be different from that in adjacent substrate. However, leaves are also a food source, and the artificial addition of detritus to reaches can lead to increased densities of invertebrates in the reach (Reice, 1980; Dobson and Hildrew, 1992; see also Chapter 6). As mentioned earlier, the abundance of large woody debris has been

Table 3.3 Some general patterns of relative macroinvertebrate—substrate relationships, based on data from various sources

Substrate type	Species richness	Biomass	Density
Mineral			
Bedrock	*	*→**	*→**
Mud	*	**	***
Sand	**→***	*→**	**
Gravel	***	**	***→****
Cobble/Pebble	****	***	***→****
Boulder	**	**→***	***
Organic			
Moss	***→****	****→*****	*****
Macrophyte	**→***	****→*****	****
Filamentous algae	**	**	**→***
Leaves	***→****	****	***→****
Wood	**	****	**→****

*, very low; **, low; ***, intermediate; ****, high; *****, very high.

positively correlated with a high diversity of both macroinvertebrates and fish, but in this case the particles are more likely acting to increase the heterogeneity of the habitat rather than in provision of additional food sources. A summary of the rather complicated interrelationships between substrate and benthic invertebrates is given in Table 3.3.

Water chemistry and the catchment

Marine biologists work in a medium that varies relatively little in chemical composition and salinity (concentration of dissolved solids)—in general, sea water has a salinity of 35 g l^{-1}. Freshwaters, in comparison, are generally extremely dilute; rivers have a global mean salinity of between 0.1 and 0.12 g l^{-1} (Berner and Berner, 1987) and a range from 0.01 to 0.5 mg l^{-1} (Ward, 1992*b*). However, one simply cannot generalize as to the actual chemical composition of stream and river water as it depends on the interplay of several variables that are unique to every river catchment and even to tributary sub-catchments. These include:

(1) the initial chemical composition, amount and distribution of rain and snowfall related to the proximity to coast or industry and to climate;

(2) the nature of the surrounding catchment and movement of water from the catchment to the river (see Chapter 1) related to topography, geology, soils, and vegetation and to the contribution of groundwater;

(3) the distance from headwaters and time (season or even time of day or time since last rainfall);

(4) the influence of human activity and land use in the catchment, such as agriculture, forestry and urbanization.

A typical river is essentially a dilute calcium bicarbonate solution dominated by a few cations and anions (Wetzel, 1983; Table 3.4.). Other important variables to consider are pH, which measures the acidity of the water (concentration of H^+ ions), hardness (which measures the concentration of Ca^{2+} and Mg^{2+} ions), conductivity (which measures the total ionic content) and alkalinity (which measures the concentration of carbonates).

Aside from direct inputs of chemicals into the stream or river water from the channel substrate (related to the geology of the bedrock), the input of chemicals and maintenance of chemical composition is related to the hydrological cycle discussed in Chapter 1, and particularly to the movement of rainfall through the surrounding catchment to the freshwater system. Additional input sources are related to land use and atmospheric processes and involve soils, sea spray (especially Na^+ and Cl^- ions), air pollution, and volcanoes, mediated through the action of rainfall and the hydrological cycle or through dry deposition. The amount of dissolved and particulate organic matter also varies, and can be high, ranging from 0.5 to 10 mg l^{-1} (Hynes, 1970).

Rainwater

This contains a wide variety of dissolved substances, although it is usually more dilute than stream water (0.020–0.040 g l^{-1} on average, Table 3.4). Natural rainwater is normally a weak carbonic acid solution, with a pH of 5.64, due to atmospheric carbon dioxide dissolving in the water droplets. In the presence of atmospheric pollution (which can travel long distances from the source), rain can

Table 3.4 The effect of land use and catchment type on streamwater chemistry compared with rainfall in the same area. Note that the differences in streamwater quality are far greater than those for rainfall. (From Burgis and Morris, 1987. Reproduced with kind permission of Cambridge University Press).

Chemical parameters (mg l^{-2})	Igneous (insoluble) rocks, undisturbed forest: New Hampshire,USA		Chalk and glacial drift, lowland agriculture: Norfolk, UK		Thornbush, and rangeland: Rift Valley, Kenya	
	Rainfall	Stream	Rainfall	Stream	Rainfall	Malewa river
Na$^+$	0.12	0.87	1.2	32.5	0.54	9.0
K$^+$	0.07	0.23	0.74	3.1	0.31	4.3
Mg^{2+}	0.04	0.38	0.21	6.9	0.23	3.0
Ca^{2+}	0.16	1.65	3.7	100.0	0.19	8.0
Cl$^-$	0.47	0.55	<1.0	47.0	0.41	4.3
HCO$_3^-$	0.006	0.92	0	288.0	1.2	70.0
SO$_4^{2-}$					0.72	6.2
pH	4.14	4.92	3.5	7.7		

be even more acidic as a result of sulphur dioxide and nitrous oxide gases dissolving to produce sulphuric and nitric acids. So-called 'acid rain' has been recorded at pH values as low as 2.1 to 2.8 in the United States and Scandinavia. Sea salts (especially Na^+, Cl^- and Mg^{2+} ions) reach the atmosphere in spray and can also be transported long distances but, of course, the levels tend to decrease with increasing distance from the sea. Thus, rainwater reaching the land already has the complex chemical composition of a dilute, weakly acidic seawater solution modified by dust (Moss, 1998). Where rain reaches streams with little contact with soils, as in bogs or some tropical rainforest habitats, the streams will have low mineral content and be slightly more acidic than the rain itself. More usually, however, the rain has been in contact with vegetation and soils before reaching the stream or river where it undergoes considerable chemical alteration.

Vegetation effects

As we mentioned earlier, vegetation in general, and especially trees, scavenge ions (including sea salts and atmospheric pollutants) from the air. This process is particularly important in upland regions near the headwaters of most streams. Conifers in particular are known to have a greater scavenging capacity than other types of trees (Gee and Stoner, 1989). Various ions reach the leaves and needles from rainfall and dry deposition and further increase in concentration following evaporation from the canopy surfaces and canopy exchanges. Precipitation passing through the vegetation to the ground ('throughfall') picks up these additional ions, and has a different chemical composition and higher concentrations of some ions than the original rain. Once throughfall reaches the soil, root uptake for transpiration further increases concentrations of ions, and in-soil processes involving cation-exchange, mineralization of mineral and organic matter, and uptake by organisms add to the changing chemical composition of what is now soil water. An example of such changes can be seen from data from the Ballyhooly Forest monitoring site in County Cork, Ireland (Table 3.5).

The other effect of vegetation will be on selective uptake of ions and nutrient

Table 3.5 An example of the changes in ionic concentrations (μmol_c l^{-1}) in water samples, from rainfall through the tree canopy to the soil. (Data from Farrell and Boyle, 1991)

	pH	NH_4^+	Ca^{2+}	Cl^-	SO_4^{2-}
Bulk Precipitation	5.50	0.028	0.019	0.24	0.048
Throughfall	5.17	0.083	0.077	0.80	0.15
Humus Water	3.87	0.14	0.20	0.93	0.15
Soil Water at 25cm	4.15	0.003	0.077	1.10	0.17
Soil Water at 75cm	4.50	0.0043	0.087	0.92	0.16

This data set is from a sub-oceanic Norway Spruce site on orthic podzol soil in Ireland with significant marine salt influence but low to moderate inputs of anthropogenic nitrogen and sulphur compared to continental European sites. Ionic concentrations are expressed as moles of charge (often referred to as equivalents) to allow a functional comparison of concentrations of different ions (μmol_c l^{-1} = mg l^{-1} × 10^3 × charge/mass) fluxes in the soil. This is clearly illustrated by increases in nitrate and potassium concentration in stream waters following removal of riparian vegetation in stream stretches in the Plynlimon catchment, mid-Wales (Hornung and Reynolds, 1995). Similar increases in nitrate, potassium and phosphorus were found following clearcutting during the famous catchment level Hubbard Brook studies (Likens and Bormann, 1995), whereas removal of vegetation had much less effect on concentrations of calcium, magnesium, sodium, and especially sulphur in this system. Removal of the canopy also reduces the 'scavenging' ability of the catchment vegetation and hence atmospheric inputs to the catchment, such that concentrations of ions like sodium, chloride, and sulphates decrease in stream waters following clearfelling of trees. Subsequent revegetation of the catchment limits the loss of nutrients to the lotic system. In mature rainforests, in fact, streams are very dilute and most ions are released by weathering (Moss, 1998).

Geology, soils, and stream pH

The above discussion has already hinted at the role of soils in modifying the chemical nature of precipitation and throughfall before it enters the freshwater system. Different soils vary in their influence, particularly with respect to their neutralizing or buffering capacity of the acidic precipitation, throughfall, and soil water. This in turn relates largely to the nature of their parent bedrock. Table 3.4 illustrates the differences between rainwater and stream water chemistry on three different geologies and land uses.

Hydrogen ions (H^+), produced by the dissociation of carbonic acid in rainwater, are the cause of acidity and are neutralized by a solution of carbonate minerals and hydrolysis of silicate minerals as waters percolate through rocks and soils. Thus, the buffering capacity of rocks is related to the levels of calcium carbonate and bicarbonate and weatherable silicate minerals. Residence time of water in soil also influences the rate and amount of buffering (Hornung *et al.*, 1990). Buffered catchment water thus finds its way to the freshwater systems carrying carbonates and cations and supplements those released directly to the water from the channel bedrock.

Table 3.6 illustrates the buffering capacity of various rock types and the characteristics of the headwaters draining such geologies. Catchments on hard, igneous rocks tend to be low in dissolved salts and have low buffering capacity and hence surface waters tend to be soft and acidic with pH values around 3.5 to 5.5. On the other hand, catchments on sedimentary, especially calcareous, rocks are rich in carbonates and streams are usually well-buffered, hard water systems with high pH, often between 7.5 and 8.5. Similarly, soils with free carbonates, high content of weatherable silicates, or high base saturation generally give rise to circumneutral (around pH 7.0) well-buffered drainage waters. In contrast, in catchments where soils are strongly leached and have little buffering capacity left, as in most parts of Malaysia, acidic 'blackwaters' result, especially in forested areas (Dudgeon, 1995). The freshwater systems in catchments with poorly buffered rocks and soils are susceptible to the impact of acid rain (Table 3.6), caused by atmospheric pollution and exacerbated by the presence of coniferous forests.

Table 3.6 Buffering capacity of different rock types, the characteristic nature of low-order streams draining such geologies and the predicted impact of acidic precipitation on them. (Modified from Hornung *et.al.*, 1990. Reproduced with kind permission of Kluwer Academic Publishers).

Class	Buffering capacity	Major rock types	Characteristics of 1st and 2nd order stream	Impact of acidic precipitation on surface waters
1	Little or no buffering capacity	Granite and acid igneous rocks or metamorphic equivalents; granite gneisses, quartz sandstones and metamorphic equivalents; decalcified sandstones	Naturally acidic, low conductivity, poorly buffered	Widespread impact expected
2	Low to medium buffering capacity	Sandstones, shales, conglomerates and metamorphic equivalents; coal measures; intermediate igneous rocks	Weakly acidic, low conductivity, poorly buffered	Impact restricted to 1st and 2nd-order streams and small lakes.
3	Medium to high buffering capacity	Slightly calcareous rocks, (e.g. marlstones); basic and ultrabasic igneous rocks; Mesozoic mudstones; low grade intermediate to mafic volcanic rocks	Circum-neutral. Well buffered	Impact improbable except for near surface drainage in areas of acid soils
4	Infinite buffering capactiy	Limestones, chalk, dolomitic limestones, highly fossiliferous sediments or metamorphic equivalents	Alkaline, high conductivity, highly buffered	No impact

They also exhibit quite dramatic temporal change in pH over short periods associated with rainfall or snow melt events (see below).

Aside from the above, other factors can also lead to low pH stream conditions and are worth mentioning. Naturally acidic streams can arise from the presence of ironstone ferrous carbonate in the catchment geology. This results in the oxidation of ferrous to ferric iron in aerobic surface waters that in turn generates H^+ ions (Townsend *et al.*, 1983). Natural organic acids can arise from areas of *Sphagnum* bog in wet valley bottoms, swamps, and peaty areas and contribute to acidic runoff from the catchment. Systems subject to high inputs of surface runoff where there is little interaction between rain water and soil (e.g. in catchments with thin and waterlogged soils or thick forest litter), will also tend to be acidic in nature.

Acidity levels also influence the solubility and formulation of metals in the soil and stream waters. Of particular interest is aluminium which becomes soluble below pH 4.5 and can be toxic to fish when in a particular form known as 'labile monomeric aluminium' and above a concentration of 0.2 mg l^{-1}. One of the most problematic effects of acid rain seems to be related to increases in labile monomeric aluminium in catchments of low buffering capacity, especially when planted with coniferous forests (see pp. 235–6).

Land use, nutrients, and pollution

While sea spray and the weathering of rock still dominate the ionic composition of most of the world's freshwaters, man's activities, through agricultural, industrial, and urban pollution probably have the greatest effect on nutrient levels. Nutrients can be important limiting factors for plant growth and productivity in aquatic habitats, just as they are in terrestrial ones. Rainfall has small amounts of nitrogen compounds dissolved from the atmosphere (nitric acid and ammonia), but even so, this can be an important source (or even the key element) to desert stream ecosystems (Grimm, 1994). In wetter climates, as rainfall percolates through the vegetation and soil, the concentration increases and nitrogen, particularly nitrate, can find its way to stream waters. As we have seen, however, the nature and extent of vegetation and land use in the catchment regulates the levels reaching the lotic habitat. The concentration of nitrates also varies with the extent of arable land in the catchment, and large fluxes in total nitrogen (from 876 to 5000 kg m^{-2} yr^{-1}) can result from agricultural runoff (Billen *et al.*, 1995) which can potentially lead to eutrophication of freshwaters (pp. 234–5). The nature of this relationship is clearly seen in Fig. 3.5 for a European river. Dry deposition of ammonia in areas of intensive animal production supplements nitrogen levels in the catchment.

Phosphorus (P) is leached from rocks and soils in small amounts and due to its natural scarcity in the biosphere and plants' ability to absorb and retain P, it is generally found in low concentrations in stream waters (largely as phosphate). However, in agricultural areas, values can increase. For example, in Canada, levels are usually in the order of 10–40 μg l^{-1} in forests or rough pasture, rising to 50–150 μg l^{-1} in intensively farmed areas, but can exceed 1mg l^{-1} during periods of low discharge and manure pollution (Mackay, 1995). In developed countries,

Fig. 3.5 The relationship between mean annual nitrate concentration and the ratio of meadows to arable land in catchments of small streams draining agricultural areas of the Meuse river basin , France. (Redrawn from de Becker *et al.*, 1984.)

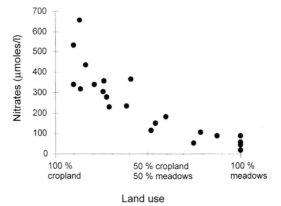

approximately half the P in middle- to higher-order rivers arises from detergents in sewage effluent.

The amount of fertilizer used has increased in many countries this century, and much is lost to surface waters. In Ireland, for example, up to one-third of fertilizers applied to pastures find their way to rivers and streams (Tunney *et al.*, 1996). pH also tends to increase with increased levels of agriculture, partly due to runoff from improved grazing farmland that has been limed. Liming can change naturally acidic soils to soils with moderate to high buffering capacity (Hornung *et al.*, 1990). The effects of this can last 60 to 100 years.

Pesticides from agriculture and forestry are not very soluble but do occur at low concentrations in drainage waters. However, biomagnification processes (see p. 232) can lead to problems and significant levels have been found in top aquatic predators such as dippers (e.g. Ormerod and Tyler, 1991). Industrial pollution introduces new substances to freshwaters as well as increasing the concentration of natural ones. Obviously, the concentrations and toxicity vary, but partly depend on the ratio of receiving to effluent volume. The impact of mine drainage can also be severe.

Atmospheric pollution can influence freshwater habitats far from the pollution source. A prime example is the phenomenon of acid rain. The impact depends on the buffering capacity of the receiving catchment soils and the nature of the catchment vegetation. However, excessive and long-term acid rain pollution can exhaust bicarbonate buffering capacity and lead to decreasing pH in freshwaters, as has been documented in Scandinavia, Canada, the northern United States, and Scotland and Wales in the United Kingdom. The various aspects of pollution are revisited in Chapter 9.

Organic matter and suspended solids

Particulate organic matter enters streams as whole branches, leaf litter, bud scales, flowers and pollen from overhanging and surrounding vegetation and as finely divided soil humus and animal wastes through bank erosion and chance inputs. At this point though, we are more interested in fine particles, suspended solids, and dissolved organic matter. As we saw in Chapter 1, enormous amounts of materials can be washed into rivers and transported long distances. Inorganic suspended solids originate from terrestrial sources, such as through soil disturbance followed by heavy rainfall, bank erosion, etc. The significance of suspended solids relates largely to the effects on subsurface light levels and indirectly to the nature of the substrate (see p. 41). The levels can vary considerably; as an example, values from 5 to 540 mg l^{-1} have been recorded in rivers in northern South America (Lewis *et al.*, 1995). The nature of suspended (and dissolved) materials conveys optical properties that can be used to classify rivers (Sioli, 1975):

- *Blackwater* rivers are poor in dissolved inorganic and suspended solids, but dissolved organic matter produces a reddish-brown colour. These are typically of low pH.

- *Whitewater* rivers have high levels of suspended solids with a muddy/silty appearance, as well as high levels of dissolved inorganic solids, tending to be alkaline.

- *Clearwater* rivers vary in acidity and have little suspended material.

In addition to highly erodible soils, poor soil conservation practices (particularly associated with agriculture) can lead to extremely high sediment levels. Removal of vegetation in the catchment, either by clearcutting forests (especially on steep slopes) or through overgrazing of the uplands (especially by sheep and goats), can lead to large-scale soil erosion and influxes of sediments to waters draining the catchment. There is thus an inverse relationship between the amount of vegetation and erosion, which generally means drainage waters in arid areas have higher concentrations of suspended solids than in wetter areas (all else being equal!). Other anthopogenic activities influence suspended solid loading, such as construction of dams, which reduce sediment transport downstream and thus influence the fertility of the downstream floodplain and perhaps even coastal marine ecosystems as found with the Aswan dam on the River Nile (see p. 226).

Variation in water chemistry over time

Regular monitoring of water chemistry at a sampling location on a stream will undoubtedly show patterns of variation. Changes in water chemistry have been documented under normal flow conditions where there are large quantities of macrophytes such as in chalk streams. Here, photosynthesis can cause diurnal fluctuations in pH from 7.4 (night) to 9.0 (day) in addition to changes in oxygen levels we discussed earlier (Westlake and Ladle, 1995). Normally, however, short-term reversible changes in chemistry follow the rise and fall of water levels associated with rainfall events, or with longer-term seasonal changes.

Base flows (normal levels) of streams usually have higher concentrations of most ions than flood flows (known as 'spates'). Discharge usually rises rapidly to a peak perhaps 2–3 hours after maximum rainfall (depending on the size of the receiving waters), and much of this water has had only minimal contact time with soil and rock of the catchment. Dilution also plays a role. However, during such increases in discharge, the concentration of H^+ ions increases and thus pH falls. This is known as an 'acid pulse'. Figure 3.6a follows such changes over a 24-hour period in a fairly well-buffered forested stream. In forested catchments on poorly buffered geologies, this decline in pH is even greater and will be accompanied by a rise in aluminium. At the same time, conductivity usually decreases (Fig. 3.6b). These episodic events can have a marked effect on the biota of streams and rivers that at base flow do not appear to be suffering acidification. Typically suspended solid levels increase during spates (Fig. 3.6c) especially where there is little riparian vegetation. If heavy rains follow a period of drought, accumulated solutes in soil water, which have increased in concentration through evaporation, undergo flushes of mineralization and nitrification. The runoff water post-drought will then contain large amounts of nitrates and other solutes (Hornung and Reynolds, 1995). Similar accumulation of materials occurs in snow, and, again, thawing allows increased mineralization and a flush of nitrification, picked up in runoff.

Fig. 3.6 Episodic changes in water chemistry associated with spates. Variation in flow (black dots) and (a) pH, (b) conductivity, and (c) suspended solids at a site in the River Douglas catchment, County Cork, Ireland, over a 2- hour period in spring. (Unpublished data, Cleneghan, O'Halloran, and Giller.)

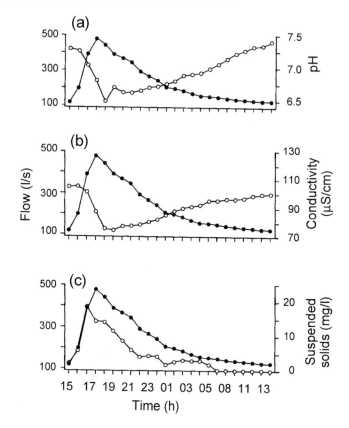

Sulphate and nitrate ions can be scavenged from the air as snow falls, and if held in long-lived snowbanks, runoff water from melting snow in spring can lead to longer-lived episodic acidification of streams, as in Canada (Hornung and Reynolds, 1995).

The effects of increased discharge are short lived, but low flow conditions last longer. Reduced discharge would normally lead to slightly elevated conductivity levels. Thus, seasonal fluctuations in concentration of many ions are expected, paralleling variation in discharge. Changes in wind direction and precipitation patterns over the year will influence inputs of marine salts or pollutants and seasonal changes in biological activity (particularly vegetation) both on land and in the water may also affect water chemistry.

Monitoring over longer periods of time can indicate directed changes in water chemistry that may fundamentally change the nature of the system, as in acidification. Directed, long-term changes in nutrients, salinity, suspended solid load and oxygen accompany gradual eutrophication of rivers caused by pollution, as in the Rhine and its tributaries in The Netherlands (van den Brink, 1994). Long-term changes in water chemistry also follow changes to land use in the surrounding catchments (e.g. afforestation or clearcutting). Under such circumstances, conditions will not revert back to previous levels unless pollution ceases or original catchment vegetation is reinstated.

Variation in water chemistry in space

Small-scale, within-reach variation in water chemistry is not easy to detect because of the generally well-mixed nature of running waters. However, high respiration and nitrogen mineralization rates in the hyporheic zone will lead to increased nitrogen and reduced oxygen levels at the upwelling zones (see Fig. 1.3, p. 8) in the channel itself (Grimm, 1994). This in turn can influence the distribution of benthic algae.

Larger-scale, within-river variation is a relatively well-known phenomenon. As a rule, the concentration of most dissolved salts (thus conductivity, alkalinity, and hardness), nutrient levels, and pH tend to increase from the river's source to its mouth. Sometimes the change is quite sudden due to the influx of a tributary or a groundwater source with a very different water chemistry, but generally there is a steady change attributable to gradual addition of salts from various drainage basins. The change in geology, soils, climate, vegetation, and in anthropogenic influence as one moves from the uplands to lowlands also plays a part. We will return to these longitudinal patterns in Chapter 6.

At a regional (between-river) scale, geology and soils are the major factors influencing water chemistry, although local climate (especially rainfall patterns) and surrounding vegetation are also important. On a biogeographic scale, geology and climate are again important. Berner and Berner (1987) give information on average concentrations of a variety of parameters from different continents. Thus in South America with extensive rainforest and highest annual precipitation, the average for total dissolved solids is the lowest in the world. However, other factors are also important, as the African average is also low, where hard geologies are common and soils weathered. European rivers seem to hold the highest concentrations largely due to agricultural and urban runoff. It should be borne in mind that these large-scale data are dominated by information from a few large rivers at downstream locations (Allan, 1995) and regional variation within continents is likely to be greater than between-continent averages.

Relationships between water chemistry and the biota

Because of the general lack of small-scale spatial variation in water chemistry, we will normally have little success in explaining distribution patterns of animals and plants at the within-reach scale on the basis of water chemistry. However, there are quite strong relationships at the larger between-catchment and regional scales that can be related to variation in water chemistry and in particular to pH and associated variables.

One major approach to the study of community patterns in streams and rivers has essentially been to correlate the distribution of species with one or more environmental factors that vary among the streams. Samples from a series of sites can be classified or projected onto axes of variation (ordination) in relation to species composition and abundance using multivariate techniques, and the resulting patterns can in turn be compared with gradients of environmental factors. Where benthic macroinvertebrate communities have been sampled from a variety of sites that extend well into the acidic range (pH < 4–6), such analyses always implicate pH and/or close chemical correlates such as hardness, alkalinity, and aluminium concentration, in the separation of sites. Other site characteristics like distance from source, stream order, discharge, and slope play a secondary role. The results are remarkably consistent irrespective of the spatial extent over which the study sites are located and compared from the regional level to individual catchments (Hildrew and Giller, 1994). Other elements of the biota show remarkably similar patterns when studied over similar suites of sites. These include benthic microarthropods (microcrustacea and mites) (Rundle and Hildrew, 1990) and macroalgae, bryophytes and higher plants (Ormerod *et al.*, 1987*b*).

The ecological patterns that underlie these multivariate patterns are that mean species richness and total species pools increase with pH (Hildrew and Townsend, 1987). Several invertebrate families are absent from low pH sites (e.g. mayflies, molluscs) while others are usually well represented (e.g. stoneflies, blackflies). Similarly, many algal, moss and higher plant species seem to be confined to either hard or soft waters. Streams with a pH as high as 6.5 but low alkalinity (low Ca^{2+}) often show similar features to more acidic waters (pH <5.5, Willoughby and Mappin, 1988). Low calcium levels can cause osmotic problems and affect shell or cuticle secretion in invertebrates (especially macrocrustaceans, crayfish, and snails). Physiological effects of low pH have also been demonstrated on chironomids, mayflies, and crustaceans. Fish are also strongly influenced by pH particularly in streams with higher concentrations of aluminium. Using experimental manipulation of streams, Ormerod *et al.* (1987*a*) showed that mortality of salmon and trout was dramatically increased in the presence of aluminium (0.35 mg l^{-1}) at pH 5.0, but mortality was low at pH 4.3 with no additional aluminium. There are clear physiological effects of low pH and high aluminium on salmonids (e.g. Bowman and Bracken, 1993).

In addition to all these physiological effects, ecological factors are influenced by pH. For example, there often appears to be a greater diversity of food available in less acid streams, allowing for a greater trophic diversity. Macrophytes are more common, large detritus particles decompose more rapidly enhancing the supply of FPOM (Hildrew *et al.*, 1984) and the quality, quantity and availability of suitable algal foods are also enhanced in less acid streams (Willoughby and Mappin, 1988). Indeed, this latter study has shown that lack of suitable foods restricts otherwise acid-tolerant species from acid water sites.

In sharp contrast to acidic waters, streams which are broadly circumneutral to slightly alkaline (pH >7.0) are much less influenced by chemical factors. Surveys of macroinvertebrate communities conducted over wide areas naturally show biogeographic groupings of sites, for instance by biome for all macroinvertebrates (Corkum, 1991) or drainage basin for Simuliidae (Corkum and Currie, 1987). Other factors implicated in various studies include climate, geology, land use, nutrients, conductivity, temperature, stream area, and distance from source. There is a great problem with interpretation however. Many of these factors are intercorrelated and are probably surrogates for both regional (including history and chance) and local effects (including flow, productivity and detritus inputs, and processing which are in turn affected by climate, land use, and riparian vegetation). Interpretation is also complicated because, in general, these are one-off studies and the potential influence of biotic factors such as disease and parasites on populations is overlooked or unknown.

Flow and hydraulics

Both terrestrial and aquatic habitats consist of a fluid medium overlying a solid. The lives of terrestrial animals and plants are largely decoupled from the motion of the medium in which they exist, the air. However, for aquatic organisms, the medium, water, influences all aspects of their existence. Water has a higher density than air, leading to more mechanical support but making it harder to move in. In lakes, much of the biota are free from contact with the 'ground', while in lotic systems the biota is much more closely associated with the 'ground', the substrate. Flow forces are undoubtedly the major architects of the physical habitat in streams and rivers, where they influence the particle size and nature of the substrate and channel morphology, the supply of dissolved oxygen, affect the distribution and turnover of food and other resources, and create direct physical forces within the water column and on the substrate.

Nature of flow

Flow in natural channels is three-dimensional; each fluid particle may travel longitudinally, laterally, or vertically. It is also complex in both space and time, as the motion of individual water molecules is inherently unpredictable and even chaotic. At the same velocity, flow can be either turbulent or laminar (related to depth and roughness of the stream bottom), which as Statzner *et al.* (1988) point out, presents lotic organisms with almost two different worlds. Laminar, hydraulically smooth flow conditions can exist over solid, smooth surfaces (mud bottoms, flat bedrock) or through dense strands of weeds or over flat blades of macrophyte leaves. Here, fluid moves in parallel layers which slide past each other at differing speeds but in the same direction. Pure laminar flow is rare and most usual at low velocities. Turbulent, hydraulically rough flow occurs in areas of coarser substrate and high velocity and involves chaotic eddies and swirls in every direction that disrupt the orderly laminar flow and that have an important mixing effect on heat, water chemistry, and oxygen into areas close to the substrate.

Two other properties of a fluid influence the nature of flow: viscocity and inertia. Viscosity is related to how rapidly a fluid can be deformed, the resistance due to the coherence of its molecules. Colder water is more viscous (syrupy) than warmer water. Inertia reflects the resistance of fluid particles or objects in a fluid to accelerate or decelerate when force is applied or ceases. High inertial forces promote turbulence, high viscous forces promote laminar flow. The ratio of inertial to viscous forces within a fluid produces the dimensionless Reynolds number (Re) which can be estimated for the stream channel or an individual organism:

$$Re = U\,L_a\,\nu^{-1},$$

where U is the average velocity of fluid or movement or swimming speed of the object (m/s), L_a is some length dimension (either the depth of flow or some characteristic length (m) of an object, such as an organism, immersed in a flowing fluid), and ν is the kinematic viscosity of the fluid—another way of describing how easily the fluid flows. The kinematic viscosity is the absolute viscosity divided by the density; this changes with temperature and for water at 15° C, $\nu = 1.141 \times 10^{-6}$ and at 25° C, $\nu = 0.897 \times 10^{-6}\,m^2\,s^{-1}$ (Gordon et al., 1992).

For a fluid, a large Re, where inertial forces dominate, indicates turbulent flow. For example, a small babbling brook with a current of $0.1\ m\ s^{-1}$ has an Re of 10 000 (Reynolds, 1994). In contrast, a small Re, where viscous forces dominate, indicates laminar flow, with a transitional range between 500 and 2000. For any given depth, flow becomes laminar when velocity decreases such that Re drops well below 2000. Re also indicates the forces experienced by an animal. Both the movement of the fluid and the movement of the animal will govern the Reynolds number. In general, small organisms close to the stream bed where velocity is low have low Re values and will be more subject to viscous forces. Large organisms in greater velocity conditions have higher Re values and will be subject to more inertial forces (see p. 114).

Another dimensionless quantity, the Froude number, is more often used to characterise flow habitats. This represents the ratio of inertial to gravitational forces, where gravitational forces encourage water to move downhill and inertial forces reflect the water's compulsion to move or not (Gordon et al. 1992). Froude number (Fr) is defined as

$$Fr = U/\sqrt{gd},$$

where U is the average velocity of the fluid (as above), d is water depth and g acceleration due to gravity. Where Fr <1, flow is slow or tranquil, but when Fr >1 it is fast and invariably turbulent.

Although one may question the relevance of this excursion into the physics of flow, the importance will become clear when we consider how current changes with depth and how animal size influences life in flowing water later.

Discharge and current

River or stream discharge (D) is simply a measure of the amount of water moving down the channel past a given point per unit time $(m^3\ s^{-1})$. It is related to stream width, depth, current velocity and roughness of the substrate. Discharge will obviously increase downstream due to the addition of tributaries, the increase in depth and change to a smoother substrate. As an example, mean annual discharge increases from 0.013 $m^3 s^{-1}$ for 1st order streams to 466.1 $m^3 s^{-1}$ for 9th order rivers in boreal forests of Canada (MacKay, 1995). The actual values reached depend on the length of river, size of drainage basin, amount of runoff, and climate. Discharge will also vary in response to rainfall or drought events (see below). While organisms are likely to be affected by mean and range of discharge (especially the extremes), discharge itself is of less biological interest than the current velocity where the organisms actually live, and the associated flow forces such as drag, lift and shear.

Current velocity is measured in metres per second and mean velocities rarely exceed 3 $m s^{-1}$. The gradient of the stream bed (difference in surface level between two points in the channel), the nature of the substrate, and water depth all affect current velocity. At a given discharge, the velocity of flow at any one point in the river decreases exponentially with depth, giving a vertical velocity profile or gradient (Fig. 3.7a). This results from a thin layer of fluid in contact with the substrate being prevented from moving by frictional drag. This is the so called 'no-slip' condition (Vogel, 1994) and is exactly the same reason why dust can collect on the blades of electric fans. The flow above this in nearby layers is also slowed but the influence diminishes with distance and the current is faster the further it is from the substrate (see below). Similarly, friction from the channel sides and surface tension will cause transverse velocity gradients. Thus, highest current speeds across a river will tend to occur just below the surface at the deepest point of the cross-section (Fig. 3.7b). Average velocity is close to that at 0.6 of depth from the surface and is around 80–90% of surface velocity.

Boundary layers and dead zones

The sharpest part of the vertical velocity gradient is close to the bottom where current speeds tend to approach zero. A so-called boundary layer exists from where the fluid contacts the stream bed to where the fluid is no longer significantly influenced by the presence of the substrate (Gordon et al., 1992). The thickness of this layer shrinks with increasing current velocity. Within the boundary layer is a viscous laminar sublayer which varies in thickness depending on the nature of the stream bed. Where substrate irregularities are small in comparison to water depth (such as bedrock streams, or deep lowland rivers with fine particle substrates, Fig 3.7a) hydraulically smooth conditions occur, leading to a relatively thick laminar sublayer where viscous forces overcome turbulent momentum. Most streams though have large surface irregularities and hydraulically rough conditions, so near-bed patterns then become extremely complex and high velocities can occur relatively close to the stream bed (Fig 3.7a). Where flow hits an object protruding from the bottom (like a cobble or boulder, Fig. 3.7c), the front edge is fully exposed to flow, but on the top and sides the current is fast but has a thin laminar layer which progressively thickens as one passes along the object (Statzner et al., 1988). At the downstream edge, flow 'separates' and eventually the current becomes less or non-existent behind the object, forming a so called 'dead zone' which leads to a depositional microhabitat (Fig. 3.7c).

Fig. 3.7 Velocity gradients in a stream. (a) Vertical gradients over hydraulically smooth and rough substrates (modified from Hynes, 1970, and Gordon *et al.*, 1992). (b) A transverse section through a smooth channel showing velocity contours (v_3 high, v_1 low velocity) (modified from Newson, 1994). (c) Distribution of currents around a boulder (modified from Maitland, 1990).

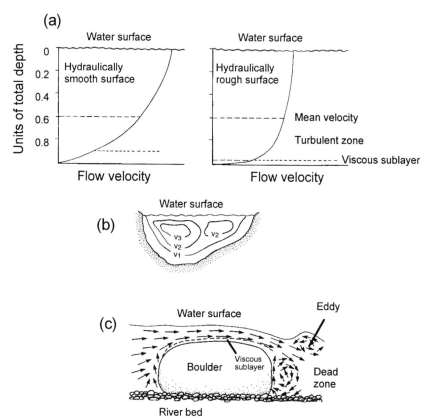

Shear stress

Flow velocity gradients produce shearing forces close to the stream bottom that are largely characterized by shear stress—the force acting parallel to the surface per unit area of stream bed. This relates to the erosion potential for mineral and biotic particles and to the energy required to be expended to withstand the forces. Thus, as water flows over a solid surface, be it a substrate particle or an organism, it generates lift and drag forces, and if the stress is large enough, the substrate particle or organism is set in motion. Particles may roll or bound along the stream bed (substrate moved in this way is known as 'bed load') or may be carried in suspension (entrained) by turbulent eddies (particles moved in this way are known as 'suspension load'). Shear stress (τ) is related to the specific weight of water (1000 kg m^{-3}), depth of fluid (D) and slope of the channel (S):

$$\text{thus } \tau = 1000DS \text{ (kg m}^{-2}).$$

The magnitude of shear stress thus increases as the depth of a waterbody increases. Shear stress is also correlated with the square of current velocity, so high flows exert a large force on the stream bed and influence the particle size (as discussed earlier) and the quantity of bed load. Fine material will be entrained at current speeds above 20 cm s^{-1}. Sandy beds, which form in flows between 20–40 cm s^{-1}, will tend to be scoured during flooding events when depth and current velocity increase, and will refill as they decline (see also Table 3.1, p. 39).

Variability in flow and shear stress over space

One of the main habitat characteristics of streams and rivers is the spatial variation in flow and shear stress. At the scale of the individual cobble or boulder, the boundary layer thickens with distance along the surface as mentioned earlier, thus shear stress generally decreases with distance back from the leading edge. Within a stream reach, changes in gradient and stream depth lead to fast riffle (higher shear stress) and slower pool (lower shear stress) sequences and as the stream meanders, flow becomes disturbed and is faster on the outside than the inside of a bend. Irregularities in the stream bed or the banks, woody debris, and changing substrates also result in complex current patterns (eddies, reverse flows, etc.) even in low gradient streams. The stream and river reach is thus a mosaic of water bodies travelling at different current velocities and exerting different shear stresses on the stream bed and organisms (Fig. 3.8). Larger-scale longitudinal

Fig. 3.8 Patchiness in flow in a river system. Depth (a) and current velocity (b) contours for a low gradient reach of the River Coln, England. (Redrawn from Mackey *et al.* 1982.)

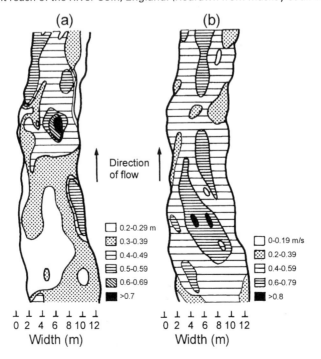

patterns in flow occur from headwaters to source. As we saw in Chapter 1, rivers typically originate from springs and rivulets which in turn form fast-flowing turbulent streams in high gradient uplands. Tributary streams then gradually coalesce resulting in larger, smoothly flowing, deep but low gradient rivers that wind their way towards the sea. We know discharge is greater downstream, but contrary to first impressions, average current velocity (and Reynolds number) steadily increases downstream also (Statzner *et al.*, 1988). At a constant slope, current velocity will increase with size and depth of channel. Although stream slope declines downstream, channel width and depth increase and substrates become finer and offer less resistance to flow than the coarse substrates upstream, offsetting the declining gradient. A turbulent fast-flowing upland stream is probably travelling more slowly than the larger, deeper, smoother flowing, lowland river. On the other hand, shear stress is highest in the turbulent shallower headwaters and decreases downstream.

Variability in flow and shear stress over time

In addition to the spatial heterogeneity, most natural running waters show marked temporal variability in flow and shear stress. All lotic systems, including large rivers, increase in discharge following individual rainfall events (spates) and on average would naturally flood (where discharge fills the channel—bankfull discharge) approximately every 1.5 years (Leopold *et al.*, 1964, and see later). In contrast, the flow at a single point can fluctuate over a few seconds due to local surges in response to passing eddies and turbulent water movement.

Most rivers continue to flow during periods of no rainfall due to inputs from groundwater or from lakes. This is known as 'base flow'. Rainfall events in the catchment supplement this base flow, and produce what is known as a flood hydrograph—in headwaters this usually takes the form of a quite rapid rise to peak discharge and a more gradual fall to base flow once the rainfall event ceases (Fig. 3.9). The response time relates to catchment size, shape, gradient, and vegetation and basically depends on how much and how quickly water runs off the catchment and into the stream channel. Small streams will show considerable short-term variation in discharge but the larger catchment area and greater volume of water in lowland rivers dampens the effects of local storms.

Obviously, periods with more continuous rainfall will lead to higher discharges and low rainfall to lower discharges, thus seasonal/annual discharge patterns, known as flow regimes, are apparent. The controlling factors tend to be large scale, such as climate, drainage basin geomorphology, and geography. As Fig. 2.2 (p. 17) illustrated, there are a variety of flow regimes world-wide based on different annual precipitation patterns, the shape of the annual hydrograph and season of peak flow. Figure 3.10 presents some detailed examples. By monitoring at the fine scale of daily records and over several years, we can get a better categorization of flow variation and predictability. This approach has been used by Poff and Ward (1989) to classify three types of intermittent streams and six types of perennial streams (Table 3.7). Two examples are shown in Fig. 3.11.

Fig. 3.9 A flood hydrograph showing the change in stream discharge over time in relation to rainfall during a storm event at two sites near Cork, Ireland: Kilworth, a forested catchment stream and Araglin, a moorland catchment stream. (Unpublished data, P. Morris and G. Kiely.)

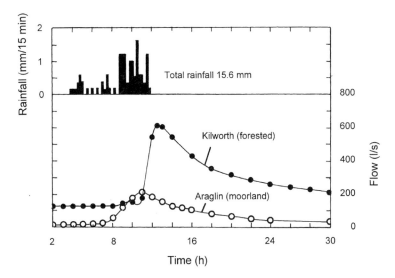

Table 3.7 Different catagories of flow regime with respect to intermittency and predictability of flow and flood frequency. The predicted relative contribution of abiotic and biotic control of stream communities is also shown. (Modified from Poff and Ward, 1989)

| | Intermittent streams | | Perennial streams | |
	High intermittency	Low intermittency	Low flood predictability	High flood predictability
High flood frequency	Harsh intermittent	Intermittent flashy	Perennial flashy Low flow predictability	Snow and rain Low flow predictability
	Abiotic	*Abiotic*	*Abiotic*	*Seasonally biotic*
Low flood frequency	Harsh intermittent	Intermittent runoff predictability	Perennial runoff Low flow predictability	Winter rain runoff High flow
	Abiotic	*Abiotic*	*Abiotic* Mesic groundwater High flow predictability *Biotic*	*Seasonally biotic* Snow melt High flow predictability *Seasonally biotic*

Flow fluctuations, especially high and low extremes, can potentially act as quite severe disturbances to lotic communities. Flood and drought disturbances will, of course, differ in their effect—the former are episodic and short-term, the latter build up slowly and are often longer lasting. Zero flow conditions can occur in normally perennial systems during rare droughts, but are a regular and 'normal' feature of intermittent streams which rely on precipitation rather than ground

Fig. 3.10 Examples of annual hydrographs from around the world. (a) Scandinavia: monthly means: (i) warm temperate rainy climate with low summer flow; (ii) cold snowy climate with appreciable runoff all year; (iii) cold snowy climate, low winter flow and peak discharge in spring (adapted from Peterson *et al.*, 1995). (b) Tropical Asia: monthly means for monsoonal climate with winter (i) and summer (ii) monsoons (redrawn from Dudgeon, 1995). (c) More detailed records fron desert conditions with flash flood events and periods of very low flow (redrawn from Grimm, 1994). (d) Tropical South America: detailed records for a small rainforest stream showing high short-term variation in discharge superimposed on a seasonally variable base flow (redrawn from Lewis *et al.*, 1995, (a), (b), and (d) reproduced with kind permission of Elsevier Science).

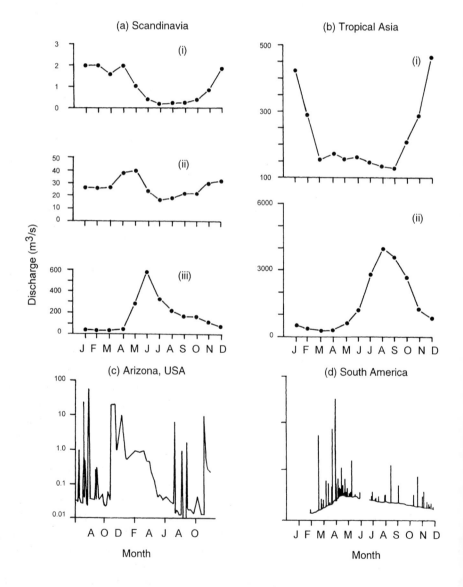

Fig. 3.11 Two extremes of the categories of river flows of Poff and Ward (1990): (a) perennial flash-flooding river;(b) mesic groundwater stream. Discharge data is available for each day of the year, for each year of records, and when plotted, produces the three-dimensional figure that illustrates the amount and timing of variation in discharge.

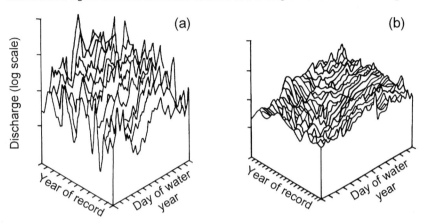

water to maintain flow. The smaller the stream and the drier the climate, the more likely the lotic system will be intermittent. In the southwestern United States deserts, for example, modal discharge varies from 0.01 to 0.05 m^3 s^{-1} in summer to 0.1–0.5 m^3 s^{-1} in winter (Grimm, 1994). Drying starts with shrinkage of the wetted channel and continues to a series of isolated pools and perhaps to complete loss of surface water, although subsurface flow may persist. An even greater abundance of intermittent streams occurs in Australia, which is the driest continent. While regulation of rivers for irrigation, water supply and hydroelectric power can reduce variation in flow (see pp. 223–4), it can also lead to decreased flow and even zero flow below dams. Many countries now provide for 'stipulated minimum flow' in regulated rivers, a practical means to retain some minimum ecosystem function and aesthetic nature.

Floods, on the other hand, are just as much a feature of tropical Mediterranean and desert streams as of those in wetter climates. The variability of floods in Australia, for example, is far greater than elsewhere (Lake, 1995) and large storm hydrographs (flash floods) are common in the rainy season in desert areas (Fig. 3.10). At the other extreme, large floods occur following snow melt in upland alpine and subarctic regions, or during monsoon rains in Asia. These floods, which can also affect rivers in the lowlands, are predictable, and occur during the same seasons, year in year out, and thus can be 'accommodated' to by the lotic community. Unpredictable flood events are common in other systems, and can cause severe disturbances to the biota. Even though floods may be predictable, exceptionally high floods can also cause major disturbances. The likelihood of large (catastrophic) floods increases with time, and such floods are actually de-scribed as 1 in 50-year or 1 in 100-year floods on a regional basis. Discharge may reach 1–3 times bankfull and thus burst the banks, often with devastating results to agricultural land and urban developments (Table 3.8). In general, flooding inevitably leads to increased average current velocity within the channel and in

Table 3.8 Examples of flood disasters world-wide. (Adapted from Giller, 1996*a*)

Date	Location	Disaster impact
1887	Hwang Ho, China.	900,000 deaths
1911	Yangtze Kiang, China	100,000 deaths
1971	India	£300m damage
1972 June	USA (Hurricane Agnes)	$3000m damage
1973 August	Mexico (Hurricane Brenda)	200,000 homeless
1973 August	Pakistan	1500 deaths, £400m damage
1974 January	Eastern Australia	650,000 km inundated, A$100m damage
1974 August	Bangladesh	5 million homeless
1974 September	Honduras (Hurricane Fiji)	10 000 deaths
1988	Bangladesh	80% land mass covered
1995 January	The Netherlands	250 000 persons evacuated.
1997 June	Poland	100,000 ha inundated (1 in 1000-yr event)
1997 November	Somalia	Over 1 million persons affected (1 in 50-year event)

turn increased average shear stress. However, this change in velocity and shear stress is not equal over all parts of the stream reach, as Lancaster and Hildrew (1993*a*) have shown (Fig. 3.12). 'Slow' patches of a stream showed low shear stress and velocity across a 10-fold increase in discharge; 'fast' patches always had high shear stress which showed a distinct increase with discharge. 'Variable' patches lay between the two extremes, as shear stress and velocity were low and undetectable at low discharge but increased with discharge to become more like 'fast' patches.

Effects of flow on biota

The most obvious effect of flow on lotic organisms is the risk of dislodgement and transport downstream. In this regard, the most important hydraulic characteristic for an individual organism is the prevailing current velocity striking the organism head-on (Statzner *et al.*, 1988). The forces acting on the organism in a given flow depend on its Reynolds number, which varies with organism size.

Large creatures like fish, with high Reynolds numbers (e.g. trout 50 000–200 000; Vogel, 1994), live in conditions where viscous forces are less significant than inertial forces and a flip of the tail can propel the fish through the water. The fish must expend energy equivalent to the shear stress to retain its position in the flow. For microscopic creatures which, due to their small characteristic length, operate at very low Reynolds numbers (10^{-4}–10^{-5}), viscosity dominates their lives and movement is like swimming in treacle and stops immediately propulsion ceases (Gordon *et al.*, 1992). The advantage of 'life at a low Reynolds number' is

Fig. 3.12 Flow velocity and shear stress relationships with discharge in a small stream in southern England. Three patch types can be distinguished (slow, variable and fast; see text for details). Bars show means ± 1 SE. (After Lancaster and Hildrew, 1993*a*.).

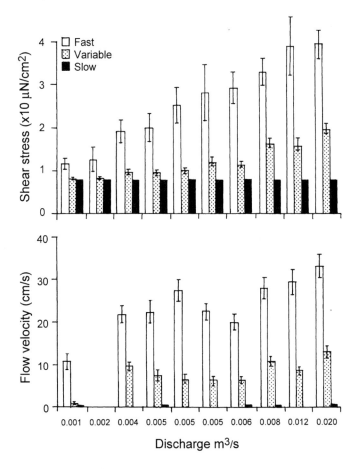

that the organism is largely protected from the action of turbulence by its 'coating' of viscous fluid. Statzner *et al.* (1988) point out that macroinvertebrates start life at low Re (1–10) and when they reach fully grown size, Re is higher (~ 1000). Evolution must therefore compromise between life at low and at higher Re.

Individual species have a variety of adaptations to overcome or escape from flow, which will be explored in detail in Chapter 5. In the present context, what is clear is that species do react differently to current velocity, show differential preferences and hence different flow conditions lead to divergent assemblages of organisms. The well-documented species differences between pools and riffles is a case in point. In a detailed survey, boundary layer Re was the most strongly correlated individual variable with invertebrate distribution and taxon richness in two New Zealand streams (Quinn and Hickey, 1994) but a combination of mean velocity, substrate size, and depth gave a stronger correlation than any single variable. It appears that the interaction between current velocity and stream substrate size is important in determining invertebrate distribution. The general relationships between species distributions and flow relate to the need for current for feeding, respiratory requirements, and metabolism or indirectly to substrate preferences.

Current velocity also has a strong influence on behavioural characteristics of lotic animals including body posture, case- and net-building, locomotory activity and drift, territoriality and respiratory movements (see Statzner *et al.*, 1988). For example, there is considerable evidence linking the distribution of caddisflies to current velocity such that velocity preference curves can be constructed. One of the problems with any studies of this kind is measuring flow at the proper scale (i.e. the flow in which the individual actually lives). Edington (1968) measured currents next to nets of caddis larvae and found certain species concentrated within certain velocity ranges. *Hydropsyche instabilis* constructed nets in faster water (15–100 cm s^{-1}) than *Plectrocnemia conspersa* (0–20 cm s^{-1}). This related to the efficiency of net construction and filtering, so when baffles were constructed in the field to divert current from the nets of *Hydropsyche*, individuals vacated the original nets and moved to areas of higher currents. Hydraulic conditions also clearly influence the distribution and abundance of periphyton (Poff *et al.*, 1990) not only at the reach scale but also at the scale of the individual boulder. Statzner and Bouchardt (1994) have also drawn attention to zones of transition of *hydraulic stress* along river systems which, although they may be at a rather coarse level of analysis, seem to be related to major longitudinal changes in species composition.

Aside from the general properties of flowing water we have just considered, the

Fig. 3.13 A postulated relationship between frequency of disturbance and productivity and some structural features of the benthic invertebrate communities of riffles. (After Hildrew and Townsend, 1987.)

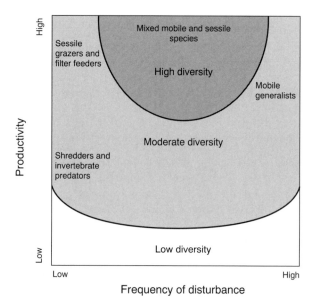

variation in discharge also makes rivers and streams quite risky places to live. It is believed that flow variation and predictability are important components of the physical habitat and may have an influential role in controlling the overall nature of lotic communities (Hildrew and Giller, 1994). Table 3.7 (p. 61) shows a conceptual model of how control of stream communities switches from abiotic to biotic factors in relation to flow predictability and flood frequency under the various flow regimes identified by Poff and Ward (1989). In a similar way, Hildrew and Townsend (1987) have modified the habitat templet concept of Southwood (1977) for lotic communities (Fig. 3.13) and postulated how species diversity and productivity may be related to frequency of disturbance. But, it is not only the frequency of disturbances that is important—the magnitude and predictability of disturbances must also be considered. This can be shown on a small scale experimentally (Fig. 3.14a). On a larger scale, natural catastrophic flood disturbances at the 'wrong time of year' can cause dramatic and relatively long-term impacts on

Fig. 3.14 (a) Recolonization of macroinvertebrates on stones which have been subjected to a small simulated flood that decreased periphyton (brushed; dot-dash line, B) or a large simulated flood that removed periphyton (acid-scoured; dashed line, C) compared to controls (solid line, A) (redrawn from Boulten *et al.*, 1988). (b) The effect of a catastrophic flood on macroinvertebrates in the Glenfinish river, a 2nd order temperate stream in County Cork, Ireland. Open squares show mean macroinvertebrate density ± 1 SE; closed circles show taxon richness. The arrows indicate major (1986) and minor (1988) flooding events (redrawn from Giller *et al.*, 1991).

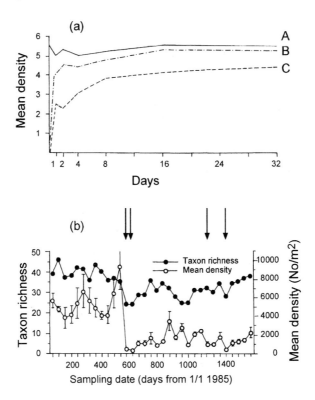

stream biota, as shown by the results of a 1 in 50-year event in late summer in a temperate, winter-rain stream (Fig. 3.14b).

Biological interactions

Ultimately, organisms in streams and rivers are limited to specific ranges of physicochemical environments by their physiological tolerances. Given these larger-scale limitations, organisms may be further restricted to particular current velocities, substrates or areas of food availability and physical disturbances may play a further role. Biological interactions, such as predation and competition, will be dealt with in some detail in Chapter 7, but we should not end this chapter on the habitat templet without at least illustrating how such interactions can influence the distribution and abundance within otherwise suitable habitats.

One of the many advances in stream ecology in recent years has been the increasing awareness of the importance of biotic interactions in the ecology of lotic organisms. However, most of the work has concentrated on the effects at small-patch scales. There are now many examples demonstrating interspecific competition for space in the benthos (e.g. Dudley *et al.*, 1990; Hemphill, 1991; and see pp. 187–9) most often involving the more sedentary components of the fauna such as fixed retreat-building caddis and blackflies. But competition between more mobile animals has also been shown. Field experiments by Kohler (1992) showed strong interactions between the dominant grazing cased caddis *Glossosoma* and the mayfly *Baetis* as well as with more sedentary forms. Large-scale effects of such competition have been revealed following the decline of such dominant competitors following pathogen outbreaks (Kohler and Wiley, 1997; see p. 188). Similarly, experiments by Kennedy and Strange (1986) clearly demonstrated the impact of trout on the distribution of young salmon in relation to flow and depth. Removal of the competitively dominant trout led to increased usage of slower deeper areas of the stream by the salmon.

Predators, such as fish and large predatory insects, consume a considerable proportion of the standing crop of the benthos and clearly affect prey behaviour (see Chapter 5), yet it has proved difficult to demonstrate resultant changes in habitat use and distribution of prey. Experimental approaches manipulating predation rates in small patches of stream bed using cages or enclosures have often led to equivocal results, possibly because of the continual exchange of organisms between the manipulated and surrounding areas (see pp. 184–5). There is, however, some evidence for restricted habitat use by prey (Allan, 1995). Clearer effects can be seen as a result of grazers feeding on periphyton. Benthic grazers tend to aggregate in patches of high food abundance or quality (see Chapter 5) and grazing, especially by caddis larvae and snails, does seem to have a significant effect on algae (see Gregory, 1983 for an early review). At the small scale of individual stones, sessile insect grazers can control the composition of algae in their immediate vicinity (Hart, 1985), whereas grazing minnows can control the abundance of filamentous algae in pools (Power *et al.*, 1985). Interestingly, when predatory bass were also present, algae were abundant as minnows emigrated, hid, or were eaten!

Parasitism and disease may have larger-scale influences on the distribution of organisms, especially when introduced to a region. Notable examples are the introduction of the 'crayfish plague' which has lead to a massive disease-mediated decline of the British crayfish *Austropotamobius pallipes* (Holdrich and Reeve, 1991) and the Noble crayfish *A. asticus* in Europe, and the impact of episodic outbreaks of microsporidian pathogens on caddis in Michigan trout streams mentioned above (further details are given on p. 188).

The accidental introduction or invasion of other exotic invertebrates, fish and mammals has often resulted in substantial changes to the native fauna. In the lower Rhine, for example, invading ponto-caspian amphipod crustaceans, especially the tube-building *Corophium curvispinum*, have undergone dramatic population explosions at the expense of native *Gammarus* and caddis and bivalve species (van den Brink *et al.*, 1990). Similarly, the arrival of the notorious zebra mussel (*Dreissena polymorpha*) in the Hudson river, New York state, has had some profound effects. Since first identified in May 1991, mean densities reached $600–3900 \text{ m}^{-2}$ by 1995 and locally up to $10\,000 \text{ m}^{-2}$. In reponse, unionid clam densities dropped by up to 50% in three years and recruitment dropped by 90% as a result of both competition for food and fouling of shells by zebra mussels (Strayer and Smith, 1996). We discuss the problems of exotic species introductions further on pp. 239–41.

Table 3.9 A summary of the nature of the variation in streams and rivers on the different spatial and temporal scales

Scale	Space	Time
Small scale	*Within-stream reach:* influences flow, substrate, particle size, organic matter retention and vegetation	*Daily/short-term variation:* temperature and oxygen; flow—related to current, shear stress and substrate; chemical changes—related to pulses of increased velocity and sediment and reduced pH; flood disturbances
Medium scale	*Longitudinal distance within river:* longitudinal change in temperature, oxygen, water chemistry, flow and flow variability, substrate, and energy inputs	*Seasonal changes:* temperature and climate, water chemistry, discharge and current velocity, energy inputs, pollution and flood disturbances
Large scale	*Differences between streams:* water chemistry, pariculary pH, related to geology and land use	*Interannual and decadal:* water chemistry and temperature related to changes in land use, directed chemical changes involving pollution, acidification and eutrophication; climatic variation
Very large scale	*Biogeographic patterns:* catchment area; river length; history and chance, not related to habitat	*Historical–evolutionary time:* development of river and succession processes in the surrounding landscape; major climatic changes

Summary

Flow and water chemistry (including oxygen) are the primary factors governing life in lotic systems. But environmental variation in time and space is the key characteristic of running waters that moulds the habitat templet and thus underpins our understanding of the influence of the environment on lotic organisms. Different scales of variation have different effects on where the biota live and which biota are present and these are summarized in Table 3.9.

This variation in space and time in the major environmental factors that create the lotic habitat sets the stage on which lotic animals and plants have evolved and must be adapted to in order to survive. From this background, we can now explore the various types of lotic animals and plants (Chapter 4) and consider their adaptations (Chapter 5) before moving on to patterns and processes and more applied issues.

4 Life in running waters

Running waters harbour a multitude of species ranging in size from viruses and small bacteria to large vertebrates. Small organisms are ubiquitous in running waters but large aquatic animals are naturally more or less confined to large rivers. A quick glance into a stream might reveal a few fish but little else. However, picking up a stone from the stream bed will provide a glimpse of the thriving life in the stream. Because of the continuous downstream flow of water, few organisms are able to dwell in the water column unless the current is slow. Instead most species are associated, in one way or another, with the substrate. This includes micro- and filamentous algae attached to rocks, higher plants rooted in the substrate, and invertebrates often living in the interstices between mineral particles, on rock faces or in leaf packs.

To the curious layman (often an angler) the most obvious inhabitants of a stream or small river (other than fish) would be filamentous algae, mosses, and the larvae of many insects, notably mayflies, stoneflies, and caddisflies. A closer examination would reveal a large number of other species, belonging to many other taxonomic groups. And if this closer examination was microscopic, a vast array of microbes, microarthropods, and minor phyla would be found. In the following sections we will give an overview of the more important organisms living in streams and rivers. In doing so we emphasize those that are either more or less restricted to running waters, or that may also be very important for biological processes there, even if they are also associated with lentic or terrestrial habitats. We have deliberately restricted our consideration of fish and other vertebrates in this overview, partly because such information is fairly easy to obtain elsewhere. On the other hand, there is a distinct bias towards the invertebrates. Aside perhaps from fish, the invertebrates as a whole, and the larger macroinvertebrates in particular, are without doubt the best-studied organisms in running water systems. Not suprisingly, they are also, on the basis of present knowledge, clearly the most diverse group of organisms and play a hugely important role in the functioning of lotic systems.

The reason why we find certain species in a particular aquatic habitat has to do with the ability of these organisms to utilize and survive under the special set of biotic and abiotic conditions that characterize the habitat. We will deal with adaptations to the lotic environment in Chapter 5, including morphology, reproduction, life history patterns, communication, and behaviour. But apart from the adaptations to the habitat, there is a further vital component that is essential for understanding the distribution of taxa, and that is their biogeography. We have included a brief account of biogeographical patterns of lotic organisms in Chapter 8.

Microorganisms

Due to their small size and the relatively specialized techniques required to study them, our understanding of the biology of microorganisms in freshwater systems has been rather limited until fairly recently. With the development of new micro-biological methods for identifying and culturing these microbes, this situation is changing and for the first time we are beginning to see their true role and importance in the functioning of running water ecosystems (see p.151).

Bacteria

As in all other habitats on this planet, bacteria are often present in large numbers in running waters but the ecology of bacteria in streams and rivers still remains relatively poorly understood. What is known, however, is that bacteria are the major utilizers of dissolved organic matter. Free-living bacteria are mainly associated with decomposing organic material, but also occur in the biofilm on the surfaces of rocks and vegetation, in the interstices of the substrate and suspended in the water (see Chapter 6 concerning their role in energy flow and decomposition). In addition, bacteria occur as gut commensals and parasites in lotic animals.

Among the free-living bacteria, Gram-negative rods predominate (i.e. those not retaining the violet dye when stained with Gram's method), and in experimental culturing on different substrata, leaf-pack-inhabiting bacteria have been shown to degrade pectin and cellulose matter (Simon and Jones, 1992). Bacteria suspended in the water column of running waters derive mainly from growths associated with instream decomposition and from terrestrial inputs, thus the seasonal dynamics in bacterial counts clearly reflects the connection to autumnal leaf fall. Concentrations of suspended bacteria in streams and rivers range from 5.2×10^4 to 2.5×10^7 cells ml^{-1} (Lamberti and Resh, 1987). Densities in sediments may exceed 10^7 cells ml^{-1} and annual production has been estimated to be as high as 70 g m^{-2} dry weight in a British chalk stream (Sleigh et al., 1992).

Bacteria are known to be sensitive to low pH, although this may not be expressed in biomass, which can be similar on detritus in acid and circumneutral streams. However, their effect on decomposition seems to be significantly reduced in acid streams (Simon and Jones, 1992).

Fungi

While a number of fungal types occur in streams and rivers, hyphomycete fungi are by far the most important and will be considered here. The conidia of hyphomycetes (i.e. asexual spores cut off externally at the apex of specialised hyphae) are relatively large, being 10–40 times longer than average terrestrial spores. They typically have four diverging arms (they are 'tetraradiate'), or, more

Fig. 4.1 Hyphomycete conidia have characteristic tetraradiate, or occasionally S- shapes. (Redrawn from Ingold, 1975.)

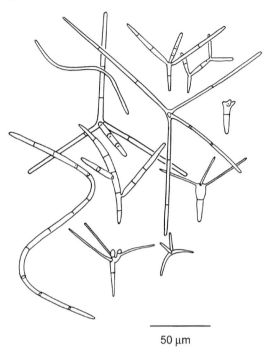

50 μm

rarely, a sigmoid shape (Fig. 4.1). These shapes may help the conidia to avoid being washed away by the current (Webster, 1981).

Hyphomycetes colonize the dead leaves that fall into streams and their hyphae penetrate the leaf tissue in an important process called *conditioning*. This makes the leaf more palatable and nutritious to detritivores as shown by increased preference and growth rates in these animals (see pp. 159–61). Hyphomycetes begin to 'skeletonize' dead leaves by macerating cells using pectinases. This type of sceletonization may be recognized by fine pin-prick holes. Wood is also attacked. In addition to the hyphae, the fungal spores are consumed by detritus-feeding animals. This resource may be substantial since nearly one million spores can be produced from a single dead leaf. Chapter 6, pp. 158–63, deals with decomposition in more detail.

Hyphomycetes are distributed from the tropics to the Arctic Circle. Their effects in tropical forests are not well known, although it appears that relatively more processing takes place here before the leaf material enters streams than in temperate areas. Our knowledge from higher latitudes is also very restricted, although large numbers of species are sometimes present (Marvanová and Müller-Haeckel, 1980). Many of these species are freeze-tolerant. Local distribution seems to be closely coupled to the kind of riparian vegetation and to water chemistry. In acid streams, low species diversity and reduced decomposition rates have been observed, suggesting that low pH may limit them. More detailed studies have shown, however, that the negative effects may be caused by chemical inhibition, perhaps from high aluminium levels, rather than by low pH *per se* (Chamier, 1987).

Plants

Plants have a multifaceted role in the biology of streams and rivers. Not only do they supply oxygen and contribute to the physical habitat of animals, they also act as a major conduit of energy flow. In their own right, aquatic plants are a diverse and interesting group with a range of adaptations that specialize them for life in running waters.

Algae

Algae are the most significant primary producers in most streams and rivers. Macroalgae are primarily filamentous forms occurring as tufts on rocks. Most other algae are microscopic, but often occur in colonies forming visible layers on the substrate or suspended in the water column as phytoplankton. Assemblages of species of algae and cyanobacteria attached to the substrate are collectively called periphyton. The main algal periphyton, that is, microalgae, includes diatoms, green algae, and phytoflagellates (Fig 4.2). Diatoms especially make up a species-rich group which is often considered as the most important food for many benthic herbivores. Primary production by benthic algae often makes up the major energy pathway in unshaded streams and in rivers with low turbidity (see p. 150).

Epilithic algae either form thin crusts (e.g. *Hildenbrandia, Lithoderma*) or occur in 'meadows' several mm thick (e.g. many pennate diatoms) on hard surfaces like stones. Algae living just beneath the surface of softer rocks are called endolithic (e.g. *Schizothrix*). Although the instability of finer sediments makes life more risky for algae, populations of many species can at least temporarily occur there in dense aggregations (e.g. *Oscillatoria, Phormidium, Microcoelus, Mastigocladus, Hydrodityon, Nitzschia*). Epiphytic species of algae live on higher aquatic plants. Phytoplankton occur chiefly in lowland rivers. In low-order streams most of the suspended algae

Fig. 4.2 Examples of microalgae: (a) stalked epilithic diatom *Achnanthes*; (b) *Nitzschia*, a diatom found in finer sediments; (c) the crustose red alga *Hildenbrandia*; (d) the filamentous green alga *Cladophora*; (e) the tubular green alga *Lemanea*. (From Hynes, 1970.)

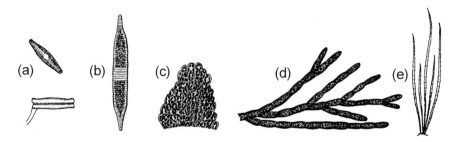

(a)   (b)   (c)   (d)   (e)

derive from benthic growths, but others may sometimes originate, as inocula, from standing water in the system.

Macrophytic algae occur as threads or filaments (e.g. *Cladophora*, Fig 4.2), tufts (e.g. *Oedogonium*, *Ulothrix*, *Stigeoclonium*), or as branched organisms with carbonate reinforcements (e.g. *Chara*, *Nitella*). Tubular algae may also be present (e.g. *Enteromorpha*, *Lemanea*). The amount of algal biomass reflects light conditions, flow rate, availability of nutrients, and grazing pressure at a site. Because of spatial variability in these factors large differences of algal growth may occur over small distances of stream bottom and even on a smaller scale over the surface of a single stone or boulder.

Mosses

In rivers with a stable substrate mosses may be very important inhabitants sometimes entirely covering rocks, boulders, and bedrock. They are especially abundant where low light levels constrain periphyton growth. Sometimes, as in some boreal, forested watersheds, they may contribute more to the primary production than periphyton (Naiman, 1983). Some moss species are truly aquatic, while others are semi-aquatic (i.e able to withstand prolonged periods above the water) and can often be found on exposed boulders along riverbanks.

In addition to flow stability, flow velocity is an obvious and important factor for moss production, and therefore, perhaps not surprisingly, different species of moss are differentially sensitive to flow variation. Studies in Finnish streams indicate that competition between different species is also of importance (Muotka and Virtanen, 1995). Large perennial species like *Fontinalis* spp., *Rhyncostegium riparioides*, and *Hygrohypnum ochraceum* appear competitively superior in stable environments, whereas smaller forms, including fast-colonizing *Blindia acuta*, prevail in disturbed habitats. With respect to life histories, the former group reproduces mainly vegetatively, while the latter has sexual reproduction. This means, at least in streams with stable beds, that moss communities are largely *dominance-controlled*. Species richness in such communities (in contrast to that in *founder-controlled* communities) result from dominance relationships rather than the colonization process (Yodzis, 1989).

Moss growth makes up a three-dimensional habitat of much greater structural complexity than bare rocks provide (Fig 4.3). This is expressed in the very high densities of invertebrates which are favoured by the protection from flow, the increased living space, and food in moss-rich habitats (Englund, 1991*b*). Moss tissue itself is rarely eaten, while periphyton growing on the moss and fine particles trapped in the plants constitute the main food source for the invertebrates (see also p. 42).

Flowering plants (Macrophytes)

In most running water systems, flowering plants (Angiospermae), such as the examples in Figure 4.3, are generally restricted to those areas where the gradient and hence flow rate is low. Only here is there sufficient accumulation of fine

Fig. 4.3 Types of morphological forms of submerged plants: a) moss, which adheres to stone surfaces and rooted plants; (b) *Vallisneria spiralis*, with its smooth linear leaves; (c) *Myriophyllum spicatum* with its finely divided leaves.

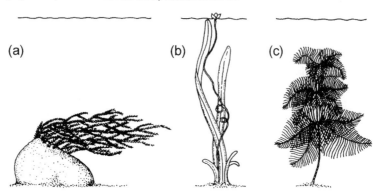

materials to provide the necessary substrate for rooting, and the eroding power of the water low enough. Submersed plants are also dependent on sufficient light reaching them. Therefore, increased turbidity reduces the maximum depth at which plants can photosynthesize. When the water is very clouded from suspended particles, submersed vegetation may be completely absent. Low-order streams are often heavily shaded, which also eliminates the extensive primary production other than from algae.

Under certain circumstances, however, lush macrophyte communities develop, and the best examples are perhaps the chalk streams of southern and eastern England. Just as in the case for mosses, the development of a truly lotic and lush flora seems to be dependent on stable flow conditions. For these reasons, the reed *Juncus bulbosus* expands in regulated rivers where flow variation is moderated. Enriched lowland rivers (e.g. within an agricultural landscape) can also develop thick macrophyte communities especially during the summer.

While species diversity of aquatic flowering plants is, in most cases, quite low, the riparian zone of rivers often abounds with species, which are more or less dependent on the river water seasonally inundating this zone. High water levels bring nutrients to the riparian system. It has been shown that in regulated rivers where the spring flood is reduced due to storage in large reservoirs, the development of river margin vegetation is greatly impeded (Nilsson and Jansson, 1995).

Higher plants influence the lotic systems in different ways. They reduce the current velocity, thereby increasing sedimentation. They also provide substrate for an epiphytic microflora, which in turn attracts grazers. In fact, some plants (e.g. *Ceratophyllum*) emit chemicals that signal their presence to grazers. Attracting grazers may reduce periphytic growth and thereby their shading effect, thus benefiting the plants (Brönmark, 1985). In contrast, only few herbivorous stream invertebrates seem to feed on living aquatic plants, possibly because they contain secondary compounds rendering them poisonous or at least unpalatable (Otto and Svensson, 1981). Some insect larvae, however, do feed substantially on macrophytes, such as the limnephilid cased caddis larva *Anabolia nervosa* on the pond weed *Potamogeton* (Jacobsen and Sand-Jensen, 1992, 1994, 1995). Vertebrates, including the rare manatee, ducks, and the grass carp can consume substantial amounts of submerged plants. Otherwise, these plants probably contribute predominantly to the river system energy flow in the decomposer food chains.

Invertebrates

As we mentioned at the start of the chapter, the invertebrates are the best studied and most diverse animals in streams and rivers. We therefore devote rather more space to discussing the various invertebrate groups than to other groups of organisms and make no apology for doing so!

Protozoa

The Protozoa is a heterogeneous group of microscopic unicellular or colonial eukaryotes that includes all heterotrophic and motile species, but also photo-trophic species. This is a rather pragmatic classification as it neglects the fact that member species may even belong to different phyla, but serves zoologists and ecologists, who often focus on functional units (Taylor and Sanders, 1991).

In streams, protozoans occur where the water velocity is restricted, particularly in interstitial habitats, in association with plants, and where organic matter settles. Protozoa includes two phyla. Members of Sarcomastigophora have a single type of nucleus, and pseudopodia and/or flagella for locomotion. The subphyla Mastigophora (e.g. dinoflagellates, eugleniids, cryptomonadids) and Sarcodina (e.g. *Amoeba*) belong to this phylum. The other large phylum is Ciliophora, the members of which have two types of nuclei, and simple cilia or ciliary organelles for movement.

In planktonic communities, both in freshwater and marine systems, Protozoa have a well-documented role as predators. In running waters, however, information is more meagre. Microflagellates especially may consume significant amounts of bacteria in some streams (Bott and Kaplan, 1984). Other protozoans also forage among particles in depositional areas of the stream bed, ingesting bacteria and algae. Ciliates can feed extensively on bacteria and flagellates, leading to high productivity. For example, on soft sediments in a British chalk stream, it was estimated that 12 g ciliate dry weight was produced per square metre of stream bed per year (Sleigh *et al.*, 1992). Another important microhabitat for Protozoa in chalk streams is the leaves of macrophytes. The total production by a protozoan population was similar to that of the amphipod *Gammarus*, and greater than those of simuliids and fish, which are all important animals in the stream.

Due to their lack of body structures, protozoans are often not recorded from predator guts despite the fact that they may well be eaten by many different species of scrapers, filterers, and deposit feeders or by young stages of predatory macroinvertebrates. For many small invertebrates, like naidid worms and orthoclad midge larvae, protozoans may indeed make up the bulk of the diet.

Turbellaria

In lotic environments, Tricladida (planarians) appears to be the most important of the seven orders into which the Class Turbellaria (flatworms) is customarily divided. Several of the other six orders, in combination referred to as Micro-turbellaria, are also found in running waters. About 400 species of micro-turbellarians are known world-wide and there are some 100 species of planarians.

Triclads are flattened, 5–30 mm long animals that glide on the substrate. Movement is produced through the action of cilia on the ventral body surface beating in a thin layer of mucus that is secreted from special glands. A majority of the stream-living triclads are cold-loving species, hence they are most abundant in headwater streams. The optimal temperature, for example, for *Crenobia alpina*, a European species, is 7°C. These animals are predators and scavengers. Turbellarians have a great capacity to detect food chemically and are quickly attracted to injured invertebrates. In some lotic systems they catch insect larvae such as simuliids. The pharynx is protrusible through the ventrally positioned mouth and digestion is often external to the body. Triclads are only rarely fed on by other predators. Reproduction may be sexual or asexual but most turbellarians are hermaphrodites (i.e. they possess both male and female sex organs). Turbellarians are well known for their remarkable regeneration capacity. If they are cut into pieces, each piece will regenerate into a whole flatworm.

Mollusca: Gastropoda

Snails (Gastropoda) are widely distributed in the stream environment. Many representatives from the subclasses Prosobranchia (with a horny operculum that closes the entrance to the shell) and Pulmonata (without an operculum) occur in flowing waters. More common examples include members of the families Pleuroceridae (Prosobranchia), and Ancylidae, Lymnaeidae, Physidae, and Planorbidae (Pulmonata). Generally, snails favour streams with high calcium carbonate concentration, since this is essential for the construction of the shell. A notable exception is the family Valvatidae, which is most common in waters with low carbonate concentration (Pennak, 1989).

Most snail species are found in shallow waters. Different species vary in their habitat preferences. Ancylids (freshwater limpets, Fig. 4.4) occur on rock surfaces.

Fig. 4.4 Lotic Mollusca include (a) the freshwater limpet (*Ancylus*) and mussels such as (b) *Margaritifera margaritifera* , the Pearl mussel, and (c) the smaller pea-mussel *Pisidium* sp.

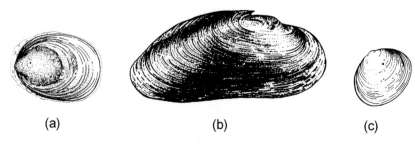

(a)   (b)   (c)

Spired, spiral-shelled snails include pleurocerids found on rocky or sandy sediments, physids and hydrobiids on vegetation, and lymnaeids that are quite unspecialized with regard to habitat.

Snails' preferred food by far is periphyton which is scraped away with a special toothed or file-like rasping organ (the radula). Some physids and planorbids may, however, include large amounts of detritus in their diet. The abundance and biomass of snails may be very high in streams. *Juga silicula*, a North American pleurocerid, can make up more than 90% of the invertebrate standing crop in some streams. At such densities, they must clearly influence other invertebrates. This has been shown by negative relationships between the snails and other benthic taxa, and in increases of other taxa following snail removal (Hawkins and Furnish, 1987). One of the mechanisms involved is exploitation competition. Some studies have also shown the capacity of snails to reduce algal abundance and also to influence algal production and community structure, including a shift from filamentous to adnate (flattened) forms.

Mollusca: Bivalvia

The most important freshwater bivalves are unionaceans (the freshwater mussels including Unionidae and Margaritiferidae) and sphaeriids (including *Sphaerium* and *Pisidium*) (Fig 4.4). Out of the 260 native and six introduced freshwater species in North America, which represents the most diverse bivalve fauna in the world, 227 are unionids. Europe has some 50 species. Unionidae contains many species with very restricted distributions making them vulnerable to extinction. For example, the number of species in the Tennessee river dropped from 100 prior to construction of a large impoundment in 1936 to less than 45 today (Pennak, 1989). Throughout most of its distributional range, *Margaritifera margaritifera*, the pearl mussel (Fig. 4.4), is threatened with extinction and subject to conservation measures. Mussels in general have a long lifespan and pearl mussels can live for more than 100 years.

In contrast to unionaceans, sphaeriids have wide distributions. Such differences suggest that the dispersal capacities may be fundamentally different (McMahon, 1991). Unionaceans spread primarily in their larval (glochidia) stage, which is parasitic on fish (see Fig. 5.11, p. 127), a fact which limits their capacity to disperse to where fish cannot go. In contrast, sphaeriids may disperse efficiently as passengers on birds, salamanders, and insects. Their establishment is facilitated by the fact that only a single individual is needed to found a new population, as they are self-fertilizing hermaphrodites.

Many unionaceans inhabit large rivers with a coarse sand or gravel substrate and high current velocities that prevent siltation. In contrast, members of the most species-rich genus of sphaeriids, *Pisidium*, prefer a substrate consisting of finer particles; their species diversity has been estimated to be maximal at a mean particle diameter of 0.18 mm.

Most mussels feed on small suspended particles that are filtered from the water. Cilia, and perhaps mucus, are instrumental in the capture of particles. Some species may feed from organic matter that is resuspended from the stream bed

Fig. 4.5 Crustacea: (a) Decapoda (noble crayfish *Astacus astacus*); (b) Asellidae (*Asellus*, the water hoglouse); (c) Gammaridae (*Gammarus*); (d) Atyid shrimp; (e) and (f) micro-crustacea (copepod *Cyclops* ≈ 1mm and cladoceran *Bosmina* ≈ 0.5mm). (e and f redrawn from Hynes, 1970.)

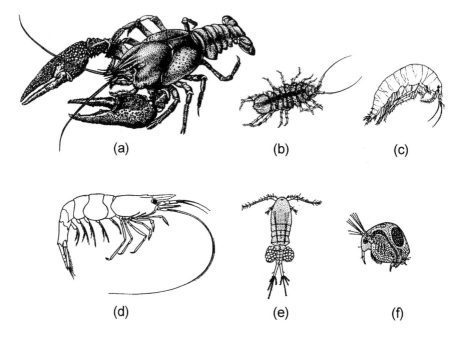

through 'pedal feeding'. Bivalves may also be significant as consumers of phytoplankton. Many of the larger predators, most importantly perhaps fish, feed on bivalves.

Crustacea

Many kinds of crustaceans are associated with running waters. Here we emphasize the larger forms belonging to the class Malacostraca including the orders Decapoda, Amphipoda, and Isopoda (Fig. 4.5), primarily because these are all very important in various lotic communities. We also briefly present some smaller, but important, members of the meiofauna like cladocerans, ostracods, and copepods.

Malacostraca

Decapoda are among the largest invertebrates to be encountered in running waters. They may conveniently be divided into shrimps, crayfish, and crabs. Decapods inhabit all sorts of aquatic environments, but many species are confined to lotic environments.

Shrimps are common in more tropical and subtropical latitudes, especially in streams with lush vegetation and slow currents. Atyid shrimps (Fig. 4.5(d)) may be the dominant organisms in tropical headwater streams instead of the insects which dominate the temperate systems. This is especially so where fish diversity and abundance are low, which often is the case on islands, such as Puerto Rico, and in peninsular areas. These species are primarily filterers or scavengers and they tend to modify the substrate by removing silt. This in turn favours algal growth and thus influences the benthic community, especially collectors and grazers (Pringle *et al.*, 1993).

Palaemonid shrimps also prefer sluggish water. About 100 species of *Macrobrachium* occur in the world. Species belonging to this genus are cultured in many places. The second important genus, *Palaemonetes*, seems to be excluded by *Macrobrachium* from locations between 30° N and 30° S, except at higher elevations.

Freshwater crabs also appear to be restricted mainly to the warmer parts of the world. In Africa, for instance, the river crab genus *Potamonautes* contains more than 40 species. Europe is the home of three crab species (genus *Potamon*), while North America only has one (*Platychirograpsus typicus*), which occurs along the Mexican east coast and into Florida.

Out of 382 extant species of freshwater crayfish, more than 80% are found in North America north of Mexico. In striking contrast, Europe has less than half a dozen indigenous crayfish species. A majority of crayfish live in lentic environments, although some species are confined to flowing, sometimes even fast, streams. Many of these live where shelter is abundant, while some burrow into the stream bed or into the stream banks or hide under boulders and cobbles.

Crayfish (Fig. 4.5(a)), like shrimps, can have significant influence on lotic communities. Most species are omnivorous and may be key processors of organic material, primarily allochthonous plant litter. They may also have strong effects as herbivores. Hart (1992) showed that at current velocities below 50 cm s^{-1} crayfish (*Orconectes propinquus*) efficiently removed *Cladophora*, thus indirectly changing the habitats for other invertebrates (see p. 204 for further details). While crayfish are also capable of depleting macrophytes and macroinvertebrates, they are themselves fed on by a range of predators including herons, muskrat, mink, reptiles, amphibians, and dragonfly larvae, although the importance of their predation is rarely quantified. Fish, however, have a documented strong impact, which is often shown in a negative relationship between densities of predacious fish and crayfish. Man is also a heavy predator on crayfish in some parts of the world. This, however, rarely seems to cause extinction but could certainly change population structure. As we mentioned in Chapter 3, populations of European crayfish (*Astacus astacus* and *Austropotamobius pallipes*) have been severely reduced over most of their distributional range by the 'crayfish plague'.

Amphipods (order Amphipoda) are common in many freshwater systems around the world. In total, about 900 species are known, and they occur in many types of habitats including streams, rivers, springs, and subterranean habitats. Their distribution pattern suggests that they are cold stenothermic. Europe has about 350, and America about 150 species. The most important family is Gammaridae (Fig. 4.5(c)). Although some gammarids appear to be favoured by high calcium bicarbonate levels, most amphipods appear to be restricted to streams with low or moderate concentrations.

In some headwater streams amphipods may be very abundant, especially where there is a stable substrate and ample food. Pennak (1989) reports *Gammarus* densities above $10\,000\ \mathrm{m}^{-2}$ in spring brooks with abundant, rooted vegetation, and densities of several thousand individuals per m^{-2} may be encountered in vegetation-free, second-order forest streams. Basically amphipods are omnivores, consuming both dead organic material and periphyton. Gammarids are frequently found in great numbers in the downstream drift, which makes them an important food item for drift-feeding fish in certain streams.

Asellidae (order Isopoda) occur in freshwaters, although this family is less diverse than Gammaridae. Like the Gammaridae though, many species are confined to groundwaters and the constantly dark environments of caves. They then often lack eyes and pigmentation. *Asellus aquaticus* (Fig. 4.5(b)) is perhaps the best-known species in Europe. It is detritivorous and appears to thrive in a wide range of habitats ranging from acidic forest streams to heavily polluted rivers.

Meiofaunal Crustacea

Microcrustaceans (Fig. 4.5(e, f)), which include members from the classes Ostracoda, Branchiopoda (including Cladocera), and Maxillopoda (including Copepoda), are important components of the fauna of most lentic freshwater systems but it has only recently been discovered that they may also play an important role in the food webs of stream and river communities. Many of these species have tiny drought-resistant eggs which can be carried in the wind as aerial plankton and hence disperse easily over land, a fact which helps explain why these species often have a very wide geographical distribution.

Ostracoda are small, usually about 1 mm long, and have a bivalve-like carapace. They are found in both marine and fresh waters, and they may be quite common in inland saline waters. About 300 species are known in the United States and a little over 400 in Europe. Some species have an interstitial lifestyle, while others move actively around on the stream bed feeding on bacteria, algae, and fine detritus. Some species are restricted to groundwater, others are clearly stream living. Often only female ostracods are found. In fact, no males have ever been found of many species and parthenogenetic reproduction appears to be widespread. Interestingly, ostracods have the largest sperm of any animal. Little is known about the importance of ostracods in the ecosystems they inhabit, but they are significant from a palaeontological perspective, since their carapaces preserve well in the sediments.

Cladocerans inhabit virtually any kind of freshwater habitat, including riverine and interstitial environments, and occur in the plankton of large rivers and in the benthos, although fast-flowing habitats appear to be avoided. Species of the family Chydoridae dwell in the interstices of stream gravel deposits, although they appear to lack particular morphological adaptations to this habitat.

Many Copepoda are planktonic, and as such may be found in large rivers and in lake and reservoir outlet streams. Small copepods of the suborder Harpacticoida (also to some extent members of Cyclopoida and Calanoida) occur on or in the stream bed. They are only rarely found in swift waters. Food, which consists of organic particles or unicellular plants and animals, is acquired by raking, grabbing, and scraping. Some species are parasitic and these have extreme morphology, making them very unlike other copepods.

Other non-insect macroinvertebrates

Three frequently encountered groups in lotic environments are Oligochaeta (worms), Hirudinaea (leeches), and Acari (water mites). They are by no means restricted to lotic conditions and the great majority of them occupy slow-flowing marginal habitats where the sedimentation of fine organic materials takes place.

Oligochaetes are deposit-feeding collectors which may be very abundant in situations when other macroinvertebrates are absent, particularly where high amounts of organic material are decomposing resulting in low oxygen tensions. This makes them excellent animals for monitoring water quality in polluted rivers and Tubificidae are a well-known indicator organism.

In contrast, most leeches are predators, feeding on various invertebrates, although a few are parasites of amphibians, fish, birds, and mammals. Others may be predators or parasites depending on the size relationship between the predator and its prey. Leeches do not generally appear to be important food for other stream-living animals.

Water mites are frequent members of both benthos and meiofauna (Smith and Cook, 1991). Over 5000 species of water mites are known in the world, many lotic. *Sperchon* and *Aturus* are the most diverse genera in North American streams. Acari develop through several stages and have a complex life cycle. The eggs are laid into plant stems or into the tissues of sponges or mussels. The larval stage developing from the egg is parasitic, often on the terrestrial stage of an aquatic insect (predominantly chironomids). A succession of other stages follows, including the quiescent 'nymphochrysalis', the predatory 'deutonymph', the again dormant 'imagochrysalis', and finally the adult stage which is predaceous. Smith (1988) found the prevalence of insect infestation by larval water mites (i.e. the total number of parasitized hosts to the total number of potential hosts) frequently exceeded 20 % for a variety of adult insects including Corixidae (water bugs), Dytiscidae (beetles), Libellulidae (dragonflies), Culicidae and Chironomidae (mosquitoes and midges).

Insects

Insects are among the most conspicuous inhabitants of streams and rivers. In most cases, it is the larval stages of these insects that are aquatic, whereas the adults are terrestrial. Typically the larval stage is very extended, while the adult lifespan is short. Lotic insects are found among many different orders and brief accounts of their biology are presented below. The most important insect groups in running waters are the Ephemeroptera (mayflies, Fig. 4.6), Plecoptera (stoneflies, Fig. 4.7), Trichoptera (caddisflies, Fig. 4.8), Diptera (true flies, Fig. 4.9), Coleoptera (beetles, Fig. 4.10), Hemiptera (bugs, Fig 4.11), Megaloptera (alderflies and dobsonflies, Fig. 4.11) and Odonata (dragonflies and damselflies, Fig. 4.11). The identification of these different orders is usually easy and there are many keys available to help in the identification to species. In contrast, some genera and species, particularly among the Diptera can often only be diagnosed by specialist taxonomists. In Table 4.1 a simple key to the main insect groups in lotic systems is presented along with a listing of the major families.

Table 4.1 A simplified key for the dominant lotic insect orders including a listing of the major families. Terrestrial adults have been excluded. Note that exceptions will exist in such a simplified key

---

1. **Wings present**

Adults

1.1 Mouthparts forming beak on underside of head: BUGS (Hemiptera)
Gerridae (water striders), Veliidae (water crickets), Notonectidae (back swimmers), Corixidae (lesser water boatmen)
1.2 Head without beak, front wings hardened, lack veins: BEETLES (Coleoptera)
Elmidae (riffle beetles), Psephenidae (water penny), Dytiscidae (diving beetle), Gyrinidae (whirligigs), Dryopidae

2. **Wings absent**

Larvae

2.1 Wing pads (developing wings) present (hemimetabolous insects)
    2.1.1 Mouthparts form beak: BUGS (Hemiptera). (See above for families)
    2.1.2 Leaf-like gills on abdomen, tarsus 1 segmented with 1 claw, usually 3 'tails':
        MAYFLIES (Ephemeroptera)
        The large families which have at least ten genera, all represented in running
        waters, include Baetidae, Siphlonuridae, Oligoneuriidae, Heptageniidae,
        Leptophlebiidae, Ephemerellidae, and Caenidae
    2.1.3 No gills on abdomen, tarsus 3 segmented with 2 claws, 2 'tails': STONEFLIES
        (Plecoptera)
        Northern hemisphere Euholognatha (detritivores) includes Leuctridae,
        Capniidae, Nemouridae, Taeniopterygidae. Systellognatha (predators)
        includes Chloroperlidae, Peltoperlidae, Perlidae, Perlodidae and
        Pteronarcidae (although a few of the latter are detritivores). In the southern
        Hemisphere two further suborders occur, Eusthenioidea (Eustheniidae,
        Diamphipnoidae) and Gripopterygoidea (Austroperlidae, Grypopterygidae)
    2.1.4 Hinge-like lower lip below head: DRAGONFLIES and DAMSELFLIES (Odonata).
        Important families of dragonflies are Gomphidae, Aeshnidae,
        Cordulegasteridae, Corduliidae and Libellulidae and of damselflies include
        Calopterygidae, Lestidae, and Coenagrionidae
2.2 Wing pads absent (holometabolous insects)
    2.2.1 Jointed thoracic legs present
        2.2.1.1 Prolegs present on last abdominal segment. Long lateral filaments
            absent: CADDISFLIES (Trichoptera)
        Net-spinners include Hydropsychidae, Polycentropodidae, Philopotamidae,
        Psychomyiidae. Case-building caddis include Limnephilidae,
        Sericostomatidae, Goeridae, Lepidostomatidae, Helicopsychidae,
        Glossosomatidae. Roving caddis include Rhyachophilidae
        2.2.1.2 Prolegs present (Dobsonflies) or single 'tail' (Alderflies). Long lateral
            abdominal filaments: MEGALOPTERA. Sialidae, Corydalidae
        2.2.1.3 Prolegs absent from abdomen, no single 'tail': BEETLES. (See above for
            families)
    2.2.2 Jointed thoracic legs absent: TRUE FLIES (Diptera)
        2.2.2.1 Obvious head capsule (midges; family Chironomidae, blackflies;
            family Simuliidae)
        2.2.2.2 No obvious head capsule (e.g. craneflies; family Tipulidae)

Table 4.2 The number of identified species of selected aquatic insect groups. Note that the exact figures are subject to constant changes due to new discoveries and revised taxonomies

	World	Europe	N. America
Mayflies	>2000	217	575
Stoneflies	1800	387	608
Caddisflies	>9600	895	1340
Blackflies	1650	190	169
Chironomids	c.20 000	1404	2000
Odonates	5000–6 000	127	650

Insects are ubiquitous in freshwater and are often represented by many species. We indicate the size of selected orders with respect to their number of species in Table 4.2. Although the numbers refer to aquatic species, a majority are to be found in running waters.

Ephemeroptera (mayflies)

Mayflies have a world-wide distribution. In 1990, 371 valid genera (61 as fossils) were known in the world (Hubbard, 1990) comprising more than 2000 species. This represents a 60% increase since 1976 when only 231 genera were known and shows our very rapidly increasing taxonomic knowledge of this insect order. Streams and rivers are generally inhabited by many species of mayflies and, in fact, most species are restricted to running waters. Baetids, heptageniids, and ephemerellids are usually the most frequently encountered families in lotic habitats (Fig. 4.6). Larval mayflies are just as likely to be found on stony substrate as on higher plants or burrowing in the sediments.

Larval mayflies are characterized by the presence of three 'tails'; two cerci, and between them usually a terminal filament. Mayflies are hemimetabolous insects (where larvae or nymphs resemble wingless adults) going through many post-embryonic moults, often in the range between 20 and 30. For the heptageniid *Ecdyonurus dispar*, body length increases about 15% for each instar (Humpesch, 1981).

Mayfly nymphs are mainly grazers or collector-gatherers feeding on algae and fine detritus, although a few genera are predatory (e.g. within the families Siphlonuridae, Metretopodidae, and Behninigidae). Some members of the families Ephemeridae, Heptageniidae, and Siphlonuridae filter particles from the water using hair-fringed legs or maxillary palps. Shredders are rare among mayflies, but they do occur in the Ephemerellidae and Leptophlebiidae.

Those species feeding on periphyton are often found grazing on the upper surfaces of the substrate where they are exposed not only to visual predators, but also to the direct action of the water current. This partly explains their high propensity to occur in the drift together with the fact that baetids, especially, often probe for

Fig. 4.6 Representatives of some important mayfly families: (a) Baetidae (*Baetis*); (b) Siphlonuridae (*Ameletus*); (c) Ephemerellidae (*Ephemerella*); (d) Caenidae (*Caenis*); (e) Heptageniidae (*Heptagenia*).

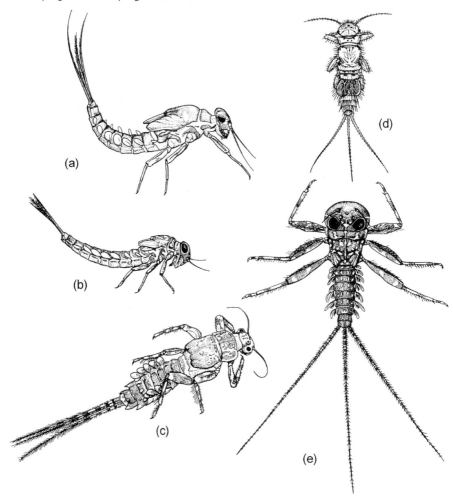

better food patches using drift (see p. 178). As part of the drift, mayfly nymphs are important prey to drift-feeding fish, especially young salmonids.

Respiration is facilitated by the gills, which are paired organs on up to seven abdominal segments (clearly seen in Fig. 4.6). In many species gills beat to aid water movement over their surface. Since larval mayflies of different species vary strongly in their tolerance of low oxygen concentrations, they are useful indicators for monitoring pollution in streams and rivers. They also possess a well-known sensitivity to acid conditions, although a few mayflies can tolerate low pH, and some leptophlebiids have been found in waters of a pH below 4.

The adult lifespan is short, ranging from a few hours to a few days, rarely up to two weeks, and the adults do not feed. Mayflies are unique among insects in having two winged stages, the subimago and the imago. The emergence of adults tends to be synchronous, possibly in order to swamp their predators (Sweeney and Vannote, 1982).

Plecoptera (stoneflies)

This is a relatively small, rather homogeneous order with more than 1800 species belonging to 15 families. Stoneflies are characterized by two long cerci ('tails') and a hemimetabolous life cycle. They have largely an antitropical distribution, being best represented in the temperate region of either hemisphere. Members of some important stonefly families are illustrated in Fig. 4.7.

Stonefly larvae are characteristic inhabitants of cool, clean streams of low orders, although several taxa occur in alpine and high-latitude lakes. While they are sensitive to organic pollution, or more precisely to low oxygen concentrations accompanying organic breakdown processes, stoneflies seem rather tolerant to acidic conditions. Lack of extensive gills at least partly explains their relative intolerance of low oxygen levels.

There are four suborders, which are listed in Table 4.1. Most stoneflies occur in stony habitats, often in the interstices of the substrate or in leaf packs. Their importance for ecosystem processes is two fold. One group of Northern

Fig. 4.7 Representatives of some major stonefly families: (a) Perlodidade; (b) Perlidae; (c) Leuctridae; (d) and (e) Nemouridae.

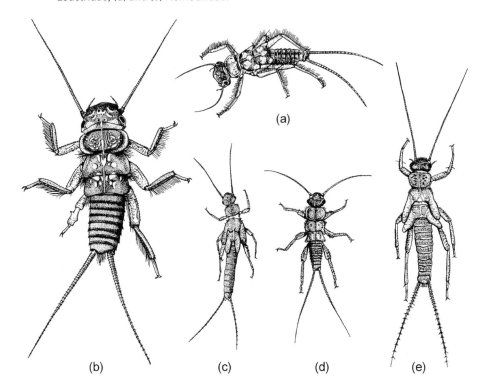

Hemisphere families, including Capniidae, Leuctridae, Nemouridae, and Taeniopterygidae, is largely detritivorous and their life cycle is well timed to utilize the autumnal leaf fall. Another significant northern Hemisphere group, including Chloroperlidae, Peltoperlidae, Perlidae, Perlodidae, and Pteronarcyidae, consists chiefly of predators of many smaller inhabitants, especially larval midges and blackflies. Many predatory species may shift from herbivory to carnivory in the course of their ontogeny, others may feed opportunistically on whatever is available.

Many stoneflies have reduced growth rates in winter, but it is striking that many also grow well at temperatures near 0° C. This ability seems to pertain to detritivores in particular, and therefore may reflect an adaptation to the seasonality in food availability. Some stoneflies reach considerable size; for example, the detritivorous nymphs of North American *Pteronarcys* may measure 50 mm in length and the development takes several years. At the other end of the size spectrum, full-grown nymphs of several families are found that barely exceed 5 mm in length and the life cycles of these are completed within a year.

Adult stoneflies are poor fliers. This probably explains their virtual absence on oceanic islands. Often stoneflies have short wings (brachyptery) or complete wing reduction (aptery). It has been shown that stoneflies may use the wing flaps for sailing on the water surface and for aerial gliding: the larger the wings the better the performance. These observations have been put forward as a hypothesis of how powered wings for insect flight may have evolved from articulated gill plates (Marden and Kramer, 1995). Some stonefly species feed in the adult stage from algae, leaves, and buds. Interestingly, adults attract partners by drumming their abdomens against leaves or wood.

Although many freshwater biologists would maintain that the Plecoptera is a well-studied group of insects, Stewart and Stark (1988) argued that, despite their importance, less than 5% of the species are well known with respect to life history, trophic interactions, growth, development, spatial distribution, and nymphal behaviour.

Trichoptera (caddisflies)

This is one of the most diverse insect orders living in the freshwater environment, and caddis-flies have a world-wide distribution (apart from Antarctica). Caddis-flies may be categorized broadly into free-living (roving and net-spinning) and case-building species. More than 9600 living species are known, belonging to 45 families and 626 genera (John Morse, personal communication, January 1996). Trichoptera is taxonomically close to Lepidoptera and the discovery of new caddisfly taxa is still proceeding at a relatively high rate. At the same time, there are many instances where solely the adults have been described, hence it is often not possible to identify all larvae with certainty. Figure 4.8 illustrates some of the caddis families.

Caddisflies are holometabolous insects (where the larvae undergo a complete metamorphosis to the adult stage during pupation) having five to eight larval instars. Being a very large family, larvae of various species occupy the whole range

Fig. 4.8 Larvae of some important caddisfly families: (a) Limnephilidae; (b) Glossosomatidae; (c) microcaddis Hydroptilidae; (d) Sericostomatidae; (e) Philopotamidae; (f) Lepidostomatidae; (g) Polycentropodidae, (h) Hydropsychidae; (i,j) Goeridae; (k) Rhyacophilidae.

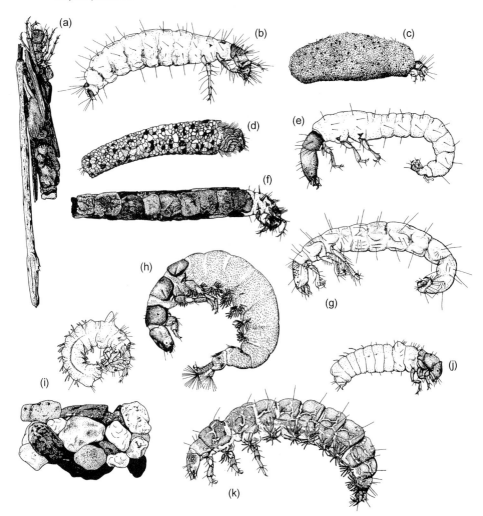

of major freshwater environments. Their success is undoubtedly related to their capacity for spinning silk, which is used for case-building, net-spinning and pupation (see pp. 118–21). The materials of the cases range from pure silk to the gluing together of sandgrains and organic particles, often in generic-specific or species-specific fashion (Fig. 4.8).

Many species are found where the current is slack and organic debris accumulates on the bed. Others occupy patches of vegetation, gravel bars, and rocks in a more or less selective manner. The habitats that various species utilize are partly reflected in their diet. While many species ingest a wide variety of food, their means of acquiring the food may be highly specialized. This has implications for their ecological functions, which include predation (e.g. the families Rhyacophilidae, Polycentropodidae), shredding (e.g. the cased families Limnephilidae, Lepidostomatidae, Sericostomatidae), piercing (e.g. Hydroptilidae), filtering-collecting (e.g. the net-spinning Hydropsychidae, Philopotamidae), and grazing/scraping (e.g. the cased Goeridae, Glossosomatidae, Helicopsychidae). In addition, some taxa (e.g. the family Psychomyiidae) may actually garden microalgae and protozoa in their galleries or defend algal patches on stones. Adults of some Trichoptera feed on nectar. They live for less than a month, but limnephilid species inhabiting temporary waters may live for more than three months to 'wait out' the drought (Wiggins, 1973).

The roving green rhyacophilid caddis larvae are generally present in low-order streams, where they feed extensively on other insects, primarily chironomid and blackfly larvae. They have strong claws which enables them to withstand fast currents. The cased Limnephilidae is the most species-rich family and they occur in many different habitats. Their cases are very variable. Limnephilids are likely to play an important role in the processing of organic matter in many lotic environments. Hydropsychids are well represented in most lotic environments where they spin a small net that is continuously tended. Other net-spinners, like Polycentropodids, construct large sack-like nets from which they remove small animals, and they tend to occupy slower-flowing and deeper waters. There is further information about adaptations in net-spinning caddis larvae in Chapter 5. Larval caddisflies often represent the highest biomass of the macroinvertebrate communities of streams and so they are an important food for various fish species and birds such as dippers.

While many caddis larvae attain considerable sizes (e.g. the cased Phryganeidae can reach up to 5 cm), others are notoriously small. Hydroptilidae (microcaddis) rarely exceed 6 mm. Members of this family may occur in very high densities, especially in association with filamentous algae, which they pierce and suck out the cellular content. While the first four instars of hydroptilids are free-living, the fifth one builds purse- or barrel-shaped cases (Fig. 4.8(c)). This last instar is also morphologically strikingly different from the earlier instars.

Diptera (true flies)

This is a very diverse order of insects to which many aquatic forms belong. A few families are uniquely lotic, such as Simuliidae, Athericidae, Blephariceridae, and Deuterophlebiidae. Chironomidae is the largest family, found in a great variety of habitats from temporary to permanent, from the smallest trickle to large rivers to lakes, and even marine habitats. Larvae of Thaumaleidae and several Psychodidae develop in madicolous habitats. In Tipulidae both aquatic and terrestrial larvae occur. The larvae of aquatic dipterans are readily recognized by their lack of jointed thoracic legs, although two types of 'false legs' may be present: ventral prolegs on the thoracic and anal segments (sometimes also on the abdominal segments) and creeping welts, which are transverse ridges most commonly found on the ventral margins of the first seven body segments. Many species of one

Fig. 4.9 The larvae of the two main families of Diptera. Chironomidae, the non-biting midges; (a) and (c) Diamesinae; (b) Orthocladinae and (d) Tanypodinae; (e) Simuliidae (blackfly).

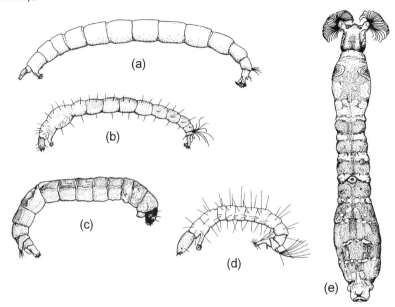

suborder (Nematocera, mostly aquatic) have a sclerotized head capsule with stout, toothed mandibles moving in a horizontal plane. In contrast, members of a second suborder (Brachycera, mostly terrestrial) lack a head capsule, and their mandibles are claw-like, move in a vertical plane and can be withdrawn into the head. In the following sub-sections we present a more detailed account of three of the most important lotic families: Simuliidae (Fig. 4.9(e)), Chironomidae (Fig. 4.9(a)–(d)) and Tipulidae.

Simuliidae

About 1650 species of blackflies have been described. The true number may be much higher because of the family's propensity to form cytospecies. These are morphologically identical but cytologically distinct, that is, having fixed amino acid sequence differences in inversions and other chromosomal characteristics, as well as meeting other criteria for a species status (e.g not forming hybrids in sympatric populations).

The family is a homogeneous group of superficially similar members. The larvae attach to the substrate via a silk pad to which they anchor their abdominal proleg, which carries large numbers of hooklets (Fig. 5.5, p. 113). More details on the use of silk by simuliids is given on pp. 116–17. With few exceptions the larvae are restricted to the lotic habitat, where they filter small particles from the water using labral fans (Fig. 4.9(e)). Collecting and scraping feeding modes have been demonstrated, and in a few genera (*Twinnia, Gymnopais, Crozetia*), which lack labral fans, filtering is of course not possible. The larvae of a few African and Central

Asian species are obligately associated with other arthropods including crabs and mayflies.

Blackfly larvae are important components of running waters and may sometimes occur in astounding densities. Their large numbers make simuliids important prey; they are frequently consumed by larval stoneflies and caddis-flies, but also fish such as sculpins, and by birds such as dippers and harlequin ducks. Another significant role of simuliids is through their impact on stream particle transport. The larvae collect large quantities of minute suspended particles, mainly smaller than 5 μm, which rapidly pass through the gut and are transformed into faecal pellets of >50 μm diameter. Where blackfly larvae are abundant, as in lake outlet streams, this process contributes strongly to the retention of organic matter in the stream by retarding its downstream transport and by increasing its propensity for sinking. With abundances which may amount to more than 100 per square centimetre their impact on carbon cycling, or 'spiralling', may be highly significant. We will come back to this topic in Chapter 6 (pp. 164–5).

Adult blackflies are often considered as pests and in some tropical areas the adults transmit a nematode parasite that causes 'river blindness' (onchocerciasis) in humans and cattle, a serious although not lethal disease. They also transmit leucocytozoonosis, a protozoan blood parasite often fatal to birds. This has economic consequences for the American turkey industry. The bites of some species cause allergic reactions in humans. On mass attacks, cattle may be killed for the same reason, and serious reductions in milk yields and egg production are known.

Chironomidae

With perhaps some 20 000 species world-wide, the Chironomidae (midges) is the most speciose freshwater group. This important family is subdivided into nine subfamilies, but we will only consider the main ones here: Tanypodinae, Diamesinae, Prodiamesinae, Orthocladiinae, and Chironominae.

Chironomids are the most widely distributed and often the most abundant group of insects in freshwater. They are found in cold, glacier-fed streams, springs, madicolous habitats, and from the smallest stream to the largest river. They occur at elevations up to 5600 metres in the Himalayas, and their distribution spans between continental Antarctica (68° S) and Ellesmere Island (81° N) in the Northwest Territory of Arctic Canada, near the northern-most extremity of North America. Despite the fact that a host of papers and books have been devoted to the chironomids, detailed ecological knowledge about most species does not exist (Pinder, 1986). A recurrent problem to aquatic entomologists is the difficulty of correctly identifying the chironomids: keys are incomplete and only work for last larval instars or certain regions.

The many representatives of Chironomidae cover most of the functional feeding groups, although a majority are collector–gatherers (Berg, 1995), including both tube-building and free-living forms. Their tubes are often the most obvious indication of their presence, which on closer examination can be seen on rock surfaces, plant leaves, and muddy bottoms. Often the tubes show regular distributional patterns, indicating that their inhabitants are territorial. In the subfamily Chironominae several genera, including *Chironomus* and *Rheotanytarsus*, spin silken catch nets associated to their tubes (see Fig. 5.7, p. 117). After a certain time of exposure the nets are entirely, or partly, consumed by the larvae. Many orthocladiines (most tube-living) and diamesines (free-living) scrape algae from rocks and higher plants. Diatoms are the most frequently found food in the gut. A number of Orthocladiinae feed on living vascular plants and macroalgae, and shred leaf litter. Some orthocladiines and chironomines also feed on wood. Predators are mainly found in the subfamily Tanypodinae, which have the largest head capsules.

Grazing chironomids may cause depletion of their food resource because of their high abundances and rapid growth rates (e.g. Wiley and Warren, 1992), and they could also bring about changes in periphyton community structure (Eichenberger and Schlatter, 1978). Several species mine the leaves of aquatic macrophytes. Yet others live as commensals or parasites. For example, *Epoicocladius ephemerae* lives on the body of the burrowing mayfly *Ephemera danica*, and *Eukiefferiella ancyla* builds tubes on the inner rim of the shell of the limpet *Ancylus fluviatilis*.

The sheer numbers of chironomids indicate their importance as potential prey animals. Indeed, most studies on predation in running waters clearly show that chironomids are ingested by virtually all predators, often more than any other prey.

Tipulidae

The Tipulidae (craneflies) is a very large family. Although about 15 000 species are known world-wide (Byers, 1996), a majority of these have larval stages restricted to terrestrial or semi-aquatic environments. Yet many species do occur in lotic systems in a wide variety of habitats, from madicolous systems to small streams and large rivers. Our ecological knowledge of tipulids is, however, rudimentary for most species. Tipulids have four larval instars and the life cycle can be completed in a period of time ranging anywhere between six weeks and five years, although most aquatic larvae require 6–12 months (Byers, 1996). Development over several years is found in species inhabiting high-latitude environments.

The head capsule of larval tipulids is characteristic in the sense that its rear part is incompletely sclerotized and can be retracted into the thorax. Larvae of the subfamily Tipulinae are large (some reaching several centimetres in length) and tough-skinned (sometimes called 'leather jackets'), while most Limoniinae have an almost transparent cuticle. The most important role of the aquatic tipulids is probably in the decomposition of organic material, thus many tipulids, including the subfamily Tipulinae, are shredders feeding on decaying leaf detritus. *Tipula* may be quite dependent on a specialized flora of bacteria residing in the hind gut (Pritchard, 1983). In Limoniinae, there are also some important predaceous genera, notably *Dicranota*, *Hexatoma*, *Limnophila*, and *Pedicia*. Cylindrotominae are mainly herbivorous (moss, higher plants) or shredders.

Coleoptera (beetles)

The beetles are one of the few groups of insects whose aquatic members normally live in water both as larvae and adults. They are by far the most speciose order of terrestrial insects but surprisingly this diversity is not so apparent in freshwaters.

The well known riffle beetles are an arbitrary collection of taxa primarily including the entire family Elmidae (Fig. 4.10) and riffle-inhabiting members of Dryopidae, the genus *Lutrochus* (Lutrochidae), and the water penny (family Psephenidae *sensu latu*). Most riffle beetles are small, generally slow-moving species clinging to the substrate. The elmids have aquatic adults, whereas the water penny has terrestrial adults. Both adults and larvae of most species feed on fine detritus with associated microorganisms that is scraped from the substrate, although others may be xylophagous, that is, wood eating (e.g. *Lara*, Elmidae). Predators do not seem to include riffle beetles in their diet, except perhaps for their eggs, which are sometimes attacked by flatworms. Ecologically, their main role therefore seems to be in the breakdown of organic material indicated by their rich faecal production.

Other beetle taxa may also be important in running waters, particularly in slow-flowing sections. Among these, the Dytiscidae (diving beetles) is the most diverse family, with more than 2500 species (White and Brigham, 1996). Both larvae and adults are predators: larvae are engulfers and adults are piercers. Hydrophilid larvae are also predatory, while the adults are omnivores. Gyrinid (whirligig beetles) larvae are benthic predators, whereas the adults live on the water surface, attacking dead and living organisms trapped in the surface film. Dryopids are detritivores, and hydraenid adults mainly grazers.

Hemiptera (bugs)

This is the other main group of insects that utilizes freshwater habitats as both larvae and adults. Water bugs belong to the large, mainly terrestrial (>90 % of the

Fig. 4.10 Riffle beetle (Elmidae) larvae (top) and adults (bottom) of (a) *Elmis aenea* and (b) *Limnius volckmari*.

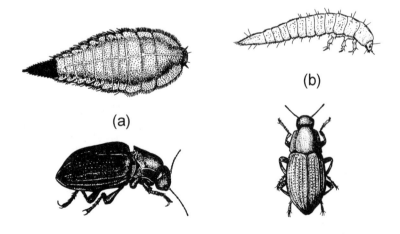

(b)

(a)

species) order Hemiptera and all are found in the suborder Heteroptera. In total, more than 3300 species belonging to 15 families are either aquatic or semi aquatic. Few are lotic, but several are semiaquatic in the sense that they live on the water surface (Gerromorpha or 'water striders'). In lentic waters and in slow-flowing streams some species are truly aquatic (e.g. backswimmers and corixids—'water boatmen'). There are only a few lotic species in Europe, but in tropical streams and rivers one often finds quite a number of species, particularly in pools. Individual species of *Anisops*, a mainly subtropical and tropical genus of backswimmers, often seem to coexist by swimming at different depths.

Hemipterans are hemimetabolous insects, most of which are predatory on other insects. They plunge their piercing maxillary stylets into the captured prey and the often highly toxic compounds in the saliva rapidly paralyse the prey. Gerromorpha prey on terrestrial or emerging insects caught in the surface film, the prey being located through vision and by vibrations on the water surface.

These surface forms are themselves prone to predation especially by fish. *Velia* (Fig. 4.11(b)) possesses a repertoire of anti-predatory behaviours (Brönmark *et al.*,

Fig. 4.11 Other insects: a)*Sialis* (Megaloptera); (b)*Velia* (the water cricket, Hemiptera); and the dragonfly *Zygonyx* (Odonata) with labial mask folded (c) and extended (d).

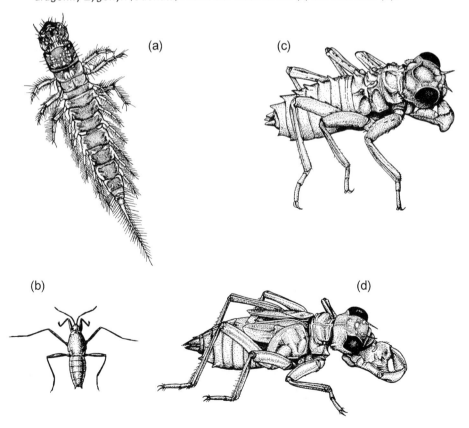

(a)

(c)

(b)

(d)

1984*b*), including thanathosis (death feigning) and rapid propulsion through the addition of a detergent which rapidly decreases the surface tension, leading to an instant flight over several centimetres. The aggregatory behaviour characteristic of the water striders *per se* may also be advantageous against predation. *Gerris* also avoids predatory fish by jumping. In European streams, water crickets, *Velia caprai*, forage in small flotillas. When an individual has captured a prey, it rapidly swims to the stream margin. Neighbouring individuals may detect its success and if the prey is big enough several individuals may share the same prey. Individuals may compete for the best position on the surface with regard to prey availability (see p. 130).

Adults of one of the few riffle-dwelling bugs, *Aphelocheirus aestivalis*, respire by using a permanent physical gill consisting of a dense pile of short hairs that holds an air bubble forming a 'plastron' (see pp. 108–9). Elmid beetles have similar adaptations.

Megaloptera (alderflies, dobsonflies)

Megaloptera is a medium-sized order with less than 5000 species world-wide. Most species are terrestrial; in North America 64 aquatic species occur but in Europe only six (all in Sialidae). Sialids also occur in Asia.

In running waters, members of the families Sialidae and Corydalidae are particularly important, as they are all voracious predators, having large mandibles with sharp teeth. Sialids (Fig. 4.11(a)) feed on a variety of aquatic invertebrates, in particular small insects such as chironomids, oligochaetes, and molluscs. Smaller larvae also include microcrustaceans, and in the first instar, microorganisms and detritus, in their diet. Larval sialids prefer soft-bottom habitats in lakes as well as in streams and rivers, while corydalids occur over many different habitats including springs, streams and rivers, and lacustrine habitats. They can even survive in temporarily dry stream beds. The development of sialids can involve up to 10 moults over 1 to 2 years. In corydalids, which can reach 65 mm, the number of instars is 10–12, and the larval lifespan 2 to 5 years. Pupation takes place in soil.

Odonata (dragonflies and damselflies)

These are conspicuous, hemimetabolous insects (lack a pupal stage). About 5500 species occur world-wide, the larvae are aquatic, the adults terrestrial. Adults are often large, colourful and day active, and are efficient predators that are territorial and usually found patrolling around aquatic habitats. There are three suborders: Anisoptera ('dragonflies'), Zygoptera ('damselflies') and the less well-known Anisozygoptera. Anisoptera adults are stout, strong-flying insects; the fore- and hindwings are of different sizes and always held open. Important families are listed in Table 4.1 (p. 84). In contrast, Zygoptera adults are slender animals with similar-sized fore- and hindwings that are held closed above the body at rest. Aniso-zygoptera, which are confined to the Himalayas and Japan, are intermediate between the other two suborders in many respects.

In the larval stages most dragonflies are found in lentic or slow-flowing habitats, although some are lotic specialists (e.g. *Zygonyx torrida*, Fig. 4.11(c)). From a review of the relative representation of species in different habitats, it appears that Australia and Malaysia have the greater share of species confined to running waters (40%), whereas South Africa, North America and Europe have fewer (20–25%; Watson *et al.*, 1991). Few species, however, are found in rapid flow.

Respiration in larval Anisoptera takes place through pumping water in and out of the rectum, which is foliate and richly provided with tracheae (air-filled tubes). In Zygoptera, 2–3 caudal lamellae aid respiration which, however, is believed to be chiefly through cutaneous diffusion. Development involves 10–15 moults, which can involve a larval life between a few weeks in some Zygoptera and Libellulidae and five years in some Anisoptera.

Dragonfly larvae are voracious predators and they include various invertebrates as well as small aquatic vertebrates in their diet. Prey are grasped with the long, hinged labium that is thrust against them (Fig. 4.11(d)). Prey are either stalked or captured using a sit-and-wait strategy (Zygoptera, Aeshnidae) in the vegetation or pursued by more active hunters (most Anisoptera) sprawling among fine organic material. They possess binocular vision which aids in prey capture. Due to their size, odonates are at risk of being eaten by fish. In fact, many species thrive best in the absence of fish.

Vertebrates

Representatives from all vertebrate classes (most notably fish, of course) are found associated with lotic habitats. Because of their size, ease of identification, economic importance, conservation status, or general interest, vertebrates are generally well studied and have been the subject of many specialist texts. We will introduce the groups here and give some of the more interesting aspects of their biology relevant to life in streams and rivers.

Fish

These are the best-known inhabitants in freshwater systems. This is no doubt conected with their importance as food; river fishery for domestic use and commercially has world-wide importance. It is also related to their value for recreation—fishing is perhaps one of the most popular hobbies in the Northern Hemisphere, and as such it has considerable economic importance for tourism.

Most of the 8500 species of freshwater fish (Lowe-McConnell, 1987) occur in rivers or connected floodplains. In North American streams and rivers, darters (Percidae), minnows (Cyprinidae), and suckers (Catostomidae) are the most important components. Two groups of fish are especially important and diverse in South America: Characidae and catfish. Families of cyprinoids, including cyprinids, loaches (Cobitidae), and hillstream loaches (Homalopteridae) contribute notably to the diversity of Asian rivers. European waters have relatively few true freshwater fish because of the recent glaciations. Some characteristic taxa are shown in Fig. 6.8 (p. 168).

Many fish species have life cycle stages in both fresh and marine waters, others migrate between these habitats (diadromy). Species reproducing in freshwater and having a growth phase in the sea are called *anadromous* species. Several species of lampreys and salmonids belong to this category. Species of salmon are important anadromous fish in northern rivers, which they populate hundreds of kilometres from the sea. In the Atlantic, *Salmo salar* is the chief species, while in the Pacific, species of the genus *Oncorhynchus* play a similar ecological role. Man has negatively impacted on the populations of salmonids by habitat destruction and damming, as well as overfishing. Eels are *catadromous*, that is, they spawn in the sea and migrate as larvae to freshwater where their main growth takes place before they return to their place of birth in the sea. Galaxiids in New Zealand reproduce in freshwater, but young fish spend a relatively short period in the sea. The Hawaiian freshwater fish fauna consists only of diadromous gobioid species. In these, newly hatched fry leave the streams in which they hatch to spend a period in the sea as part of the zooplankton community (Radke and Kinzie, 1996). Postlarvae return to streams and metamorphose. Juveniles and adults live in freshwater, where they spawn.

Buried in a sandy substrate, larval lampreys (a primitive jawless fish-like vertebrate) filter the water both for organic particles to support their slow growth and for respiration. Larval lampreys are restricted to running waters, whereas after metamorphosis the adults of many parasitic species migrate to lakes or the sea. After a period of parasitic feeding, predominantly on fish, they return to the running waters for reproduction and after spawning they die. Their adult life is restricted to one or two years, but their larval life may be extended over many years. Non-parasitic species do not feed as adults; they spawn in the spring after transformation.

The most characteristic fish species of European streams is probably the brown trout, *Salmo trutta*. Other salmonids play a similar role in the stream systems of other continents, such as in North America (e.g. cut-throat and brook trout). In parts of the world where trout is not native, one or another species has often been introduced. Trout feed on a wide range of aquatic invertebrates on the stream bed or drifting in the water column, and, especially during the summer and autumn, on terrestrial insects that have fallen onto to the water surface. Other fish species feed predominantly on invertebrates associated with the stream bed, including sculpins (Cottidae), darters, and minnows.

Trout tend to be particularly important in the smaller, mountain headwater streams. Lower down in the systems, they appear to be replaced by other species, a pattern that was observed quite early this century and has been used in the classification of streams (see Fig. 6.8, p. 168). One such classification ranked stream segments of European rivers (from upstream to downstream) into trout, grayling, barbel, and bream zones, primarily on the basis of the habitat selection of these species with respect to slope and temperature (Huet, 1954). Not only does the composition of the fish fauna change downstream, but it also tends to become more diverse, often with several species of Cyprinidae appearing. Still further downstream, bottom-feeding suckers (Catostomidae), larger species of cyprinids and catfish (Siluroidei) appear, which feed mainly on vegetable matter. Most species of suckers live in running water where they play the same role as Gobioninae in East Asia and the Danube basin and running water barbs in southern Asia (Banarescu, 1990).

A majority of temperate fish species are predators on macroinvertebrates, whereas in tropical/subtropical areas detritivorous and grazing fish species also play key roles in lotic habitats. The impact of these predatory fish on macroinvertebrates has generated numerous adaptations by the latter to avoid being captured and eaten (see Chapter 7, pp. 184–7) and can potentially influence the distribution of invertebrates (see Chapter 3, pp. 68–9).

Extensive disturbance of rivers and streams, including pollution, habitat destruction, damming, and introduction of exotic species, has severely affected natural populations of freshwater fish. We will return to this in Chapter 9.

Reptiles and amphibians

Most freshwater amphibians, including Urodela (salamanders and newts) and Anura (toads and frogs), lay eggs and have their larval development in water, and they are relatively short-lived. After a metamorphosis several remain in or near water. Respiration in larvae is through gills and skin, in adults through skin and lungs. There are nearly 4000 species of amphibians.

Few amphibians are restricted to habitats with flowing water. Of those that are, the most spectacular examples include two species of giant salamanders belonging to the genus *Andrias* (Cryptobranchidae) living in Chinese and Japanese cold water streams. They grow to reach a length of up to 1.5 metres. The North American hellbender (*Cryptobranchus alleganiensis*) belongs to the same family, and shows a similar affinity to fast-flowing streams with rocky substrate, where they feed on snails, crayfish, and worms. Other salamanders spend time as larvae in stream pool habitats.

Most reptiles are terrestrial. Those found in freshwater habitats (snakes, turtles, and crocodiles) are air-breathing. Most of them lay eggs, and then not in water. Reptiles have fewer, but longer-lived species than the amphibians. Among the reptiles, the Concho water snake (*Nerodia paucimaculata*) of central Texas is classified as an endangered species that is only present in riffles along the Concho and Colorado rivers. This species served as an example of the utility of metapopulation dynamics to analyse the viability of populations of the species (Soulé and Gilpin, as quoted by Quammen, 1996). By damming the river, riffle habitats were separated by extended slow-flowing areas, where competing species excluded *N. paucimaculata*, thus breaking up its population into relatively isolated subpopulations (together forming metapopulations).

Crocodiles and their relatives are among the largest vertebrates of tropical and subtropical rivers. They are likely to have significant impact as predators of fish. Many of them occur in slow-flowing rivers, although the dwarf caymans found in South America do prefer fast-flowing streams.

Birds

Although many species of birds use the margins of streams and rivers for foraging, few are exclusively aquatic. Many of those associated with fast-flowing water primarily feed on adult stages of insects. These birds occur in different parts of the world and include European grey wagtail, North American black phoebe and water thrushes, Asian water redstarts, forktails and whistling thrushes, and Central and South American buff-rumped warblers and Andean torrent tyrannulets, tyrant flycatchers and wagtail tyrants. Species occurring on larger rivers often also occur on lakes or marshes. Truly lotic species, in the sense that they explore the water column or the benthic habitats of streams and rivers, are the dippers and half a dozen species of ducks.

Dippers

There are six species (Fig. 4.12) of dippers in the world; one in Europe, two in Eurasia, two in the Andes and one in eastern North America and Mexico. These birds are unique among passerines in the sense that they are able to swim underwater, exploiting invertebrate prey. Dippers have many physiological and morphological adaptations, including dense, waterproof plumage and strong bills, legs, toes, and claws. Their wings are designed to be used as flippers that can bring them to the bottom and help maintain their position there against the current. Dippers have nasal flaps that stop water from entering (like other aquatic birds).

Fig. 4.12 World distribution of dippers. Note the absence from important regions such as Australia, major parts of Africa and eastern North America. (Redrawn from Tyler and Ormerod, 1994. Reproduced with permission of the Academic Press, London.)

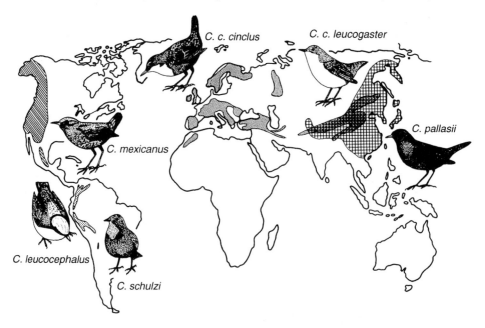

Andean dippers do not swim or dive, but catch prey by wading in belly-deep water or from rocks in cascades and waterfalls by dipping their heads under the water surface. The white breast patch of the European dipper may act as a light reflector to aid in the hunting for small prey on dark rocks on the stream bed. Dippers feed mainly on aquatic insects, especially the larvae of mayflies, caddisflies, simuliids, and stoneflies, but also on some fish, crustaceans, and molluscs.

Ducks

Many species of waterfowl utilize riverine habitats, but as mentioned earlier only a limited number of species are truly lotic in the sense that they live and forage in fast-flowing streams and rivers. These include the harlequin duck found in Iceland, Greenland, Labrador, north-western North America, and north-eastern Siberia; the torrent duck of the Andes; the blue duck in New Zealand; and the Brazilian merganser which has populations at inaccessible forest torrents in headwaters of the Paraná and Tocantins rivers in southern Brazil, eastern Paraguay and north-eastern Argentina. Like the dippers, ducks all exploit in-vertebrate prey which they capture in fast-flowing habitats. Although the harlequin ducks breed on fast-flowing streams and rivers, they spend the non-breeding seasons on rocky coasts. In Iceland their diet consists almost exclusively of blackfly larvae and pupae (Bengtson, 1972). Interestingly, the Andean torrent duck feeds in a way similar to most dippers, while the two Andean dipper species have a different mode of foraging to other dippers, perhaps as a consequence of interaction with the ducks (Tyler and Ormerod, 1994). Salvadori's duck of New Guinea favours rushing mountain streams at altitudes up to 4000 metres, but more rarely it also occurs in sluggish rivers and lakes. The African black duck is found in less torrential wooded streams and rivers of hillier parts of tropical Africa, and the bronze-winged duck occurs in rivers of southern South America.

Kingfishers and sandpipers are other examples of birds that are often found along rivers, but most species are not restricted to a life in these habitats.

Mammals

Rivers provide drinking water for all sorts of mammals. Therefore many species, especially in arid areas, are found in riparian habitats along rivers. Few species, however, actually live in the water, and there are only a few specialists which spend an extensive part of their lives in slow-flowing rivers. The foremost representatives are the beavers of northern boreal regions, otters, hippopotamus, river dolphins, and the peculiar monotreme, the platypus of Australian waters.

Beaver

The beaver (genus *Castor*) is one of the most important mammals associated with lower-order stream habitats, because of its capacity to modify water flow and stream morphology by building dams across streams. This habit can lead to the forming of braided channels, which were probably more common in times when beavers themselves were more abundant. Furthermore, the creation of ponds behind the complete dams gives the channel gradient a step profile. The damming activities also create wetlands and lead to an increased retention of organic matter in the streams. Naiman and co-workers (1986) estimated the magnitude of sediment retention by beaver (*C. canadensis*) dams in some Canadian streams to be about $10\,000\ \mathrm{m}^3/\mathrm{km}$ of stream. Nutrient cycling is also affected, and so is the composition and diversity of the biota (Naiman *et al.*, 1988). Beavers feed to a large extent on the fresh bark of riparian trees, which are felled with the aid of their powerful teeth. They also build spectacular lodges using branches and twigs, completed with mud and rocks. The removal of mature trees in the riparian zone opens up the canopy, thereby increasing the potential for primary production in beaver streams (see Chapter 3, p. 36).

As mentioned above, beavers were formerly abundant but after extensive hunting their populations dropped to a small fraction of their former densities. Beavers have since been given some protection through legislation and now populations are increasing rapidly again in North America and in northern Europe. These changes have, not unexpectedly, had important consequences for the stream ecosystems. Other rodents, such as muskrats, coypu, and voles can also influence channel patterns through their burrowing activity into banks and, in the case of the coypu, through their destruction of macrophyte and reed beds. The South American coypu (*Myocastor coypus*) was accidentally introduced into many countries in Europe as it escaped from fur farms and established free-living populations. In Britain, they led to such severe damage in the Norfolk Broads region that the species was actually proscribed and exterminated.

Otters

Otters (genus *Lutra*) are torpedo-shaped mammals (about 1 metre in length), which live in association with aquatic habitats such as streams and rivers, and lake and sea shores. Different species are found in Europe, Asia, and North and South America. The European otter (*L. lutra*) and the North American river otter (*L. canadensis*) have similar lifestyles which include a heavy reliance on a fish diet (particularly eels and salmonids), but seasonally expand their diet to include amphibians, birds, and crayfish. Both species are suffering great population reductions and shrinking range largely related to habitat destruction through dredging, channelization, and loss of riparian cover, but also through water pollution and the accumulation of toxins (e.g. PCBs). The European otter in particular is now almost extinct in much of mainland Europe. Otters are territorial, marking territory boundaries with faecal deposits ('spraints') and live in underground holts. They prefer habitats with a good riparian cover, especially deciduous trees with large rooting systems. Individual territories can exist along river lengths up to 15 kilometres (Fig 5.13, p. 131). The related mink (*Mustela vison*), a native of North America, has a similar lifestyle although it has a less specialized diet and can forage inland. Introduced into Europe, there is some evidence of competition with the otter, but the intensity is not clear.

Fig. 4.13 The river dolphin Ganges susus (*Platanista gangetica*). The long 'beak' bears numerous pointed teeth and the neck is extremely flexible to aid movement among vegetation. (From Evans, 1988.)

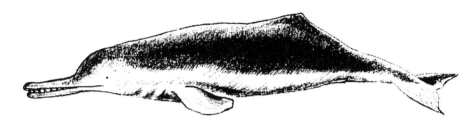

Other mammals

The hippopotamus (*Hippopotamus amphibius*) is a very large mammal that spends most of the daylight hours in rivers. The animals' impact on African river systems must have been highly significant but these days populations are reduced. For example, in Kruger Park, South Africa, there are 2–10 per kilometre of river. They graze on land at night but defaecate in the water, thereby increasing the input of allochthonous matter (Davies *et al.*, 1995). They actually cause more human deaths than any other large mammal in Africa.

The platypus, in contrast, is a small and extraordinary animal inhabiting a wide range of freshwater habitats in eastern Australia. This egg-laying monotreme mammal feeds on benthic invertebrates such as freshwater shrimps, which are located by its bill-shaped organ carrying numerous electrosensors.

The only totally aquatic mammals in freshwater are the river dolphins (Fig. 4.13). Five species occur in parts of the Yangtze (Chineese river dolphin or Baiji, *Lipotes vexillijer*), Indus (Indus susus, *Platanista minor*), Ganges, Brahmaputra, Kharnapuli and Meghna river systems (Ganges susus, *P. gangetica*), and the Amazon and Orinoco river basins (Amazon river dolphin or Boto, *Inia geotrensis*). One species (Franciscana, *Pontoporia blainvillei*) occurs more in river estuaries than freshwaters of South American rivers. River dolphins have poorly developed vision (the Indus and Ganges susus are virtually blind), which may reflect the fact that they live in turbid rivers and estuaries where vision is of little value. Food, mainly consisting of fish, molluscs, and crustaceans, is located by sound (echolocation). Several populations of these mammals are small and decreasing due to pollution and mortality in fishing nets.

5 Adaptations to life in running waters

From one perspective, terrestrial and aquatic habitats are similar in that they consist of a fluid (gaseous atmosphere or liquid water) overlying a solid (land surface or river or lake bed sediments). However, the greater density of water provides mechanical support that allows a vast array of aquatic organisms to live 'free from contact with the ground' suspended in the fluid medium, particularly in the oceans and lakes. It also means that any movement of the denser water is also of much greater and more immediate importance for aquatic organisms than air movements are for terrestrial ones. The challenges to life in streams and rivers are therefore going to be different from those in terrestrial systems, and as a consequence, we find unique adaptations among the lotic biota, some of which we explore in this chapter.

Flow refuges

It will be clear to the reader from what has gone before that current is the most significant factor for life in running waters. The very fact that we do not find masses of animals collecting at the downstream end of river systems attests to the ability of organisms to cope in some way or another with the forces exerted by flowing water. From laboratory studies (see Statzner *et al.*, 1988) it seems that a large number of lotic animals can actually withstand quite high flow velocities, many in excess of 150–200 cm s^{-1}, without being dislodged and washed away. These velocities are higher than generally occur in running waters, especially close to the bottom. Body shape, size, and a range of other adaptations such as hooks and grapples, friction pads, ballast, and silk are important in this context and are discussed on pp. 110–21. But these cannot provide the complete answer. First, trying to resist flow appears to be energetically expensive. For the caddisfly *Micropterna*, for example, a large part of the entire energy budget is expended simply by moving against the flow (Bournaud, 1975). Second, flow forces fluctuate over time and the increased flows and shear stress during spates and floods would exceed the ability of most organisms to simply resist the imposed drag and lift forces. Attempting to withstand the current is one tactic for coping with life in running waters; escaping or avoiding the current is another.

For a long time, it was generally assumed that the boundary layer (p. 57) provided a refuge for organisms to escape flow forces and that many of the morphological characteristics we will discuss later were adaptations to this end. Unicellular algae, crustose or felt-like turfs, a few tens of micrometres thick, can exploit this microzone. This might be true also for the smallest animals that have a considerable portion of their body within the viscous sublayer of the boundary layer, thus mainly experiencing friction drag. But it is now clear that the viscous sublayer is probably thinner than previously thought and that most benthic macro-invertebrates, including streamlined and dorsoventrally flattened taxa, probably experience rather complicated turbulent flows within the boundary layer and consequently endure the forces of flow rather than escape them (see pp. 111–15).

Current speed declines markedly within the substrate and organisms living beneath rocks or in the hyporheic habitat will be less exposed than those on the surface. We know that fauna can occur deep in the beds of streams, particularly in gravel substrates. In fact, highest benthic densities are usually found at between 5 and 20 cm depth (Fig. 5.1). Microcrustaceans, oligochaetes, and chironomids are clearly the most abundant taxa here, whereas baetid and heptageniid mayflies and caddis larvae are more abundant at the surface of the substrate. However, the surface layers offer certain resources for lotic invertebrates (e.g. periphyton for the grazers, coarse detrital particles for shredders, and suspended particles for filter-feeders) hence the hyporheos cannot be a permanent refuge from flow. In fact, there is a large body of evidence showing diel patterns of activity on the upper surface of stream substrates due to vertical migrations in lotic invertebrates (see p. 171).

If invertebrates are actually using the hyporheos as a refuge, one could expect densities to increase there as flows increase during spates. The evidence to date is equivocal, with some studies showing such trends (Dole-Olner and Marmonier, 1992) while others showing almost the opposite, with losses of 50–90% of animals from the hyporheic zone during spates (Palmer *et al.*, 1992). The substrate can be

Fig. 5.1 The distribution of macroinvertebrates (mean ±95% confidence intervals) with depth in the substrate over two seasons in Salem Creek, N. America. (After Godbout and Hynes, 1982. Reproduced with kind permission of Kluwer Academic Publishers.)

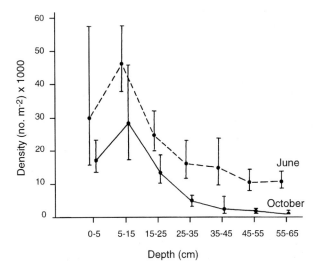

scoured to quite a depth during severe spates, thus the hyporheos is not a guarantee of safety. Similarly, to avoid low flows or drought conditions in temporary streams, one might expect invertebrates to seek refuge in the hyporheic zone, but again evidence is equivocal. Certainly, microcrustaceans move to deeper areas (100 cm) but generally macroinvertebrates do not (Clinton *et al.*, 1996).

On a larger scale, lateral extensions of channels onto floodplains can offer refugia during flood disturbances. These are known to be important for fish (Schlosser, 1991), but there is little information on the extent of use by invertebrates. There is, of course, always the risk of stranding when the flood subsides and in any case, extensive lateral habitats are usually lacking in headwater areas, particularly where the valleys are narrow and steep.

A fourth and perhaps the most convincing type of flow refuge is related to the great spatial heterogeneity of flow within the river or stream channel, both laterally and longitudinally. Certain macrophytic plants provide protection and shelter from the current for a variety of animals. *Myriophyllum*, with finely divided leaves and large surface area, *Potamogeton crispus* with its crenulated leaves and clumps of mosses (see Fig. 4.3, p. 76) all have high invertebrate densities, whereas plants with smooth, linear leaves like *Vallisneria* are generally the least populated. Similarly, use of leaf packs and marginal areas can offer protection from the current during normal flow conditions. We also saw in Chapter 3 that if the bottom is rough, flow is weaker downstream of individual substrate particles (e.g. cobbles, boulders) or other obstructions, and small recirculating eddies are established. Larger animals, like fish, can utilize such areas behind large particles whereas smaller animals can reside in the lee of smaller substrate particles, or within crevices and holes. There are also other types of low flow regions, or *dead zones*. These include turbulent eddies generated by larger-scale bottom irregularities, large slowly moving recirculating zones along the sides of pools, and side pockets to the main channel. Such low flow patches can be of the order of few hundred square centimetres on the stream bed (see Fig. 3.8, p. 59) and flow rate remains low and largely unchanged even during increased or peak discharge during flood events (see Fig. 3.12, p. 65). In rivers, these 'dead zones' can be even more substantial (Reynolds *et al.*, 1991) and are crucial to the maintenance and dynamics of phytoplankton.

As with the hyporheos, to be satisfied that these low flow patches are acting as refugia, it is necessary to show that animals actively or passively aggregate in them during periods of increased discharge. Sampling macroinvertebrates from the three 'patch types' we discussed earlier (Fig. 3.12, p. 65), Lancaster and Hildrew (1993*b*) found that the relative density of several taxa (particularly stoneflies) increased in the 'slow' refugia patches over a seven-month period in which discharge and flow events gradually increased (Fig. 5.2). The results were taxa- and-size specific—small individuals showed no response, whereas large stoneflies did. More recent experiments, based on artificial flow refugia in enclosures, monitored invertebrates over shorter time periods where discharge varied widely, and demonstrated clear movement of invertebrates into the experimental dead zones during spates (Winterbottom *et al.*, 1997).

Fig. 5.2 The relative movement of two species of stonefly larvae between patch types of varying flow (F, fast; V, variable; S, slow; see text for details) as discharge gradually increases from August to April. (From Lancaster and Hildrew, 1993*b*.)

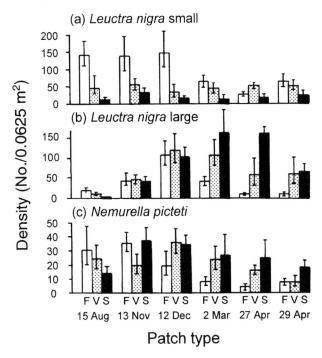

Flow refugia are scale-dependent phenomena. Small-scale elements (like a single substrate particle) may provide protection from low-intensity local disturbances. Patch-scale refugia may provide protection from higher-intensity disturbances. Both operate within the normal range of an individual (i.e. within-habitat, Hildrew, 1996*b*). For intense, widespread disturbances between-habitat flow, refugia are needed at the species population level. Within the full drainage basin, the variety of channel forms, the floodplain, marginal habitats, and the great overall length of the drainage network make it unlikely that there will be catastrophic mortality simultaneously throughout the system. So, through dispersal in space among and within the various habitats and dispersal in time through, for example, extended oviposition or egg hatching, the risk of population extinctions throughout the drainage basin is reduced (Hildrew and Giller, 1994). The provision of flow refugia is dependent on within- and between-habitat heterogeneity, both of which can be compromised through the activities of man, as we will see in Chapter 9.

Physiological adaptations

The physiological tolerance limits of different stream organisms influence their ability to cope in a specific situation or habitat. We will discuss just a few physiological systems here to illustrate some of the more interesting adaptations to running waters.

Feeding

A particularly significant aspect influencing feeding is the type of digestive enzymes that are present. These restrict the kinds of food that can be digested and affect the way different temperatures and food qualities influence digestion. Snails are among the few animals possessing cellulase, which enables them to break down the cell walls of algae and plant detritus. Detritivores feed on a material with low levels of assimilable protein, carbohydrate, and lipid. Cargill *et al.* (1985) showed that in later instars caddisfly shredders develop a preference for lipid-rich food, frequently found in hyphomycetes. An alternative source of lipids is utilized by those caddis larvae which shift from shredding to predation in the last instars (Giller and Sangpradub, 1993).

Temperature affects the feeding rates of lotic animals in the same manner as animals living in other systems. This means that metabolic rates normally increase with temperatures up to a certain species-specific value above which inhibition starts (see pp. 34–5). In winter though, feeding may be minimal or even discontinued. However, many lotic organisms are quite capable of growing even at temperatures near to freezing point. For instance, Short *et al.* (1980) reported that considerable processing of leaf litter took place under the ice cover in a Colorado stream, most likely due to shredding by the stoneflies which occurred at high densities in leaf packs. Brinck (1949), in a classic study of Swedish stoneflies, described how many stoneflies showed a 'hiemal' growth, (i.e. they have their main growth from autumn to spring, often with only a slight retardation in winter).

Respiration

This takes place largely through diffusion across the body walls of most of the smaller invertebrates. Insects, in addition, possess tracheal systems, which are networks of internal tubing of decreasing dimensions carrying oxygen to all parts of the body. In adults these open to the outside via spiracles, but in larvae the spiracles are closed. Like many lentic forms, lotic insect larvae often respire with the help of external gills, which provide a large surface area to volume ratio to enhance diffusion of oxygen into the body. Examples are common in the Ephemeroptera, Plecoptera, Trichoptera, and Odonata (see for example Fig. 4.6, p. 86). Since oxygen levels are only rarely a problem in streams, the gills are often relatively small or immobile. Under oxygen stress though, respiratory movements do occur (see p. 124). Taxa which utilize air bubbles (including adult beetles and bugs) sometimes have very specialized respiration in more fast-flowing environments where ascending to the surface to replenish the bubble would be perilous. This is the case in some elmid beetles and in the Palaearctic water bug *Aphelocheiris aestivalis*, which both have a 'plastron' consisting of a very dense pile of hydrofuge hairs forming a permanent physical gill. The density of the 6-μm long hairs in

A. aestivalis is as high as 2.5 million per square millimetre (Thorpe, 1950). Oxygen diffuses into the air bubble from the water and then enters spiracles and the tracheal system. The spiracular gills of blackfly pupae are filled with water, but the outer cuticle of the gill wall is hollow and forms an air film, providing another example of a plastron that is linked with the tracheal system of the pupa. In contrast, larval blackflies, like most stream invertebrates without gills, absorb oxygen through the body wall. Other aquatic insects breathe atmospheric air brought from the water surface (e.g. dytiscid beetles, hemipterans, and some dipteran larvae), although this is understandably much rarer in lotic than lentic environments.

Gills are also found associated with the legs of amphipod and isopod crustaceans and in molluscs. Freshwater prosobranch snails, which have a horny operculum or 'trapdoor' to shut the shell, have a single gill (ctenidium) located in the mantle cavity with leaf-like plates richly supplied with blood vessels. Oxygen-poor blood passes through the ctenidium in the opposite direction to oxygen-rich water currents created by cilia, a counter-current mechanism ensuring a positive diffusion of oxygen from the water to the blood (Brown, 1991). Pulmonate snails, which have re-invaded freshwater from the land, have instead a 'lung', a richly vascularized pocket in the mantle. They either rely on surface breathing or in some species of Lymnaeidae or Physidae, the pocket is filled with water and acts as a gill. Ancylidae and Planorbidae have a conical epithelial gill as a further adaptation to aquatic life.

In higher aquatic plants, mechanical support is offered by the water, so the epidermis can be thinner and thus facilitate gaseous exchange across the surface. Extensive spaces within the tissues facilitate the transport of gases internally. Fish have a very efficient respiratory system involving gills and counter-current systems, while most amphibians can breathe under water either through their body surfaces or via gills which are retained generally only during the juvenile stages. Other aquatic vertebrates, like reptiles, birds, and mammals, breathe air directly, and effectively 'hold their breath' while swimming under water, with associated changes in blood flows to various parts of the body.

Osmoregulation

Animals in freshwater are hypertonic (body fluids are more concentrated) in relation to the medium in which they live. This causes osmotic problems, with surrounding water striving to dilute the internal salt concentration and salts tending to diffuse into the surrounding water, both of which will disturb the biochemical integrity of the animals. This is exacerbated by the permeability of the respiratory surfaces that allow oxygen uptake. To counter the risk of a diluted body fluid, several structures have evolved to differentially retain and uptake salts. In aquatic insects these ion absorption sites include: (1) chloride cells (Ephemeroptera, Plecoptera, Heteroptera); (2) chloride epithelia (abdominal—Trichoptera: Limnephilidae, Goeridae; anal—Diptera: Tabanidae, Stratiomyidae, Ephydridae, Muscidae; rectal—Odonata; (3) anal papillae (Diptera: Nematocera, Syrphidae; Trichoptera: Glossosomatidae, Philopotamidae); and (4) gut wall epithelium of drinking insects (Sialidae, Dytiscidae) (Ward, 1992a). Bivalves eliminate excess water as urine via the kidney and recover lost ions via active transport over the gills and other epithelial surfaces (McMahon, 1991). Freshwater fish also have specialized membranes to retain salts and they produce copious amounts of dilute urine to eliminate the large amounts of water that enter the body through the gills.

Drought resistance

An ability to survive adverse conditions often relies on physiological adaptations. For example, animals have a varying capacity for withstanding drought. Most aquatic macroinvertebrates rapidly succumb in the absence of water, while other taxa can tolerate long dry periods, but then usually only in a resting dormant stage. Encystment is a feature of many protozoan life cycles, especially in systems that have a propensity to dry out, or when conditions otherwise become un-suitable (Taylor and Sanders, 1991). Sponges can also undergo dormancy when active tissue transforms into dry gemmules during periods of environmental stress (p. 141) and rotifers have a great ability to tolerate desiccation (anhydro-biosis), reviving in as little as a few minutes even after a couple of decades (Wallace and Snell, 1991). Triclads undergo encystment as entire animals or have eggs that are tolerant of desiccation, a feature of many other invertebrates, especially among inhabitants of temporary streams. Most notable are the Crustacea. For example, ostracod eggs may remain viable for years and in some species the eggs even require a dry period to hatch. Some species of blackfly larvae have eggs that survive dry seasons. For example, in the widely distributed *Simulium vernum* complex, females lay eggs in stream channels after the seasonal flow has ceased (Crosskey, 1990). Life history adaptations also play a role, as discussed later (p. 143).

Body form, size, and other features

Body size and shape

There are, of course, evolutionary constraints on the body plan of organisms, yet many factors can still influence their shape. Since stream organisms live in an environment characterized by moving water, it is perhaps not surprising that this can be traced to various aspects of their morphology. The lifestyle and micro-habitat of a species are also crucial. Thus, for a small invertebrate, it is important whether it lives on the surface of the substrate or among crevices or in the stream bed, whether it lives exposed to fast currents or in slack waters, or if swimming behaviour occurs. In animals that are directly exposed to flow, the near-bed hydrodynamic forces (drag, lift, and shear) are critical for the animals' ability to move on the substrate, and, not least, to avoid being swept away. Filter-feeders are, of course, directly dependent on the current and its supply of food, and they may have to balance the positive effects of food delivery rates with the negative action of the various flow forces. Whether grazing or filter-feeding, taxa dwelling in or utilizing exposed microhabitats would be expected to have evolved some means of coping with the flow. In particular, blackfly and blepharocerid fly larvae, some mayfly and caddis larvae, and riffle beetles (both adults and larvae) do inhabit torrential habitats, and have special adaptations to deal successfully with this environment.

Shape

Body shape plays an important role in in the biology of running water organisms. Even in diatoms, which are generally very small, their morphology is variable and can be used to distinguish several different guilds (Table 5.1). These guilds in turn show clear patterns with respect to location, from headwaters to high-order rivers, hence the shape clearly influences their ecology. Turning to stream animals, many have a strikingly flattened body that is held against the substrate, perhaps best exemplified by heptageniid mayfly larvae. Originally it was believed that such flat-bodied animals could avoid the impact of the current by crouching inside the

Table 5.1 Diatom guilds from three Kentucky River tributary streams, USA, distinguished on the basis of morphological characteristics (From Molloy, 1992.)

Guild	Distinguishing morphological features
Achnanthes spp. (1)	Small in size, monoraphid*, generally prostrate orientation to the substrate
Cocconeis spp. (2)	Concave monoraphid; prostrate orientation to substrate and large amounts of mucilage combine to give this taxon a unique mode of adherence
Centric (2) (3)	Centric diatoms: *Cyclotella* and *Stephanodiscus* Filamentous centric diatoms are not included in this group
Filamentous (2) (3)	Filamentous centrics found almost exclusively in chains in most samples: *Melosira* and *Skeletonema*
Adnate (1) (2)	Adjacent to substrate surface without being prostrate or erect: *Rhoicosphenia, Amphora, Surirella, Rhopalodia, Denticula, Cymatopleura*
Erect (1)	Perpendicular to substrate without stalks, often forming rosettes. Generally araphid or pseudoraphid: *Fragilaria, Diatoma, Synedra, Asterionella, Meridion*
Biraphid/prostrate/ non-motile	Taxa generally biraphid, prostrate, non-motile: *Anomoeoneis, Diploneis, Gyrosigma, Stauroneis, Amphipleura, Neidium, Caloneis, Frustulia, Bacillaria paradoxa, Nitzschia,* and *Hantzschia amphioxys.*
Navicula spp. (1)	Biraphid, generally prostrate, frequently motile, arborescent or stalk-forming genera; *Cymbella, Gomphonema* and *Gomphocymbella.* Selected species within *Gomphonema* without stalks are included here
Eunotia spp. (1)	Araphid; adhere to substrate by means of one or more jelly pores

(1) are guilds common in small, headwater streams; (2) are guilds common in downstream (3rd–5th order) communities; (3) are guilds common in high (6th) order rivers.

* A raphe is a cleft (usually sigmoid) running along the frustule of a diatom.

boundary layer, or even that the current helped to press them down against the substrate. Statzner and Holm (1982, 1989) changed this view by using laser-doppler anemometry to show how flow behaves around the bodies of various animals. Not only does flow separate above a flattened animal, but it is also much more complex than was first thought. Flow separation reduces lift, but at a cost of increased drag which, however, is a price that may well be worth paying to stay attached. For the heptageniid larvae, certain features of its body design may in fact lead to negative lift in flowing water. This is accomplished by lowering its head shield and by using its femora as spoilers (Weissenberger *et al.*, 1991) (Fig. 5.3). An alternative explanation for the flattened body of these insects could be that it increases the potential for movement in narrow interstices of the substrate, although the long thin bodies of other invertebrates, like many stoneflies and, of course, worms, are perhaps better adapted to this.

The most flattened animals in streams are flatworms and water pennies. Flatworms, however, are probably flat because of evolutionary constraints in body shape, and they do in fact seem to avoid fast-flowing microhabitats (Hansen *et al.*, 1991). The water pennies, which are larvae of the riffle beetle family Psephenidae, seem to adhere to the substrate through suction. Sucker-like mechanisms are also formed by the gills of some heptageniids. Leeches have suckers, but they are not adapted for life in flowing water, and they appear to be unable to move against the current. Suckers are also found in blepharocerid fly larvae (Fig. 5.4), which enable them not only to withstand very rapid currents, but also to move against currents of up to 2.4 m s^{-1}. Some madicolous psychodid fly larvae also have suckers, but true suckers are rather rare in lotic invertebrates, perhaps because they only work on smooth surfaces, and thus afford little flexibility in habitat choice.

In contrast, baetid mayfly larvae have streamlined shapes held off the substrate. As streamlining reduces drag (lift is also reduced), this shape enables these mayflies

Fig. 5.3 A nymph of the *Ecdyonurus venosus* group. The lowered positioning of its head shield and use of the femura as spoilers decreases lift.

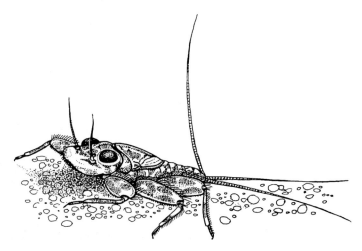

Fig. 5.4 Ventral view of a blepharocerid fly larva showing the suckers.

to cope well in fast-flowing environments. Mayfly species found in very fast-flowing waters tend to be small and have relatively large legs, while other appendages (gills and cerci) are smaller than in lentic species.

Larval blackflies, which live exposed to currents ranging from almost lentic conditions to torrential cascades, also have a distinctive body shape and are attached to the substrate with a large number of small hooklets that are anchored onto a pad of silk produced by the larva (Fig 5.5; p. 116). The current deflects the streamlined body in a downstream direction; the deflection is almost zero in a larva feeding in very slow currents, whereas in very fast currents, the body is held almost parallel to the substrate. Blackfly larvae seem to be able to control their feeding posture to balance the conflicting demands of drag and feeding to some extent (Hart *et al.*, 1991). By bending up against the current, larvae hold their labral fans higher up where velocity, and hence particle flux, are higher. The

Fig. 5.5 Larval blackfly, showing the distinctive body shape (a) and details of the system of hooklets around the tip of the abdominal proleg (b, c) with which they are attached to the substrate (pp, posterior proleg; rh, row of hooklets).

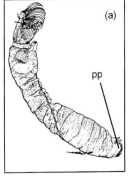
(a)
pp

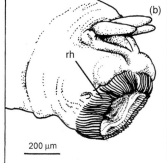
(b)
rh
200 μm

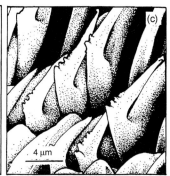
(c)
4 μm

abdomen is widest at about one-fifth of the distance from the hind end. It has been speculated that this shape may help reduce drag, but probably it also determines where vortices will form from which the larvae feed (Chance and Craig, 1986). In contrast, the middle part of the blackfly larva is narrow, which facilitates bending and rotating.

Size

The size of lotic organisms is important not only with respect to factors such as hydrodynamics and the ability to move within the stream bed, but also to biotic factors such as predation risk. Nevertheless, body size is first and foremost related to the nature of the organism. For instance, cladocerans, ostracods, and chironomids rarely exceed a few millimetres in length and fish or crayfish are normally 10–100 times larger. We discussed in Chapter 3, (p. 56) how the relative importance of viscous and inertial forces of the flow around organisms is described by the Reynolds number (Re) and that Re increases with inceasing body size. Thus, small animals live in a world of low Reynolds numbers. That is, they experience an environment where viscoscity is very important. Movements are impeded and gas exchange slowed down, whereas they have the benefit of a water layer that surrounds the organism and provides a protective shield from the buffeting of the current. In contrast, large animals, such as fish, experience higher Reynolds numbers, which means that inertial forces are much more important than viscous forces and so large animals have relatively few problems related to locomotion and gas exchange. The effects of flow will, therefore, not only change with the type of organism, but also with the body size of a single individual as it grows. Life for small insect larvae with a Re of 1–10 is dramatically different from that of fully grown larvae with a Reynolds number of around 1000. Such ontogenetic changes have implications for the microhabitats that different stages of a species should select, and in fact may help to explain some of the distributional patterns observed in the field.

There appears to be a vertical distributional change in relation to mean body size so that, in general, the larger inhabitants of a stream dwell in the water column or on the stream bed and the smaller ones, to a greater extent, within the substrate. The diverse meiofauna that resides entirely within the stream bed are all small organisms including nematodes, mites, and small crustaceans. Mites living in running waters are also smaller than those living in lentic environments. It is also reasonable to expect a similar body size gradient when moving from coarse to fine substrates. Exceptions to these body size-habitat patterns include some relatively large organisms that bury into a finer substrate, such as larval lampreys, and the inverse situation of small organisms suspended in the water column in the case of river plankton.

Body size can influence predation risk. Large invertebrates suffer a much greater risk of being captured and eaten by fish than very small ones for two reasons. First, as fish primarily use vision for prey detection, larger prey can be spotted at a greater distance than small prey. Second, since larger prey contain more energy than small prey, it is often more energy-efficient for the fish to select large prey.

There are therefore important implications for where and when invertebrates should be active in order to minimize the risk of being captured and eaten (see pp. 184–6).

Finally, body size is also related to life history patterns. Large animals develop slowly; for instance large stonefly or odonate larvae may take several years to complete their larval growth, whereas small ones can reach maturity in the course of only a few weeks. The blackfly *Simulium sirbanum* can pass through its entire larval life in only four days under favourable temperatures near 30° C (Séchan, 1980). Huryn (1990) found clear differences among leaf pack-developing chironomid species; the small *Corynoneura* (2 mm) completed eight or more cohorts in a season, whereas larger species managed fewer. The largest, *Pseudorthocladius* (7 mm), had a single generation per year. We will return to life history adaptations on pp. 139–46.

Hooks, bristles, hairs, and filaments

The tarsi of aquatic insects all have terminal claws. In riffle beetles, the claws are large and stout. This enables them to retain their position even at high current velocities. The posterior prolegs of the caddis *Rhyacophila*, the megalopteran *Corydalus*, and lotic chironomid midges, in addition to blackfly larvae, have hooks or hooklets that likewise help to stop larvae from being swept away when they move over exposed surfaces. Most insects also have bristles and hairs of various kinds and functions that are scattered in intricate patterns across their legs, head, thorax, and abdomen. These assist the larvae to monitor their immediate surroundings. For instance, a cased caddis larva can assess whether the case is in place and is provided with continuous information with respect to flow with the aid of setae connected to nerve cells. In burrowing insect species, a dense cover of bristles and hairs helps to keep the sediment particles away from the body and in the stonefly *Capnopsis schiller* even the eyes are covered (Fig. 5.6).

Cerci (the 'tails' extending from the abdomen of insects) help provide sensory information and most likely assist swimming and other movements. In ephemerellid mayflies, following disturbance, the end of the abdomen and cerci are often raised over the head and pointed forwards. This is known as the 'scorpion posture' and is believed to have evolved to deter predators (Peckarsky and Penton, 1988).

Insect silk: an important building material for lotic insects

Silk is a generic term used for all fine, chiefly fibrous, protein threads extruded by all sorts of arthropods even though the threads may differ in chemical composition. In caddis-flies at least, silk is composed of long unbranched polypeptide chains of fibroin. In lotic animals, silk is particularly important in the larvae and pupae of blackflies, chironomids, caddis-flies, and butterflies. It has the unique property of being liquid when stored in the animal but sticky in water. The silk is used for attachment, tube, case, and catch net construction, and could serve as lifelines. Silk strands, although they are soft, have an extremely high tensile strength, greater even than that of mild steel.

Fig. 5.6 The head and thorax of *Capnopsis schilleri*. Note the degree of hairiness and that even the eyes are covered.

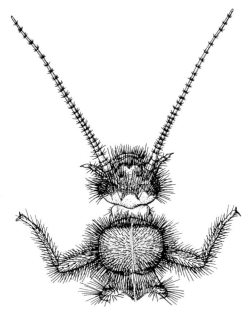

Blackflies

Blackfly larvae, even when very small, produce large amounts of silk which serves several purposes. First, silk is used for anchorage and explains the extraordinary capacity of blackfly larvae to remain attached or move in fast-flowing micro-habitats. The larvae have numerous hooks, arranged in characteristic rows, encircling the tips of the anterior (thoracic) and abdominal prolegs (Fig. 5.5, p. 113). These help larvae to anchor firmly onto silk pads attached to the substrate. In species dwelling in particularly fast flow, the number of hooks on the abdominal proleg may exceed 8000, compared to only 500 in species living at slow velocities (Crosskey, 1990). By producing new pads blackfly larvae are able to move over surfaces, much in the same way as the terrestrial geometrid moth larvae loop, although the body of a blackfly larva is held nearly parallel with the substrate during movement. Just before looping starts silk is secreted onto the thoracic proleg, the larva swings forward and attaches the silk to the substrate. When anchored at two points, the larva enlarges the silk pad, releases its hold on the first pad, and swings the abdomen forward placing its abdominal proleg onto the new silk pad.

Blackfly larvae can also drift away by quickly releasing the hooks' grip from the silk pad. A larva about to drift almost invariably attaches a string of silk to the substrate before letting go. This mooring line, only a few micrometres in diameter, enables larvae to, at least partially, control the risky business of drifting. When departure is caused by a disturbance, such as a physical contact with a predator, the lifeline allows the larva to climb back and return to its original position.

Silk is also an important prerequisite for the construction of pupal cocoons. Interestingly, the chemical composition of silk in blackfly silk glands appears to change when approaching the last larval instar (Barr, 1984). This can be seen in a shift of silk colour, apparently associated with the changed functions of the silk through the life cycle.

Chironomids

Many species of midges build larval and pupal tubes using silk. Depending on the species, these vary in shape and the materials that are glued together by silk (plant fragments or mineral particles). The larvae of some chironomids construct catch nets that can either be placed inside the tube (tribe Chironomini) or on extending arms from the tube (tribe Tanytarsini, Fig. 5.7). The larvae of Tanytarsini are widely distributed filter-feeders in streams. One such species, *Rheotanytarsus muscicola*, uses three different kinds of silk (Kullberg, 1988). One has a fine texture and is used for constructing and lining its tube. The second and third types are used for constructing the catch net; one is thicker and is used for making the framework and the other is finer and used to spin the net. The former arises when silk is ejected through the mouth while the latter is produced when silk is forced through grooves on the anterior edge of the ventromental plates of the head. The catch net consists of irregularly spun strands which seem extremely sticky and are suitable for capturing colloids and particles measuring 0.01–10 μm. Collected particles are either eaten or incorporated into the case.

Fig. 5.7 The tube of chironomid larvae of the tribe Tanytarsini. Note the silken net spun between the extending arms of the tube.

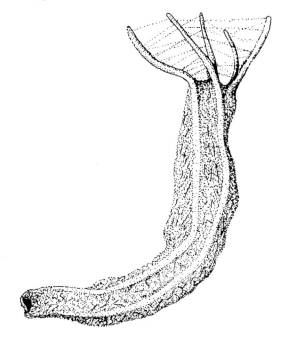

Caddisflies

In caddis larvae, silk is secreted through an opening at the tip of the labrum (the 'upper lip'), and plays an important role for net construction, case-building, and attachment.

Nets

The larvae of many species of caddisflies belonging to several different families construct catch nets, predominantly among the Hydropsychidae, Polycentropodidae, and Philopotamidae. The nets are primarily used to passively collect living or dead food items from the flowing water in a manner similar to spiders' webs and they usually include a retreat tube. Most polycentropodids construct relatively large nets with irregular and coarse meshes. *Plectrocnemia conspersa* is probably the most well-studied species. Typically larvae sit in a silken tube from both ends of which funnel-shaped catch nets widen towards the current. They only exploit habitats with currents below 20 cm s^{-1} and at very slow velocities below 4.5 cm s^{-1} the net type constructed depends on the depth. At depths of 5 cm or less, much of the silk is attached to the surface film, while in deeper water the larvae spread out silk strands radially from the openings of the retreat tube onto the stream bed resulting in an area of meshwork in which small animals are trapped when moving across the substrate (Townsend and Hildrew, 1979). Newly hatched larvae of *Plectrocnemia* use a colonial net for a short period after hatching. Such nets may be large (10 cm^2) and harbour more than 300 larvae (Hildrew and Wagner, 1992). Silk in this instance probably helps larvae to obtain their first meals and affords protection from flow forces. Similar aggregations on communal nets have been observed in blackfly larvae.

Larvae of other Polycentropodidae build large bag-shaped nets, like *Polycentropus flavomaculatus*, which are often positioned on the lower face of rocks. It has been suggested that this species, in contrast to *P. conspersa*, has a restricted option as to where it can construct its net, since it dwells in habitats where the larvae face much greater risks of being eaten by fish. Very large, up to 20 cm long, funnel-shaped nets (Fig. 5.8b) are found in *Neureclipsis bimaculata*, a common species in

Fig. 5.8 The nets of the caddis larvae *Hydropsyche* (Hydropsychidae) (a) and *Neureclipsis* (Polycentropodidae) (b).

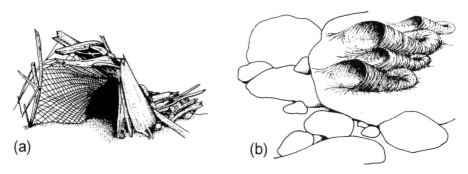

(a)   (b)

lake outlets. The size of the aperture of the funnel appears to depend on both current velocity and food density. Thus, larvae inhabiting outlets from eutrophic lakes will construct much smaller nets, especially when occupying fast-flowing microhabitats, than larvae in oligotrophic (or slow-flowing) outlets.

The elongated net bags of philopotamids have extremely fine meshes, often only about 1 μm, and a small aperture. This leads to a very slow flow through the net. It is conceivable that the matrix-like structure supports a rich growth of algae, bacteria, and protozoa, which could provide food for the larva. 'Gardening' has also been discovered inside the galleries that are attached to solid substrate by members of the family Psychomyiidae (see below).

Hydropsychids are probably the most widespread net-spinning caddis larvae in the world. They typically inhabit faster-flowing parts of streams and rivers than do polycentropodids. Their nets are small and built next to the anterior entrance of their retreat tubes. The larvae continuously tend their nets. These are often constructed using support from small plant fragments and gravel, and they have a characteristic bilaterally symmetrical configuration (Fig. 5.8a). *Macronema* larvae, however, build a sophisticated 'house' with a funnel facing the current. The larva sits inside the house feeding on an in-house positioned fine-meshed net (Fig. 5.9).

Meshes of hydropsychid catch nets are rectangular and typically measure 300×200 μm, although mesh size varies between species. This variation has

Fig. 5.9 *Macronema* larvae build a sophisticated net with a funnel facing the current. The larva sits inside the net feeding on material collected on the fine-meshed net. (After Sattler, 1963.)

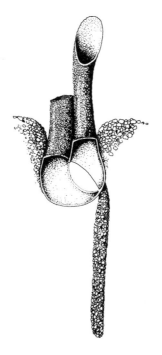

received a great deal of attention, since it has interesting implications for larval distributions in relation to suspended particle size distributions and current velocities, and thereby habitat partitioning (Loudon and Alstad, 1990). However, the situation is somewhat complicated for several reasons. First, species with coarse meshes largely feed on drifting animals, whereas those with smaller meshes are primarily detritivores (e.g. Wallace *et al.*, 1992). Moreover, the distribution of hydropsychids is apparently also influenced by the varied temperature optima of different species (see Fig. 3.3, p. 35). Catch nets even function differently at different temperatures due to the increasing viscosity of the water as temperatures decrease. This effect has greatest significance for small mesh nets. However, computer simulations of the function of nets in relation to capture rates suggest that the benefits from the increased flow through nets resulting from less viscous water at high temperatures are probably limited, as metabolic costs tend to increase more rapidly with temperature (Loudon and Alstad, 1990). This may explain why larvae appear to spin larger nets at higher temperatures. Temperature also plays an important role in determining whether a larva should spin a net or not; at very low temperatures net-spinning is unusual.

Two further factors complicate the relationships between mesh sizes and microhabitats in hydropsychids. Mesh size increases during ontogeny. Early instars of all species have relatively small meshes: in the second instar they are typically about 100×50 μm. Mesh size for fifth instar larvae may be two orders of magnitude larger. Mesh size also varies within a single net. Parts of the net positioned closest to the substrate (and being exposed to the slowest currents) appear to have smaller meshes (Malas and Wallace, 1977).

Hydropsychid nets are interesting for at least one more reason. While slight distortions of the net architecture occur naturally, especially at very low or very high temperatures, these net anomalies increase dramatically in nets in streams which are polluted by heavy metals and organic toxins (Petersen and Petersen, 1983). The presence of distorted nets in a stream therefore suggests environmental stress.

Cases and galleries

Silk is also used for the construction of larval cases in many caddisflies and in some instances it is the sole building material. More commonly, however, silk is used for lining cases and glueing pieces of plants or mineral particles together. Caddis cases are usually made into species-specific, elongated shapes and frequently taper towards the posterior end (Fig. 4.8, p. 89). Exceptions include the spiral-shaped Helicopsychidae cases, superficially resembling snail shells. Cases are most often carried around, although some species fix them to the substrate.

There are different ideas as to the benefits caddis larvae may derive from their cases, and how the strategy of building cases evolved. They do make respiration more efficient, since cased larvae are able to create an active current through the cases using undulatory behaviour moving relatively large volumes of water unidirectionally over the abdominal gills. This may have facilitated the invasion of lentic habitats. Another popular hypothesis is that cases may have developed as anti-predatory devices. Caddis cases are often augmented with larger pieces of stones or sticks. Otto and Svensson (1980) observed that trout repeatedly ingested and spat out cased caddis larvae. Sometimes they managed to expel and get hold of a larva in this way, but often, when the fish was small relative to the case, the larva resisted these attempts.

Sometimes, notably in Psychomyiidae, larvae construct attached tubes several times as long as their bodies. The larvae lead an active life inside the galleries out of which they rarely move. By allowing larvae to build galleries on microscope slides, Hasselrot (1993) was able to observe from below how *Tinodes waeneri* undulated, tended the inside of the tubes, consumed parts of the gallery wall, repaired holes, and carried out other behaviours.

Lepidoptera

The larvae of some Lepidoptera use silk for spinning silken tents on rocks in streams. In North America, larvae of the algal-feeding pyralid *Petrophila confusalis* are sometimes present at high densities. They show interesting competitive interactions with other sessile insects, especially with a hydroptilid caddis larva, *Leucotrichia* (see p. 187). The silken tent apparently can help *Petrophila* to defend space from invading *Leucotrichia* (McAuliffe, 1984a). The pupal cocoon of *Petrophila* is also made of silk and has holes around the periphery to allow water circulation. The pupa itself is found in an inner cocoon.

Colour

The colouring of animals may be considered as a special case of morphology. Almost all invertebrates in the lotic environment are drab. These shades may of course help animals escape detection by predators as camouflage against a background of dark rocks and detritus on the stream bed. One experimental study suggests that the dark-banded head patterns of some caddis larvae in fact help protect them from fish through enhanced crypsis, although such colouring seems rarer in lotic than in lentic environments (Otto, 1984). Taxa exposed to fish predators within stream vegetation, such as several chironomid and simuliid species, are frequently greenish in colour, which may make them less visible to the predators. Some fish in turn do seem able to alter their general shading to match the substrate. In the same stream one can find both light and dark trout depending on where the individuals were caught. Presumably this too is an example of crypsis to avoid predators.

Overall, one may reasonably conclude that the general lack of colour among invertebrates results in little communication in the stream environment via visual cues. This interpretation is enhanced by the fact that most species are active only in darkness. Birds, which have superior colour vision and capacity for learning, and against which probably most warning colouration is directed in terrestrial environments, are also relatively unimportant predators on invertebrates in freshwater systems (Hutchinson, 1981). Moving to the vertebrates, colour becomes much more important, especially with respect to reproduction and sexual behaviour.

The males of many fish species have brightly coloured fins and occasionally bodies, at least during the reproductive period. Sticklebacks and guppies are the most obvious examples. Amphibians also often adopt mating colours.

Behaviour

Few of the morphological adaptations we have just discussed will function successfully unless they are properly used. Hence the important role of behaviour. Broadly speaking, behaviour is any activity that alters the relationship between an organism and its environment (both the physical environment and other organisms). The diversity of behaviour is testimony to the diversity of challenges posed by life in running waters (Wiley and Kohler, 1984). In plants, behaviour is simple, innate, and obviously restricted, for example growth movements in macrophytes or motility in planktonic algae towards or away from light. Animals have more complex behavioural patterns that tend to be innate in lower invertebrates, but involve learning in higher forms, especially the vertebrates. There have been a few reviews of behavioural adaptations, mostly based on aquatic insects (e.g. Hynes, 1970; Wiley and Kohler, 1984; Vogel, 1988). As it is not easy to give a comprehensive description of all types of behaviour, we have instead concentrated on a few themes to illustrate the role of behaviour in the biology of running water animals and to give the reader a taste of this fascinating area.

Flow relations

We have already discussed the many morphological adaptations that help counteract flow forces. Behaviour is another weapon in the armoury. The general lifestyle adopted by an animal will influence the effects of flow. One of the primary functions of any adaptation to flow is to help the organism maintain its location and this can be related to *modes of existence*, a generalized scheme developed by Cummins (see Cummins and Merritt, 1996a) for insects that incorporates habit, locomotion, attachment, and concealment. We have added other life forms to this general scheme and outline the categories in Table 5.2. In addition to general habit and selection of microhabitats to avoid currents, many taxa show changes in body posture in response to changes in flow. Crayfish, for example, help maintain position by altering body posture to counteract the effect of drag when exposed to an increase in current velocity (Maude and Williams, 1983). *Ecdyonurus* mayflies lower their large head shield, as mentioned earlier. We also saw how many organisms respond to increased flow rates by moving to flow refugia. Presumably such a response is either passive and due to dislodgment and deposition in low flow areas or through active behaviour, dependent on an ability to detect differences in flow and respond accordingly.

Behavioural taxes

Running water animals show a number of behavioural taxes (active movements in response to various environmental stimuli) that singly, or in combination,

Table 5.2 Modes of existence of lotic animals. (Adapted from Cummins and Merritt, 1996. From *An Introduction to the aquatic insects of North America*, (eds. R. W. Merritt and K. W. Cummins) © 1996, Kendall/Hunt Publishing Company. Used with permission.)

Category	Description	Examples
Skaters	Adapted for life on the water surface where they feed on organisms trapped in the surface film, low-order streams or margins of high-order rivers	Water striders/pond skaters (gerrid bugs) adults and juveniles
Planktonic	Inhabiting open water, slow-flow or still, in high-order rivers	Planktonic crustaceans (Cladocera, Copepoda)
Divers	Insects adapted for swimming in slow-flowing pools, by 'rowing' with hind legs coming to surface to obtain oxygen, and often clinging to macrophytes or submerged objects	Water boatmen (Corixidae and Notonectidae) and diving beetles (Dytiscidae) (adults and juveniles)
	Semi-aquatic vertebrates; including those that forage underwater but spend most time on the water surface (birds) or land (mammals)	Diving ducks, dippers, other waterfowl, otters, mink, platypus
Swimmers	Insects adapted for 'fish-like' swimming, clinging to substrate between short bursts of swimming (height to width ratio near 1). Fully aquatic vertebrates that maintain position by swimming or using flow refuges	Streamlined mayfly nymphs (Baetidae, Leptophlebiidae), fish, lotic amphibians, reptiles
Clingers	Possess behavioural (e.g. silk nets, pads, fixed retreats) or morphological (claws, dorsoventral flattening, suckers) adaptations for attachment to substrate surfaces, or that are sessile and colonial	Net-spinning caddis larvae (*Hydropsyche*), simuliid larvae, heptageniid mayflies (*Ecdyonurus*), gastropod snails (*Ancylus*), leeches, Bryozoa, sponges
Sprawlers	Inhabit the surface of floating leaves of vascular plants or fine sediments in depositional habitats with modifications for staying on the substrate (e.g. wide bodies) and maintaining respiratory surfaces free of silt	Mayfly (Caenidae), dragonfly (Libellulidae) larvae
Climbers	Living and moving on vascular plants or detrital debris (e.g. overhanging branches, roots, and vegetation)	Damselfly (Coenagrionidae), mayfly (Ephemerellidae), midge (Chironomidae) larvae
Burrowers	Inhabiting fine sediment (and hyporheos), some constructing discrete burrows, or ingesting their way through the sediments, either very small-bodied or filiform (long and thin, e.g. cylindrical shape)	Microcrustacea (copepods, ostracods), rotifers, stonefly larvae (Leuctridae), burrowing mayfly larvae (Ephemeridae), Chironominae midge larvae, worms (Oligochaeta), bivalve molluscs (Sphaeridae, Unionidae), lampreys

help them to overcome problems associated with flow, as well as other adverse conditions. Response to light (*phototaxis*) is widespread. Some baetid mayfly larvae (swimmers) actually show a strong positive phototaxis which leads them to occupy the top of rocks in illuminated stream reaches where their algal food is abundant. However, most invertebrates (especially clingers and burrowers) are negatively phototactic, avoiding bright light by moving into the substrate or under stones (and indirectly out of the current). Examples include crayfish, mayfly larvae, and flatworms. At night, many insects emerge onto the surface of the substrate to graze, a diel rhythm controlled by light (see pp. 171, 176). However, under respiratory stress, these insects move towards the light to exposed surfaces to allow access to faster currents and more oxygen (Wiley and Kohler, 1980). Diving insects also use light as a cue for respiratory regulation, as they must return to the surface to collect a new air bubble. Two other behavioural taxes that help overcome problems of dislodgement by current are *rheotaxis* (the ability to orientate towards currents) and *thigmotaxis* (active response to touch). Most amphipod and isopod crustaceans, for example, are negatively phototactic and positively rheotactic and thigmotactic such that they avoid bright light, moving into crevices or under stones, and movement tends to be in an upstream direction as compensation for involuntary displacement downstream and to reduce drag (Covich and Thorp, 1991). In flatworms, thigmotaxis plays a role in a range of behaviours such as choosing substrate, hunting prey, and avoiding predation.

Responses to adverse conditions

Most aquatic macroinvertebrates depend on diffusion of oxygen into respiratory tissues from the surrounding water. However, oxygen concentration will inevitably decline over time in the immediate vicinity of these surfaces. For invertebrates that have a physical gill or plastron or that live in fast-flowing water, replenishment of oxygen to respiratory surfaces is automatic. However, in slower-flowing water or when oxygen levels decline (e.g. through pollution, or increased water temperature) and/or oxygen demand (metabolism) increases, behavioural ventilation is necessary, which creates additional water currents across the respiratory surfaces. Many mayfly larvae, for example, can beat their abdominal gills. Some large stoneflies, like the perlids, do 'push-ups', forcing fresh water over the thoracic gills situated at the base of their limbs. Many caddis and dipteran larvae undulate their abdomen to create water movement across the body.

These respiratory movements usually show an inverse relationship with oxygen levels and current velocity, and a positive relationship with temperature. Although they aid regulation of gas exchange, they are also costly in terms of both energy expenditure and preclusion from other activities such as feeding. Movement from sheltered, low-current areas to surfaces exposed to the current (as mentioned above) can reduce the cost of ventilation and help species that cannot ventilate (obligate fast-flowing water dwellers or 'rheophiles' depending totally on currents to renew oxygen). As a final recourse, when ventilation and changing location cannot satisfy oxygen requirements, active entry of individuals into the current has been documented. In fact, active drift in the current is a common response to all kinds of stressful situations (see p. 178).

Behavioural responses to flood disturbances were discussed earlier (pp. 106–7 and Chapter 3), but in some ephemeral, running water habitats, organisms may also have to contend with drying up of the channel. Burrowing into the substrate to take advantage of subsurface flows offers one mode of escape but is not utilized much by macroinvertebrates (see earlier). Timing of production of tolerant life stages (eggs or terrestrial adults) offers another. Alternatively, physiological adaptations involving dormancy can increase survival, as seen in many of the lower invertebrates (see p. 110).

Reproductive behaviour

We will leave our discussion of life cycles to the final section of this chapter and concentrate here on some of the interesting behavioural adaptations associated with reproduction in running water organisms. As far as most insects are concerned, the aquatic juveniles are the main feeding stages in the life history while the adults are terrestrial and mostly or entirely concerned with reproduction and dispersal activity. One may speculate that this situation has arisen to aid dispersal. In the sea, dispersal of sessile and benthic species is often by planktonic larvae carried in currents. In lakes and streams, the isolation of individual systems means that dispersal between catchments or even between streams within catchments is normally only possible through the aerial route. Significant upstream movement is usually only possible during adult stages. Terrestrial adult stages are also advantageous for ephemeral habitats such as desert streams. In many fly families (e.g. mosquitoes, blackflies, biting midges), terrestrial existence also enables adult females to obtain blood meals from vertebrate hosts that provide sufficient protein for egg maturation (see later).

Reproduction of most aquatic insects is thus in either aerial or terrestrial habitats, not aquatic ones. Aerial swarming is a typical mating behaviour especially among midges, mayflies, and caddisflies. The swarms are generally male-dominated; females enter swarms, are mated then leave to oviposit. Other taxa, such as stoneflies, mate on surrounding vegetation or, as in the case of some Odonata and Diptera, have mating territories. In the odonates, males defend a territory that includes prime oviposition sites through ritualized threat behaviour and aggression. The male seizes any female that flies into the territory, grasping her by her head or pronotum and the female loops her abdomen forward and upward to receive sperm from the male.

Insects exhibit a wide range of tactics in oviposition. In odonates, it is the male that determines the oviposition habitat where young will live, but in most other insects, the female determines oviposition site and hence larval habitat. Many caddis and some mayfly species actually enter the water and lay eggs in masses under stones while other insects oviposit at the stream edge. Larvae subsequently migrate to preferred habitats. Eggs can also be deposited in a mass on the water surface and then sink as in some stoneflies, or be deposited singly by females dipping their abdomen into the water while flying as in some ecdyonurid mayflies. Alderflies and some caddis even lay eggs on vegetation overhanging the water and larvae hatch and fall in. A spectacular reproductive strategy is shown by *Atherix ibis* (the ibis fly), whose females aggregate in large clumps under bridges or on branches over fast-flowing water (Fig. 5.10). The aggregations remain for a long time after the females have deposited their eggs and died.

The reverse journey must be made when insect larvae mature. For species that have no pupal stage (e.g. mayflies and stoneflies), nymphs simply move towards the banks and crawl out of the water to undergo the final moult on land or rise to the surface to moult and then fly off. Other insects must pupate prior to metamorphosis (see p. 140). Where pupae are free and active, as in some Diptera, they rise to the surface to emerge. Other species metamorphose inside a pupal case fixed to the stream bed and thus need to free themselves. In caddis, the *pharate* (pre-) adult has large crossed mandibles used to tear open the pupal case (which is usually constructed with gravel, small stones or pieces of vegetation), then it swims to shore. The pupation site is often different from the larval microhabitat.

A browse through the literature reveals a wide variety of reproductive strategies and behaviours among other lotic groups. Protozoans mainly exhibit asexual binary fission but sexual reproduction occurs, usually associated with environmental change. Rotifers can be parthenogenetic (females producing clones of themselves) but can also show sexual reproduction and distinct mating behaviours. All leeches are hermaphrodites (both sexual organs in each individual)

Fig. 5.10 Larva (a), adult female (b), and aggregation of dead females (c) of the Ibis fly. (From Malmqvist, 1996.)

(a)

(b)   (c)

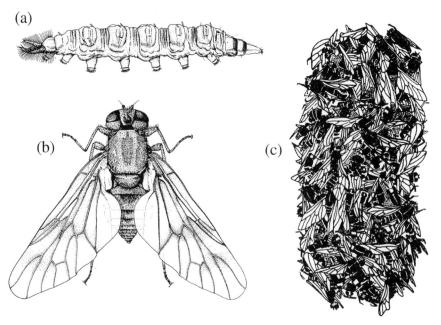

but cross fertilization occurs, whereas a majority of nematodes are bisexual (separate sexes). Perhaps the most unique reproductive behaviour among the invertebrates is shown by unionacean bivalve molluscs, whose larval stage (the glochidium) is an obligate ectoparasite in the mouth or on the fins, gills, or scales of fish of particular species (although one North American species is known to parasitize the aquatic salamander *Nechurus*; McMahon, 1991). The glochidia, like the parents, have a bivalved shell and are released once per year. Some species produce vast numbers of larvae that drift passively in streams until they contact a fish. These glochidia usually have hooks that attach to the fish surfaces. Other species exploit predator–prey relationships by luring the potential fish host with encased mucous packets of glochidia (called conglutinates) in various forms, shapes, and colours that resemble food items such as leeches, insect larvae, or even small fish (Haay *et al.*, 1995). One intriguing example is shown in Fig. 5.11. Females of the *Lampsilis* species of North America release a discrete mass of larvae resembling the shape and colour of a small fish, even with an 'eye spot'. This remains tethered to the female by a long transparent mucous strand and moves in a darting motion through the action of the current. Predatory fish like the bass are attracted to, and consume the 'lure', which leads to the release of glochidia in the buccal cavity from which they are carried to the gill filaments of the host by respiratory currents. Glochidia encyst in host tissues within 36 hours of attachment, and juvenile metamorphosis ranges from 6 to 160 days depending on the species (Kat, 1984). Water mites have a similarly complicated reproductive strategy as described on p. 83.

Fish exhibit a wide range of reproductive behaviours. The most spectacular are the anadromous salmonids that spend their early years in streams, rivers, and lakes, undergo the *smoltification* process that involves dramatic physiological changes allowing them to go to sea to mature, before returning again during migratory runs upstream in their home river to spawn (see also p. 98). The reverse behaviour is seen in catadromous fish such as the eel, which matures in rivers then descends to the sea to spawn. For the European eel *Anguilla anguilla*, this entails traversing the Atlantic from Europe to the Sargasso Sea off the east coast of Florida, north of the West Indies. Fish have also been grouped according to their within-river migratory movements, particularly those that utilize the flood plain

Fig. 5.11 The superconglutinate produced by a female *Lampsilis perovalis* (uninacean bivalve.) The vertical bands represent contents of individual conglutinates and with the 'eye-spot' the whole superconglutinate mimics a small fish. (After Haay *et al.* 1995.)

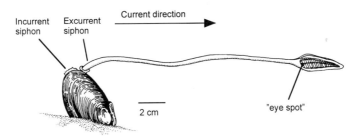

habitats for reproduction (Welcomme, 1985). In south-east Asia, so-called 'black fish' that can tolerate low oxygen conditions and prefer more lentic habitats, undertake local migrations between floodplain habitats in response to water level changes. These are generally bottom-feeding species often of dark colour (e.g. order Siluriformes that includes catfish) and tend to be multiple spawners, nest-builders, and show parental care. Silvery-scaled 'white fish', including some cyprinids and perciformes, are generally pelagic and planktivorous or piscivorous and undertake longitudinal upstream migrations within a river. They tend to be annual spawners and egg-scatterers, producing huge numbers of eggs and breed in well-oxygenated waters. Some species use the floodplain for spawning or feeding in nursery areas, others spawn in the main channel. Non-anadromous phenotypes of the brown trout in Europe also show marked upstream migration to breed in headwaters.

A final interesting reproductive behaviour is mate-guarding by males. This is well known among the adult dragon- and damselflies. Males essentially defend females to avoid sperm competition with other males and try to ensure their sperm fertilizes the females' eggs. The male genitalia are specially designed to scoop out sperm deposited by a different male before introducing its own sperm into the female's reproductive organs. The male will then hold the female 'in-tandem' or 'contact guard' her by watching over the female within its territory to prevent other matings. The crustacean amphipod *Gammarus* also shows mate-guarding, where the larger male carries the female before, during and after mating until the female has shed her old cuticle and the new one has hardened. The male should maximize the size of the female it guards to increase the number of eggs it fertil-izes, but cannot carry and move with too large a partner—the compromise seems to be a male:female size ratio of pairs of 1.3:1! (Adams and Greenwood, 1983).

Communication and sensitivity

An important component of behaviour is communication between individuals. The nature of running waters places some obvious constraints but nevertheless aquatic animals show a considerable range of communication activity.

A surprising communication medium for running water forms is sound. The water bugs are the best-known exponents, particularly the Corixidae, where the males have well-developed stridulatory apparatus involving a strigil plate on the abdomen and one or two rows of pegs on the enlarged front tarsi which differ on a species level (Fig. 5.12). *Hydropsyche* caddis larvae are also known to communicate by sound under water, stridulating using forelegs on ventrolateral striations of the head capsule (Jansson and Vuoristo, 1979). Adult stoneflies locate mates through acoustic signalling on land, where males drum specific calls on vegetation using their abdomen, which are answered by females (Ziegler and Stewart, 1979). Water surface vibrations are utilized by the gerrid water striders both to detect struggling prey and to signal to conspecifics. They possess sensillae on the femora and trochanters of their limbs that detect vibrations on the surface film, and generate surface waves using their legs for mating behaviour and courtship

Fig. 5.12 Examples of the male fore tarsi of five different corixid species to illustrate the species-specific rows of pegs that are used for sound communication by rubbing on a strigil plate located on the abdomen. (After Macan, 1976. Reproduced with permission of the Freshwater Biological Association.)

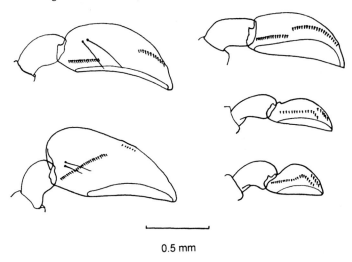

0.5 mm

(Wilcox, 1972). Water crickets (Veliidae) and some Gerridae also possess stidulatory mechanisms to produce sound.

Sight is an important sense particularly in terms of predator avoidance. For example, large stonefly and mayfly larvae, which would be prey for fish, move when approached by an observer or when a shadow falls on them. Many crustaceans are also sensitive to small differences in light intensity and ecto-parasitic leeches can respond to changes in the shadows to help locate a host. In turn, anyone trying to watch fish from a stream bank knows that it is exceedingly difficult to approach them without disturbance. Trout tend to be nocturnal, staying relatively immobile in shelter or deep pools during the day, foraging at night. This may also be an anti-predator response to avoid visual predators like birds and otters and possibly larger fish.

However, it is the production of, and response to, chemical cues and pheromones that offers the most striking mode of communication and sensitivity. Stream flow can potentially produce a persistent, unidirectional chemical signal that can provide a basis for orientation and communication. The use of pheromones as sexual attractants has been documented from a number of running water groups such as nematodes and crustaceans as well as among terrestrial adults of insects with aquatic larvae. Chemical detection of prey plays a role in feeding of several different types of invertebrates. Injured prey attract triclad flatworms and parasitic and predatory leeches can react to chemical stimuli in the water as well as to vibrations (Davies, 1991). Eels that forage nocturnally also use chemoreception (Tesch, 1977).

In laboratory experiments, McIntosh and Peckarsky (1996) found that mayflies altered their behaviour according to the presence or absence of brook trout odour.

Mayfly larvae from a trout stream maintained nocturnal drift periodicity regardless of the presence/absence of fish odour, but decreased the intensity of drift when odour was present. Mayfly larvae from a fishless stream initially reduced daytime activity in drift and on tops of rocks in the presence of fish odour, but after one day this effect disappeared and fish odour had no further effect on behaviour. A similar study by Tikkanen *et al.* (1996) also found no avoidance responses to chemical cues by *Baetis* mayfly nymphs from a fishless stream, but an immediately increased refuge use when the mayflies were exposed to live fish (like minnow). They then re-emerged on to the top of the substrate as soon as the predator was removed, while mayflies from a fish stream remained in refuges even when the risk of predation was not acute. This behaviour has been encapsulated in the 'risk of predation' hypothesis for explaining nocturnal drift patterns (see p. 178). Previous experience is obviously important, and the observations that larvae from trout streams continued to show diel drift periodicities even when all predator cues were removed indicate this behaviour may be a fixed evolutionary response in some populations (McIntosh and Peckarsky, 1996). In contrast, the mayfly nymphs from fishless streams seem to possess flexible avoidance responses and to be able to adjust their behaviour according to the prevailing level of predation risk. In crayfish, experiments have also shown that the combined effects of visual and chemical cues from predators increase shelter use, and decrease walking compared to responses to a single cue. Chemical stimuli lower the response threshold for avoidance behaviour in reaction to visual stimuli (Blake and Hart, 1993).

Other anti-predator behaviours do occur. Interestingly, several different groups including snails, crayfish, amphibia, and fish deploy alarm chemicals (low molecular weight hydrocarbons) in the presence of predators (Smith, 1992). On encountering a predator, some mayfly species become highly active and enter the drift or swim (e.g. *Baetis*) while others like *Ephemerella* reduce activity and adopt the 'scorpion like' posture (see p. 115).

Territoriality and aggression

A territory is a defended area that includes important resources for the organism(s) concerned. Such resources may include mates, as we have seen for adult dragonflies, but more usually food and associated resources. Territoriality is clearly involved in competition and more detail is given on pp. 187–9. Here, we simply illustrate the behavioural aspects. For example, dominant individuals (adult females) of *Rhagovelia scabra* defend optimal locations on the water surface at the head of pools where prey capture rates are highest (p. 190). Feeding territories are important for more sessile organisms as well. Examples include filter-feeding net-spinning caddis larvae that defend fixed-feeding sites (Hildrew and Townsend, 1980); chironomid larvae such as *Cricotopus bicinctus* that construct retreat tubes from which they forage and defend the surrounding area (LeSage and Harrison, 1980); and algal-grazing cased caddis larvae such as *Leucotrichia pictipes* that live in fixed shelters and aggressively defend the surrounding territory that extends as far as the larva can stretch out of its case to forage (Hart, 1983). Territoriality is also well known among the vertebrates. Many fish species defend territories while they are breeding (especially when associated with nest-building) but riffle-dwelling fish like darters and sculpins, and especially trout, defend feeding locations.

Riverine birds such as the dipper are also territorial, especially during the 3–4 week breeding season. The length of territory varies with productivity of the river or stream, which in turn can be related to water chemistry. For example, in acidic sites, territories extend over 2.5 kilometres of stream bank, whereas in upland calcareous streams, average length can be as short as 780 metres (Ormerod and Tyler, 1991). Otters also are well known for their territoriality and territory size is variable depending on the river system. An example from a 4th order river in southern Ireland is shown in Fig. 5.13, showing three large territories with two families and a single male.

The defence of territories and feeding sites inevitably leads to some form of conflict between individuals, either in threat displays or in direct physical inter-actions and aggression. A few examples will suffice to illustrate the phenomenon. Among filter-feeders, net-spinning caddis larvae frequently attempt to displace the resident to secure both the net and a better foraging location. In *Plectrocnemia*, both individuals rear up and strike with their mandibles occasionally causing severe bites—the conflict ends when either the intruder backs away and enters the drift, or the resident leaves the net through the 'back door' at the rear of the retreat tube of the net (Hildrew and Townsend, 1980). Generally, the larger individual wins such contests especially if it is a 'defender', but larger intruders are likely to oust smaller residents. Stridulatory alarms supplement physical aggression in *Hydropsyche* and stridulation increases the probability of victory by the resident especially if it is larger (Jansson and Vuoristo, 1979). *Simulium* larvae can maintain an even spacing between individuals through aggressive biting and head banging, particularly directed upstream where other larvae may interfere with the delivery of food particles (Hart, 1986). Crayfish also show aggressive behaviour and

Fig. 5.13 The distribution of otter home ranges in the Araglin valley, Co. Cork. Home range 3 holds a single male, 2 a family and 1 an adult pair. (After Ottino, 1997.)

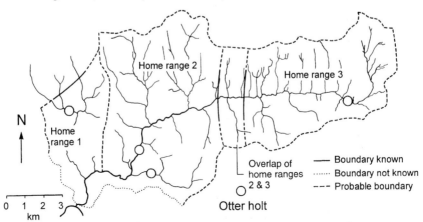

occupy and defend crevices that function as a refuge. There is a clear sequence of behaviours involving threat and submission displays and signals and fighting during encounters between individuals.

Aggression among grazing invertebrates is also well documented, where again space is important in relation to access to algal food. For example, the mayfly *Paraleptophlebia mollis* shows aggressiveness towards conspecifics by beating its abdomen from side to side, striking at adjacent individuals, or by raising and lowering its forelegs and antennae in direct contact with another nymph. Such fights end in one individual withdrawing or being chased (Peckarsky, 1983*b*). Encounters like these are likely to be a frequent occurrence in streams and rivers, especially where food resources are patchily distributed.

Distribution and foraging

The patchy distribution of food and other resources will naturally influence where organisms feed and how long they stay in certain areas. Various behavioural strategies can enhance the likelihood of locating good quality patches and of maximizing food intake. Grazers seem to select food patches of higher algal abundance and spend more time there. We have carried out experiments examining the foraging behaviour of the small-cased caddis *Agapetus fuscipes* on stones of different sizes with and without periphyton arranged to produce patches of different area and different profitability (Sangpradub and Giller, unpublished). The results clearly show a tendency for individuals to move from less to more profitable patches and to spend more time in these latter patches. Such behaviour may provide the underlying proximate cause for the aggregated microdistribution pattern found in natural streams. Limnephilid caddis may also spend significantly more time on ungrazed periphyton food patches than on previously grazed areas (Hart, 1983).

One suggested mechanism to explain such behaviours is area-restricted search. This involves increased rates of turning or decreased speed of movement in response to the presence of food. The movement patterns of *Baetis tricaudatus* illustrates this behaviour well (Fig. 5.14). Another possible explanation lies in the concept of 'giving-up rules' developed in association with optimal foraging theory (e.g. Charnov, 1976), where an individual would abandon a patch after a certain time interval following the last encounter with prey or food, or when the intake rate falls below some threshold level (such as average value for the habitat). While this has not been tested rigorously in stream systems, one elegant study does come to mind involving the net-spinning caddis *Plectrocnemia* (Hildrew and Townsend, 1980). After a certain threshold time interval during which they had not captured a prey (on average 41 hours), larvae usually abandoned a net site, thus larvae tended to remain at more profitable sites where prey were encountered frequently. *Rhyacophila* shows similar behaviour in relation to use of refuge sites, but the giving up time is shorter (10 hours on average) (Malmqvist, 1993). Animals do not always obey the rules, however. The semi-aquatic bug *Velia caprai* feeds on prey trapped on the water surface. As mentioned earlier, such prey are more plentiful in certain areas of the stream than others yet in one study there was no

Fig. 5.14 Examples of area-restricted search by baetid mayfly larvae on (a) natural substrate and (b) artificial patches of periphyton. Positions of the larvae were recorded every 30 seconds. (From Wiley and Kohler, 1984. Reproduced with permission of Greenwood Publishing Group, Inc, Westport, CT.)

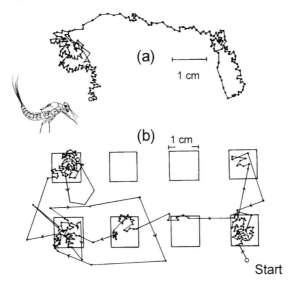

relationship between group size and prey availability and *Velia* appeared to be randomly distributed with respect to prey distribution. In fact, as group size increased, individual capture rate declined due to competitive interactions (Erlandsson and Giller, 1992). Clearly, there is still much to be learned in this fascinating area.

Trophic adaptations

Functional feeding groups

A large proportion of stream-living invertebrates are omnivorous but different animals process the various kinds of food resources present in the lotic environment in different ways. On this basis, Cummins (1973) categorized animals into a number of functional feeding groups. The concept was developed for insects, but has frequently been extended to include other invertebrates.

Six functional feeding groups are identified; shredders, collectors, scrapers, macrophyte piercers, predators, and parasites. The dominant food and feeding mechanisms of the different categories are listed in Table 5.3. Feeding mode and behaviour, rather than phylogeny, determine this functional classification but it is possible to discern some major patterns in the representation of different insect orders among the different functional feeding groups (Table 5.4).

Despite the great appeal of this general scheme, it is not without flaws. Although some taxonomic groups tend to be specialized with respect to feeding modes, for instance blackfly larvae as filterer collectors, many other taxonomic groups

Table 5.3 Functional feeding groups of aquatic larval stages and adults and their dominant food. (Modified from Cummins and Merritt, 1996. From *An introduction to the aquatic insects of North America*, (ed. R. W. Merritt and K. W. Cummins). © 1996, Kendall Hunt Publishing Company. Used with permission.)

Trophic group	Food	Feeding mechanism
Shredders	Leaf detritus, wood, living aquatic plants	Chewing of detritus and macrophytes, mining of macrophytes, and gougers of wood
Collectors	Fine particulate organic matter	Suspension feeding (filterers), deposit feeding (deposit collectors/gatherers)
Scrapers	Attached algae and biofilm	Grazing/scraping of mineral and organic surfaces
Macrophyte piercers	Cell and tissue fluids of living plants	Piercing and fluid sucking
Predators	Tissue of living animals	Engulfing, piercing
Parasites	Tissue and fluids of living animals	Internal and external parasitism

Table 5.4 Functional feeding groups and their principal representation among selected insect orders. (Modified from Cummins and Merritt, 1996. Permission as above.)

Insect order	Shredders	Collectors	Scrapers	Macrophyte piercers	Predators	Parasites
Plecoptera	+				+	
Odonata					+	
Ephemeroptera		+	+			
Hemiptera					+	
Megaloptera					+	
Trichoptera	+	+	+	+	+	
Lepidoptera	+		+			
Coleoptera	+	+	+		+	
Hymenoptera						+
Diptera	+	+	+		+	+

contain genera, or even species, with widely disparate food resources. The problems include how to categorize such clearly omnivorous species and those which shift from one functional group to another during their ontogeny (see pp. 138–9). Food availability and hence diet also change as a function of habitat, season, or even sex, which can further complicate classification of organisms. Moreover, it is the functional aspect of foraging that is used for classification; the food of different functional groups is not defined. For instance, when a shredder feeds on fragments of plants it also consumes a whole garden of attached algae, bacteria and fungi. Nevertheless, this functional group approach has become popular for a number of reasons. Foremost, functional feeding group classification provides a way of linking the structure of aquatic communities (in terms of relative abundance of different groups) with their resources and ecosystem processes, particularly in the face of environmental change. It also illustrates the coupling between morphological adaptations of the animals and their food resources.

Morphological aspects of feeding

Since morphology integrates ecological relationships over time and space, this is a particularly important facet of animal ecology to investigate (Ricklefs and Miles, 1994). In particular, the mouthparts of lotic insects demonstrate very interesting and revealing adaptations. Moreover, the morphological characteristics show a high repeatability of measurement among individuals and can be examined independently of the environmental background. Therefore, mouthpart morphology is well suited for comparative studies, perhaps even more so than behaviour, diet, substrate use, and habitat selection, all of which have been more extensively used.

A similar morphology may reflect common ecological relationships, although it is important to bear in mind that this may also be a result of a shared ancestry. On the other hand, variation in morphology is often assumed to reflect environmentally induced natural selection, although this is often untested. Therefore, experimental studies showing how fitness varies with morphology are needed. The morphology–fitness relationship has several important links, including how structure connects with function, function with potential resource use, and how these in turn relate to the realized niche (actual niche occupied) and, ultimately, to fitness (Arnold, 1983).

The mouthparts of aquatic insects show a tremendous variability including piercing, biting, sucking, scraping, brushing, browsing, filtering, holding, and grinding structures. Two examples are shown in Fig. 5.15. As mentioned above, to an extent mouthpart organization reflects phylogenetic relationships, but significant variation also occurs within orders. In closely related taxa, the design may be superficially identical, but on closer scrutiny interesting adaptive patterns

Fig. 5.15 Detailed structure of the mouthparts of a larval stonefly (a) and mayfly (b).

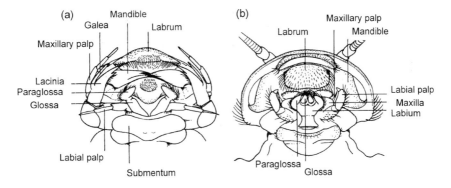

emerge. For example, a comparison of the labral fan morphology of blackfly larvae showed that fan area, ray length and thickness, and other measures, varied systematically among species inhabiting a range of habitats from slow streams to large rivers (Zhang and Malmqvist, 1996). There are also clear examples of convergence of mouthpart morphology among unrelated taxa. Thus, it has been shown that the larvae of several grazers, including coleopteran and trichopteran families, have almost identical mandible structures (Cummins and Merritt, 1996a).

Predatory insects, such as many stonefly and caddis larvae, have simple stabbing/cutting mouthparts for seizing and cutting pieces of the prey. In stonefly larvae it is the laciniae which are used to capture prey. Normally, the prey is engulfed in one piece, but partial consumption has been observed, where the softer parts have been ingested and sclerotized parts rejected (Malmqvist and Sjöström, 1980). In rhyacophilid caddis larvae the prey is seized with the mandibles, and subsequently often fragmented to such a high degree that it is difficult to identify the remains in the gut contents (Martin and Mackay, 1982). Alderfly larvae, including *Sialis*, also have biting mandibles with sharp teeth.

Piercing mouthparts are found among a variety of insects. The mandibles are the weapons in dytiscid beetles and are provided with a channel through which enzymes can be injected into the prey and the dissolved nutrients can be sucked out. Hemipteran prey are typically 'harpooned' by mandibular stylets. The longer barbed maxillary stylets reach deeper into the prey and operate by lacerating prey tissue. The predatory water bugs use a toxic saliva to paralyse their prey and the larval ibis fly (see Fig. 5.10, p. 126) also immobilizes its prey with a toxic injection before sucking out the contents. Not all piercing/sucking lotic insects are, however, predators. For instance, hydroptilid caddis larvae have mouthparts modified for breaching living algal cells and sucking out the contents. Although most hydroptilids feed from filamentous algae, periphyton, and fine organic particles, larval *Orthotrichia* have been observed sucking out the contents of pupae and eggs of blackfly larvae (Disney, 1972).

Freshwater snails scrape periphyton from rocks and macrophytes using the rasping movements of a file-like organ, the radula. This consists of many minute teeth arranged in regular patterns in species-specific configurations. Filter-feeding invertebrates also show extensive morphological specialization. Some of the most striking examples are found in blackfly larvae, whose mouthparts are modified to passively remove fine organic particles from the water. The fans, which are modified from labral mouthparts, are situated anteriorly on the head (see Fig. 4.9, p. 91). These organs are quite complex and each fan is in fact composed of three different fans in addition to the large primary fan. The fans, that is, the three small fans and the primary fan, are attached to a common stem. The primary fan, when fully extended, has the shape of a hemisphere (rather than a two-dimensional fan), concave against the direction of flow, and has 30–70 fan rays (depending on instar and species). The fans are periodically folded in and cleaned by the mandibles and labrum. Most other lotic filter-feeders use other organs or devices to trap food particles (such as silken nets, see earlier).

Generalists and specialists

Scrutiny of the gut contents of many stream invertebrates often indicates a very low level of food specialization, which suggests that they are indiscriminate opportunistic feeders. This may be true to an extent, but we cannot exclude the possibility that what we recognize down the microscope as amorphous detritus in the guts of various species may in fact vary qualitatively. Detritus is a complex material consisting of microorganisms and dead organic material. Experimental studies have indicated that some detritivores, such as *Gammarus*, *Asellus*, and limnephilid caddis larvae, are quite capable of discriminating between leaves colonized by different fungal species, and between patches on a single leaf (see pp. 159–62).

Predator species in streams show a considerable diet overlap and are apparently opportunistic in the sense that they appear to eat what they can catch. Trout are a prime example. This means that a combination of habitat overlap between predators and prey, the capabilities of different predators and the defence mechanisms of the potential prey governs the diet of the predators. For instance, blackfly larvae often inhabit microhabitats having high current velocities, which may preclude predators not apt to hunting in fast flow, such as perlodid stonefly larvae. Rhyacophilid predators cope better with such microhabitats and can therefore capture blackfly larvae over a larger velocity gradient than do perlodids (Malmqvist and Sackmann, 1996).

In cases when a predator's phenology is tuned to that of a major prey species, it would be legitimate to talk about specialization. One good example of this is *Rhyacophila obliterata*, the larvae of which develop simultaneously with its blackfly prey in Finnish lake-outlet streams near the Arctic Circle. These well-fed predators pupate just as the blackfly larvae population dwindles due to pupation and emergence around midsummer (Muotka and Penttinen, 1994).

Through the dynamic nature of stream communities, the prey base is constantly changing, which may help to explain the low degree of specialization that is often reported for lotic predators. In many cases, chironomid larvae make up the bulk of the prey, but they are a very heterogeneous group consisting of many different species, all with their own phenologies, microhabitats, and behaviours. For instance, some chironomids have rapid development, and are therefore only available for a short time, while others grow slowly or have multiple, successive cohorts and could therefore be encountered over longer periods of time.

The most specialized stream-living species are probably found among parasitoids and commensals. For instance, hymenopterans of the genus *Agriotypus* are almost exclusively found on caddis hosts in the family Goeridae (see p. 191), and *Epoicocladius ephemerae* is a chironomid species associated phoretically with members of the burrowing mayfly genus *Ephemera*. While the latter has a specialized microhabitat, we do not know much about its food specialisation. The same is true for those several species of blackflies that live as larvae and pupae attached to other animals, including crabs, shrimps and mayflies. Perhaps these phoretic species may have to be more flexible in terms of food acquisition than other simuliids (Crosskey, 1990).

Ontogenetic changes

Both the size of their mouths and the size of their food influence those organisms ingesting entire food items, living or dead. Above a certain particle size, ingestion is impossible, a phenomenon which is referred to as 'gape size limitation'. At the other end of the size spectrum, most animals avoid food that is considerably smaller than they can readily ingest. It thus follows that food particle size tends to increase with the size of the consumer. The upper limit is, however, better defined than the lower size limit, and sometimes we merely see an expansion in the range of food sizes with increasing consumer size (Fig. 5.16).

Many lotic animals do not eat the same food throughout their development. Predatory invertebrate species often start out as herbivores or detritivores. In the stonefly genus *Isoperla* there are species ranging from complete herbivory to carnivory as they grow. A study of two sympatric *Isoperla* species in southern Sweden indicated that the diet not only differed between the species, but also according to season, locality, and sex (Malmqvist *et al.*, 1991*b*). There are also clear ontogenetic diet shifts in Trichoptera, especially among the cased caddis where a shift from mainly detritivory to predominantly predatory behaviour has been recorded in some species (Giller and Sangpradub, 1993).

For a majority of lotic insects more dramatic shifts take place when they emerge from and leave the aquatic environment as terrestrial adults. Clearly, this phase

Fig. 5.16 Changes in prey size with predator size (head width, mm) in two isoperlid stoneflies. (From Malmqvist, 1991. Reproduced with the kind permission of Kluwer Academic Publishers.)

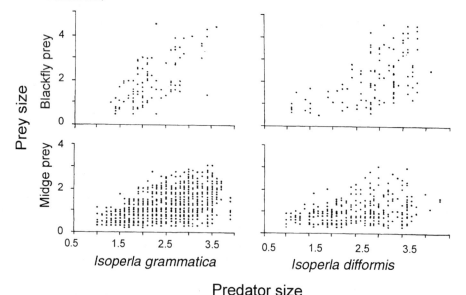

involves a complete change in most aspects of their biology, including trophic relationships. A few examples will illustrate this. Many species of blackflies shift from a larval diet consisting of fine organic particles, including colloids and bacteria, to the ingestion of blood in the adult stage which is required for egg production. Some species are capable of developing a first egg batch without blood-feeding, but all subsequent egg batches are dependent on it. Adult blackflies also ingest nectar, although this food is only for providing flight energy. Many adult chironomids appear to feed on nectar, but fresh fly droppings, pollen, and aphid excretion (honeydew) are also included in their diet (Armitage, 1995).

The adults of most stoneflies migrate after emergence to the nearest forested area where they stay from a few days up to several weeks. Species which have short adult lives mate and oviposit without feeding, whereas the more long-lived species feed on algae, leaves, twigs and dead insects (Lillehammer, 1988). Adult caddisflies have sucking mouthparts and some species are known to feed on nectar. In contrast, adult mayflies do not feed at all. Whereas most insects thus shift from one food resource to another when entering the adult stage, dragonflies retain their predaceous nature as adults, when they patrol over territories taking all sorts of flying prey. Semi-aquatic bugs and dytiscids are also predatory in both larval and adult stages.

A final example of drastically changing diets is found in lampreys. Larval lampreys live buried in the substrate of running waters where they feed from a current of water created by the pumping movements of the muscular velum and the expansions and contractions of the branchial region. This current provides water for respiration and also brings small food particles from the water column and the surface of the stream bed. The particles are trapped in a network of mucous strands in the pharynx, which gradually carry the particles down into the oesophagus. Larval lampreys go through a metamorphosis after several years. During the transformation, which lasts for several months, lampreys cease to feed. After transformation, lampreys migrate downstream, either to the sea or to lacustrine or riverine habitats depending on the species, where most species assume a parasitic life on suitable species of fish. Non-parasitic lampreys do not feed in their adult stages and, following a period of about nine months without food, they spawn in spring the year following the onset of the transformation. In many ways the life cycle of parasitic lampreys reminds one of anadromous salmonids, which also go through diet shifts, albeit less dramatic, connected, at least partly, with habitat changes.

Life history patterns

Any freshwater ecologist who has studied a temperate stream site over a year or two will be aware of the clear seasonal succession of benthic species, many species appearing, others disappearing as the seasons progress. They will also have been struck by the clear sequence of changes in the size of individuals of various species over time. These patterns reflect the growth and development of individuals through their life cycle. Even in the largely aseasonal tropics, life cycle patterns are evident as organisms develop towards maturity. A *life cycle* is the general sequence of morphological stages and physiological processes through which an individual of a species passes during its life, effectively linking one generation to the next. The qualitative and quantitative details of events associated with the life cycle make up the *life history*, such as growth, development, dormancy, dispersal, number of generations per year, etc. (Butler, 1984). While the life cycle is essentially fixed for the species, the life history can vary. For example, all aquatic Diptera pass through a life cycle involving egg, larval, pupal and adult stages, but as far as life history is concerned, the duration of stages, number of larval stages, activity of the pupa and emergence and flight duration of the adults can all vary within and between populations and species of flies. Two aspects of life history patterns are especially important: *voltinism* refers to the frequency with which the life cycle is completed within a year, and *phenology* refers to the seasonal timing of the various life cycle processes and the population synchrony of these. To determine life histories, biologists try to follow the development and progression of individuals derived from one reproductive period (a *cohort*) through the various life cycle stages or size classes over time (based on linear measurements of body parts such as head capsule width, body length, etc.). There is a vast body of literature based on such approaches, which we can only touch on here. Readers should consult Thorp and Covich (1991) and Wallace and Anderson (1996) for further details—although these are based on North American freshwater invertebrates and insects, respectively, they are nevertheless widely applicable.

Variation in life history patterns can be attributed to two broad sets of factors:

1. *Intrinsic factors* including physiology, morphology, and behaviour, which tend to restrict life history traits within certain genetically and phylogenetically (evolutionary) determined ranges. Thus freshwater crustaceans, rotifers, fish, and molluscs spend their entire life cycle in water, whereas most aquatic insects and some amphibia are only aquatic during larval stages and spend their adult life on land. Among the insects themselves, species show either complete or incomplete metamorphosis. In the former, holometabolous, life cycle (Megaloptera, Neuroptera, Diptera, Coleoptera, Lepidoptera, Trichoptera) individuals pass through egg, larval, and pupal stages before metamorphosing to the adult stage. In the latter, hemimetabolous life cycle (Ephemeroptera, Plecoptera, Odonata, Hemiptera) individuals pass from egg through immature nymphal stages that resemble the adult but lack wings and reproductive organs, and in some enter a sub-imago stage, before the adult. The larval or nymphal stages are usually the dominant part of the life cycle and individuals progress through a series of instars as they grow; between each successively larger instar, the insect sheds its old exoskeleton and subsequently grows into the new larger exoskeleton during that instar (growth is therefore a series of step-like increases in size). The number of larval instars varies among insect orders, from 3 in Neuroptera, to 4–5 in Hemiptera, 4–7 in Diptera, 5–8 in Trichoptera, 12–22 in Plecoptera, and 15–50 in Ephemeroptera. The length of each instar varies among taxa but generally later instars last longer. In other arthropod taxa, like Crustacea and Arachnida, life cycles are more complex, sometimes with more than one stage of metamorphosis (see Chapter 4).

2. *Extrinsic factors* such as temperature, photoperiod, nutrition, degree of habitat permanance and presence of other taxa can influence most life history parameters (Sweeney, 1984). As we saw in Chapter 3 (pp. 34–5), temperature can influence growth and development rates, metabolism etc. as well as indirectly affecting food availability. Diverse life history patterns have evolved to enable species to exploit seasonally available food (e.g. primary production, leaf fall), ensure emergence of adults into appropriate environmental conditions, and to evade unfavourable physical conditions (such as drought and floods) or minimize limiting biotic interactions (Wallace and Anderson, 1996). Even in non-seasonal tropical areas, somewhat surprisingly the natural environment exhibits some seasonality (e.g. Wolda, 1987) and life cycles must be adjusted in time so that critical stages can be matched with the appropriate environmental conditions (Butler, 1984).

Voltinism and longevity

Very small organisms have a short life cycle and can proceed through many generations relatively rapidly whereas the development of large organisms naturally takes longer. However, even within a species, prevailing conditions can determine how many generations can be squeezed into the year. For example, the short summers at high latitudes allow fewer generations than at lower latitudes.

Univoltine species, with a single generation each year, tend to be found only in certain seasons, and generally have non-overlapping generations. Sponges, for example, show annual life cycles with periods of active growth and dormancy, sexual (separate sexes, leading to the production of larvae), and asexual reproduction (Frost, 1991). This latter process produces clones through fragmentation or gemmules which remain dormant during harsh conditions and hatch and grow vegetatively into a new sponge (Fig. 5.17). Many seasonally occurring turbellarian flatworms are univoltine, especially in temperate habitats and extremes of geographical ranges (Kolasa, 1991). An annual life history is found in pulmonate gastropod snails such as *Lymnaea* and *Physa*, which reproduce in spring and die with complete replacement of generations. This once-off reproduction is known as *semelparous*. Most amphipod and isopod crustaceans also tend to be annual and semelparous species. Among the northern temperate insects, including many mayflies, stoneflies, and true flies, an annual cycle is again the most common, although the life cycle itself can vary from a few weeks to several months. Some other groups are clearly univoltine and annual but various life cycle stages do overlap at one time. Few Trichoptera species are missing for long periods, a situation also found among amphipods, freshwater limpets, and some leeches.

Multivoltine life histories involve several generations per year. Microscopic taxa like protozoans, rotifers, and microcrustaceans have rapid development. Hermaphrodite flatworms are generally multivoltine (Kolasa, 1991) and tropical and subtropical gastropods tend to have two or three reproductive intervals a year with various degrees of overlap in generations (Brown, 1991). In insects, multivoltinism is not very common and largely depends on the favourableness of the climate. A number of tropical mountain rainforest stream insects, however,

Fig. 5.17 The general life cycle of freshwater sponges showing the switch between sexual and asexual phases. Gemmule formation occurs under stressful conditions. (After Frost, 1991. Reproduced from *Ecology and classification of North American freshwater invertebrates* (ed. J. H. Thorp and A. P. Covich), Fig. 4.8, by permission of the Academic Press, London)

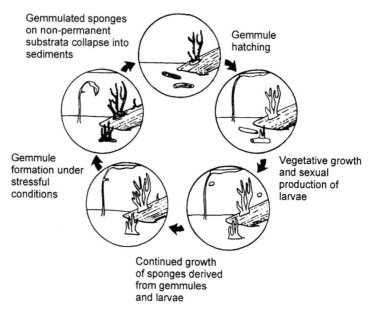

Gemmulated sponges on non-permanent substrata collapse into sediments

Gemmule hatching

Gemmule formation under stressful conditions

Vegetative growth and sexual production of larvae

Continued growth of sponges derived from gemmules and larvae

show aseasonal life cycles with continuous hatching and larval growth (Marchant and Yule, 1996); in these cases, the larger the insect, the longer the life cycle.

Many taxa, however, show life cycles exceeding one year, either reproducing many times during their life (an *iteroparous* cycle) or having a relatively long pre-reproductive period before their single reproductive event. A two-year life cycle is known as semi-voltine. Some tubificid worms may mature in their first year, reproduce, resorb gonads, mature, and reproduce again in the second year and then die (Brinckhurst and Gelder, 1991). Many gastropod molluscs are perennial, especially prosobranchs (e.g. Hydrobiidae) and the unionacean bivalves we discussed earlier can live for over a century and do not mature for over 20 years. Decapod crustaceans, like crayfish, live for several years, undergoing up to 11 moults of the exoskeleton and tripling in length in the first year (Covich and Thorp, 1991). Among the insects, it is usually the relatively larger and often predatory taxa that live for more than one year. Perlid stoneflies and some caddis species may live for three or four years, Odonata even longer.

Among the vertebrates, similar variability in the length of life cycles exists, again largely related to size, with small amphibians and fish being annuals, larger fish and reptiles perennial and often long lived. In terms of voltinism, most vertebrates will tend to have distinct breeding seasons and be univoltine but it is difficult to generalize regarding iteroparity and semelparity. Even within a species, individuals may differ (see below).

Phenology and life history responses to environmental conditions

If the prevailing environment plays a major role in the timing of various life cycle processes, one would expect the greatest modifications to life history and the closest relationships between life cycle and environmental conditions, to be shown by the fauna of temporary running water systems. Small size, rapid development and egg and/or larval diapause are commonly cited as adaptations to life in temporary habitats. Mayflies in temporary streams in western Oregon begin to hatch in late autumn with the onset of flow, but the hatching period tends to be extended, and development lasts 5–7 months (Dietrich and Anderson, 1995). Those larvae that delay hatching till spring, survive summer drought in the few remaining permanent pools. Emergence of adults also tends to be extended, although peak emergence precedes the summer drought. Stoneflies, which are more usually associated with cold perennial streams, do occur in temporary and desert streams as well. Like the mayflies, they are winter-active, hatching in late autumn but tend to diapause for several months when streams dry up. In New Mexico, the eggs of stoneflies are deposited when the stream is flowing and remain in the substrate for several months before resuming development when water flows again (Jacobi and Cary, 1996). In the Oregon streams, stoneflies tend to be semivoltine, spending the dry summer in surviving sections of the stream and only resuming growth in late autumn when water levels recover, emerging as adults the following spring (Dietrich and Anderson, 1995). However, mortality is high during this period. Dormancy is thus an important feature of the life cycle under such conditions.

Even in more benign conditions, life cycles must be temporally adjusted to seasonal variation in temperature, oxygen, food levels, and to optimal conditions for dispersal and reproduction. Two taxa may show identical life cycles and voltinism, yet their phenology may differ substantially in seasonal scheduling. There are often long periods of the year when many taxa are absent in samples (usually winter or summer) or are only present as small individuals. This often involves a resting egg or pupal stage, or cessation of growth during either summer or winter. Phenological differences between species may also be related to interspecific interactions. Elliott (1995), for example, has suggested that avoidance of competition among 12 species of carnivorous European Plecoptera could be achieved through differences in egg biology which relate to development rates, timing of hatching, etc. Such differences also occur among species of mayflies and caddis such that, at any one time, immature larvae or nymphs of similar species are at different stages of growth and hence different sizes. One species thus always has larger individuals than another similar species. We see this among coexisting grazing caddis larvae, where larval size relates to food type utilized (Sangpradub and Giller, unpublished data). Whether this is temporal partitioning to avoid competition or due to some other factor remains to be seen. The timing of life history with that of the major prey organism, as shown by *Rhyacophila* (see p. 137) might also explain phenological differences between predator species.

In an attempt to classify life cycles of invertebrates from temperate streams, Hynes (1970) distinguished three main types:

1. *Slow seasonal cycles* show a distinct change in size distributions with time and are common in cool streams. The eggs may hatch soon after laying, with growth occurring over a long period towards maturity, nearly a year later (e.g. Fig 5.18a), or hatching may extend over a relatively long period resulting in continuous recruitment over time, with life cycles spanning the winter (e.g. univoltine crustaceans, many stoneflies, mayflies, and caddis species).

2. *Fast seasonal cycles* occur through rapid growth following a long egg or larval diapause (a genetically programmed dormancy initiated in a particular life cycle stage) or after one or more intermediate generations. Cycles may reach maturity in spring, early and late summer, or autumn and several fast cycles can succeed one another. Typical fast cycle insect species include representatives of the mayfly *Baetis* and many blackfly genera, while some caddis show rapid growth after a long egg diapause.

3. *Non-seasonal cycles* where individuals of several stages or size classes are present in all seasons (e.g. the caddis *Rhyacophila*, Fig. 5.18b). Such life cycles may result from lifespans exceeding one year (e.g. large stoneflies) or taxa which have multiple overlapping generations (e.g. many molluscs). This type of life cycle is the predominant one in the Southern Hemisphere and Tropics in marked contrast to the northern temperate zone (Wallace and Anderson, 1996).

Fig. 5.18 Life history patterns of two caddis species (a) *Agapetus fuscipes* and (b) *Rhyacophila dorsalis* over a three year period. The diagram shows the number of individuals per square metre from samples collected monthly over the study period. *Agapetus* shows a clear univoltine life history, *Rhyacophila* a complex bivoltine pattern with overlapping generations. (instars I–VII, PP, pre-pupa; P, pupa; A, adult). (Sangpradub and Giller, unpublished.)

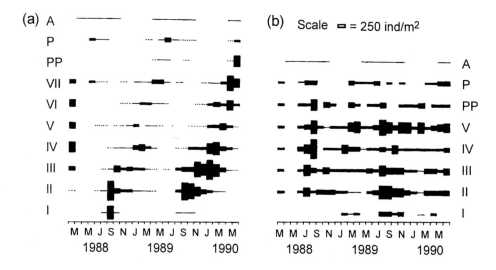

Life history plasticity

What should be evident from the preceding discussion is that there is great variation and flexibility in life history within and between populations, including egg diapause, duration of larval stages and growth rates, degree of synchrony in emergence, and number of generations per year. This plasticity in life history can occur from intrinsic differences among individuals within a population or as a response to environmental differences between populations across the geographical range of a species. Temperature, for example, is inversely related to duration of egg development in non-diapausing invertebrates and faster development of arthropod instars occurs at higher temperatures (see pp. 34–5). Nutritional effects can also influence voltinism (Butler, 1984). Thus, in response to different climates, many insect species may display more generations a year at lower altitudes and latitudes. This is most apparent in widely distributed species like *Baetis rhodani*, where life cycles vary from relatively synchronous and univoltine to less synchronous and multivoltine with overlapping cohorts (Clifford, 1982). This is not always the case, as genetic constraints may limit voltinism, as in the mayfly *Leptophlebia* which is always univoltine over a wide climatic and geographical range (Brittain, 1982), but variation does occur in most species. For the stonefly *Nemoura trispinosa*, life cycle patterns vary from a univoltine, slow seasonal type, to a univoltine fast seasonal type with extended egg development dependent on maximum annual water temperature (Williams *et al.*, 1995). This species exhibits eurythermal egg development—the ability to show major differences in the number of degree-days needed for egg development among local populations of the same species (Lillehammer *et al.*, 1989). This enables the species to switch between one- and two-year generation times depending on the local temperature range and food supply.

This kind of ecological generalization may also be the best adaptation for life in waters with unpredictable flow. The basic components for life cycle plasticity are prolonged hatching and emergence periods and a wide range of larval stages at any one time. This spreads the life cycle stages over time and thus decreases the risk of eradication by short-term catastrophes (Dietrich and Anderson, 1995). Drought during the summer is predictable and life cycle adaptations such as drought-resistant eggs ensure rapid recolonization following the drought. But unpredictable winter or spring droughts do not allow such adaptations and hence the great value of life cycle plasticity. Similarly, the value of such plasticity is also evident in temperate systems that are subject to unpredictable spates. Coexisting caddis in the Glenfinnish River in Ireland, demonstrate a wide degree of life cycle flexibility (Sangpradub, Giller, and O'Connor, unpublished). *Agapetus fuscipes* hatch fairly synchronously, but show variable development rates (Fig. 5.18a). *Silo pallipes*, *Plectrocnemia conspersa*, *Philopotamus montanus*, and *Sericostoma personatum* show great variation in development rate between individuals, some extending to a two-year cycle and leading to split cohorts. *Glossosoma conformis*, *Drusus annulatus*, *Potamophylax cingulatus*, and *Halesus radiatus* have delayed egg hatching and the appearance of first instars over several months. *Rhyacophila dorsalis* (Fig. 5.18b) and *Odontocerum albicorne* both show two cohorts a year and overlapping generations.

Flight periods also vary among the caddis species from one month in a grazing species to nine months in a filterer with most extending over five months. These variations in rate of development, the wide range of size classes present at any one time, the ability to overwinter in different larval stages and the asynchronous, extended flight periods give great flexibility to cope with year-to-year differences in weather and unpredictable disturbances, so-called 'spreading of risk' (c.f. den Boer, 1968).

Similar plasticity is evident in other animal groups and often involves a combination of sexual and asexual reproductive strategies, as in protozoa and sponges. Variable growth rates within populations of salmonids are well known, leading to some individuals being able to smoltify and go to sea after just one year, while others take two years. Individuals usually die following reproduction but others even within the same species (e.g. steelhead trout and Atlantic salmon) may return to sea a second time and then return again to freshwater to reproduce (Bayley and Li, 1996). Both sedentary and anadromous phenotypes occur among charr and trout (e.g. brown trout and sea trout are the same species, but the latter individuals go to sea). However, such flexibility is generally less evident in longer-lived, higher vertebrates, apart from the ability to vary the number of offspring and social controls on the individuals that reproduce (e.g. in territorial mammals like the otter, or birds like the dipper).

While the study of adaptation might be considered by some as rather 'old hat', there is clearly still much we do not know about how animals and plants survive in running waters. Linking behaviour, physiology, and morphology of individuals to population patterns and processes is a big step, but one that is begining to be thought of as an important stage in the development of our understanding of lotic species.

6 Energy and nutrients

So far we have examined the nature of the running water habitat and the organisms and their adaptations. We now turn to the population, community, and ecosystem levels and in the next three chapters explore the various patterns and processes that are found in streams and rivers. Flowing water and the intimate link between the stream and its valley leads to some of the unique structural and functional features of the lotic system. To set the scene, we will explore the processes involving energy, nutrients, and decomposition in this chapter before turning to movement, colonization, and species interactions in Chapter 7, and then discuss community structure, species diversity and distribution at the biogeographic scale in Chapter 8.

Food sources and energy flow

All ecosystems require a continual input of energy to function and, for most, this is based on the production of organic matter by plants via photosynthesis using solar radiation. Energy, in the form of organic matter, is then passed on to consumers. This can be directly through grazing food chains to herbivores thence to carnivores, or indirectly, following the death of plants or loss of plant parts like leaves, through decomposer food chains involving microbes, detritivores, and, again, carnivores. At each stage in the movement of energy through food chains, a proportion is lost through respiration (dissipation of heat via metabolism and to provide energy for work). Further energy is lost to the consumer in faeces or excretory products and only the energy held in the body itself or as reproductive products is available to the next consumer level (Fig. 6.1). This results in a continual reduction in available energy for successive consumers as one moves up the trophic levels in an ecosystem.

The ecosystem is thus an open system with respect to energy, and running waters, with their unidirectional flow, are particularly open. They are sustained energetically, as we shall see, not only through the continual influx of energy in the form of solar radiation, but also through the intimate relationship between the streams and the surrounding terrestrial ecosystems that lie within their catchments. This movement of energy drives the movement of nutrients, which is dealt with later (pp. 162–5).

Fig. 6.1 Gains and losses of energy in an energy budget of an individual animal, in this case a sturgeon.

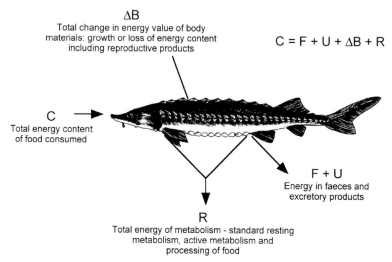

ΔB
Total change in energy value of body materials: growth or loss of energy content including reproductive products

$$C = F + U + \Delta B + R$$

C →
Total energy content of food consumed

F + U
Energy in faeces and excretory products

R
Total energy of metabolism - standard resting metabolism, active metabolism and processing of food

General considerations

There are essentially four sources of energy to streams and rivers and these are utilized by a range of producers and consumers (Fig. 6.2). Solar radiation supports instream (termed *autochthonous*) primary production. The other sources are based on organic matter produced elsewhere (termed *allochthonous*) and imported into the running water ecosystem. Table 3.2 (p. 40) defined the nature and size catagories of this organic matter. Adjacent riparian ecosystems produce coarse particulate organic matter (CPOM) like leaves, twigs, flowers and wood which enters the lotic system via direct litter fall or lateral litter blow. Fine particulate organic matter (FPOM) can enter through windblow, surface runoff, bank erosion and, along with dissolved organic matter (DOM), in groundwaters via subsurface drainage or from rainfall through the overhanging canopy. Seasonal floods onto floodplains can lead to the deposition of organic matter from rivers but can also liberate nutrients and organic matter from the soil which can be pulled back into the lotic system as floods subside. Finally, due to the transport properties of running water, upstream sections of the stream export both CPOM (e.g. dead macrophytes and some of the allochthonous matter it received itself), FPOM (faeces and material resulting from the partial breakdown of detritus) and DOM (such as extracellular exudates from primary producers and most of the DOM it received itself). These exports in turn become an allochthonous energy source for downstream sections.

Some of the autochthonous organic matter is passed through a series of consumers via grazing food chains. The allochthonous organic matter tends to be somewhat resistant to breakdown and while some is processed and degraded via detritivory and decomposition (e.g. leaves), the rest may enter the detritus storage pool and remain in one place for extended periods of time (e.g. woody material) or be displaced downstream from its origin (Fig. 6.2). Just as for the individual organism

Fig. 6.2 Components of the energy budget of a stream reach. The budget is given by: Import (I) + Primary Production (P) = Export (E) + Community Respiration (R) + Change in Biomass of organic matter in the system [Δ(D + Bf + Bp + Bc + Ba)]. (Adapted from Fisher and Likens, 1973.)

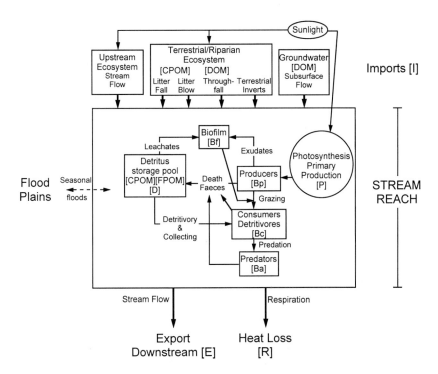

or population, an energy budget can be constructed for the ecosystem with imports and primary production balanced by export, respiration and change in the detritus storage pool or biomass of producers or consumers (Fig.6.2). We give some examples later (pp. 157–8).

The relative contribution of autochthonous and allochthonous resources is expected to change with successive stream segments. Low-order, particularly forested streams, will be subject to considerable shading, hence low primary production. On the other hand, they will experience large inputs of allochthonous CPOM in the form of leaves and other particulate matter which will form a major energy source for macroinvertebrates and microbial decomposers. Higher-order, wider rivers may experience much less influence from the riparian vegetation (see Fig 3.4 p. 37) and hence light levels and primary production can increase while direct input of organic matter may be reduced. Likewise, the balance between primary production and ecosystem respiration (P/R ratio) is an important feature of any stream segment. The relevance of these features to the functioning of the stream or river system will become clearer later, but before dealing with such issues, we examine the various food sources in more detail. Various studies express production levels or quantities of organic matter in different units. We have converted most values to gram of carbon per square metre (g C m^{-2}) using a standard conversion of 1g C m^{-2} per 2 g ash free dry mass (AFDM) (Webster and Meyer, 1997) or used dry weight (DW) of organic matter.

Autotrophs and primary production

We introduced the different types of autotrophs in Chapter 4 (pp. 72, 74–7) and looked at some of the factors that influence them in Chapter 3. Chemosynthetic bacteria are largely restricted to hot springs where they utilize chemical energy sources involving hydrogen sulphide and carbon dioxide as the carbon source to produce organic compounds. Otherwise, autotrophy is dominant only where conditions favour high productivity of plants. For periphyton this would include unshaded stream stretches, small rivers in dry areas like deserts and grasslands, or in headwater streams above the tree line. Seasonally, periphyton may grow well prior to spring opening of leaf buds. Bryophytes may also be prominent in low-order streams above and below the treeline. Most aquatic macrophytes are confined to low gradient streams and rivers with some fine sediments for root establishment. Rooted plants can have high-standing stocks per unit area especially in summer and in lowland eutrophic rivers. The flowing nature of rivers and the short passage time of water largely preclude phytoplankton except in sluggish lowland streams, river side channels and backwaters, within macrophyte beds or in dead zones.

Primary production can be limited by light, flow rate, temperature, grazing, and availability of nutrients (see Chapter 3 and pp. 162–4). There is no clear latitudinal trend and in fact there is greater variation in primary production within latitudes than between them (Benke *et al.*, 1988). Allan (1995) gives some tentative values of average lotic production of 0.01–0.1 g C m^{-2} d^{-1} for shaded and 0.25–2 g for open canopy areas in deciduous biomes, and maximal values of 1–6 g C m^{-2} d^{-1} in systems with limited riparian vegetation such as grasslands, deserts, and open coniferous biome streams. In a recent comparison of primary production in stream ecosystems, Lamberti and Steinman (1997) also showed highest gross production in desert streams and greater production in deciduous than boreal and montane coniferous streams. In large rivers primary production can vary from close to zero when turbid to >2 g C m^{-2} d^{-1} when clearer. Seasonal variation can also be considerable as illustrated by one extreme example from a cold desert stream in the central United States, where gross primary production of benthic algae and bryophytes varied from 3.8 in winter to 18 g C m^{-2} d^{-1} in summer (Brown and Matthews, 1995).

As to the fate of autochthonous production, it is largely only periphyton and phytoplankton that is directly consumed. While benthic algae offer a potentially good quality nitrogen-rich food for invertebrates, with a relatively low carbon to nitrogen ratio (C:N of 9.1–10.1:1), bryophyte and macrophyte tissues are only grazed by a few herbivores (see p. 76). They do, however, trap fine detritus and submerged macrophyte surfaces are usually covered with a diverse epiphyte community which can itself be highly productive in shallow eutrophic lowland streams in summer. Dissolved organic compounds can be exuded and used by bacteria (as we discuss below), but most macrophyte production is processed through the decomposer food chains within the stream stretch or is exported to stretches downstream.

Microorganisms and biofilms

Bacteria can be found in the water column, mostly attached to fine particles in suspension. However, it is the benthic microbes, especially those associated with biofilm, that have received the most attention and seem to be the most active and productive of those studied. Biofilms occur on most surfaces in streams and rivers including inert substrates like stones but also on the water surface and on organic substrates like wood and, as we will see later, on leaves. Biofilms consist of autotrophic filamentous algae, cyanobacteria, and diatoms; heterotrophic bacteria, actinomycete or hyphomycete fungi; amorphous, detrital, and silt particles and exoenzymes often enmeshed in a gelatinous polysaccharide matrix. Biofilms appear to be major transducers of energy and matter in lotic systems (Lock *et al.*, 1984). Not surprisingly, the biological components of biofilms on leaves and wood differ from those on stone. Higher biomass, especially of fungi, and higher metabolism, occur on wood (Sinsabaugh *et al.*, 1991). The nature of the biofilm can vary with site and seems to be related to stream chemistry. Nutrient availability can also limit microbial biomass as shown by nutrient diffusion experiments (Tank and Winterbourn, 1995).

Bott and Kaplan (1985) estimated that production by benthic bacteria can reach 9–40% of primary production, although Rosenfield and Roff (1991) suggest bacterial production can exceed primary production in forested sites. Values of $0.03–0.11$ g C m^{-2} d^{-1} were found in the forested sites, and higher values (0.2–1.22) in open sites in this latter study. The major energy source for bacteria in the biofilm appears to be dissolved organic carbon (DOC) leached from detritus, released by aquatic microalgae and macrophytes, excreted by consumers, and released by their own enzymatic degradation of detritus (if attached to an organic substrate) (Miller, 1987). Protozoans (such as ciliates and flagellates) and perhaps micrometazoans (like rotifers and microcrustaceans) can consume bacteria directly and the consumers in turn release exudates and faeces which are used by the bacteria. There is thus considerable nutrient cycling and energy fluxes and transfers within the biofilm matrix which represents the so-called 'microbial loop'. Some macroinvertebrates (scrapers, see Tables 5.3 and 5.4, p. 134) can feed directly on organic biofilms in the same way as they consume periphyton, and these biofilms may represent the major source of 'amorphous detritus' frequently found in gut contents of invertebrates (Winterbourn *et al.*, 1985).

Coarse particulate organic matter

CPOM includes all particles greater than 1 mm in size. Autumn-shed leaves are a major energy input for temperate and tropical forested streams, and blossoms, fruit, and pollen can also be important. Coarse organic detritus is also produced within the lotic system from the death of macrophytes or aquatic animals. Once in the stream, particles collect in front of boulders, snags, and small woody debris as leaf packs or larger debris dams or settle in slow-flowing areas like pools. Woody material that enters the stream is a relatively poor food source (with a C:N ratio of 220–1340:1) but represents a large pool of energy and nutrients that is released over time through its slow decomposition. Large woody debris (like logs, fallen trees, and branches) also plays an indirect role in the energetics of streams and rivers by modifying the physical character of the stream (see Chapter 3, pp. 43–4), and in helping to trap and thus increase the residence time of other detritus, especially leaves, in the stream (i.e. increasing the retentiveness of the stream reach).

The distribution of CPOM is highly variable in time and space. Autumn leaf fall in temperate deciduous forests may be highly synchronized, but in the tropics, leaf fall is affected by seasonality of rainfall, types of trees, and episodic storm events (Covich, 1988). When salmonids die in the headwaters following reproduction, they can provide a predictable and vital source of energy and nutrients especially to nutrient-poor systems. Other sources such as large mammal carcasses and faeces from aquatic mammals are, however, unpredictable in time. It is obvious that the nature of riparian vegetation affects litter input, but surprisingly the overhead riparian area at a site is not a good predictor of the quantities of suspended leaves or leaf fragments at that site. Dense stream bank vegetation can reduce the amount of litter blow reaching the water by trapping material on or adjacent to the bank. Some tropical trees (the so-called 'container trees' like tree ferns and palms) entrap leaves even before they reach the ground, especially in steep sloped mountain catchments (Covich, 1988). Storms or floods can release such leaves into the stream. In a novel study using Landsat and geographical information systems (GIS) approaches, amounts of leaves in an Oklahoma prairie river were best explained by mesoscale parameters such as percentage of riparian forest cover for 500–1000 m upstream reach lengths (Johnson and Covich, 1997). The percentage of whole leaves at sites decreased with distance downstream while leaf fragments increased. This study gives a hint as to the fate of CPOM and of leaves in particular in lotic systems.

As one might expect it is difficult to generalize about the amount of CPOM entering stream systems. The average input for the eastern United States based on data reviewed by Webster *et al.* (1995) was a total mass of 335 g C m^{-2} yr^{-1} but this ranged from 40 to 700 g C m^{-2} yr^{-1}. A general trend is for higher inputs, as expected, in low-order streams. For example, Connors and Naiman (1984) calculated values of 150–250, 100–150, and 7.5–8.5 g C m^{-2} yr^{-1} for 1st, 2nd, and 6th order tributaries of the Matawek-Moise river in Canada. Another expected pattern is for significantly lower inputs in more open streams than forested ones. Values of 35 g C m^{-2} yr^{-1} were found in open forest streams of Australia whereas values for tropical rain forest streams reached 480 g (Lake, 1995).

The quantities or standing stocks of CPOM in streams and rivers also vary and depend on a number of factors including inputs, retentivity of the stream bed and qualities of the decomposer community. For a range of stream sites in the United States, non-woody CPOM varied between 17 and 2600 g C m^{-2}, whereas woody

CPOM standing stocks ranged from 200 to 14 500 g (Webster and Meyer, 1997). There is generally a clear decrease in standing stocks of CPOM with increasing stream order. This is partly due to the higher inputs and processing of litter in low-order systems but also due to the storage of material behind debris dams, which are themselves more abundant in low order systems. Standing stocks also vary with season, related of course to the seasonality of inputs. At the microhabitat level, pools tend to accumulate organic matter, and less is found in riffles and very little on rock outcrop substrates. There is also evidence that standing stocks vary in different parts of the world across at least two orders of magnitude. New Zealand, in particular, which has streams with few debris dams and little woody debris, has low retention characteristics and hence low quantities of benthic organic matter (Winterbourn, 1995).

Fine particulate organic matter

FPOM includes all particles smaller than 1 mm down to 0.50 μm. Although FPOM can enter streams from adjacent terrestrial areas, it is primarily generated from the breakdown of the larger coarse particulate organic matter (CPOM) by the activity of shredders, microbial processes and physical abrasion. Crayfish, for example, consume the equivalent of 36 g C m^{-2} of leaf litter a year in an Appalachian stream (4–6% total litter input), and produce 12 g C m^{-2} of FPOM (Huryn and Wallace, 1987). Scouring of algal cells or biofilm from the substrate by the current or as a result of feeding activity of grazers or scrapers provides another source. Large rivers and lake outlet streams also contain suspended algae. In view of the poor quality of CPOM as food for shredders, and the consequent high ingestion rates, there is a high production of faeces which, together with its associated microflora, can be an important source of FPOM and lead to coprophagy. Some filter-feeders, such as simuliids, which capture FPOM, actually produce masses of faeces of larger particle size than ingested—an interesting reverse to shredding which may have great significance in both lake outlet streams and large rivers (Wotton *et al.*, 1998). Flocculation of dissolved organic matter by physical and chemical processes produces small particles which contribute another source of FPOM.

FPOM has its own microbial community associations, and microbial biomass per unit weight of organic matter tends to increase with decreasing particle size (Sinsabaugh *et al.*, 1992) but this is due to bacteria rather than fungi. FPOM occurs on, or associated with, the substrate or in suspension. The amount varies from stream to stream and with season and has a positive relationship with stream order. Flow regime and disturbances and the presence of debris dams and other instream structures play a major role in FPOM availability and transport. Studies by Naiman *et al.* (1987) in Canada identified standing stocks of benthic FPOM from 2 to 43 g C m^{-2}, and the presence of beavers and their dams increased these amounts by over 100-fold. Plants with narrow leaves or that grow in tufts can trap FPOM, and values of up to 1000 g C m^{-2} have been recorded for *Ranunculus* (Statzner and Kohmann, 1995). Mean levels of suspended organic material generally fall within a narrow range of less than one to a few mg l^{-1} (DW), but rivers draining peatlands in Finland can reach values >10 mg l^{-1} (DW), levels which have previously only been reported from tropical blackwaters (Peterson *et al.*, 1995). Concentration of suspended matter is clearly related to discharge and can increase rapidly following spates (see Fig. 3.6, p. 52)

Filter-feeders, like the net-spinning caddis and blackfly larvae, feed on suspended FPOM, whereas collector/gatherers, like mayflies, cased caddis flies, chironomids, and oligochaetes, feed on benthic FPOM in or on the sediments. The interesting studies of Winterbourn *et al.* (1984) using stable carbon isotope analysis, identified the primary source of food of these animals as being ultimately of terrestrial origin, again stressing the importance of allochthonous inputs and CPOM breakdown.

Dissolved organic matter

The majority of all organic material transported in streams and rivers would actually pass through a filter with a pore size of 0.45 μm and hence is, by definition, dissolved organic matter. Of course, DOM is very heterogeneous in composition and ranges from small identifiable organic molecules such as sugars, lipids, amino acids, and proteins to large humic molecules and colloids. The former constituents play a role in the energetics of lotic communities, but constitute <30% of total DOM (Bott *et al.*, 1984). The remaining and dominant fraction is of little biological importance. This material is transported downstream, hence the fraction tends to increase with increasing stream order.

Most DOM originates from terrestrial decomposition processes and enters streams and rivers from the land (p. 148). Instream sources, such as detrital leaching, exudates from algae, higher plants, and heterotrophs, and animal excretions offer the most biologically useful components. The relative importance of these various sources is related to the nature of the catchment, especially whether or not it is disturbed. The input of soil organic matter is highest from grassland catchments, lowest from desert catchments and intermediate from forested ones (Allan, 1995). A general world-wide review by Thurman (1985) concluded that concentrations of dissolved organic carbon (DOC) in small streams vary around 1–4 mg C l^{-1}, larger rivers 2–10 mg C l^{-1} and highest values of 10–30 mg C l^{-1} were found in tropical blackwaters. Values can be much higher than expected, as in the low-order, but short and steep rivers in New Zealand, where DOC levels in fully forested catchments can reach 18–38 mg l^{-1} (Winterbourn, 1995). While the concentration of DOC is known to be closely related to discharge, there is relatively little information on seasonal fluctuation within rivers. A study of the lower Rhine showed, rather surprisingly, that the concentration appears to be a more or less stable over the year (around 3.6 mg C l^{-1}). In this study, a slow downstream increase in DOC was evident (Admiraal and van Zanten, 1988), but other studies are equivocal on this pattern.

Only a few specialized animals appear to be capable of directly assimilating DOM, thus the incorporation of DOM into food webs largely relies on the microbial uptake of smaller labile components of DOM within biofilms and subsequent transfer to consumers. DOM can, however become aggregated into particles by flocculation, often as a consequence of mechanical forces. For instance, Petersen

(1986) observed that the amount of fine particulate organic matter (FPOM) increased by 66% below a waterfall from such flocculation. This amorphous particulate material is readily colonized by microorganisms and is in turn fed on by a variety of suspension feeders. Wotton (1996) postulated that flocculated DOM bound together with fibrils of mucopolysaccharides exuded from bacterial cells, algae, and animals, may play a much more significant role than previously thought in the trophic biology of running waters, and especially lake outlets.

Animal food

Little need be said about animals as a food source. Micro- and macroinvertebrates provide a high calorific and protein content to predators and thus generally offer the highest quality food resource of all. Such food sources are not confined just to aquatic prey either, as surface-dwelling predators and scavengers like the water cricket and surface-feeding fish can take advantage of a further allochthonous energy source in the form of terrestrial invertebrates falling into or trapped on the water surface (see Fig. 6.2). This can provide the major source of food for stream-dwelling fish such as trout, especially in summer and autumn in small temperate streams and rivers (Bridcut and Giller, 1993). Other lotic predators feed from the benthos or from suspension or both. Most are polyphagous (feeding on a variety of prey types) and predator–prey interactions can form an important component of the functioning of lotic communities. These will be explored later (pp. 182–7).

Secondary production

This represents the net production of living organic matter or biomass by a consumer population, a critical parameter if we wish to quantify energy flow. The basic factors that control secondary production (P_c) are illustrated in Fig. 6.3. In

Fig. 6.3 A schematic outline of the factors that may affect the secondary production of a consumer population. Standing stock biomass (B) is the product of mean organism weight (W) and population density (N), both of which may affect consumption. Internal and external stream factors and biotic feedback are also important. Production (P_c) is the product of mean daily biomass growth rate (g), time interval (Δt) and standing stock biomass (B). (Modified from Benke *et al.*, 1988.)

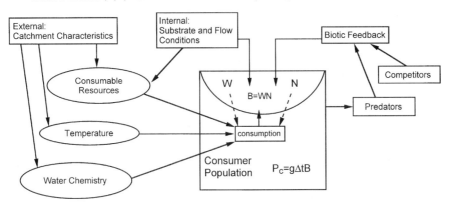

the figure, the consumer could represent an invertebrate, fish or even a microbial population if modified somewhat. For macroinvertebrate communities, most data is from low-order streams and the annual high values of secondary benthic production are usually in the region of 25–50 g C m^{-2} yr^{-1} (Benke, 1984). The well-studied desert stream Sycamore Creek in Arizona has one of the highest recorded values at 68 g C m^{-2} yr^{-1} but cool desert streams in eastern Washington and Utah shaded streams have values ranging from 6 to 12 g C m^{-2} yr^{-1} (Fisher, 1995). Much lower values of <1 g C m^{-2} yr^{-1} have been recorded in some Canadian streams (Mackay, 1995). There is very little information for large rivers, but the work of Mann *et al.* (1972) for the River Thames gives estimates of planktonic production of around 12 g C m^{-2} yr^{-1}, which was approximately 70% of benthic production.

Most studies, however, are on specific populations of animals and some of the levels of production are quite astonishing. Artificial recirculating channels in southern England were colonized by the fast-growing chironomid *Orthocladius calvus* which reached over 68 000 individuals per m^2 after just 16 days before disappearing at around day 32. This gave a productivity of 17 g C m^{-2} for the short period (Westlake and Ladle, 1995). Other high values can also be achieved by species with high biomass under certain conditions, such as filter-feeding *Hydropsyche* and dipteran larvae below impoundments, which have been recorded as exceeding 12 g C m^{-2} yr^{-1}.

Another important measure is the annual P$_c$/B ratio; secondary production divided by mean standing stock (the amount of biomass per unit area at a given point in time). This gives a rate of biomass turnover and can approximate mean growth rate. While most taxa have significantly lower production rates than those mentioned above, P$_c$/B ratios can be quite high, especially for short-lived species. Low latitude temperate and subtropical stream invertebrates can show ratios close to 100 whereas in higher latitudes, values rarely exceed 10. The high ratios are related to short development times and invertebrates with long lifespans have low P$_c$/B ratios; the crayfish, for example, with a life span of 3–11 years has a P$_c$/B ratio of only 0.58 (Huryn and Wallace, 1987). In general, therefore, the production of the benthos is many times greater than the standing stock biomass present at any one time. The importance of this was highlighted by studies on trout in a New Zealand stream which appeared to consume up to 30 times more prey biomass in a year than was available in the benthos at any one time (Allen, 1951)—the so-called 'Allen's Paradox' (Hynes, 1970). The solution to the apparent paradox would require P$_c$/B ratios which are generally higher than most studies would suggest, but the important role of terrestrial prey to trout, as mentioned earlier, was possibly overlooked. In fact, estimates of the potential annual energetic contribution of terrestrial arthropods to some headwater streams are comparable to annual production values of aquatic macroinvertebrates in such streams (Cloe and Garman, 1996).

Not surprisingly, there has been a considerable amount of work on fish production, given the value of fish as a natural resource. J.M. Elliott, for example, has been following trout populations in Black Beck, a small Lake District stream in the United Kingdom for over 25 years (Elliott, 1994). Secondary production (measured as biomass change) ranged from 8.86 to 33.9 g m^{-2} yr^{-1} over the period. Mann and Penczak (1986) summarized production values for eight species of salmonids and identified values between 0.14 and 57.7 g m^{-2} yr^{-1} for brown trout and between 0.22 and 11.1 g m^{-2} yr^{-1} for salmon. Production of other fish species would generally fall within these limits. Nutrient concentrations and availability of preferred habitat (such as pools for salmonids) will influence population size and hence production. Food levels, and more importantly temperature, seem to be key factors affecting growth rate. It is surprising, therefore, that tropical waters do not seem to have higher levels of fish production than temperate ones (Welcomme, 1985). A comparison of 17 tropical and 26 temperate rivers showed P$_c$/B ratios did not vary much more than twofold across latitudes. Indeed, average annual fish production of a number of rivers and streams in tropical Asia are low by comparison to European waters (Dudgeon, 1995). Biomass and production on river floodplains may be an exception, but would also be subject to considerable annual variation depending on inundation extent.

Community metabolism and energy budgets

To model the energy flow in lotic systems, we need measures of all inputs (allochthonous and autochthonous), all outputs (export and respiration), and changes in biomass or energy content of biotic and detrital standing stocks. Of course, this is not an easy task. We thus have relatively few complete annual energy budgets, and those available are mostly based on short-term studies of small stream segments in northern temperate systems. Nevertheless, it is instructive to look at the few North American examples in Table 6.1.

Two important parameters that tell us a lot about the functioning of the system are the primary production:community respiration ratio (P/R) and the exports:import ratio (E/I). Closed-canopy forested headwater streams like Bear Brook have very low primary production, a very low P/R ratio and imports which exceed exports (E/I<1). Such systems would be classified as heterotrophic, dependent on production from elsewhere. Wider river channels with reduced influence of riparian vegetation or arid streams (e.g. Deep Creek) have much greater primary production relative to detritus input, so P/R>1 and exports are near to or exceed imports. These systems would traditionally be classed as autotrophic. As Allan (1995) quite rightly points out, P/R values greater than 0.5 indicate that over 50% of respired energy is attributable to autochthonous primary production, thus this value may be a more sensible one to distinguish between heterotrophic and autotrophic systems. P/R values will fluctuate on a seasonal basis, particularly in the more autotrophic systems due to variations in primary production. Even in low-order stream reaches with a low annual P/R ratio, primary production may dominate during part of the year. P/R will also tend to vary longitudinally with distance from the headwater. This shows a clear pattern in undisturbed temperate North American streams with forested headwater catchments and has been incorporated into the River Continuum Concept (RCC) we discuss later (pp. 167–9)

Table 6.1 Estimated energy budgets for five North American streams. (Modified from Cummins *et al.*, 1983).

Parameters	Bear Brook	Augusta Creek	Deep Creek	White Clay Creek	Fort River
Order	2	1	2	3	4
Catchment type	Deciduous	Deciduous	Arid	Deciduous	Deciduous
Scale	Reach (1700 m)	Catchment	Reach (Station 3)	Reach	Reach (1700 m)
Inputs (Import)					
POM	3226	2317	142758	3030	36000
CPOM	(2733)	(355)	(2490)	(2153)	(2250)
FPOM	(493)	(1962)	(140268)	(878)	(33750)
DOM	2807	1974	149085	4117	100125
GPP	10	38	14245	3782	2700
Subtotal	6043	4329	306088	10929	138825
Outputs (Export)					
POM	1201	858	169099	3286	31500
CPOM	(927)	–	(2469)	(1894)	(900)
FPOM	(274)	–	(166639)	(1392)	(30600)
DOM	2797	1022	149085	4117	101700
Respiration	2035	2449	12124	3031	5625
Subtotal	6033	4329	330308	10434	138825
Balance*	0	0	-24220	495	0
E/I	0.66	0.44	1.09	1.04	0.98
P/R	0.01	0.5	1.18	1.25	0.96

(POM, particulate organic matter, >0.45 μm particle diameter; CPOM, coarse particulate organic matter, >1–2 mm; FPOM, fine particulate organic matter, < 1–2 mm > 0.45 μm; DOM, dissolved organic matter, < 0.45 μm; GPP, gross primary production. Storage was not measured but assumed to be in steady state. All values kcal m^{-2} yr^{-1}

* No difference reported in some because some values obtained by difference.

Leaf litter breakdown and detrital processing

The breakdown of detritus is an important process in stream and river ecosystems, both in terms of energy flow and nutrient cycling. Leaf litter is a major component of lotic detritus and considerable attention has been placed on the way it is processed and decomposed.

Phases of processing

Leaf litter from riparian vegetation is chemically very different from living vegetation and basically consists of cellulose, lignin, other resistant carbohydrates, and polyphenols. It is thus quite a poor food source and may also retain some of the tannins and toxins that performed anti-herbivore functions when the leaves were alive. Fresh litter is therefore not readily consumed by most aquatic animals but once in the stream, it starts to be processed by a combination of physical and biological factors that fall into three phases (Webster and Benfield, 1986):

1. *Rapid leaching* of dissolved organic matter (DOM) and soluble inorganic constituents of up to 25% initial dry weight over the first 24 hours and more gradual losses for a further extended period.

2. *Microbial colonization and decomposition*, which can start even before the leaf litter enters the stream and initially involves hyphomycete fungi which gradually give way to bacteria as the decay progresses. The reverse pattern of colonization occurs on macrophyte detritus. Hyphomycete hyphae are important in the decomposition of plant material, spreading over and penetrating the surface of the leaves using hydrolysing enzymes that are capable of degrading cellulose, pectin, chitin, etc. Laboratory studies have shown hyphomycetes can convert up to 75% of actual leaf mass to fine particulate organic matter (FPOM) over a relatively short (6-week) period (Suberkropp and Klug, 1980). Kaushik and Hynes (1971) more or less prevented any loss of leaf mass using antibacterial and antifungal antibiotics, with loss of fungi having the greatest effect. Typically, four to eight species dominate the fungal community but there does not appear to be any succession of species (Maltby, 1992). In addition to the direct decomposition, the leaves are 'conditioned' by microbial activity becoming softer, chemically modified (C:N ratio decreases to around 20–80:1 due to the microbial protein) and more palatable and readily assimilated by detritivores (see below).

3. *Mechanical and biological fragmentation.* Physical fragmentation and abrasion through the action of the current reduces the particle size. But more importantly, invertebrate shredders bite out the softer parts between leaf veins leaving a vascular skeleton which is abraded or consumed. The feeding activity of shredders speeds up the breakdown of coarse particulate organic matter (CPOM) to FPOM through skeletonization, and the creation of smaller particles through fragmentation or in the production of faeces. Small-scale experiments using leaves held in fine mesh bags that exclude macroinvertebrates show their contribution to decomposition is generally in the order of 24–40% and breakdown rates of CPOM are higher when invertebrates are more abundant (Webster and Benfield, 1986; see also Fig. 6.7, p. 166). The activities of shredders, in turn, enhance the surface area to volume ratio for microbial colonization.

Detritivore–detritus relationships

When given the choice, shredders prefer leaves that are 'conditioned' and that have the highest microbial growth. This is partly due to the conditioning process itself but the microbes also offer an additional food source. Microbial cells are actually more nutritious than dead leaves—the assimilation efficiency of consumers for detritus is lower (6–35%) than for microbes (42–97%) (Merritt *et al.*, 1984) and they do provide some important nutrients such as lipids.

However, not all fungal species are highly palatable and preferences for different types of leaves (see below) can be reversed by changing the colonizing fungal species (see Bärlocher, 1985, for a review). Seemingly, microbial biomass constitutes a relatively small percentage (0.03–10% biomass) of the diet of detritivores. Radio-tracer studies have shown that the main food components contributing the bulk of energy used in growth does come from leaves (Findley, Meyer, and Smith, 1986). Extracellular enzymes from microbes may retain activity in the animal gut and enhance digestion (Benke *et al.*, 1988) and thus add to the value of consuming the microbes. Overall, however, it seems that most of the energy requirements of the shredders comes from the detritus itself, but as this offers a relatively poor food source, shredders must process relatively large quantities to obtain sufficient nutrients for growth. We might therefore expect strong relationships between shredder abundance and quantities of detritus.

Stream faunas are well adapted to the annual input of autumn-shed leaves which is not surprising given its importance as a major energy resource. For instance, life cycles are well timed to the litter fall period in a multitude of taxa, particularly among shredders. Many species, especially among the Plecoptera, are also able to actively process leaves under the ice at near-freezing conditions as we mentioned earlier (see Chapter 5, p. 108).

Recent experimental studies have shown that leaf litter may, at least sometimes, be a limiting resource. In an elegant study by Richardson (1991), the amount of leaf litter was manipulated in a number of streamside channels. In treatments where levels were elevated, there was evidence for increased detritivore adult mass, increased densities of shredders, and a decreased emigration rate. In particular, a chironomid, *Brillia retifinis*, responded strongly and rapidly to the food supplementation. This kind of response has not always been found. In an extensive field experiment carried out in a North Carolina stream, Reice (1991) manipulated sections of the stream to contain 1% and 400 %, respectively, of background litter levels. Despite the magnitude and long duration (19 months) of the manipulation, there were no detectable effects in either breakdown rates or macroinvertebrate richness, or diversity in leaf pack samples. The absence of a response appeared to be related to the poor representation of shredders in this stream. However, in a series of larger-scale field experiments carried out in experimental catchments at the Coweeta Hydrological Laboratory in the Appalachian mountains, Bruce Wallace and co-workers have shown that shredder abundance dwindles if their food resource becomes scarce. In one of their most spectacular experiments (Wallace *et al.*, 1997), litter fall into the stream was restricted by placing fencing over a 180-metre stream reach, which, of course, had been studied in detail prior to the manipulation. The experimentally reduced leaf input decreased the secondary production of total benthos to 20–40% of pre-treatment levels. Only scrapers and filterers were unaffected. In addition to the drop in shredders and deposit-feeding collectors, predators declined in a manner that suggested that these in turn were limited by their food resource (i.e. other invertebrates). If representative of detritus-based systems, this leaf exclosure study suggests that headwaters can be strongly controlled by bottom-up processes cascading to trophic levels above the primary consumers (see pp. 202–4).

Leaf preference and breakdown rates

Leaves from different plant species vary in breakdown rates and in food quality thus it is not surprising to find detritivores showing clear preferences for leaf type when given the choice. In one of the earliest studies (Kaushik and Hynes, 1971), preference by *Gammarus* and stonefly and mayfly nymphs was in the order elm–alder–oak–beech–sugar-maple. More detailed, recent studies have confirmed this general pattern. The dipteran shredder *Tipula lateralis* preferred and had highest growth rates on alder but no growth and high mortality was observed when larvae were fed eucalyptus or oak. Preference and growth rates on chestnut fell in between (Canhoto and Graça, 1995). Alder has relatively high nitrogen levels and low levels of indigestible compounds, whereas oak and eucalyptus have thicker cuticles, higher tannins (oak), toxic oils (eucalyptus) and lower fungal colonization. Clearly, the differences in nutritional quality affect not only preference but also growth, survival, and larval development time in this shredder species.

Leaves with the lowest C:N ratio tend to have highest disappearance rates in streams and rivers. Monitoring the fate of leaf material from autumn to spring showed only 5% of alder leaf (C:N ratio 15:1) remained intact with 48% partly eaten and 47% skeletonized, whereas 61% of beech (C:N ratio 51:1) was intact, 29% eaten and 10% skeletonized (Haeckel *et al.*, 1973). Woody debris obviously has much slower breakdown rates, varying from 1 to >100 years, depending on size from twigs to tree trunks. This is due to the high C:N ratio (200–>1000:1), resistance to leaching, and low surface area to volume ratio for microbial decomposition.

Precise values of breakdown rates of leaves vary with exposure method, temperature, pH, water chemistry, flow, and other factors, but the summary in Fig. 6.4 illustrates the relative rates across a wide selection of woody and non-woody plants. One interesting feature is the relatively faster decomposition of riparian species and aquatic macrophytes, which can be related to their relatively low C:N ratios and for the macrophytes, the lack of the supporting tissues found in terrestrial leaves. Other patterns include faster decomposition in small headwater streams than in larger ones and interestingly, leaf breakdown appears faster in streams than in all other kinds of ecosystems (Webster and Benfield, 1986). Slower breakdown rates are found in small temporary streams compared to permanent ones and also in pools compared to riffles, related to the reduced shredder abundance and reduced physical abrasion.

The rate of detritus processing appears to decrease with increasing latitude. This has been explained as an effect of decreasing temperatures, but when the temperature effect is accounted for, actually a positive relationship remains, suggesting that the overall relationships are not simply a matter of temperature (Irons *et al.*, 1994). There appear to be changes in the relative contribution of microorganisms and shredders to the decomposition process with latitude (and possibly altitude). At high latitudes (and thus low temperatures) shredders appear to be more important in the breakdown rate of organic matter, perhaps as a

Fig. 6.4 Leaf breakdown rates for a range of woody and non-woody plants. Breakdown rates are assessed by exponential coefficients (−k, expressed as d^{-1}) calculated from regressions of log$_e$% ash free dry weight remaining against time the leaves have been exposed in stream water. Leaves can be classed as having fast, medium or slow breakdown (Petersen and Cummins, 1974). (Modified from Webster and Benfield, 1986. Reproduced with permission of the Annual Review of Ecology and Systematics, Vol. 17(c) 1986.)

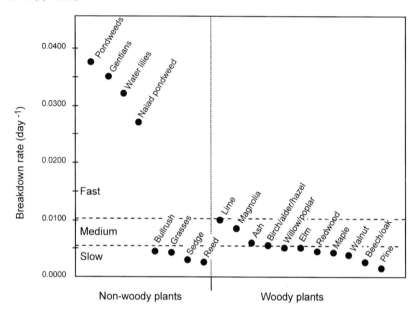

consequence of their origin in cool lotic systems. Conversely, microorganisms seem to be relatively more important at low latitudes (and altitudes), because their metabolic rates are assumed to be retarded at low temperatures (Fig. 6.5).

Nutrient–producer relationships and nutrient spiralling

The concentration of plant nutrients is extremely variable in freshwaters, due to the strong influences of the surrounding catchment discussed in Chapter 3, pp. 49–50. In this section, rather than simply comparing nutrient levels, we concentrate on nutrient–producer relationships and nutrient cycling.

Nutrient limitation

Nutrient relationships in streams are different from those in lakes. In lentic environments the dependence on nutrients is strong and normally limits the production and turnover of primary producers (Brönmark and Hansson, 1998). Productivity of stream producers is also influenced by nutrient concentrations, particularly phosphorus and nitrogen, but sometimes light limitation is more important. This is particularly so in upstream, low-order systems, which are often

Fig. 6.5 Latitudinal trends in the relative importance of microbes and macroinvertebrates in leaf breakdown. Microbial processing, expressed as the percentage of total leaf litter breakdown, apparently declines with increasing latitude, whereas the biomass of shredders on leafpacks (mg/g) shows an opposite trend. (Modified from Irons *et al.*,

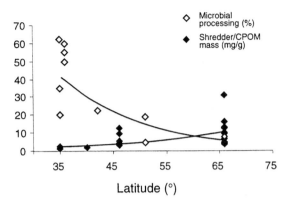

shaded by a closed and dense canopy. The production of submersed macrophytes and periphyton also often declines at high stream orders. Here, nutrient levels are normally relatively high, especially in catchments that are influenced by agriculture, but increasing turbidity and depth reduces light penetration through the water resulting again in a production limited by light (Wetzel and Ward 1992). Another difference between streams and lakes is that often nearly all available lake nutrients in the photic zone are sequestered by phytoplankton, reducing concentrations in the water column, while the open nature of stream ecosystems results in a continuous input of nutrients from the watershed (Newbold, 1992).

Where light is not limiting, abundant phosphorus or nitrogen does increase production and algal growth, as has been demonstrated in many studies involving experimental enrichment with these nutrients. This has been especially obvious in systems where the background concentrations of soluble reactive phosphorus have previously been below 15 μg l^{-1}, and those of inorganic nitrogen below 60 μg l^{-1}. Thus, many clearwater systems, and habitats positioned at intermediate stream orders, appear to be nutrient-limited, whereas others, in particular small shaded and large turbid systems are not.

One of the most thorough investigations of the importance of nutrients for a stream ecosystem has been carried out in the Kuparuk river in Alaska. Here, fertilization experiments have been conducted over a number of years by Bruce Peterson and co-workers. In this pristine, high latitude (68° N) river, phosphorus clearly limits primary production but the situation is quite complex. Bryophytes, for instance, which are known to enhance macroinvertebrate populations (see Chapter 3, p. 52), responded strongly and their biomass increased nearly 20-fold in comparison with control reaches after the first 7–8 years of fertilization (Bowden *et al.*, 1994). The effects of fertilization observed on diatoms were initially strong, but declined after the first two years (Miller *et al.*, 1992). Moreover, the composition of diatom species changed from erect to more prostrate forms. Using stable isotope techniques (carbon 13 and nitrogen 15), Peterson *et al.* (1993) were able to demonstrate that the nitrogen and carbon in the animals originated from the experimental fertilization of the plants and thus the decrease in algal biomass and change in diatom form was probably caused by grazing. The simple macro-invertebrate community in Kuparuk river is dominated by one species each of blackfly and caddisfly (filterers), midge and mayfly (grazers), and fish (grayling, a predator). Primary production obviously plays a key role in the energetics of the system in comparison to the large quantities of peat and dissolved organic matter (DOM) entering the river from the surrounding tundra. The Kuparuk river study is a straightforward example of 'bottom-up' regulation of aquatic ecosystems (see Chapter 8, pp. 202–4). Experience tells us that it could be difficult to assess the effects of fertilization experiments because of such indirect effects over several trophic levels. Therefore, the timescale of an experiment is important. Short-term experiments may show rapid positive responses in primary producers. However, if the experiments are allowed to continue over several consumer generations, fertilization may favour higher grazer and/or predator densities, while the biomass of primary producers remains at levels similar to those prevailing before the experimental treatment was initiated.

Spiralling

Nutrients are not only taken up by organisms but also released, and therefore can potentially be cycled within the system. What is so different about lotic systems compared to terrestrial ones, is that the internal biotic cycling of matter is small compared to the throughput of material, and thus the biological community only gains a temporary hold on nutrients (Winterbourn and Townsend, 1991). This is because of the unidirectional flow of water, so cycling in stream systems has a spatial component through a net downstream loss for each cycle. The release of organic and inorganic nutrients in one stream or river segment represents a component of the imports to another segment downstream. This downstream cycling has been termed 'spiralling' (Wallace *et al.*, 1977), and the storage–cycle–release pattern of energy and nutrients through a succession of stream segments is a fundamental feature of lotic systems.

Spiralling length is determined by the combination of uptake length (average distance a released atom is transported until it is captured again) and turn-over length (the downstream distance moved while in an organisms, Fig. 6.6). Spiralling length (i.e. the distance between two consecutive uptakes) has been estimated at 190 m for phosphorus in a Tennessee stream (Newbold *et al.*, 1983). The major part (165 m) was as transport in the water, 25 m was in micro-organisms associated with CPOM, FPOM, and biofilm, but less than 2 m was in the consumer component. However, phosphorus retention was high, in the sense that a large portion of phosphorus was bound up in biota, increasing the retention 300 times more than if biota had been absent. Much of this retention was due to a pleurocerid snail species, *Elimia claeviformis*, which not only accumulated relatively high levels of phosphorus, but also was displaced very slowly downstream (less than 1 cm d^{-1}).

Fig. 6.6 A schematic figure of nutrient spiralling. The irregular line indicates the path of a dissolved nutrient atom that is regenerated from biota at point (a) and carried by the water downstream to a point (b) where it is taken up by an organism. The organism typically moves a short distance downstream before the atom is mineralized and returned to the water (c). The spiralling distance is the sum of S_W ('uptake length') and S_B ('turnover length'). (Modified from Newbold, 1992.)

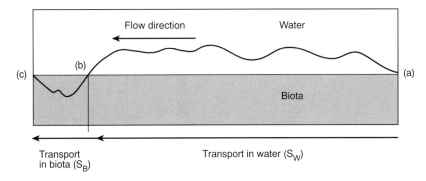

The spiralling of carbon is also very important because it increases the retention of energy in stream systems. Retentive streams show low turnover lengths as shown in a compilation of data from streams in the eastern United States (Webster *et al.*, 1995). In another study, Wotton *et al.* (1996), using fluorescent dye as an inert marker in a shallow stream, showed that high densities of blackfly larvae were not only able to intercept downstream transport of fine particles, but also to repeatedly ingest and egest faecal material containing the dye particles. As mentioned earlier, simuliids egest larger particles than they ingest, and since larger particles are more readily captured by the larvae, recapture after the first interception was more efficient. Spiralling length in this experiment was estimated to be 5.6 m, a remarkably short distance. Naturally, as pointed out above, spiralling length is not only a consequence of uptake and release intensities, but also of abiotic factors. Not surprisingly, low current speeds and pools tend to conserve material locally, while high velocities displace particles over much longer distances before they are recaptured.

Longitudinal patterns

We saw earlier how the unidirectional flow of water sets up longitudinal patterns in physico-chemical factors (Chapter 3). It is now opportune to revisit the concept of longitudinal patterns in the light of the discussion of energy and nutrients and the role played by the biota. In a series of innovative studies, J. Bruce Wallace and colleagues used the insecticide methoxychlor to virtually wipe out the insect community from a headwater stream (without affecting most other invertebrates and microorganisms) in order to study the relative importance of benthic insects in the decomposition and transport of detritus (e.g. Wallace *et al.*, 1982; Cuffney *et al.*, 1990; Fig. 6.7). The experiment resulted in a strong reduction of the downstream export of organic material, particularly FPOM, because the fragmentation of the material was slowed down leading to a build up of benthic

Fig. 6.7 (a) Treatment with an insecticide led to a significant decrease of insect (but an increase in oligochaete) numbers and different leaf types. (b) A consequence of reduced macroinvertebrates was a lowered transport of suspended organic matter (bottom right panel) and increased accumulation of benthic detritus (bottom left panel). Values given as ash free dry weight (AFDW). Error bars show the upper 95% confidence limits. (Data from Wallace *et al.*, 1982. Reproduced with kind permission of Springer–Verlag.)

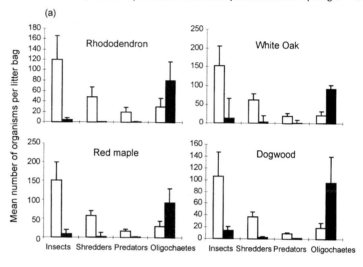

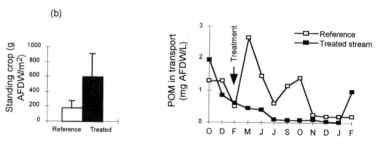

detritus (Fig. 6.7b). This instructive experiment clearly demonstrated how important the intact biota of headwaters is to downstream communities. It is significant that this evidence of an upstream/downstream link comes from a low-order stream, because it is in the headwaters that carbon storage primarily takes place, due to the high retentivity of these systems. In contrast, much of the carbon consumption may take place by the communities of higher stream orders (Naiman *et al.*, 1987; see also p. 157).

The loss of organic materials to downstream parts of a system depends on the interaction of a number of factors including the dominant size classes of the organic material, the topography influencing the retentive capacities (i.e bed roughness and slope), as well as the faunal composition. It is often assumed by implication that the fragmentation of organic material by shredders in low-order streams would favour the feeding and growth of collectors in downstream sections through the production of FPOM, and indeed, this has been shown experimentally (Cummins *et al.*, 1973; Short and Maslin, 1977). Food for collectors is also produced by several other processes and thus the relative contribution from shredders could theoretically be small (Heard and Richardson, 1995). Nevertheless, the large impact of insects in the above-mentioned experiments by Wallace and his collaborators indicates that shredders do play a highly significant role, at least in the types of systems they manipulated.

Another interesting longitudinal change involves microbial assemblages. Leachates from riparian vegetation are a readily available form of organic carbon to stream microbes but leachate chemistry and nutritional quality varies with leaf species. Bacterial assemblages thus appear to change qualitatively in response to alterations in riparian vegetation as one proceeds downstream along a river system (Koetsier *et al.*, 1997).

The River Continuum Concept

From a different starting point to Wallace's above, and on a larger scale, Vannote *et al.* (1980) postulated that the structure and function of river communities change in a predictable way between source and sea. Their approach was to consider that the apparently predictable geomorphological–hydrological downstream changes, including energy input and organic matter transport, act as the template upon which biological communities are adapted. The authors argued that in effect, stream communities, much as their hydrological counterparts, are systems in a dynamic equilibrium. Their 'River Continuum Concept' (RCC) included a number of predictions of longitudinal changes along the continuum. The most important ones concerned temperature amplitude, the relative proportion of different functional feeding groups, species diversity, and ratios between production and respiration, and between CPOM and FPOM (Fig. 6.8). According to the RCC, low-order streams are predicted to have a low P/R value (<1), because of shading by the dense canopies and the provision of leaf inputs. As a consequence these streams are also predicted to have a large proportion of shredders. In mid-order streams, improved light conditions, due to a broader stream channel, favour algal and macrophyte growth driving the P/R ratio above 1, and thereby enhancing the relative abundance of grazers/scrapers. At these intermediate stream orders, according to the RCC, temperature amplitudes are greatest and therefore maximum species richness is predicted as more taxa will experience optimal temperatures compared to sections of the river where temperature variation is less. The high turbidity and great depth of high-order rivers reduce light again, thus P/R<1. Some primary production by phytoplankton is assumed to occur, and in the absence of coarse organic material, which has been largely broken down to fine particles upstream, collectors will be the dominating invertebrates in these large rivers.

These ideas stimulated a prolific debate on the organisation of lotic communities. Numerous attempts were made to test the predictions of the RCC and some strong support was established at several sites in the United States and Canada (see the review in Benke *et al.*, 1988). However, it soon became evident that the

Fig. 6.8 A schematic representation of the changes in macroinvertebrate functional feeding groups predicted by the River Continuum Concept and the fish communities as the river progresses from forested headwaters to higher-order, lowland river. The fish illustrated (from left to right) are sculpin (bullhead), trout, grayling, bream, river lamprey (fish-like vertebrate), barbel, and pike.

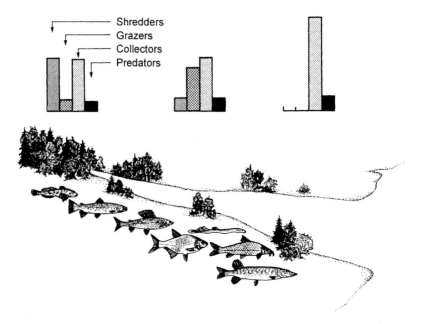

concept was too idealistic, particularly in only addressing pristine rivers. Anthropogenic alterations and changes in land use have strongly affected many river systems (see Chapter 9), thus rendering the RCC inapplicable to a number of other situations. Another weakness concerns the fact that the RCC was developed by researchers active in areas with deciduous forests in the temperate parts of North America. In other streams, such as in New Zealand, for example, shredders are poorly represented due to the low tree line, low retention of CPOM, and unpredictable flooding (Winterbourn, 1995). The RCC also disregards the strong effects of tributaries, lakes, and other local or regional features such as extensive floodplains within the river system, which often cloud distinct longitudinal patterns.

One of the underlying hypotheses, that of a gradual downstream physical change, has also been questioned because stream sections of high hydrological stress apparently interlace with sections of lower stress and major changes in ecological patterns seem to occur at such junctions (Statzner and Borchardt, 1994). The RCC prediction that maximum species diversity would occur in intermediate stream orders where variation, especially temperature, is greatest has also been criticized by Statzner and Higler (1985) on several points. The main ones are the fact that the RCC only relates to macroinvertebrates and disregards the fact that fish and plankton diversity, for example, is greatest in the highest stream orders, and that in tropical areas low-order streams have the greatest temperature amplitudes. Finally, the RCC rests heavily on the assumptions that low-order streams have high loads of CPOM (and hence a large share of shredders) and that they are heterotrophic systems, while in fact, many stream systems in the world have source areas devoid of forest, as in very dry or high altitude (above the tree line) landscapes.

A good deal of work has been undertaken to modify the RCC to accommodate these criticisms and the RCC has been used as the organizing theme for the excellent *Ecosystems of the World* text on streams and rivers (Cushing *et al.*, 1995). Grubaugh *et al.* (1996) strongly defended the RCC from much of the criticism by pointing out that many workers have studied only a single habitat type, such as cobble riffles, which cannot be expected to reflect the overall changes throughout the stream continuum. These authors also argued that it is essential that the biomass of different functional groups should be studied, and not just the relative abundances. In support of these arguments, they showed that the mass of the different functional groups met the predictions of RCC when data were weighted for relative habitat availability along the continuum. Their study was conducted in a 1st through 7th order stream in the Appalachian Mountains, which co-incidentally is within the geographical area where the RCC probably is most applicable. Today, it is widely considered that the greatest asset of the RCC was its tremendous success in provoking productive discussions, and it still remains one of the few theories undividedly concerning the lotic environment.

7 Movement and interaction

Having concentrated in the previous chapter on ecosystem patterns and processes, we now turn to the population level, and in this chapter discuss the mobility and colonization patterns of lotic organisms and species interactions.

Movement, drift, and colonization

Just peering into a stream or river would leave one with the impression that there is little movement of organisms apart perhaps from fish. But this impression is wrong. Pick up a stone and turn it over and you will notice many of the invertebrates, especially large heptageniid mayflies, scuttling away to the under-surface. Set up a net in the stream and overnight it will collect hundreds of individuals that have been drifting past that point in the channel. Place artificial substrates on the stream bed and within days they will be colonized by an assemblage that closely resembles the communities of the adjacent substrate. Follow the recovery of a stream reach disturbed by a pollution incident or a catastrophic flood or drought, and you will be surprised at the rate of recovery. Clearly, therefore, there is a lot of activity in the stream over a range of spatial and temporal scales. The benthic macroinvertebrates have actually been described as being in a state of 'continuous redistribution' (Townsend and Hildrew, 1976). A lot of the work has been done on the invertebrates, but the colonization of allochthonous leaves by hyphomycete fungi and of stones by algae clearly demonstrates the mobility of other types of organisms.

One obvious reason for movement relates to the flowing nature of the water in rivers and streams. The drag force of flow (especially during high flow events) can cause dislodgement and subsequent downstream transport of individuals. But as we will see, other physical, chemical, and biological factors are involved, and movements are not purely passive in nature. For macroinvertebrates, movements include downstream drift in the water column, swimming or crawling from upstream, downstream or lateral areas, vertical movements through the substrate, and for insects aerial movements by adult stages along or between river channels involving oviposition or flying in of aquatic adults. Stream and river invertebrates are generally considered to have high dispersal capabilities, but these dispersal and mobility capabilities do vary considerably among invertebrate taxa. The variation in mobility could even be viewed as one aspect of resource partitioning (Hildrew, 1996b; see pp. 193–5) as species may differ in their ability to colonize disturbed or newly formed patches or reaches.

Small-scale movements

There are many different phenomena which illustrate the extent of small-scale movements. Many insect larvae appear to show small-scale diel changes in their distribution on individual stones, tending to occupy lower surfaces during the day, but upper surfaces at night (Elliott, 1971a; Glozier and Culp, 1989). This activity is usually seen for grazer/scraper species (such as many mayflies) and is associated with diel patterns in feeding. Short-term, small-scale movements in response to the presence of predators or competitors and movements of individuals between food patches were discussed earlier (see Chapter 5, p. 132). The colonization of bare substrates (either scoured natural ones, or implanted artificial ones) over 24-hour periods also attests to the degree of these small scale movements and movements into artificial refugia during periods of peak flow (see pp. 106–7) are of a similar scale. Studies on individual fish have shown they too show daily movements, swimming between pools and riffles. Tiny PIT tags (passive-induced transponders, which carry a unique individual code) were implanted in individual trout held in enclosures, and each time they swam over detector plates placed on the stream bed between pool and riffle habitat, the direction and time of movement was recorded (L. Greenberg and P. Giller, in prep.). Some fish remained in the enclosure's pool, some in the riffle, while others moved into the pool at night and stayed in the riffle during the day, or vice versa.

Medium- to large-scale movements

Monitoring movements of individuals over relatively longer time periods than discussed above gives us some idea of the potential size of the home range of the individual (the area over which the animal normally travels) and perhaps the net movement over the lifetime of an individual. This is best done using some form of unique marking of individuals. Erman (1986) took advantage of the fact that the cased caddis larvae of *Chyranda centralis* marked themselves by incorporating pieces of coloured plastic into their cases. By setting up marking stations of differently coloured plastic, it was possible to estimate distances covered up- or downstream. Some individuals, especially younger larvae, showed little movement, but older larvae generally did move. The greatest movement over 24 hours was 3.6 m upstream, and over 4 days, 7 m upstream, 4.2 m downstream. Over 12 days, three larvae made net gains of 3.4 m upstream and the longest known distance travelled upstream was 56.9 m over seven weeks. The sequence of colours on the case of another individual indicated it had travelled 42 m downstream, then upstream again at least 42 m. Several larvae made such up and down movements during the course of the study.

In another example, 1000 late instars of the large stonefly *Pteronarcys californica* were individually marked and their positions monitored in a 360-metre stream stretch through recaptures over a three-month period (Freilich, 1991). Most nymphs stayed within a few metres of where they were first captured, with a mean displacement of 1.8 m downstream. Eighty-five percent of movements were of 12 m or less although some individuals did show extremely rapid upstream movements of 6–22 m per day. The distribution of these grazing nymphs was markedly clumped and they tended to stay many days in these 'centres', then move quickly between them. Overall, tagged insects were confined to fast-water riffles and low velocity silt-bottomed pools acted as barriers as there was no evidence of any tagged individuals crossing pools.

This kind of evidence for rather limited within-stream movement links elegantly with some interesting genetic studies by Bunn and Hughes (1997). If there is high dispersal between populations, high gene flow would lead to little genetic difference and vice versa. For three insect species (a mayfly, a gerrid, and a cased caddis), the degree of genetic differentiation at the between-reach scale within a stream, was greater than at the larger between-stream scale. This finding seems to indicate that in these Australian tropical rainforest streams, larvae apparently move very little within the stream (although the degree of genetic differentiation suggests the active swimming *Baetis* moved more than the cased caddis), but dispersal among streams through adult flight is high. It is also thought likely that larvae present in each reach are the result of only a few matings (where females lay many eggs). Small shrimps in similar streams also showed high levels of genetic differentiation between sub-populations within and between different sub-catchments, but in this case differentiation increased as one moved to larger spatial scales (Hughes *et al.*, 1995). Shrimps do not have the power of flight between catchments!

One might expect that larger animals will have larger home ranges and move over larger areas or distances than the smaller invertebrates. While this is probably true in the case of mammals and birds (e.g. consider the size of otter home ranges in Fig. 5.13, p. 131), for fish this is not necessarily the case. For brown trout, estimates of home range lie between 15 and 50 m^2 in area, and 9 to 18 m stream length (Hesthagen, 1990). Other fish, such as sculpins and guppies, also show restricted movements (see Power *et al.*, 1988). However, other studies based on individual marking and recapturing of fish (Bridcut and Giller, 1993) have identified three categories of brown trout: those that remain within the same pool or riffle and sometimes even associated with the same rock; those that remain faithful to a certain habitat type; and those that move between habitat types and sometimes over several kilometres up- and downstream. Brown trout fry also show extensive movements, and there is evidence of large numbers of fry moving downstream, influenced by water temperature, discharge, turbidity, prey availability, and territoriality of larger fish (Elliott, 1987).

Downstream movements of trout fry might perhaps be better considered as within-stream migrations. Migrating fish, decapods, and amphipods are found in many large rivers and long migrations in tropical and temperate fishes are associated with reproduction in upstream spawning sites (see p. 98) particularly in anadromous species. Rivers also function as dispersal corridors for riparian plants. In a series of experiments using model diaspores (reproductive elements of dispersal), Nilsson *et al.* (1993) examined the distances they were transported and the riverbank characteristics where the model diaspores (sunflower seeds and wooden cubes) stranded. Diaspores could be carried up to 140 km, but dams formed significant barriers to transport and travel was considerably shorter on windy days because the diaspores were blown ashore. In contrast, river curvature, current velocity, the presence of floodplain, and tree and shrub cover did not influence diaspore deposition on the banks. Natural diaspores, of course, will vary in floating capacity, which is also important to riparian plant dispersal.

Larger-scale dispersal between streams and rivers normally requires some terrestrial or aerial movement and is thus largely restricted to insects, birds, and mammals. The extent of such movements, for insects at least, is relatively poorly studied, but is clearly the most important route of colonization of severely disturbed catchments or new channels. We will come back to colonization a little later (see pp. 181–2). Seeds or spores of aquatic plants can disperse between waterbodies in air, or in animal faeces or on animal bodies. The colonization of remote, especially volcanic, islands clearly requires large-scale dispersal over the sea. The sea will pose a severe barrier to many taxa and hence lead to unique and often depauperate communities (see pp. 213–14).

Drift

One of the most ubiquitous and widely studied processes in running waters is the downstream drift of organisms. While it is easy to measure and has strong diel patterns, the question as to how upstream populations can be maintained in the face of such downstream losses has challenged stream biologists over the past 50 years or so. Surface drift contains largely allochthonous material dependent on the riparian vegetation (e.g. terrestrial insects) plus emerging adults of aquatic larvae. True drift (the downstream transport by the current of organisms normally living in or on the substrate) is found in both small streams and large rivers. Drift is monitored by placing drift nets across the flow of the stream or river. There are numerous designs, some simple with a rectangular opening fixed to a simple net, others more complicated with a narrow slit-like entrance leading to an expansion box, then the net. The time of day and location (see below) and mesh size will influence what and how many individuals are collected.

Drift involves most kinds of benthic invertebrates at some stage in their life cycle as well as fish fry and algae like diatoms. However, some species have a far greater propensity to drift than others, and some taxa rarely drift if at all, thus the drift differs in composition from the benthos. Drift samples tend to be dominated by a relatively few taxa. In a study on a headwater Australian stream, for example, 194 taxa were identified from drift samples but 11 contributed almost half the total number of invertebrates (Schreiber, 1995). Similarly in the River Rhine in France, 25 of the 138 taxa represented 98% of the total drift (Cellot, 1996). These dominant taxa tend to be similar irrespective of where the samples are taken from. Baetid and leptophlebiid mayflies, the amphipod *Gammarus* and simuliid and chironomid fly larvae in particular are always among the most abundant animals in the drift of streams. In riparian and slow flowing areas of large rivers, chironomids, oligochaetes, and *Hydra* dominate (Cellot, 1996). Some caddis larvae are usually common (e.g. Hydropsychidae and Polycentropodidae). In contrast, systellognathan stoneflies, heptageniid mayflies, planarians, cased caddis, and molluscs tend to be rare or absent in the drift. Wilzbach *et al.* (1988) tried to integrate drift potential with mode of existence (Table 5.2, p. 123) and functional feeding group (Table 5.3, p. 134) and suggested that in general, scrapers tend to be clingers and rarely drift (mainly accidental entry and passive drifters), while gatherer–collectors tend to be swimmers and sprawlers and show more active drift behaviour. Among the mayflies, for example, *Baetis* and *Ephemerella* would fall in the latter group, *Ecdyonurus* and *Heptagenia* in the former (Giller and Campbell, 1986). For many species therefore, drift is part of their life history and, for lotic communities, drift provides a mechanism for the continuous redistribution of individuals over the substrate and for the colonization of denuded areas as well as a food source for other animals (such as net-spinning caddis larvae and fish).

Based on Waters (1972) we can classify drift into three categories:

1. *Constant drift*: continuous, accidental displacement at low densitites.

2. *Catastrophic drift*: pulsed, high density movements resulting from major physical and chemical disturbances such as high or low water levels or pollutants.

3. *Behavioural drift*: periodic, resulting from diel patterns of activity or avoidance of predators, competitors or other stressors.

The main area of debate among freshwater biologists lies in whether entry to drift is active or passive, which in turn relates to the various causes of drift (see below).

Drift distances and densities

The number of individuals drifting per m^3 is the *drift density*. Non-catastrophic drift densities vary widely from place to place but in general, numbers are surprisingly low (Table 7.1). Typically, oligotrophic streams have very low drift densities [see S. Sweden (a) example in Table 7.1] and highest densities tend to be from streams which have relatively high discharge. The mesh size of the drift samplers can be critical to estimated drift density (see Georgia example in Table 7.1) and up to 5 times the numbers collected using 234 μm mesh are caught with mesh size 143 μm (Smith-Cuffney and Wallace, 1987). Densities vary with time of day and season (see below). Numbers of drifting animals also tend to increase from mid-channel to nearer the bank and from the water surface to the bottom (larger organisms tend to drift nearer the bottom) (Cellot, 1989). At any one time therefore, the percentage of the benthos drifting is very small and most values will tend to fall in the range 0.002–0.008%. Nevertheless, when one considers the total drift of individuals past a point per day (*daily drift rate*), the number is often quite impressive (Table 7.1), particularly for large rivers with their greater discharge and larger area of river bottom. In most systems this daily drift rate over an area of bottom is often many times greater than the benthic standing crop of that area.

Drifting animals generally travel only short distances (from less than one to maybe tens of metres) but this varies with taxa and current velocity (Table 7.2, and see Lancaster *et al.*, 1996). For passive drifters with no special ability to return to the bottom (e.g. *Ecdyonurus*, *Hydropsyche*), drift distances are similar for live and dead specimens (i.e. individuals eventually settle out of water). Allan (1995) suggests

Table 7.1. Ranges of drift density and daily drift rate past a single point from streams and large rivers from around the world. The S. Sweden (a) example represents an oligotrophic stream and the Georgia example is based on drift samples using extremely fine mesh (143 μm) which collects large numbers of very small drifting animals.

Geographical area or river	Drift density (mean no. individuals per m³)	Mesh size (μm)	Daily drift rate (number individuals per day × 10³)
Smaller streams			
Low altitude Nepal[a]	0.37–0.76	400	0.285–5.78
High altitude Nepal[a]	0.23–3.46	400	0.087–0.73
Malaysia[a]	1.56–1.79		
Ghana[a]	0.10–1.90		
Georgia, USA[c]	31.0–116.3	143	
Florida, USA[a]	0.03–0.49		
Equadorian Andes[a]	0.85–3.28		
Queensland, Australia[a]	0.31–3.98	400	
S. Sweden (a)[d]	0.02–0.08		
S. Sweden (b)[e]	1.45–11.34	200	
N. Sweden[f]		1000	5.04–192.0
High altitude Sweden[g]	1.6–4.2	145	2590–9000
Canada[h]	0.60–5.40		20.0–366.0
Wales, UK[b]	0.06–7.80	440	8.0–1373.0
N. England, UK[b]	0.33–0.41	275	20.0–11970.0
Larger rivers			
Lower Mississippi[b]	0.60—1.10	505	
Lower Missouri[b]	0.44		64000.0
Volga[b]	0.70–4.60		1397500–7873630
Upper Rhone[b]	0.06–10.5	500	44000.0
Danube[i]	0.12–0.31	400	13600.0

[a] References in Brewin and Ormerod (1994); [b] References in Cellot (1989); [c] Smith-Cuffney and Wallace (1987); [d] Kullberg and Petersen (1987); [e] Malmqvist and Sjöström (1987); [f] Müller (1954); [g] Ulfstrand (1968); [h] Bishop and Hynes (1969); [i] Anderwald *et al.* (1991).

10–20 m is the norm at moderate current velocities of 30–60 cm s^{-1}. Even algal cells seem to travel short distances before recolonizing the substrate (Müller-Haeckel, 1973). The turbulent eddies probably contribute to this. Active drifting taxa are capable of leaving the drift even more rapidly (such as *Baetis rhodani*). Older fish fry in good condition travel only one-third the distance at night and half the distance during the day of new or dead fry before returning to the stream bottom (Elliott, 1987). Older fry in poor condition seem to extend drift distance.

Table 7.2 Examples of drift distances of some stream organisms in field experiments under two current velocity regimes

Species	Distance (m)	
	10 cm s^{-1}	50 cm s^{-1}
Agapetus (cased caddis)[a]	0.13	1.9
Baetis rhodani (mayfly)[a]	1.0	4.41
Ecdyonurus spp. (mayfly)[a]	1.59	8.33
Hydropsyche spp. (caddis)[a]	1.99	11.49
Newly emerged trout fry[b]	7	37
Poor condition older trout fry[b]	12	65
Good condition older trout fry[b]	3	12

[a] Elliott (1971*b*); [b] Elliott (1987)

Drift distance may also be extended through pools or in the face of chemical or physical stressors. *Baetis* larvae, for example, are clearly in control of drift distances, and using a combination of parachuting (where an individual has uplifted abdomen and outstretched legs) and swimming, can readily drift through a pool (Cambell, 1985).

Temporal patterns

Peaks of drift can occur over short periods such as one hour or less (Schreiber, 1995) in response to sudden changes in discharge but by far the strongest temporal pattern in drift is the diel pattern. In tropical and temperate regions alike, drift generally displays a distinct circadian rhythm with maximum drift over night, and low levels of drift during the day. Most invertebrates (meiofauna and macrofauna) show a nocturnal peak just after sunset (Fig 7.1a), some with a second peak just before dawn. The most common exceptions are the Chironomidae which tend to be aperiodic drifters and the water mites (Hydracarina), which are actually day drifters. The diel patterns suggest that drift is not simply a result of low level passive drift caused by hydraulic forces but that it has a strong active behavioural component which is largely related to light intensity. Strong moonlight, for example, can depress drift and the constant light of polar summers also seems to extinguish the drift rhythm. Vertebrates also show diel patterns, as seen in trout fry which typically drift downstream at night (Elliott, 1987). Diatoms and uni-cellular green algae, however, drift most during the day (Müller, 1974) possibly be-cause they grow rapidly in the light and slough off more easily with increasing size.

Among the taxa that show highest drift levels (e.g. *Baetis* and *Gammarus*) nocturnal drift is most pronounced in the largest size classes (Fig. 7.1c), which are perhaps the most at risk from predatory fish, but more about this later. In most groups however, drift overall seems to be greatest in the earliest instars which is why using fine mesh drift nets leads to such high estimates of drift density. Life history characteristics of the drifting taxa also contribute to longer-term seasonal patterns

Fig 7.1 Examples of drift patterns of larvae of the caddisfly *Rhyacophila nubila*: (a) diel drift patterns showing the nocturnal peak; (b) seasonal drift density showing the summer/autumn peak and winter minimum; (c) changes in drift periodicity with size, where larger instars become increasingly nocturnal in their drift activity. (Redrawn from Fjellheim, 1980.)

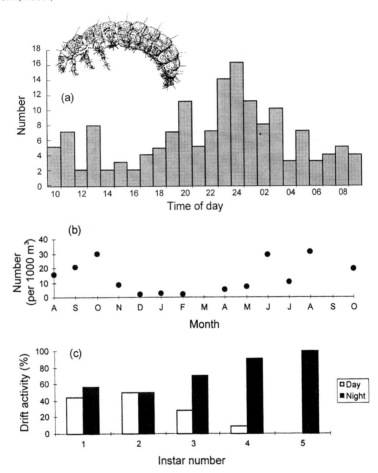

(Fig 7.1b) which show a general trend in temperate systems towards a peak in summer and to a lesser extent autumn and spring and a minimum in winter. This pattern has been found in small streams (e.g. Fjellheim, 1980) as well as large rivers (e.g. Cellot, 1996). In other parts of the world, seasonal drift patterns may differ, as for example in Australian rainforest systems, where drift peaks in the wet season and is lower and less variable in the dry season (Benson and Pearson, 1987).

Causes of drift

Natural drift represents the combination of many activities of invertebrate taxa and as such is likely to be influenced by many factors. These include daylight, moonlight, temperature, discharge and current velocity, substrate, turbidity, benthic density, food resources, and predators. Even parasitism can influence drift, as seen in the enhanced drift of *Gammarus* parasitized by the acanthocephalan *Pompharhynchus laevis*. Fish that feed on *Gammarus* are the primary host of this parasite (McCahon *et al.*, 1991).

Passive (constant) drift can occur through simple accidental erosion by the force of moving water during the course of normal activity and increasing shear stress in laboratory studies generally leads to increased population loss via drift (Borchardt, 1993). Increasing the abundance of refugial space in these studies mitigated against the impacts of increasing flow. Other physical stresses such as rapid flow reduction, temperature shocks, low oxygen, chemical toxicants, and pesticides also increase drift rates. Treating a stream stretch with the pesticide methoxychlor led to an estimated 2–5 billion animals drifting past a particular site during a 4-hour period (Flannagan *et al.*, 1980). Experimental acidification can lead to a similar response. A recent study has indicated that exposure to increased ultraviolet radiation may also increase drift rates (Kiffney *et al.*, 1997).

One problem in determining what causes drift is that it can be difficult to prove whether entry to the drift is accidental or not. In some of the above responses to stressors, active entry is probable, as it provides an immediate escape mechanism. We saw earlier (p. 130) how individuals can escape from predators (in response to contact or chemical cues) and competitors by actively drifting away. The use of drift may also provide a useful mechanism of actively searching for new food patches or preferred substrates as shown by Kohler (1985) who found that *Baetis tricaudatus* drifted actively when food levels fell below some threshold value. Any behaviour that increases the probability of exposure to the eroding current can increase the chances of passive drift entry, however. This may occur if animals, especially the larger ones, increase their activity on the top surfaces of stones at night to forage. Drift entry is almost certainly determined to an extent by accidental dislodgement resulting from such diel changes in foraging movements and activity. However, the increase in use of upper surfaces demonstrated in experimental studies would not account for the massive increase in numbers of individuals drifting at night, so drift periodicity is not solely the result of passive release from the substrate (Glozier and Culp, 1989).

But why just forage or be active at night? How do we account for the occurrence of some taxa on stone surfaces in the daytime but only in the drift at night? Allan (1978) suggested that nocturnal foraging and periodicity in drift can be explained by the 'risk of predation' hypothesis. By being active and drifting at night (either passively or actively), individuals reduce the risk of predation by visual predators such as fish. A number of studies lend support to this hypothesis (see Allan, 1995, and p. 130). The nocturnal activity of invertebrate predators (such as large stonefly larvae) can also contribute some 60–90% of the night-time drift of their prey through contact where these predators are abundant (Malmqvist and Sjöström, 1987). Perhaps the best kind of support for the predation hypothesis comes from the study of drift patterns in streams that lack predators. On the island of Madeira, the lotic fauna is depauperate with no predatory stoneflies or native fish. *Baetis* showed no significant difference in drift rate during the day or night in a fishless stream, but in a stream holding introduced trout, the usual nocturnal periodicity was strong, and larger nymphs were virtually absent from drift during the day (Malmqvist, 1988). Flecker (1992) studied the drift in a series of Andean piedmont and mountain streams. Again, drift was nocturnal where visually hunting drift-feeding fish were abundant but in mountain streams historically devoid of fish, drift was aperiodic. Where rainbow trout had been introduced, *Baetis* did show nocturnal drift, suggesting that evolutionary changes can take place quite rapidly in these mayflies in response to introduced fish. Likewise, in Nepal, fish are absent at high altitude sites, where drift is aperiodic, whereas in middle elevation and lowland stream reaches, which have fish, drift is strongly nocturnal (Fig. 7.2). Palmer (1992) showed strong nocturnal drift in meiofauna (copepods, small oligochaetes, and rotifers) which are clearly too small to be at risk from larger predatory fish. As they live in the hyporheos, their entry to the drift is obviously active. Perhaps here too, they may be avoiding smaller visual hunters such as odonates or fish fry.

Fig. 7.2 Drift periodicity of total macroinvertebrates and Baetidae only in Nepal comparing lowland (open) and upland (shaded) sites (with and without fish, respectively). Night-time hours are shown by the shaded section of the horizontal bar at the top of the figure. (From Brewin and Ormerod, 1994.)

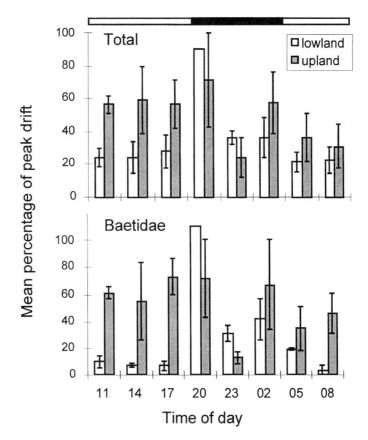

While drift may be unavoidable to some taxa, it is clearly not just a passive phenomenon and has a highly active component. To many taxa it appears to be a controlled behavioural activity (governed by light intensity) that may be beneficial to individuals as a form of locomotion, to enhance foraging opportunities and to avoid predators or competitors or other stressors.

Compensating mechanisms

There is no evidence to show that upstream areas become depopulated in the face of the vast numbers of animals that drift each day. It was speculated quite early on that the reason for this was that drift simply represents the surplus production of populations over the carrying capacity of the area (Waters, 1972). This theory would gain some support if there was a clear positive relationship between benthic density and drift density but in fact there is not. On the whole, drift appears to be largely density-independent, both at the individual species and at the community level. The relatively short drift distances and movements described earlier could provide some explanation for the maintenance of upstream populations. In addition, upstream movements have been found in a wide range of organisms. Amphipods like *Gammarus* are renowned for this and positive evidence of upstream migration by crawling has been found in mayfly, stonefly, and caddisfly larvae (Müller, 1974). The surface-living water cricket (*Velia*) is also able to move considerable distances upstream. For taxa that rarely drift, such upstream movements can probably compensate for any downstream drift. For more drift-prone taxa, however, small-scale studies using directional traps suggest that <30% of drift is compensated for by upstream crawling (Elliott, 1971a; Bird and Hynes, 1981). Rather than larvae moving upstream, Müller (1954) suggested in his 'colonization cycle', that upstream insect populations are maintained by adults migrating to oviposit in headwaters. Certainly, adult flight provides great mobility and there is evidence of the adults of many insects showing upstream-directed flight (Müller, 1982), although non-directed flight has also been documented. It only requires relatively few females to fly upstream and to lay a lot of eggs to offset the quantitatively greater downstream drift (Otto and Svensson, 1976).

The processes that maintain upstream populations in the face of downstream drift losses are still the subject of debate and the relative importance of surplus production versus upstream crawling and flight by ovipositing females is yet to be fully evaluated (Power *et al.*, 1988). A recent theoretical study, however, maintains that upstream migration may not be necessary to avoid upstream depletion (Anholt, 1995). Computer simulations indicated that population persistence can be achieved by random dispersal of adults coupled with density-dependence acting on birth and death rates during some life stage. Through such density-dependence a population may persist at equilibrium without emigration having to be balanced by immigration. Upstream migration could then be viewed rather as a behaviour to enhance individual fitness than as a compensatory mechanism. Overall, drift may well constitute a net loss of individuals downstream, but clearly not to the extent that populations are unable to maintain themselves (Allan, 1995).

Colonization

The mobility of most lotic organisms underlies another of the strong patterns in streams and rivers, that of the relatively rapid re-establishment of communities and recolonization of disturbed areas. The rates of recolonization depend on the size of the disturbed area and the proximity of a source of colonizers and hence distance that colonists must travel. Thus small-scale experimental patches (<1 m^2) of cleared or implanted artificial substrates can be recolonized in a couple of days to a few weeks based on local immigrants. Severely denuded or stressed systems recovering from large floods, drought, or pollution may require 70–150 days or if the disturbance is catastrophic, a year or more (see also Fig 3.14, p. 67). For example, following the Mount St. Helen's volcanic eruption, which carpeted stream bottoms with volcanic ash, recovery took over five years (Anderson and Wissema, 1987). In addition to area affected, the time to recovery depends on the nature of the disturbance and the proportion of original residents surviving in more local refuges may also play a role.

As well as recolonization of disturbed systems, colonization of new stream and river channels has been widely reported and is often quite rapid. A new stream channel receiving pumped water from a lake was rapidly colonized over a few months by insects flying in and reproducing (Malmqvist et al., 1991a), and after a year the 'colonization curve' had almost levelled off. In the case of streams formed following glacial recession, which also offer new channel areas for colonization, a clear succession of species occurs over several years as the physical and biological environment changes (see p. 199).

Rates of colonization also depend on the taxa, largely because the taxa themselves vary in their propensity to move and modes of movement, as we saw earlier. Cooper et al. (1990) suggested that one can rank colonization ability based on the relationship between colonization rates on to empty substrate trays and local benthic densities. Thus, from one study, the rank order (low to high) of colonization ability was *Ephemerella* < Chironomidae = Paraleptophlebiidae < *Amphinemura* < Baetidae. Scoured stone surfaces were first colonized by simuliid larvae in another study (Hemphill and Cooper, 1983) and substrate trays in a Swedish stream were rapidly initially colonized by baetids, simuliids, and chironomids (Ulfstrand et al., 1974). Newly opened stream channels connected to the main river can also be rapidly colonized by baetids and chironomids (Gore, 1982). What all these taxa have in commmon is a high propensity to drift. In new glacial stream channels, downstream drift as a means of colonization is of course impossible, and the initial colonizers are chironomids arriving through upstream or inter-stream flight and oviposition. These rapid colonizers have been considered as fugitive species with a high dispersal ability but poor competitive ability. One of the most extraordinary examples is the chironomid *Orthocladius calvus*, which was unknown to science before it colonized newly established outdoor recirculating streams in southern England (Pinder, 1985). It reached massive densities in the space of a few weeks (see p. 156) then disappeared and has not been seen since! Thus these examples, and many others in the literature, all point to drift and aerial oviposition as the main sources of larger-scale, longer-term colonization or recolonization of lotic systems. As we saw earlier though, crawling upstream or from lateral areas can also contribute to more local recolonization, and may be important in recovery from spates when animals move back out of flow refuges. In streams with relatively low population densities or colonization rates, drift may be responsible for most of the recolonization (e.g. 82% of colonization of substrate trays over 38 days, Townsend and Hildrew, 1976). In streams where benthic densities are higher, both drift and crawling can be important (Pearson and Jones; 1987, Giller and Campbell, 1989). Most colonizers of desert streams following scouring spate events appear to result from oviposition by flying adults (Gray and Fisher, 1981). Whatever the source, this recolonization ability contributes to the resilience of stream and river communities in the face of environmental change.

Species interactions

Interactions between organisms include predation, competition, parasitism and disease. Often such biotic processes are modified or even triggered by abiotic factors and in the stream environment it is frequently by flow. There has long been a debate as to the degree to which biotic interactions affect the structuring process of lotic communities. A traditional view is that the influence of abiotic factors is so strong in these systems that communities are constantly in a state of nonequilibrium, and thus biotic factors are of minor importance. Whether this is true or not seemingly depends in part on the rate and magnitude of disturbances acting via the flow regime. At the other extreme, in systems with stable flow regimes, benthic invertebrate populations may build up to densities where competition and predation undoubtedly matter and communities reach an equilibrium state. This would include systems fed with a constant flow of groundwater and where precipitation is low for long periods, or in outlet streams, where large lakes even out flow fluctuations. In situations where an interaction causes such a strong impact that the community structure itself is altered, the species causing this is referred to as a 'keystone' species.

We first introduced biological interactions briefly on pp. 68–9, but here we will discuss the major species interactions in more detail.

Predation

As we have seen, streams and rivers teem with organisms playing all sorts of different roles. A significant proportion of these are predators. The predators attacking prey at the water surface are primarily fish and water striders (Gerromorpha), but also include whirligig beetles (Gyrinidae), and adult flies (Empididae). Fish are generally the only predators in the water column, although many species search for prey on the stream bed along with the predatory invertebrates, like the larvae of stoneflies, rhyacophilid caddisflies, and some dipterans. Lotic predators use a variety of different cues to detect their prey. Most fish use vision, whereas species living in cloudy waters use tactile and olfactory information. The importance of vision has been taken as evidence of much of the widespread nocturnal activity of prey such as downstream drift (see earlier).

Invertebrate predators more rarely use vision. Predaceous stonefly larvae, for example, hunt primarily using their antennae and leg hairs to discover prey, despite rather well-developed eyes (Sjöström, 1985a). Also hydrodynamic cues may be involved (Peckarsky and Wilcox 1989). Surface-living insects either use vision (gyrinids) or, as in Gerromorpha, also perceive ripples propagated from prey moving on the water surface. Some net-spinning caddis, such as *Neureclipsis bimaculata*, detect movements in the net (Fig 5.8(b), p. 119) and rush to attack the prey rather like spiders. Most predatory birds and mammals use vision, but under water, the platypus keeps its eyes and ears shut, and is capable of locating prey, like small crustaceans, by sensing the weak electric currents produced by muscular activity. The Amazon river dolphins on the other hand use sonar in their turbid habitats.

Most predators show some degree of specialization with respect to diel activity, prey detection mechanism, attack and capture tactics, and microhabitats for hunting. Specialization toward particular prey taxa appears to be less common, whereas anti-predatory adaptations in prey organisms should relate in particular to their chief predators, since these pose the greatest risk.

Mechanisms of predation

Actively hunting predators are likely to aggregate in patches with high prey density (the *numerical response*). However, when prey are also highly mobile there may be no positive correlation between the abundances of predators and prey. Widely foraging predatory invertebrates include stonefly, sialid, and dytiscid larvae. Others, including drift-feeding fish, are more passive, waiting for prey to come close enough for a quick attack.

Predators also catch more prey per unit time with increasing prey densities. This *functional response* gradually levels off (a Type 2 response) as the predator becomes satiated and as handling time (the time to capture, kill, and consume the prey before resuming search) takes up an increasing amount of the foraging time available. Under some circumstances the functional response curve may take a sigmoidal shape (Type 3), where the predation rate is low at low prey density, either because it does not pay to hunt for that prey at low density, or because the predator switches to another species of prey. The rate then increases rapidly with increasing density until the curve starts to level off again. Both Type 2 and 3 curves have been found among stream-living predators (Malmqvist, 1991; Giller and Sangpradub, 1993), and increasing habitat complexity can switch a functional response curve from Type 2 to Type 3 (Hildrew and Townsend, 1977).

When predator densities are high, interactions between individual predators can reduce capture rates, as seen from experiments involving predatory stonefly larvae and baetid mayfly larvae prey (Sjöström, 1985b; Malmqvist, 1991; Peckarsky and Cowan, 1991). In experiments involving both a vertebrate and an invertebrate predator (sculpins and larvae of *Agnetina capitata*, a perlid stonefly) interesting complex responses were observed depending on which mayfly prey taxon was tested (Soluk, 1993). In experiments with baetid prey, interference between predators was observed, whereas when ephemerellid prey were used, facilitation between predators occurred. While the presence of fish is known to suppress the hunting behaviour of stonefly larvae, fish predation may be enhanced if prey are flushed out from under stones by the stonefly activity. Ephemerellids will escape from hunting predatory invertebrates in this way (in addition to the scorpion-like posturing), whereas baetids will either freeze or drift away. In fact, baetids appear to be favoured by the presence of sculpins since the fish keep stonefly larvae away from the top surfaces of the substrate, where the baetids mainly forage. Further studies (Soluk and Richardson, 1997) have shown that young trout that shared artificial streams with stoneflies gained an average of 2.4% of original body mass over a month whereas fish living without stoneflies had lost 2.6% of body mass. Apparently, behavioural relationships both between predators and prey, and between different species of predators can differ significantly from what one might predict from simply studying one prey–one predator systems.

Behavioural studies that break down the predation process into its various phases help us to understand why certain prey are captured in preference to others. For example, to what extent do predators and prey encounter each other? On encounter, what is the probability of an attack? What is the level of attack success? One example of this approach is a study by Tikkanen *et al.* (1997) on the predatory behaviour of a perlodid stonefly larvae (*Diura bicaudata*). The authors found that encounter rates were poor predictors of the preferences for different prey categories. Frequently encountered prey, such as mayfly larvae (*Baetis, Heptagenia*), were only rarely captured, and were therefore relatively safe when more stationary prey, like simuliid and nemourid larvae, were present. The latter two groups were rarely encountered, but when they were, they were captured with high success.

Antipredator adaptations

Virtually all inhabitants of lotic systems are potential victims to predators. In fact, every third or fourth species is a predator, and the predators themselves are also susceptible, at least when young or small. This predation risk is reflected in the different species' repertoires of anti-predatory devices, which include both morphological and behavioural adaptations. Heavy sclerotization, cryptic and disruptive coloration, spines and bristles, and enlarged transportable cases are frequent morphological adaptations against predators. Behavioural adaptations unveil an even more impressive list, which includes nocturnal activity, use of interstitial habitat, utilization of fast-flow refuges, drift escape, noxious exudates, thanatosis (i.e. death-feigning), threats (e.g. scorpion posturing), and retaliation. Many of these were discussed in Chapter 5.

Direct impacts of predation

For several reasons ecologists have had difficulties in clarifying whether or not predation plays a significant role in streams and rivers. Many experiments have been carried out including the use of enclosure and exclosure cages. The meshes of the cages are usually of a size that allows prey animals to move in and out while, at the same time, restricts the movements of predators. The results of these studies have shown that the importance of predation can vary from very strong to having no effect whatsoever. Cooper *et al.* (1990) suggested that the range of outcomes of enclosure/exclosure studies could be explained by the mesh size of the cages. Small meshes led to lower migration rates of prey, larger meshes to higher rates, and the low rates resulted in a visibly stronger impact of predators. In coarse mesh cages, immigration of fresh prey appeared to completely swamp any impact of the predator. An analysis of the relative importance of invertebrate and vertebrate predators based on cage studies published in the literature suggested that invertebrate predators may have a stronger impact than vertebrate predators (Wooster, 1994). This difference may, however, be illusory since the cages were significantly larger in experiments with vertebrates than in those with invertebrate predators, a fact which, if prey just move between microhabitat patches, could result in emigration from small cages, but only relocation within cages that are large (Wooster, 1994).

These experimental studies have mainly addressed the local effects of predation at the scale of a cage, and often over short periods of time. More interesting, however, is the extent to which predators influence their prey populations as a whole. This problem would be best approached by studying the effect at a larger scale, though this has rarely been done. Harvey and Marti (1993) managed to exclude American dippers from areas of about 40 m^2, and demonstrated that the dippers had a significant impact on benthic insects, in particular the large limnephilid caddis larvae *Dicosmoecus gilvipes*. Forrester (1994) observed the effects of brook charr (*Salvelinus fontinalis*) on mayfly larvae in 35 m long and 2.5–3 m wide stream sections. In this case, much of the predators' effect was caused by increasing the emigration via drift of *Baetis* and *Paraleptophlebia*. Other mayflies, such as *Ephemerella*, *Eurylophella* and *Stenonema*, were not affected, however.

As we saw in Chapter 5 (pp. 129–30), both increased and decreased activity is possible in invertebrates in the presence of predators. If prey avoid activity in the presence of predators such as fish, they may tend to be concentrated where predators are present, thereby erroneously suggesting that particularly dangerous predators have weak impacts. This has been termed the 'paradox of danger' (Sih and Wooster, 1994). Interpretations of experimental studies on the strength of predator influences in lotic environments must therefore be made with great caution.

Other investigations, however, such as those of Allan (1982) and Reice (1991), who manipulated quite large stream sections, showed that fish can have insignificant or only modest effects on the benthic fauna. In Allan's study, it could be argued that as only 75% of the fish were actually removed, this could have allowed the remaining 25% the opportunity to increase their feeding rate and hence compensate for the missing fish. However, similar conclusions can be drawn from another study where invertebrate densities were decreased dramatically (by 95%) by natural flood disturbances, yet prey intake rate and condition of trout remained unaffected (Twomey and Giller, 1991). Clearly, in such a situation the top predator population was not food-limited (but possibly habitat-limited), and under conditions of superabundant prey resources, it is unlikely that a predator population can influence prey communities unless it is strongly selective—most aquatic predators though are polyphagous (see p. 137).

An entirely different, but frequently used, approach to study predation is the analysis of predators' gut contents. As we have mentioned before, lotic predators ingest a great variety of prey, and they do so in a rather opportunistic way. In other words, they catch what they encounter and what is possible to catch. Thus, gut contents do not perfectly match prey availability, because some prey use microhabitats which the predators do not. Sometimes prey organisms also have activity patterns and behavioural adaptations which minimize the risk of encountering predators or of being captured (see above).

Flow is important for the predation process, as well as for herbivory in streams. Recently, Lancaster (1996) showed that small patches that act as flow refugia to both predators and prey (see Chapter 5, pp. 106–7) also acted as centres of predator–prey interactions for the net-spinning caddis-fly, *Plectrocnemia conspersa*, probably favoured by increased prey encounters. In contrast, the more actively foraging predator *Sialis fuliginosa* did not aggregate in these patches, and their impact was therefore lower during periods of high flow. A similar species-specific response has been observed in experiments testing whether or not blackfly larvae use high-velocity patches as refuges from predators, perhaps even at the cost of reduced feeding rates. Apparently, this is an efficient strategy against some predators such as flatworms (Hansen *et al.*, 1991). Predatory stonefly larvae too are severely restrained even at moderately high velocities, in contrast to *Rhyacophila* larvae, which showed no reduction in predation success at least up to a near-bed velocity of 53 cm s^{-1} (Fig. 7.3).

Fig. 7.3 The relationship between predation success and flow in the larvae of two perlodid stoneflies *Isoperla grammatica* and *Diura nanseni*, and the caddis *Rhyacophila nubila*. The former two species have much lower attack success on blackfly larvae than the latter at high current velocities. (From Malmqvist and Sackman, 1996. Reproduced with kind permission of Springer–Verlag.)

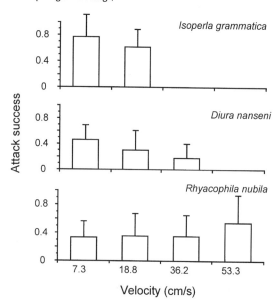

Non-lethal effects of predators

As we have seen above predators can sometimes have a direct impact on prey populations. In addition to consuming the prey organisms, predators also influence them in more subtle ways, and one cannot exclude the possibility that this effect can impact on various ecological processes. As discussed in Chapter 5 and earlier in relation to drift, predators cause prey to change their behaviour. For example, the presence of predators can affect movement rates (Malmqvist, 1992), foraging efficiency (Peckarsky *et al.*, 1993), and diel activity (McIntosh and Townsend, 1995) of grazers, causing reduced intake of algal food. This can in turn have effects both on the grazer and algal populations. As another example, water striders have been shown to use the entire surface of stream pools lacking trout, whereas they remain in the margins of pools occupied by rainbow trout (Cooper, 1984). The presence of trout could lead to increased competition for terrestrial insects falling on to the water surface both between trout and water striders and among the water striders themselves because of increased densities near the pool margins. Experiments have also shown that predator-induced sublethal effects can be instrumental in leaf packs, where the shredder efficiency in breaking down leaf material was significantly reduced in the presence of stonefly predators (Malmqvist, 1993). Disturbance of non-target animals caused by moving stonefly larvae can also be substantial. In field experiments in a southern Swedish stream, enhanced densities of the large perlid *Dinocras cephalotes* caused sizeable increases in the drift of several taxa during the night following the introduction of the stonefly larvae (Malmqvist and Sjöström, 1987).

Thus, one immediate consequence of sublethal effects is a reduced feeding efficiency. When prey organisms are exposed to predators frequently enough this may affect their overall growth rate and final body size. Retarded rates of growth may increase the risk of direct predation as a consequence of an extended larval period and thereby extended exposure to predators. Smaller final (adult) body size results in fewer eggs and thus fecundity is affected. Experiments by Peckarsky *et al.* (1993) demonstrated such a negative effect on the fecundity of baetid mayfly larvae stocked together with predaceous stoneflies. Likewise, apterous (wingless) females of the water striders in Cooper's experiments above were significantly heavier in October in pools without trout than in those with trout. In this season these insects had no eggs but varied greatly in the fat deposits, a fact which is likely to have produced differential future survival over winter and fecundity the following year.

Competition

Just as for predation, experimental studies on competition in lotic ecosystems have shown ambiguous results. Many studies have focused on local interactions, although there are few on entire populations. The most convincing cases of competitive effects have involved sessile, territorial insects, such as the larvae of caddis like hydroptilids (*Leucotrichia*) and psychomyiids (*Psychomyia*), which have attached tubes, or hydropsychids with fastened retreats with nets, and other temporarily attached animals, such as blackfly larvae (e.g. Hart, 1983; McAuliffe, 1984*a*). In these cases, space is the important limiting resource either directly or indirectly and the discussion on territoriality on pp. 130–2 is pertinent here.

Also, as for predation, the mobility of animals apparently influences the ease with which competition can be identified, although evidence is accumulating to show that food limitation and interspecific competition may be significant among mobile grazers such as certain mayfly, chironomid, and cased caddis larvae (Kohler, 1992). These studies have all shown that the grazers are quite capable of significantly suppressing algal resources, and that some taxa cause stronger effects than others, which eventually can lead to local extinction of those taxa most sensitive to depressed food resources. Another mechanism which seems particularly widespread among foragers on a stony substrate is 'encounter competition'. One example is provided by Wiley and Kohler (1981), who by using time-lapse photography, recorded natural encounters among epibenthic macroinvertebrates. Every now and then grazing caddis larvae of *Glossosoma* bumped into and displaced filtering blackfly larvae. This fact, together with observations of negative relationships between blackfly and *Glossosoma* densities, was taken as evidence for encounter competition. *Glossosoma* also appeared to influence the densities of *Rheotanytarsus* midge larvae in this way (Kohler, 1992). The strong impact of *Glossosoma* on other taxa suggests that this is a keystone competitor species in the Michigan streams where these studies took place.

A unique opportunity to delve deeper into the competitive effects of *Glossosoma* was provided by chance when a number of populations were infected by a specific microsporidian parasite, *Cougourdella* sp. This natural experiment reduced the densities of *Glossosoma* to a fraction (2.5–25%) of what they were prior to the outbreak of the parasite (Kohler and Wiley, 1997). Fortunately, this was one of those rare situations where monitoring of the benthic communities had previously occurred in several streams over a number of years. The consequences of the parasite outbreak were tremendous for the stream community and included both increased algal biomass (by about 10-fold), and other grazer and filter-feeder populations (by 2- to 5-fold). Some glossosomatids that had been rare prior to the spread of the parasite increased strongly, suggesting competitive release. Of the filter-feeders, blackfly larvae consistently increased, and hydropsychid and *Brachycentrus* caddis larvae showed large increases, presumably following an increased drift of diatoms.

One further circumstance makes the study by Kohler and Wiley remarkable. They had been conducting small-scale manipulations of *Glossosoma* densities before *Cougourdella* entered the scene. This allowed them to compare the predictions from these small-scale experiments with the large-scale effects over several years following the *Glossosoma* population crash. Reassuringly, the small-scale experiments were capable of predicting the direction of several of the larger-scale population changes, although they generally underestimated their magnitude. However, the small-scale manipulations could not have predicted some of the indirect effects such as those on hydropsychids and *Brachycentrus*.

For sessile filter-feeders, competition for attachment sites appears to be particularly important. Blackfly and hydropsychid larvae can reach very high densities, especially in stable and productive environments, such as lake outlets, where they can cover every bit of available substrate. Exploitative resource competition in such systems can be crucial if animals upstream reduce the food available to those animals that live downstream. Hydropsychids are known to effectively strip the water of zooplankton, as was shown over a distance of less than 1 km in a lake-fed artificial stream in Sweden (Malmqvist *et al.*, 1991*a*). On a much finer scale, Englund (1991*a*) constructed patches of artificial habitats with or without pre-colonized *Hydropsyche siltalai* larvae and these were implanted into a lake outlet stream. Larvae positioned below dense aggregations were much smaller than those below controls lacking larvae after just two weeks. This effect was clearly caused by the removal of seston and also by the reduction of current velocity brought about by the nets of upstream larval aggregations in the experimental treatments. The combined reduction in delivery rate of food items was nearly 50%.

In filter-feeding blackfly larvae, the situation may be similar, but not always. Some species of blackflies are territorial and these aggressively defend their attachment sites, more against upstream-positioned neighbours than those downstream (Hart, 1986). In contrast, other species appear to be favoured by high densities, and may occur in numbers exceeding 100 cm^{-2} (Wotton, 1988; Malmqvist, 1994), suggesting that the opposite of competition is taking place (i.e. some form of commensalism). Blackfly larvae also compete with algae for space as shown by Dudley *et al.* (1986), who found that the removal of macroalgae greatly favoured large simuliid larvae (small simuliids can utilize filamentous macroalgae for attachment) as well as blepharicerid dipterans.

Hydropsychids are capable of taking over patches occupied by blackfly larvae (Hemphill and Cooper, 1983; Hemphill, 1988). This may be viewed as a competition for space, although it is likely that there is also an element of predator–prey interaction in this process. Hydropsychids are aggressive animals and they fight vigorously to defend their retreats. In the closely related *Arctopsyche ladogensis* (Arctopsychidae), Englund and Olsson (1990) observed that large larvae were superior to small larvae, and that retreat owners were relatively more successful than intruders. Apparently, the size of the investment (i.e. the amount of silk used for retreat and net construction) had no influence on the outcome of fights. Unexpectedly, the larvae did not appear to use stridulation (see p. 121) for assessing information about the opponent, perhaps because the frequency of stridulation is unrelated to size, and thereby fighting ability.

Food limitation is an important impetus for intraspecific competition. There are abundant cases in the literature where such competition can be inferred from correlative data. We will just present two cases involving vertebrate predators which are apparently limited by their invertebrate food resource. Over a 13-year period, brown trout (*Salmo trutta*) abundance in the Icelandic River Laxá appeared to track, with a 1-year delay, their main food resource: larval, pupal, and adult blackflies (*Simulium vittatum*) (Fig. 7.4a; Gíslason, 1994). There was also a significant (but weaker) correlation between blackflies and one of their food resources, the nitrogen-fixing alga *Anabaena flos-aquae*. Also two duck species, the harlequin duck and young Barrow's goldeneye showed tight relationships between their population densities and those of blackfly larvae and pupae. Similarly, for the European dipper, the primary food of which is caddis larvae, Ormerod *et al.*

Fig. 7.4 Numerical responses of predators to prey density. (a) The relationship between the number of trout caught in year t + 1 and the number of adult blackflies collected in window traps in year t (redrawn from Gíslason, 1994). (b) The relationship between dipper densities and the number of caddis larvae collected in two 3-minute kick samples (redrawn from Ormerod et al., 1985).

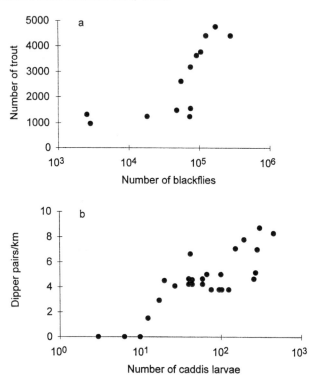

(1985) observed a fairly close relationship between the number of these larvae and the density of breeding pairs of birds (Fig. 7.4b); two to three times more pairs were observed with a 10-fold increase in prey densities. In most cases, predators do not compete so strongly for a single type of prey as found in these two studies and therefore correlations will often be weak or non-existent.

Several studies have reported lowered per-capita feeding rate and growth in hunting mobile predators, such as stonefly larvae, if they are held in high experimental densities. Intraspecific interactions are a likely cause. The defence of territories has also been demonstrated for several predator species including stoneflies (Sjöström, 1985a) and gerrid bugs (Wilcox and Ruckdeschel 1982, Vepsäläinen and Nummelin, 1985) (see also pp. 130–2). In a tropical veliid bug, *Rhagovelia scabra*, Wilson *et al.* (1979) observed an unusual partitioning of habitats. Females occupied the head of stream pools, males dominated the centre of the pools, where the current was weaker, and juveniles were furthest downstream. Interception of experimentally introduced prey (dead fruit flies) was highest by the females and lowest by the juveniles, indicating that the pool head was the most favourable habitat with respect to food. By removing all adult bugs the authors were able to demonstrate that the juveniles redistributed to the area previously occupied by the adults. Thus, females apparently held the best feeding locations through interference competition. In salmonids, juveniles are also often relegated to less preferred (shallow riffle) habitats by the presence of older fish and other species as found in an elegant field-based study on salmon and trout by Kennedy and Strange (1987).

Although all these examples suggest that competitive interactions are taking place between all sorts of organisms, and sometimes to quite a high degree, competition is likely to be most important where environmental harshness e.g. in terms of flow variation, is relatively low (Peckarsky, 1983*a*).

Parasitism

Many organisms in running waters are hosts to parasites which are mostly species-specific. A multitude of species of parasites have been described representing many different taxonomic groups including fungi, microsporidians, nematodes, mites, and insects, but the importance of these host–parasite interactions has rarely been studied. We hinted at possible effects on host behaviour earlier, and here we present just a few examples which illustrate the effects on stream communities or otherwise have a reasonably clear connection to lotic animals.

We have already described the collapse of dominant grazer populations (the caddis-fly *Glossosoma nigrior*) in southwestern Michigan streams following the infection of a microsporidian parasite *Cougourdella* sp. In fact, since this pathogen caused indirect effects on the entire community of many streams, it could be termed a keystone parasite. The study clearly showed that parasites must be considered when modelling community structure.

The 'crayfish plague', as also mentioned earlier (p. 69), virtually wiped out native European crayfish populations. Since these crayfish are a valuable food of significant economic importance, the parasite's spread has been well documented. The plague is caused by an asexual fungus species (*Aphanomyces astaci*). This fungus occurs natively in American crayfish, and was first recorded in Europe in Italy in 1860, from where it spread rapidly across the continent. Legal and illegal introductions of American crayfish have contributed to further the expansion of the plague. The lack of a common evolutionary history between the plague fungus and the European crayfish species is a likely explanation for its devastating impact.

Hymenopterans are well known as parasites in terrestrial systems but are rare in freshwater environments. One fairly widespread genus, however, is *Agriotypus*, a species-specific ectoparasitoid. The life cycle and prey–host relationship between *A. armatus* and *Silo pallipes* (Trichoptera: Goeridae) have been well documented (Elliott, 1982, 1983). *A. armatus* oviposits underwater in the case of the caddisfly pupa and the female uses the tarsi in the search for a host. A parasitized pupa is easily recognized when the parasitoid has reached its final instar as a long, springy ribbon-like structure, probably functioning as a plastron (for respiration), is extended from the caddis case. The population of *Silo* studied by Elliott suffered a pupal mortality of about 10% from the parasite.

While most adult water mites are predators, the larval stages are frequently parasites of terrestrial stages of aquatic and semi-aquatic insects. In some cases they do not actually feed on their host, although dispersal is assisted, and therefore the relationship can be classified as a *phoretic* one. The impact of parasitic mites can, however, be important either through direct mortality, or indirectly through a negative effect on egg production.

Blackfly larvae are often found to harbour parasites of various kinds (Crosskey, 1990). One of the most frequent and spectacular of these are mermithid nematodes, which often fill up a large part of the larval abdominal cavity. Mermithids are known to prevent metamorphosis, cause sterility, reduce muscle tissue, and influence adult size and longevity (Molloy, 1987). The adult mermithids, which do not feed, mate in the stream bed. Preparasitic juveniles find the blackfly larvae, which become infested. The juvenile mermithids feed by absorbing blood from the host's haemocoel. This is accomplished through the cuticle of the mermithids which lack a functional gut. If a blackfly larva becomes infested in an early instar, the parasite completes development before the blackfly larva, and as a consequence of its escape from the host, the blackfly larva is killed. When larger blackfly larvae are infested, the parasite continues to develop inside the pupa and the adult, and escapes during oviposition (Fig. 7.5). There is little information on the effects of these and other parasites on the populations of blackflies, although the high prevalences often observed indicate that mortality and induced sterility are probably considerable.

Fig. 7.5 The life cycle of the mermithid nematode parasite of blackfly. (After Crosskey, 1990.)

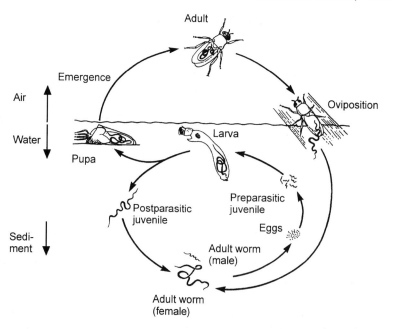

8 Community patterns, diversity, and biogeography

Freshwater biologists have traditionally lagged somewhat behind their terrestrial colleagues in studying the structure and function of communities, but in the recent past this situation has changed and there is now a considerable literature developing. However, this is not an ecology book and as such we cannot delve too deeply into this burgeoning literature. We have discussed various aspects of lotic communities elsewhere in this book, including longitudinal patterns and the River Continuum Concept (pp. 165–9) and the role of species interactions (pp. 182–92). We have also seen how various physical and chemical factors and disturbances influence aquatic communities and the distribution and abundance of species in Chapter 3. So, here, we will concentrate on a few other important community patterns and processes including resource partitioning, succession, persistence, trophic structure, and food webs, then turn to a consideration of species diversity in streams and rivers and finally to the larger scale biogeographic distribution patterns.

Community patterns and processes

Resource partitioning

The marked spatial heterogeneity of streams and rivers, ranging from the individual stone surface to the reach and whole stream segment, clearly produces a large number of microhabitats. There should potentially be, therefore, plenty of 'room' for the coexistence of species through resource partitioning. Resource partitioning refers to the different ways in which species in the same guild share resources. Schoener (1974) identified three principal niche dimensions which can be partitioned—time, food, and habitat.

Temporal segregation

This relates to the differences in life history patterns and timing of maximum growth among closely related species. Many examples among benthic insects have been cited as evidence of temporal partitioning (see Hart, 1983), particularly among the caddis (Oswood, 1976; Georgian and Wallace, 1983; see also pp. 143–5). Fish, especially tropical species, also have specialized life histories which may encourage resource partitioning (e.g. Watson and Balon, 1984). But the possibilities for such partitioning of time is of course somewhat limited and is not always evident (e.g.

among macrophyte-dwelling chironomids, Tokeshi, 1994). The other two niche dimensions offer far greater potential for resource partitioning.

Food partitioning

Despite the fact that most consumers in lotic systems are polyphagous, examples of feeding specialization and partitioning of food resources exist, particularly in relation to particle size among filter-feeders and in terms of different types and sizes of prey taken by predators. Among tropical fish in Asian streams, for example, there appears to be a high degree of morphological specialization related to feeding (Dudgeon, 1995). Dietary overlap may be reduced and fish become even more specialized when resources become scarce, as in a Panamanian stream during the dry season (Zaret and Rand, 1971). The particle size consumed by coexisting hydropsychid caddis is influenced by mesh size of their nets (Edington *et al.*, 1984; pp. 119–20), and among scraper–collector/gatherer guilds, species can be divided into at least two groups (algivores and detritivores) on the basis of diet (Rader and Ward, 1987). Even among algivores themselves, preferences for particular species of algae have been found, again particularly among the caddis larvae. What is less clear is whether or not such differences in diet are due to the use of different habitats, which by their nature may have different prey species or food resources, or whether species use different microhabitats because of their particular food preferences.

Habitat segregation

What is clear, however, is that habitat is by far the most important dimension as far as resource partitioning is concerned. Benthic organisms show clear preferences for particular microhabitat features, particularly among closely related species (Hildrew and Townsend, 1987). For example, guilds that differ in growth form and flow regime can be identified among diatom assemblages which relate to flow and substrate preferences (see Table 5.1, p. 111). Similarly, separation of species by substrate preferences has been clearly demonstrated among macro-invertebrates (see pp. 41–3) even on very small scales at the level of the single stone or boulder (see Fig 8.1). Among fish, there are also many examples, such as the almost entirely non-overlapping distribution of congeneric pool-dwelling darters within a single drainage basin (Page and Schemske, 1978), and vertical position in the water column among tropical rainforest fish (Watson and Balon, 1984; Welcomme, 1985).

Differential niche overlap

One clear pattern to arise in the study of communities is that where species overlap in resource use in one particular niche dimension, they generally differ in use of another, that is, they show differential niche overlap (Giller, 1984). Sheldon (1972) for example, showed that while four coexisting species of perlid stoneflies had minimal temporal segregation and little habitat differences, they differed in food habits. The net-spinning caddis (see Fig. 3.3, p. 35) showed some differences in longitudinal distribution in relation to thermal preferences, but where they did co-occur the species differed in the net-spinning site (Hildrew and Edington, 1979). This kind of differential overlap can be seen very clearly among three coexisting *Hydropsyche* species in a western Malaysian stream (Edington *et al.*, 1984). One species has a smaller mesh net than the other two, occupies fine gravel substrates, and collects smaller-sized food particles. The other two species occupy similar substrates but differ in microhabitat, one utilizing the upper and lateral surfaces of boulders, the other the crevices between boulders (Fig. 8.1). Stream cyprinid fish also segregate in several dimensions (Baker and Ross, 1981). Some species utilize different drainage basins, but those in the same basin or reach differ in their vertical position in the water column and in their degree of association with vegetation. A pair of species with similar habitats even showed different activity patterns over the day, one being diurnal, the other nocturnal. Another study on cyprinids, this time in Sri Lankan rainforest streams, shows species segregating among different flow regimes, position in the water column, substrate, and diet (Moyle and Senanayake, 1984).

Other species attributes such as ability to cope with disturbances and colonization ability can contribute to successful coexistence of species that otherwise show little resource partitioning. One example is the *Leucotrichia* (caddis)–*Paragyractis* (moth) interaction, where floods remove the competitively superior caddis species and allow colonization of rock surfaces by the moth, the more resilient species (McAuliffe, 1984*a*). The rapid colonization ability of certain species (e.g. blackfly and chironomid larvae) allows them to exploit temporarily empty areas created by disturbances before they are displaced by other, slower colonists (see p. 191). Colonization ability could therefore be considered another niche dimension.

Fig. 8.1 Microhabitat partitioning among hydropsychid caddis larvae. One species uses the upper and flat lateral surfaces of the boulder (points 1, 2, and 3); a second species uses crevices between boulders (points 4 and 5) and a third gravel bed sites (points 6 and 7). (After Edington *et al.*, 1984. Fig 2.(c). Reproduced with kind permission of Kluwer Academic Publishers.)

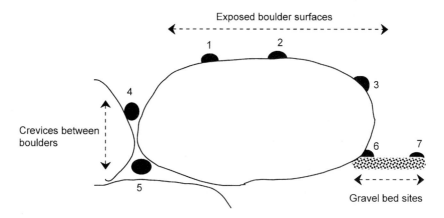

Persistence and predictability of communities

Abundance and diversity patterns occur on a number of different spatial and temporal scales in streams and rivers. Studies on headwater streams (orders 1–3) have shown a seasonal sequence of species replacement and quite characteristic seasonal cycles in community structure and function. For temperate streams not unduly influenced by floods, Hynes (1970) predicted fluctuations in biomass and density of macroinvertebrates based on life history patterns, with spring and autumn peaks, a pattern found in many studies (e.g. Stoneburner and Smock, 1979; Mulholland and Lenat, 1992; see also Fig. 3.14, p. 67). This pattern may differ in higher-order streams. In the 4th order River Awbeg in Ireland, peak abundance occurred in late summer and a smaller second peak occurred over winter with the community dominated by Simuliidae (Giller and Twomey, 1993). This may be related to seasonal changes in fine particulate organic matter (FPOM) availability. Similar increases in mean densities again largely because of summer domination by a particular taxon, have been reported elsewhere (e.g. Collier and Winterbourn, 1987).

Over longer timescales, unpolluted stream and river communities seem to be quite persistent, that is, there is a tendency for the species composition to remain unchanged in terms of relative abundance patterns and species composition (Hildrew and Giller, 1994). This seems to hold for macroinvertebrate communities over the medium term (2–10 years) despite instability in the absolute abundance of invertebrates and despite often dramatic disturbances. Similar patterns have been found for fish communities over timescales from 3 to 36 years. Of course, the degree of persistence varies with the level of environmental variability. For invertebrates in spring-fed streams in Kentucky, differences in species richness and density over a 30-year period did not exceed the annual, seasonal or between habitat differences (Johnson et al., 1994). Similarly, shaded headwater streams with a restricted temperature and discharge range also show high persistence. Greater temporal variability in flow, large fluctuations in annual rainfall, and decreased habitat stability all lead to reduced persistence levels (Townsend et al., 1987). The main reason for this overall persistence appears to be the considerable resilience shown by stream communities (the ability to return to the original community configuration quickly after a disturbance). As Niemi et al. (1990) concluded, all lotic systems seem to be resilient in the face of all kinds of disturbances, with most recovery times being less than 3 years. This resilience is related to both the characteristics of the organisms and the provision of refugia as we discussed in Chapter 5. However, under directed environmental change, such as following clearfelling of the catchment, acidification, or eutrophication, persistence is low (see also Chapter 3, pp. 52–3). The changes in the River Rhine over a 80-year period provide a dramatic example. The increasing inputs of industrial effluents and increasing levels of transportation in the river have led to a decrease in macrophytes and an increase in temperature and salinity and eventually eutrophication. In response, riverine insects decreased and macrocrustaceans increased due to the introduction and colonization of exotic species and immigration of native brackish water species (Fig. 8.2).

Fig. 8.2 Changes in the species richness of (a) macroinvertebrate fauna and (b) fish fauna of the River Rhine and its branches over an 80-year period. (After van den Brink *et al.*, 1990.)

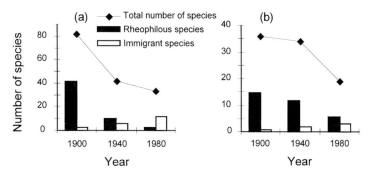

We have discussed longitudinal patterns of species and community replacement in Chapters 3 and 6 in the context of the RCC. Larger-scale, extensive spatial patterns among sites seem to be both predictable and repeatable (Hildrew and Giller, 1994) which also illustrates the persistence of lotic communities. These patterns are related to the relationships between taxa and environmental conditions that we discussed in Chapter 3. Invertebrate and diatom community structure, for example, is related to a mixture of factors such as altitude, temperature, water chemistry, surrounding land use, flow regime, area and food resources or species interactions. Where conditions are similar, community structure will also be similar. Thus, following a major survey of 268 sites in Britain, and using classification analysis, Moss *et al.* (1987) identified 15 groups of sites in relation to 28 environmental variables. These kinds of patterns have led to the development of a river invertebrate prediction and classification system (RIVPACS) which is being used in environmental assessment. The invertebrate community found at any site in the United Kingdom can be compared to that predicted based on a set of environmental variables and hence the extent of pollution or effects of river regulation can be assessed (Armitage, 1996).

Succession

Communities are not always stable in time as suggested above in relation to directed environmental change. As a response to environmental change or disturbances, communities can undergo a succession. Temporal succession is a site-specific change in a community, involving modifications in species composition and dominance, over time. It can be in response to a disturbance event on an already existing community (a secondary succession perhaps leading to recovery of the original community) or following the opening up a pristine habitat (a primary succession leading to the establishment of a new community characteristic of the habitat type and conditions). There has been a lot of work carried out on small spatial and temporal scales following the colonization of artificial substrate trays or cleaned stone surfaces (see pp. 181–2). Simuliids are usually the earliest colonizers of stones, and are later displaced by hydropsychid caddis (e.g. Hemphill and Cooper, 1983; Downes and Lake, 1991). Baetid mayflies and chironomids as well as simuliids (the major drifting taxa, see p. 173) rapidly colonize substrate trays, but subsequently reduce in abundance as other taxa colonize (Ulfstrand *et al.*, 1974; Peckarsky, 1986). At this spatial scale, the 'so-called' succession is based on short term redistribution of organisms from the source pool of potential colonizers that surrounds newly opened habitat patches.

Larger-scale, more properly termed 'successional', patterns have been documented following disturbances. Where disturbances are frequent, it may not be possible to see uninterrupted recovery and seasonal change will cloud patterns attributable to succession alone (Fisher, 1983). It all relates to the frequency of disturbances in relation to the generation time of the organisms. Much investigation has been conducted on desert streams that are subject both to intense flash floods and extensive drying up. Initial colonization by algae is largely determined by abiotic conditions during the early colonization phase and marked successional patterns occur as there is usually time for several generations between events. In Sycamore Creek, Arizona, initial post-flood colonizers are always diatoms, which are replaced by cyanobacteria or *Cladophora*-dominated assemblages (Fisher, 1983). However, in this system, five different successional patterns (A–E) have been observed following 18 successional sequences over a four-year period in Sycamore Creek (Table 8.1). The variation was partly explained by nitrogen concentration which was lowest for patterns D and E. Macroinvertebrate diversity also declined during those successional sequences with low nitrogen flux due to reduced food quality (Grimm, 1994). In addition to these species-level changes, primary production, respiration, nutrient cycling, and biomass change during these successions.

Floods also represent major disturbances that influence riparian plant communities. After alluvium is deposited following a flood in a lowland river, here too, succession can occur, with pioneeer communities developing initially, to be replaced by young soft-wood communities and then mature hard-wood communities (Décamps and Tabacchi, 1994). At any stage though, a new flood may destroy the vegetation and reset the sequence. When large floods are a normal seasonal event, as in many systems with a pronounced snowmelt hydrograph, riparian plant communities are adapted to the situation. In fact, the neat zonation of plant species characteristic of free-flowing rivers in northern Scandinavia disappears in regulated rivers when the regulation dampens seasonal variations in flow (see p. 226).

Table 8.1 Patterns of succession in Sycamore Creek, Arizona, a desert stream following flash floods (From Grimm, 1994)

Successional pattern	Length of sequence (days)
A None	11–19
B Bare → Diatoms → Diatoms + Chlorophytes	17–70
C Bare → Diatoms → Chlorophytes + Flocculent	31–57
D Bare → Diatoms + Flocculent → Flocculent + Cyanobacteria	38–118
E Bare → Diatoms → Cyanobacteria + Chlorophytes + Diatoms	14–158

Large-scale studies on whole river segments or newly created habitats show the clearest successional patterns. One example involved the creation of a lake outflow stream in Sweden. It took approximately a year before the community resembled other lake outflow communities in the area. There was evidence of competitive interactions with blackfly larvae giving way to hydropsychids again, as well as possible effects of predation (Malmqvist *et al.*, 1991*a*). But for the longest successional sequences we have to turn to Milner's work in Glacier Bay National Park in Alaska, which overall covers five streams up to 150 years old (Milner, 1994). As glaciers melt, so streams appear and new habitat is constantly being created as the ice retreats. One particularly detailed study was based on Wolf Point Creek, which was created in 1965. In 1978, the community at one site was based on six species of chironomids associated with filamentous algae (Fig. 8.3). Mayfly and stonefly species colonized between 1984 and 1986, and blackflies and caddis a few years later. Predatory stoneflies first appeared in 1988 and increased significantly by 1990. The chironomids themselves showed marked changes with the initial colonizers (like *Diamesa* spp.) disappearing, and other taxa (like *Pagastia* spp.) replacing them. Although there was a gradual increase in water temperature over this period, the evidence pointed clearly to competitive replacement. Fish (Dolly Varden Charr) first appeared around 1988 (Fig. 8.3). This is typically the first salmonid to colonize new stream habitats. Around 1000 pink salmon spawned at the site in 1991. Over the 30 years since the formation of the stream site, no non-insect invertebrate groups had established, presumably due to geographic barriers to dispersal. The insects have the advantage of flight as adults and hence aerial colonization of the new habitat.

Fig. 8.3 Successional changes in invertebrate communities and appeareance of fish populations in Wolf Point Creek, Alaska from 1977 to 1990. (From Milner, 1994.)

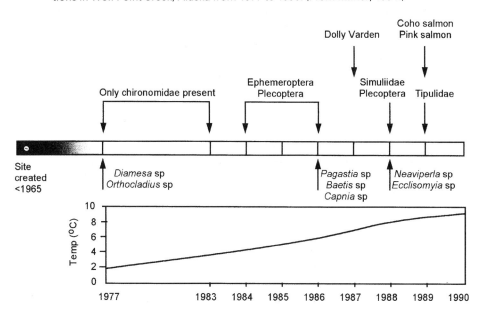

Another kind of succession worth mentioning is a longitudinal succession estab-lished downstream of organic or other pollution discharges. Changes in environ-mental conditions with distance downstream of the discharge (such as oxygen levels, temperature, or concentrations of toxic chemicals) lead to predictable patterns of community composition in space. These are discussed in more detail on pp. 233–4.

Food webs and trophic structure

Food webs can summarize all trophic links between consumers and their food categories and they are constructed around a series of interlinked food chains. They thus offer a useful conceptual approach to help us understand species interactions and to illustrate the pattern of energy flow in a community. Unfortunately, there are very few thorough descriptions of food webs for running waters, due to problems in trying to identify all the links. Gut contents analysis of larger invertebrates and fish that consume whole organisms is useful, but may not tell the whole story (Benke *et al.*, 1988). Often some components of the gut contents are unrecognizable; as we mentioned earlier (p. 137), amorphous material is common and could originate from a number of sources such as biofilm, digested periphyton, leaf detritus or FPOM. Serological or electrophoretic analysis of gut contents can be used for predators that suck out the contents of prey (such as bugs and some beetles, e.g. Giller, 1986). Radio-labelling of microbes can help identify microbial feeders (e.g. Edwards and Meyer, 1987) and use of stable isotope ratios can help to identify the consumption of detritus (e.g. Rounick *et al.*, 1982). However, all these require specialized techniques and equipment. The size of small invertebrates and consequently of their prey makes the identification of prey species at the lower trophic levels difficult, and ofter requires specialist microscopic techniques and taxonomic expertise. Consequently the taxonomic detail is usually much coarser at the lower trophic levels (e.g. at family or order) than at the higher ones (which can usually be resolved to species).

Having said all this, we are probably getting close to producing a complete stream food web, particularly following the studies in Broadstone stream (Fig. 8.4). This is an acidic, forested, stream in southern England of relatively low diversity with no fish, two major invertebrate predatory species, and one top consumer species. The majority of links among the insect fauna were identified some time ago (Hildrew *et al.*, 1985) and more recently the microcrustacea have been added (Lancaster and Robinson, 1995). Yet even for this relatively simple system, there are still gaps, such as the mites and full resolution of links to the top predator. If one starts to work on the protozoa, rotifers, and nematodes, the feeding links between these groups and the macroinvertebrates promise to complicate things further.

Despite the relative paucity of good information on lotic food webs, when we use what we have and look at their structure, a number of patterns do appear (Hildrew, 1996a). These are based around two parameters; *connectance*, which is the proportion of possible feeding links between species that is actually realized; and the *predator:prey ratio*, the ratio of number of predator species to prey species in the

Fig. 8.4 The food web of Broadstone stream, one of the most complete stream food webs published to date. Primary consumers include: e, a bivalve; f, Simuliidae; g, an amphipod; h1–h10, microcrustacean species; i, other microinvertebrates; j–l, chironomid species; m, Oligochaeta; n and o, stoneflies; p and q, chironomids; r, Tipulidae; s, cased caddis. Primary carnivores include: t–v, predaceous chironomids; aa, ceratopogonid species; bb, dytiscid beetle. Secondary carnivores include: w, a net-spinning caddis; x, an alderfly. Tertiary carnivores include: z, a dragonfly. (Diet analysis has not been carried out on aa, bb, or z.) (After Lancaster and Robertson, 1995, where details of the species can be found.)

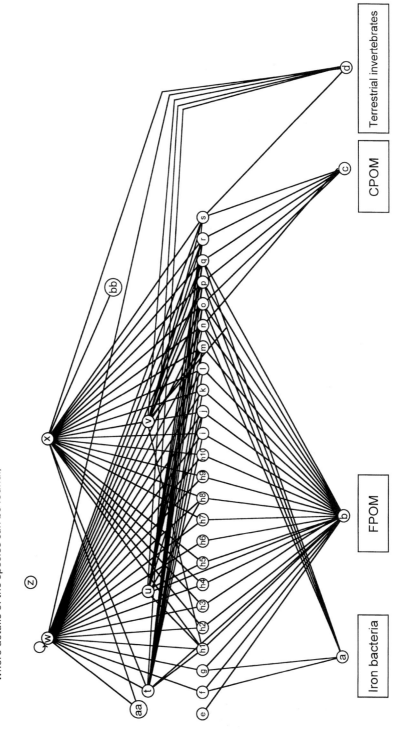

food web. In one of the most famous papers on food webs, Briand and Cohen (1987) examined 113 different data sets, from all kinds of habitats, of which nine were from lotic ones. They found that connectance (C) decreased as the number of species (S) increased. Jeffries and Lawton (1985) concentrated on freshwater systems, including many lotic ones and showed a fairly consistent predator:prey ratio, where on average, communities of freshwater invertebrates support 1 predator species for every 3 prey species. Among the lotic data sets however, the average ratio tended to be highest for pool sites ($\approx$ 0.6, n = 7), lowest for stream sites ($\approx$ 0.29, n = 26), and intermediate for riverine sites ($\approx$ 0.38, n = 12). Briand (1985) also suggested that stream food webs were shorter and more complex (more highly connected and wider) than lake and river webs, which tended to be longer, thinner, and with fewer connections. This mirrors the differences in predator:prey ratios we just mentioned. Broadstone stream only conforms to the high linkage complexity (S $\times$ C) (Hildrew, 1996a). The most complete version of the Broadstone food web has an overall predator:prey ratio of 0.21 (Lancaster and Robinson, 1995), which seems to suggest that as the resolution of the food webs improves, the ratio may decline. That is, there may actually be fewer predator species per prey species than the current data suggest, with greater linkages among the prey. Consider again the generally broad diets of stream animals.

Just looking at the number of feeding links in a food web can be misleading, however, especially if one is trying to model interactions in streams and rivers, unless the relative importance (i.e. the strength) of all the links is known, a condition which is rarely met. However, in some instances it would probably be possible to consider just certain links (i.e. those that are particularly strong). Tavares-Cromar and Williams (1996) showed that in a Canadian stream, 20–25% of all links in a stream food web could be classified as 'very strong'.

Hildrew (1996a) presented a model for lotic food webs in which he emphasised that most studies have found a strong interaction between algae and grazers, and between detritus and detritivores, at least where flow stress is minimal. Moreover, under such favourable conditions, especially in pool habitats, fish appear to have a major impact on large invertebrates. In the absence of fish (e.g. in acidified systems like Broadstone stream), large invertebrate predators are released from a top-down predation pressure and can therefore have stronger effects on lower consumer levels. Through the action of flow disturbances, the impact of the predators in these examples can be offset because population densities are too low for significant interaction (Fig. 8.5). Under such circumstances, the interactions are simply weakened but the overall shape of the web is not changed. Power *et al.* (1996) suggested a food chain architecture for a river under a Mediterranean flow regime, where food chains develop in a succession from zero to four levels following seasonal winter scouring. Their data suggested that intermediate levels of disturbance kept up food chain length because stability fostered a grazer guild consisting of armoured or sessile taxa with a high resistance to predators.

This brings us neatly into the controversy over the 'top-down' and 'bottom-up' regulation of community structure. Does the action of predators have an over-riding influence on the composition and structure of the food web or are nutrient

Fig. 8.5 A food web model of a trout stream (centre) showing strong links between basal resources and herbivores and detritivores, and between trout and large invertebrate predators. In systems with frequent flow disturbances (left) all links are weak, and in acidified systems (right) the lack of fish releases pressures on large invertebrates, which therefore suppress smaller invertebrates.The size of the category symbols represents their abundance. (Modified after Hildrew, 1996a.)

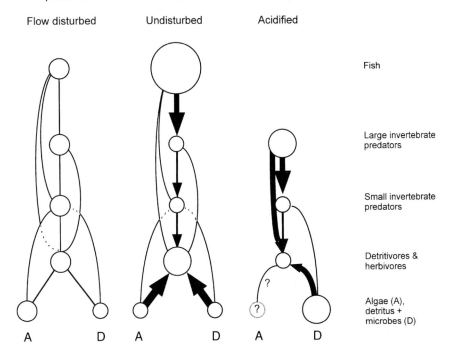

availability, productivity, and detrital inputs the main controlling factors? We discussed the influence of nutrients earlier (pp. 162–4) and the example from the Kuparuk River study illustrates bottom-up control. Similarly, the study by Wallace *et al.* (1997) manipulating detrital inputs also indicated strong bottom-up control (see p. 160). Some of the effects of predation on prey populations and communities (top-down) were also considered earlier (pp. 184–7). One of the most cited examples of top-down regulation is that of Power and Matthews (1983) who demonstrated that the piscivorous bass *Micropterus* indirectly affected the distribution of filamentous algae in stream pools by controlling the distribution of the algal-grazing minnow *Campostoma*. An extensive study of 30 sites in 20 Canadian streams demonstrated a number of effects of the presence of piscivores including decreased biomass of non-piscivorous fish, higher biomass and abundance of benthic invertebrates, and larger size of benthic invertebrate predators (Bowlby and Roff, 1986). However, the effects of fish on invertebrates was less clear, and was influenced by prey exchange rates as we discussed earlier (p. 185). A recent analysis of the pattern from a wide range of studies reaffirms the importance of prey exchange rates and suggests that benthic feeding fish have a more significant effect than drift feeding fish (see also Dahl and Greenberg,

1996), and that there is little difference in the impacts of predatory invertebrates and predatory fish on macroinvertebrate communities (Englund, *et al.*, in press).

As the above work of Hildrew (1996*a*) and Power *et al.* (1996) indicates, physical factors can play a role in regulating food webs. Hart's (1992) study in Augusta Creek, Michigan tells a wonderful story. Crayfish can eliminate the blanket weed *Cladophora* from sites with velocities $\leq$ 50 cm s^{-1}, but higher flows provide a refuge by dislodging crayfish and restricting their foraging activity hence allowing *Cladophora* to grow. If crayfish were the only limiting factor for *Cladophora*, we would expect sites with flows exceeding 50 cm s^{-1} to be monopolized by the blanket weed, but cover rarely exceeds 50%. Sessile grazers like *Leucotrichia* and *Psychomyia* can prevent such monopoly of a site if they have established prior residence. *Cladophora* in turn can inhibit the establishment of these grazers. The creation of bare space (such as by spates overturning stones, sessile grazers emerging, *Cladophora* mats sloughing off) and the nature of colonization and propagule dispersion (related to life history patterns) are thus important in this system. In addition, *Cladophora* cover positively influences the abundance of other taxa through enhancement of epiphytic algae, accumulation of fine particles, as a physical support for nets and as a refuge from flow (Hart, 1992). Amphipods, for example, are chemically attracted by the epiphytic diatom assemblage on *Cladophora* (Shannon *et al.*, 1994). The herbivores in turn consume epiphytes and detritus trapped by the epiphytic diatoms, altering the local light climate and releasing mineralized nutrients, which may enhance the growth of the host plant. In this system, therefore, crayfish not only affect other invertebrates through direct consumption but also by influencing *Cladophora* cover which in turn affects sessile grazers as well as the microalgal assemblage. Crayfish can thus act as a 'keystone' predator in this community and trophic cascades down to lower trophic levels can occur when the top of the food web is manipulated. Predatory fish can also act in this way as described earlier and as shown by Power (1990) in Eel river, California. Large fish depress small predator populations, which releases herbivorous chironomids from predation. They in turn reduce *Cladophora* to a low prostrate form with few epiphytes (which affect other grazers). Experimental exclusion of large fish allows a strong predatory interaction between smaller predators and the herbivorous chironomids, leading to tall, upright tufts of *Cladophora* with many epiphytes.

Community structure

Stream and river communities are thus governed by the interplay between physical factors and species interactions. But which are the most important? Some authors believe that the evidence indicates that stream macroinvertebrate communities are deterministic assemblages of species populations in a state of dynamic equilibrium and structured largely by species interactions (e.g. Minshall and Peterson, 1985). Others believe that physical disturbances and chance are more important, and that the systems are basically randomly assembled and non-equilibrial (e.g. Tokeshi, 1994). This debate has been ongoing in ecology in general over the last two decades, but there is a growing general consensus that a pluralistic approach is needed to explain how the diverse ecological factors govern community organization over space and time (Hart, 1992) and for freshwater ecology this is no different. As we mentioned earlier, the controlling factors differ depending on the nature of the stream or river system. While the successional patterns of the desert stream algae we described suggest that succession here may not be deterministic (Fisher, 1990), in Alaskan streams, successional patterns are highly deterministic. The difference may lie in the fact that the Alaskan stream has harsh but predictable and slow changes in conditions while the flood-induced disturbances in the desert stream are rapid yet unpredictable in time. The high resilience of stream communities is, however, an attribute found in many deterministic communities (Lake and Doeg, 1985). This link between the importance of biotic factors and abiotic severity has been termed the 'harsh–benign' hypothesis and was modified for lotic communities by Peckarsky (1983a) who was inspired by Menge's (1976) work in marine rocky intertidal communities.

Recently, Hildrew and Giller (1994) have suggested that we might be able to characterize communities into three different types based on the most important processes in each. First, in 'disturbance-dominated communities', disturbances are so intense and frequent that the dynamics of the species are essentially independent and species interactions play a minor role. The second type, 'competitive communities' can be either 'shuffled' or 'partitioning'. In the former, little ecological difference exists between species that may compete significantly in a single local patch, but chance variation in the species composition among patches reduces the risk of competitive exclusion over the entire system. In 'partitioning competitive communities' species partition resources on the basis of small-scale spatial or temporal environmental variations. Third, communities may be structured by predation. In 'patchy predation communities', prey refugia (a product of predator avoidance, separate habitat preferences or physical complexity of substrate) allow persistence in the face of intense predation by predators limited in turn by their prey (trophic cascades are possible). In 'amplified predator communities', populations concentrate in flow refugia to avoid disturbances hence predation is amplified but interactions occur in a series of 'crunches'.

These are not mutually exclusive and much work is needed to explore their validity and identify where various systems may fit. However, they do offer at least some working hypotheses.

Species diversity

Most natural running waters are diverse. Nonetheless, there have been very few attempts to construct complete species lists for stream or river systems. This is of course not an easy task. Not only do species succeed each other on a seasonal basis, but large inter-annual fluctuations in the populations of different species can also occur. Moreover, special techniques may have to be used to collect successfully different groups of taxa; what is efficient for one group is often not so for another. A further stumbling block is in the identification, which for many species, especially the small invertebrates, requires specialist taxonomic knowledge. In these times, when the preservation of biodiversity is of such great concern, detailed information about the diversity, and therefore also taxonomy, of lotic systems is badly needed.

Probably the most thoroughly studied stream in the world is the Breitenbach, a small stream near Schlitz in central Germany, where Joachim Illies, Peter Zwick, Rüdiger Wagner, and others have been sampling the entire animal community over many years. Allan (1995) offered a compilation of the data showing that 642 insect species (including 476 dipterans, 70 coleopterans, and 57 trichopterans) had been recorded. Dipterans included primarily chironomids (152 species), limoniids (86 species), ceratopogonids (61 species), and dolichopodids (50 species). Out of the additional 446 non-insect taxa, approximately half were nematodes and rotifers. It should be borne in mind that long series of sampling, as in the Breitenbach, will no doubt pick up transient species that happen to be there when sampling was performed without being true members of the local stream community. In fact, many of the species found in the Breitenbach have been taxa that inhabit lentic waters in the vicinity of the stream.

The huge effort required to produce a reasonably comprehensive list of species has necessitated a pragmatic methodology in studies of species diversity in lotic environments. Usually, this is accomplished by considering only easily collected and identifiable species, selecting one or two seasons in one or a few years, and collecting by using only a single sampling method. The experience of the investigator and his/her resources will also be crucial for the final result. Naturally, underestimates will be frequent but there have been efforts to compensate for such underestimates. Using complete data sets, Baltanás (1992) compared several methods that try to estimate how many species are missing from a sample set. All of these methods, however, showed a negative bias (i.e. the predicted species richness underestimated the true species richness). The best fit was provided by the jack-knife method (Heltshe and Forrester, 1983), which is based on the presence of unique species in the sample units:

$$\text{estimated species richness} = \Sigma o_i + k(n-1)n^{-1},$$

where o_i is the number of species observed in each sample, n the total number of samples, and k the number of unique species in the n samples. This method has been employed in studies on macroinvertebrate and moss species richness in Swedish river rapids, where the purpose was to predict changes in species richness as a consequence of altered flow regime in regulated rivers (Englund and Malmqvist, 1996). What these methods cannot do, however, is indicate which species are missing!

Frequently, studies focus only on the presence of species in the three orders Ephemeroptera, Plecoptera, and Trichoptera (referred to as EPT), which in most cases can be identified to the species level. Apart from being diagnosed relatively easily, these orders are usually better known, even in those parts of the world which have been less well studied. Also, this subset of the benthic community appears to contain sufficient information to answer most of the questions posed in various types of studies, such as in the context of monitoring changes in water quality (Wallace *et al.*, 1996).

Regional and local diversity

A host of factors contribute to the regional diversity of biota. At least two of them operate on a large biogeographic scale: speciation and glaciation–interglaciation cycles. Speciation is most likely where isolation is sufficient for colonizers to differentiate ecologically and behaviourally before re-encountering their ancestor populations.

During glaciations large amounts of water were bound in the extended polar ice caps, causing, at the same time, much lower sea levels. This situation allowed species to move across temporary land bridges between islands and larger land masses which, during interglacial periods, were isolated. Moreover, at the end of glaciations, colonization by hardy species has been possible in the wake of the retreating ice. This may have been a rapid process, as seen today in Milner's studies in Glacier Bay, Alaska (p. 199), and taxa were often left behind as glacial relicts in montane areas. Another striking feature of areas that were ice-covered during the last glaciation is, as in Scandinavia, their paucity of endemic species.

One of the most dramatic patterns on earth is the change in species diversity with latitude and altitude. How does the stream biota fit in? Many studies confirm a reduced total taxonomic richness with increasing altitude (e.g. Ward 1986; Suren 1994). The downstream increase in taxa is not universal across taxonomic groups however. Stoneflies for example, despite a threefold decrease in species richness found from 1500 to 3400 m above sea level in a pristine Rocky Mountain stream, had a marked peak in richness at 2500–2700 m, decreasing steadily with both increasing and decreasing elevation (Ward, 1986). Clear downstream increases in richness were most evident for mayflies and chironomids. Caddisflies showed reduced richness above 3200 m, but a nearly constant richness below this altitude (Fig. 8.6). As mentioned previously, Statzner and Higler (1986) suggested that transition zones between different levels of hydraulic stress have organismal elements of more than one hydraulic regime, and are therefore more species rich. Stanford *et al.* (1996) extended this contention to include several peaks in diversity in several regions of transitions (namely, headwater stream–montane floodplain, montane floodplain-piedmont valley floodplain, and piedmont valley floodplain–coastal floodplain).

Overall, the diversity of most types of organisms on earth seems to increase from the polar areas toward the tropics. Stream-living, non-fish biota have been suggested to be an exception to this rule (Patrick, 1964). Many factors, however, are likely to confound this generalization, including, for the tropics, insufficient taxonomic knowledge and greater local differences in species composition (see p. 212). A recent compilation of nearly 500 samples worldwide, suggests that richness peaks both at mid-latitudes (about 40 degrees) and near the equator but data from latitudes <20 degrees are scanty and derive, to a large extent, from oceanic islands which can be expected to have lower richness (Vinson, personal communication). There can be no doubt though that diversity is lowest at very high latitudes.

Fig. 8.6 Vertical changes in species richness over a long altitudinal gradient (metres above sea level, m a.s.l.) in the Rocky Mountains. (Redrawn from Ward, 1986.)

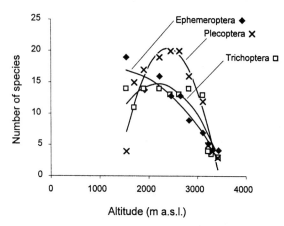

It is logical to believe that at very high latitudes and altitudes food levels may be insufficient to support a larger number of specialist species. And with decreasing harshness, in particular with respect to availability of organic material as a source of food, and increasing temperature, diversity is bound to rise at lower latitudes and altitudes. Many groups of organisms, however, show their optimal elevational and latitudinal ranges at intermediate levels, a fact that is most probably linked to temperature. While temperature variation is greatest at mid-latitudes, a second species-richness peak near the equator cannot be easily understood at present.

The regional species pool provides an upper theoretical limit to how many species could possibly colonize a single stream. In fact, the number of species found represents only a fraction of this, since it is the quality of local habitat features that determines whether a species can thrive at a site provided that it has the capacity to colonize this site in the first place. Whether colonization in turn is at all possible depends on the dispersal and establishment capacity of a species. In their review of insect diversity in streams, Vinson and Hawkins (1998) found that habitat heterogeneity affected EPT species richness at local, catchment and regional scales. Richness at one scale appeared to be directly proportional to the richness at higher scales, so that the richness of the EPT taxa at local reach scale was 50% of the catchment richness and catchment richness 34% of regional richness. The proportionality further suggests that local and catchment stream faunas are possibly unsaturated with species, truly an intriguing observation.

Determinants of local diversity

Landscape features, including the size of drainage area, vegetation, geology, soils, and gradient, together shape the habitats of a river system into a multitude of different combinations; no two rivers are alike. Island biogeography theory surmises that the system is continuously exposed to invasion of species from the regional species pool, and as species colonize, other species go extinct, maintaining an approximately constant number. Thus, the local species pool is a less extensive image of the regional pool, as seen above, and is assembled from species able to cope with the local conditions. Few species are common, but many are rare and the particular mix of species in a certain system is determined by many different features (Chapter 3). Thus in polluted rivers, oxygen levels put particular demands on the respiratory capacities of their inhabitants. Consequently, species with high oxygen requirements, such as many lotic stonefly and mayfly larvae, are unable to persist. Those which can, may thrive far better in the absence of competitors. In very stable and productive habitats, such as lake outlet streams, interactions can be of extraordinary strength for running waters. Such habitats may foster a situation where a few species outcompete others, and a comparative study suggested that the more productive such outlet streams are the more species poor they become (Malmqvist and Eriksson, 1995). It appears as if hydropsychid larvae are 'keystone' species, suppressing others, probably due to their aggressive behaviour and their sheer densities occupying most available space. However, competition or predation probably does not often lead to extinction of species from streams and rivers, although there is hardly any doubt that relative densities are influenced by these factors.

One of nature's general relationships concerning diversity that is also predicted by island biogeography theory, is the positive relationship between area and species richness described as:

$$S = cA^z$$

where S and A are species richness and area respectively, and c and z constants: c is specific for certain taxa and regions, z describes the rate by which the number of species drops with decreasing area, and since z is often near 0.3, a decrease in area by nine-tenths approximately reduces the species number by 50%. Rivers are no exceptions to the species–area relationship, as they can be thought of as islands of water in a sea of land, and species richness in a range of animals increases with drainage area or with the actual areas of the entire stream channel (Fig. 8.7). The explanation for the species–area relationship is, however, not simple. Several hypotheses have been proposed (see Hart and Horwitz, 1991 and Rosenzweig, 1995 for discussions). The two most appealing ones include a passive sampling model (area *per se*), where diversity is larger purely because of the statistically greater probability of large islands sampling more colonizers than small islands. The second one involves a diversity effect of habitats, since it is likely that larger islands (or areas) have a greater variety of habitats and that they can offer optimal conditions for a larger number of species. This is perhaps most obvious when studying very small trickling streams, which typically are poorer in species than larger streams and rivers. This factor can, however, easily be confounded with the fact that small islands have fewer individuals than large islands, and by chance, the number of species must also be smaller. There need not be just one factor explaining the species–area relationship, and it is likely that different factors contribute.

The fit between species richness and area is often relatively poor, which again suggests that factors other than size (or correlates to size) affect richness as well.

Fig. 8.7 Species–area relationships in rivers: (a) stream-dwelling mussels from south-eastern Michigan (after Strayer, 1983); (b) fish species in various river systems around the world (after Welcomme, 1979); (c) macroinvertebrates from streams on a Danish island (after Brönmark *et al.*, 1984a. Reproduced with kind permission from Kluwer Academic Publishers.)

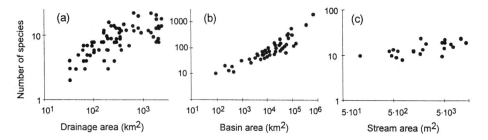

These factors probably differ between regions, although often substrate, water quality, temperature, and disturbance (e.g. flooding) seem to be among the most important ones (Chapter 3). Historical factors may also be important. Thus, the Nile harbours fewer fish species than would be expected from the species–area relationship alone. This deviation has been attributed to the presence of alternating dry and humid periods during the Quaternary, and the last dry period may have eliminated many of the species in the Nile (Hugueny, 1989).

The river continuum concept (RCC), in conflict with the species–area relationship, predicts maximum species richness at intermediate stream orders, primarily because the environment of low- and high-order streams is less variable than those of mid-orders (see pp. 167–9). However, the validity of the RCC is not clear as we discussed. Unfortunately, an additional problem when testing the RCC, particularly with regard to species diversity, is the extensive habitat destruction that has taken place in large rivers, which may have resulted in reduced species numbers today.

Function of diversity

Does the loss of diversity through pollution and habitat destruction matter? The function of diversity is in general quite poorly known and for stream systems, we can only speculate at the present time. Two features may have a considerable effect, although these can be hard to test empirically. The first is that stream food webs appear to be highly connected as we discussed earlier. This means that if species-specific parasites, or disease, attack a population of a species and drive it down to low numbers, populations of one or several other species may replace the first species functionally, and no changes in the rate of various processes would be detected. The second feature arises if the affected species happens to be a keystone species. When this is the case, a considerable restructuring of the community will follow. This happened when the caddis-fly *Glossosoma*, a keystone species, was hit by a microsporidian parasite in a number of streams in Michigan, United States (see p. 188). It is, however, premature to rule out the possibility that less spectacular species than keystone species could have distinctive and important roles. In a review of lotic biodiversity and ecosystem processes, Covich (1996) pointed at the subtle and varied roles played by different detritivores in processing leaf litter from various riparian tree species. He argued that we are barely beginning to understand the complex linkages that are necessary in order to make predictions about the effects of lost species.

Biogeographic patterns in running water biota

It is not easy to make world-wide comparisons of lotic faunas for several reasons. Foremost, as in practically any other biological habitat, Northern Hemisphere faunas are far better documented than those from the Southern Hemisphere. Recently though, there has been a rapid increase in the number of identified species for certain taxonomic groups as biologists explore more of the world's streams and rivers (e.g. in Asia and South America). Second, some taxonomic groups are better known than others, not least because more professional taxonomists work on them or they are easier to identify. For this reason, Coleoptera are better known than Ceratopogonidae (dipterans also known as 'no-see-ums'). Furthermore, with increasing amounts of data, gaps between morphologically distinct species sometimes tend to fill up with 'new species' showing intermediate characteristics, shedding doubt over existing taxonomies.

In regions where our knowledge is reasonably satisfactory for major groups, some obvious biogeographic patterns have begun to emerge. These show variation in species richness along geographical and altitudinal gradients, between islands and mainland, and between recently glaciated areas and areas not previously or recently affected by ice (see previous section). One example is the much reduced diversity of most freshwater groups in the northern and western parts of Europe in comparison with continental Europe. At the extremes, northernmost Scandinavia and western Ireland and Iceland, the fauna is accordingly the least diverse. Ireland, for example, has perhaps 75% of the taxa of Great Britain (McCarthy, 1986).

Aquatic organisms have played an important role in the interpretation of the geological history of the world, particularly concerning plate tectonics. Brundin (1988) has examined the taxonomic relatedness between stream-living chironomids from South America, South Africa, Australia, New Zealand, and Southeast Asia, and demonstrated that South Africa separated from Antarctica at a comparatively very early stage in the break-up of the southern continent, Gondwanaland. This conclusion was based on phylogenetic analyses of the subfamilies Podonominae, Aphroteniinae, and Diamesinae. Brundin showed great similarities between South American species and those from New Zealand and Australia. Some of the New Zealand groups, which all have their closest relatives in South America, exhibited pleisomorphy (primitive characters) and other indications of long isolation. The original connection was via Western Antarctica to Andean parts of South America. Studies of the Australian species showed that the bridge to South America went via Patagonia and East Antarctica, and that this was interrupted comparatively late. A similar conclusion can be drawn from analyses of the mayflies (Edmunds, 1972).

Tropical versus temperate faunas

As pointed out earlier, stream animals show great similarities across the world. Often different species belonging to the same genus play a similar role in geographically distant areas. However, one must take care not to overgeneralize as there are also clear biogeographic differences.

We discussed the latitudinal diversity gradients earlier (pp. 207–8) and while stream faunas have been seen as an exception to the general pattern of increase in diversity towards the tropics, there is a definite risk that the diversities of tropical streams are greatly underestimated. This could have at least two explanations. First, tropical running waters may have had a more diverse fauna in the past which has become depleted through human activities, more so possibly because of higher sensitivity to disturbances than corresponding faunas at higher latitudes that are more resilient to disturbance. Second, taxonomic knowledge about the lotic fauna is far more limited for tropical than for temperate systems, and very few tropical systems have been studied in detail. There can also be little doubt that as we explore more of the tropical river systems our estimates of the biodiversity of tropical lotic species will climb, just as it has for terrestrial organisms. Looking at specific groups of animals shows clearly that it is hard to generalize on temperate–tropical gradients. For instance, while the number of known blackfly species is higher in the neotropical than in the Nearctic region, the number of afrotropical species is lower than in the Palaearctic region.

Geographic ranges

Lotic invertebrates have geographical distributions ranging from very small to very large. The mechanisms underlying such variation are not known and are un-doubtedly complex. One factor certainly plays an important role—the capacity for dispersal. This is why many cosmopolitan species are often found in groups which can disperse passively as a part of the 'aerial plankton'. These are generally small taxa which frequently have drought-resistant stages and include animal groups such as cladocerans and ostracods. Small insects, like many chironomids and simuliids, are also likely to disperse widely in a passive manner. Extensive distributions may also be found among strong flying species, including odonates and caddisflies.

It is not obvious what factors make certain species rare while others are common. In fact, the rarity of a species may be defined in many different ways, such as with respect to local population size, to habitat specificity or to geographical range, which in different combinations provide seven forms of rarity (Rabinowitz, 1981). Freshwater taxa with a world-wide distribution do occur, although this is not common for most groups. Many oligochaetes belong to this category as do some ostracods, midges, and dytiscid beetles. Such cosmopolites are also generalists in relation to habitat requirements and probably are never truly just lotic. Many species have also been introduced by humans, and some of them now have nearly global distributions, such as the brown and rainbow trout. Rare species, on the other hand, may be vulnerable in the sense that small populations are more likely to go extinct. Nevertheless, there are several examples of very small populations that must have successfully persisted as such over very long periods of time. Examples include *Chlorolestes draconicus*, a damselfly species in South Africa, and the Mount Donna Buang wingless stonefly *Rickoperla darlingtoni* in Australia.

Hot spots and cold spots

Some areas of the world appear to be virtual hot spots, having very high diversities of at least some groups. One example is the number of freshwater mussels in North America in general and in the drainage area of the Mississippi in particular, which is much higher than anywhere else. This is thought to reflect the fact that freshwater mussels first developed in this area and subsequently dispersed. In contrast, oceanic islands have depauperate faunas. This has classical island–biogeographic explanations, which primarily involve the island size, distance from mainland, and geological age (see below). Clearly, few freshwater organisms tolerate the high salinity of sea water, making the dispersal to islands problematic. The island faunas therefore consist of species, or derivatives of species, which either were present on islands before they became disconnected from continents or that have managed to disperse over water. If colonization was historical, very remote faunas can have relict elements of taxa that have become extinct in the source areas. Others may have adaptively radiated into new species. The older the islands, the greater the representation of these categories. Therefore, younger islands, or those exposed to recent glaciations, are both species-poor and have widely distributed species.

Dispersal capacity is obviously a central feature for the successful colonization of islands by stream-living organisms as mentioned in the previous section. The strong flying odonates may be present within a diverse community, whereas weak fliers such as stoneflies and mayflies are often virtually absent. The mechanisms of dispersal in the latter category include wind transport of females or possibly eggs, and 'hitch-hiking' on the feet or bodies of birds (a known dispersal mechanism for amphipods as well). For small organisms spending their entire life in water and with desiccation-tolerant eggs, as is the case in ostracods, wind dispersal of eggs is most likely. In studies on rarity, dispersal capacity, such as expressed in wing character-istics, can be important for species with restricted distribution, especially if their habitats are of a temporary nature. Various forms of short-wingedness (brachyptery) or lack of wings (aptery) occur, particularly in water bugs and stoneflies.

The capacity to establish after dispersal is another important factor. Successful colonizers must be able to cope with the abiotic and biotic factors present, and the initial problem of building up a viable population must be overcome. Many colonization events certainly fail because of lack of mating opportunities and hence absence of reproduction.

Island stream faunas

Islands are rewarding areas to study from both ecological and biogeographical points of view, because they have species-poor biotas which have developed under a lower impact of predation, competition, and disease than continental biotas. In such simplified systems, it is often easier to unravel the mechanisms underlying many of the ecological processes.

Few researchers of streams and rivers have taken the opportunity to study biogeographic processes in islands other than the species–area relationships we discussed above. In a study on freshwater invertebrates in the Canary Islands, Malmqvist *et al.* (1997) showed that ostracods behave very much like terrestrial ferns from a biogeographic perspective. They have very low endemicity, which may be explained by long-distance jump dispersal of diaspores; the drought-resistant ostracod eggs are of a similar size to fern spores (i.e. about 0.1 mm), and may be readily dispersed via wind. Moreover, ostracods are widely partheno-genetic and island species of ferns are most often hermaphrodites or have self-compatible gametophytes. At the other end of the spectrum, Canarian freshwater beetles have a high degree of endemic species (about 75%) and much stronger relationships with those factors which are often considered of paramount import-ance in biogeographic contexts, such as island area, habitat diversity, distance to mainland, and island age.

On isolated insular streams, some taxa are missing because of palaeobio-geographic events and dispersal barriers. These absences leave gaps in food webs that are filled by other species (Covich, 1988). In the Caribbean, for example, predaceous stoneflies are absent in headwaters but their functional equivalents are juvenile palaemonid shrimps and crabs. Net-spinning caddis and blackflies are absent in some insular montane riffle microhabitats, but they are replaced by high densities of filter-feeding atyid shrimps.

These kinds of findings illustrate that the functions carried out by organisms are more important than the actual organism itself to the processes in streams and rivers. Man, through his various activities, has clearly influenced the patterns and processes of many ecosystems around the world and rivers and streams are no exception. In the final chapter, we will turn to these more applied issues.

9 The use, abuse, and conservation of running waters

Rivers all over the world have supported the growth of human civilization since the first towns appeared some 7000 years ago (Meybeck, 1996) but as a result of this growth and the diversification of activities, most of the world's rivers have been negatively affected. Nearly thirty years ago, H.B.N. Hynes (1970) wrote '… human activity has profoundly affected rivers and streams in all parts of the world to such an extent that it is now extremely difficult to find any stream which has not been in some way altered and probably quite impossible to find any such river'. The situation has not improved to any great extent to the present day and has, if anything, deteriorated further in many parts of the world. What has improved is our understanding of the changes we have wrought, the factors causing them and to some small degree, how we can prevent future impacts and start rehabilitating damaged systems.

The most dramatic effects have involved the continuous and directed changes in water chemistry through eutrophication and acidification, the long-term alterations to stream and river morphology and hence habitats through flow regulation, channelization, lowering of water tables and destruction of riparian zones, and the introduction of exotic species. These effects can operate at the tributary catchment of even entire river basin scale. Accidental or intentional point source pollution events generally occur at the reach scale and act as short-term disturbances. These have also increased as rivers are becoming more important as receptacles for industrial and domestic effluents. Running waters are well known for their resistance to change and can, for example, self-clean over time or with distance downstream if the pollution input is not great. However, very extensive, concentrated and/or continuous inputs of pollutants overcome even this innate ability. The fact that we can use aquatic organisms as 'barometers' of change (e.g. through biotic indices) testifies to the potential impacts these chemical and physical agents can have. All is not yet lost, however, and the introduction of strict regulations and water quality directives, the emergence of legislation requiring environmental impact assessments prior to granting of development licences, and the rising importance of the concept of biological integrity as a national environmental goal, point towards the possibility of improving the current situation.

In the following sections, we will briefly discuss some of the more important applied issues including water resources, water regulation, pollution and species introduction, and conservation.

Water as a resource

Freshwater is probably the most important resource of mankind. Not only is it vital for terrestrial life but we consume water in such a range of activities that it can aptly be regarded as a 'pillar of our civilization' (Biswas, 1996). Although freshwaters are finite, and represent only a tiny fraction of the water on earth (p. 2), they are a renewable resource, continuously replenished by precipitation through the hydrological cycle. However, on a global scale, the majority of the total annual runoff returns to the sea and some is lost to seepage and evaporation, leaving approximately 9000 km^3 of runoff per year (22%) readily available for human exploitation (Biswas, 1996). Estimated global demand rose from 1360 km^3 in 1950, to 4130 km^3 in 1990 with the growth of human populations, increased standards of living in developed countries and with the intensification of industry and agriculture and is expected to reach 5190 km^3 by the year 2000 (WRI, 1992). Theroetically therefore, there should be sufficient waters to support an even larger human population. However, much of the world's water resources is not distributed in a useful way, with largest supplies usually in areas of lowest population density. Also, overall rainfall patterns around the world have become much more erratic over the past two decades, possibly related to global climate change, destruction of rainforests, and strengthening of the effects of the El Niño–Southern Oscillation events on the global weather patterns. In addition, the increasing urbanization and development of industry and agriculture have been accompanied by problems of reduced water quality and pollution, which further reduce the availability of usable water. There are thus many areas, predictably in the more arid zones (like Africa and the Middle East) but more surprisingly also in parts of Europe, that are currently suffering (such as Poland, Romania, Ukraine), or will suffer in the future (such as Greece, Turkey) from water scarcity. The annual runoff per head of population is the key. In Ireland, for example the value is 15–20 000 m^3, in Scandanavia >20 000m^3 but in the United Kingdom only 1000–3000 m^3 and in Germany <1000 m^3. Even within a country, there are regional differences. In northern Europe, for example, western regions have higher annual runoff than eastern ones. The development of water conservation, recycling and management plans is therefore seen as vital. The importance of freshwater to the future of mankind has been recently highlighted by Cohen (1995) and in this context it is becoming increasingly important to view water as an economic resource in its own right.

Sources of water

To utilize the rainfall effectively involves interrupting the hydrological cycle by collecting it as surface water or extracting it from groundwaters. Water can be abstracted through intakes or pumping stations on streams and rivers or piping from suitable natural lakes or artifically created storage reservoirs. Groundwaters can be collected from natural springs or by constructing wells. Desalination of sea water offers an additional, albeit expensive, source of water especially for coastal arid countries (e.g. in the Middle East).

The most suitable areas for utilizing existing lakes or for delaying runoff to the sea by creating reservoirs are in the mountains. Here, the natural systems are oligotrophic and less polluted, rainfall tends to be higher and steep slopes facilitate abstraction due to the large head of water available for gravity feed. Usually, however, these sources are far from the areas where the water is needed. Groundwaters are another generally clean source, but overexploitation leads to a drop in the water table, and replenishment of groundwater supplies is far slower than for surface waters. Lowland rivers are a much less desirable source, as abstraction requires pumping and water is often polluted or carries a high suspended solid load, thus requiring pre-treatment.

These sources are often linked through management schemes. The flow of rivers can be regulated by the addition of water from reservoirs or groundwaters or alternatively water can be withdrawn from rivers at peak flows for storage in reservoirs or refilling of groundwaters. The relative importance of the various sources does vary from one country to another.

Main water uses

One can divide the main water uses (also termed *consumer processes*) into two broad categories: abstraction and instream uses (Table 9.1) which we will briefly deal with in turn. The pattern of use varies within different regions and changes with the degree of development of countries. Non-industrialized countries would use water resources for domestic supply, irrigation, transport, waste transportation, and exploitation of biological resources, while the most industrialized countries would exploit the water resources more completely. Consequently, the average amount of water used per capita per day will vary from 7000 litres in countries like the United States to <100 litres in developing countries such as Laos (Biswas, 1996).

Abstraction of water

Domestic supply: At its simplest, this would involve manual abstraction directly from the source, but at its most sophisticated, it requires reservoirs, river regulation schemes, water treatment, and extensive distribution grids to users. Some examples of water consumption for various household activities are given in Table 9.2.

Table 9.1 Main water uses (consumer processes) which can be divided into those involving abstraction and those based within the river

Abstraction	Instream uses
Domestic supply	Hydroelectric power generation (HEP)
Industry: manufacturing	Transport/navigation
Industry: cooling	Flood control and water storage
Irrigation	Waste transportation
Flushing of canals	Exploitation of biological resources
Diversion between catchments	Recreation and culture

The need is for adequate and stable quantities of clear water, free from harmful chemicals, disease organisms, and objectionable odour and taste. While it is available to a large extent from headwaters and groundwaters, it is less so near the centres of heavy population. In developing countries increased urbanization is associated with sanitation and drinking water supply problems due to pollution. This is accompanied by an increase in the incidence of a range of debilitating diseases such as bilharzia, amoebic dysentery, and cholera. In developed countries too, pollution of lowland rivers and lakes, and the need for water recycling to meet demands, has led to the requirement for water treatment to ensure quality of drinking water meets certain standards imposed by international and national law (such as the World Health Organization standards). Such treatment involves sieving, coagulation of salts, sedimentation, fine sand filtration, and sterilization (using chlorine or ozone). Sometimes 'softening' is carried out when waters have a high bicarbonate or sulphate content, or lime is added to prevent corrosion of pipes if waters are acidic.

Industrial abstraction: Commercial and industrial use varies tremendously with the product and the process (Table 9.2). The basic requirement is for a regular supply of cheap water of the appropriate quality. Smaller industries can be supplied from the domestic networks but larger ones often have their own abstraction source. Water can be used directly in processing of goods or in cooling machinery.

Table 9.2 Examples of water use for domestic, agricultural, and industrial activities. (Data from Cunningham and Saigo, 1990; Biswas, 1996 and Kiely, 1997)

Activity or product	Consumption (litres)
Domestic	
Bath	100–150
Shower (per 5 min)	100
Clothes wash	75–100
Cooking	30
Toilet flush	10–15
Industrial	
US automobile	400 000
1 kg steel	150–250
1 kg synthetic fibre	2000
1 kg paper	900
1 newspaper	500–1000
Agricultural	
1 egg	150
1 loaf bread	600
1 kg beef	16 600

Cooling of power stations is also important, although the majority of water tends to be taken from large lowland rivers or estuaries.

Irrigation: It is estimated that on a global scale more than two-thirds of all water drawn from surface resources and aquifers is used in the irrigation of crops. The demand has increased dramatically over the past 200 years from about 8 million hectares of irrigated land in 1800 to over 250 million hectares in the present day (Biswas, 1996). Most of the irrigation water is subsequently lost to the atmosphere through evaporation and transpiration. Irrigational water supplies tend to be more seasonal than domestic ones and demand tends to be greatest when regeneration of storage reserves is lowest. In arid regions agriculture is only possible if adequate water is available for irrigation. In Egypt, for example, nearly 88% of the nation's available water is used in irrigation (Newson, 1994). To meet the demand water regulation and creation of reservoirs is vital and these have their own problems as we will see later. Irrigation itself can also lead to water logging and high soil salinity, as well as providing habitats for vectors of tropical diseases such as mosquitoes (malaria) and snails (bilharzia).

Diversion between catchments: The supply–demand imbalance we discussed earlier means that local water resources are not able to meet demand at all times. For example, most rainfall in the United Kingdom falls in the west and north, and most excess rainfall (leading to surface runoff) occurs in winter, yet regions of high population and intensive industry are found in areas of low rainfall and demand for water is greatest in the summer (Mason, 1991). Similar problems are apparent throughout the world. Aside from regulating rivers through dams, etc. (see below) redistribution networks have been established to transfer water between catchments. In one example, the desert lands of southern California get most of their supply from northern California by means of a man-made aqueduct hundreds of kilometres long. Such diversion programmes are also used to supplement reservoirs and hydroelectric power schemes (see later).

Within-stream uses

Hydroelectric power (HEP): Electricity is generated using the force of gravity on water to drive turbines, usually involving storage reservoirs where water can be augmented from neighbouring catchments. The water quality is less important than the quantity and the head available. Small-scale systems are being established in many places which feed into the local electrical supply grid, but often river regulation is established for multiple purposes, including HEP and public supplies. In Sweden, HEP contributes 40–50% of the electricity supply and in Norway almost 100%.

Transport and navigation: Inland rivers are important for human transport particularly in countries through which large rivers flow. In mainland Europe, for example, the Rhine and Danube rivers are major navigational routes, serving many large inland cities in several countries and carrying huge quantities of cargo. The main requirements are for an adequate discharge that can maintain a navigable depth in the channel. Often, significant instream modifications are carried out, including construction of weirs and locks, dredging, and channel-ization to deepen and widen channels and construction of canals to extend the navigation networks

Flood control and storage: Both these processes involve major water regulation schemes. Control of floods involves any or a combination of construction of dams, dredging and canalization, flood bank and levee construction, and water weed control. Water storage also requires instream dams that are built to equilibrate water resources through the year. Because of its importance we will consider flow regulation in more detail in the next section.

Waste transportation: Domestic, industrial, and agricultural consumer processes produce large quantities of waste products for which natural water courses offer cheap and readily available conduits for disposal. Sewage and industrial effluent discharges are the most obvious and almost inevitably lead to some level of pollution of the receiving waters. This topic will also be explored in a later section.

Exploitation of biological resources: Many of the larger rivers support commercially viable populations of animals, particularly in terms of fisheries. Most rely on native species, but some fisheries are based on introduced species. The temperate commercial fisheries use traps or netting to capture catadromous and anadromous fish such as shad, salmon, trout, and eels. In tropical Asia, the cyprinids are the most important food fish, particularly the major carps in India, Indonesia, Malaysia, and China, which have been spread throughout the region by man (Dudgeon, 1995). Gouramies and catfish form a significant fishery in Thailand and Vietnam (Lowe-McConnell, 1970). Most fish production in large rivers is associated with floodplain habitats which are used extensively by fish for reproduction (see pp. 127–8). Water regulation schemes and flood control measures can thus have significant detrimental effects on such fisheries as shown by developments on the River Ganges (Natarajan, 1989).

Other resources are also exploited such as shellfish (largely in lower reaches and estuaries), mink and beaver for fur, and reeds like *Phragmites* for cellulose and thatch roofing. In addition to the exploitation of natural populations, the development of freshwater aquaculture has grown. Fish farms require suitable water sources, depending on the fish species (mainly salmonid-based in Europe and Scandinavia, and cyprinid in Asia). They also require access to natural waterbodies to remove effluents.

Recreation and culture: Freshwater systems often act as a focus for recreational activities, particularly in developed countries. These include angling, sailing, water skiing, bathing, and hunting. The conservation of features of scientific and cultural interest and aesthetic quality is also important. and can contribute significantly to tourism and thus can make a significant economic contribution to a region. Natural fisheries are often augmented by hatchery rearing and stocking (e.g. salmonids) or supplemented with introduced, exotic species (e.g. the zander in the United Kingdom) to promote angling. However, some recreational activi-ties can have detrimental effects on river and stream ecosystems (see pp. 238–9).

The management of water resources

Any particular river system is likely to be subject to a number of different consumer processes at the same time, each with their own, and often conflicting, requirements for water quantity and quality. Abstraction for irrigation and instream uses such as transportation, HEP, and waste disposal does not sit well with preserving the native flora and fauna, maintaining fish and wildlife habitat, maximizing production of recreational or commercial species for harvest, and maintaining a suitable quality of water for human consumption. The adverse pressures on the quality of the aquatic environment are particularly marked in the technologically more advanced countries, where the range of requirements for water resources is increasing in parallel with demands. Conflicts are exacerbated where water systems are shared by two or more countries. This occurs in over 200 river basins around the world (Biswas, 1996). For example, the River Danube joins eight European states with tributaries in twelve countries. The River Ganges is shared by India and Bangladesh while nine African countries compete for water from the River Nile. There are examples where whole communities are being deprived of their water resources simply because practically all the water has been diverted for use in upstream areas, leaving only a trickle of water in the old river channel (e.g. the River Jordan in the Middle East). Similarly, countries located downstream may receive all the waste products dumped in the river by countries upstream. Water conservation and management schemes, which must be established at the river basin level, attempt to preserve, control, and develop water resources to ensure adequate and reliable supplies of a suitable quality for all consumer processes in the most suitable and economic way. They should involve recycling and treatment of waste water, pollution prevention, carefully designed river regulation and storage schemes, as well as protection of riparian and aquatic habitats.

Water management has been supported by legislative instruments all over the world, such as the 1972 Clean Water Act in the United States, which had the objective 'to restore and maintain the chemical, physical, and biological integrity of the nation's rivers' (Jackson and Davis, 1994). Biological integrity in this context is defined as the 'capability of supporting and maintaining a balanced, integrated, adaptive community of organisms, having a composition and diversity comparable to that of the natural habitats in the region' (Frey, 1977). To some extent the problems arise from the need to recycle water and the inevitable input of wastes of varying types during its use that lead to an alteration of the natural water chemistry of the system. One approach towards maintaining biological integrity has been to attempt to eliminate chemical toxicity by imposing legally binding standards on effluent discharge (set at national, regional, or even local levels) and on maintaining the chemical quality of receiving waters through water treatment.

For any of the consumer processes we discussed earlier, there are a set of requirements regarding the quality of water to be used. These are usually related to concentrations of various chemicals, suspended material, and bacterial content. If water fulfils these requirements or standards, it can be said to be of good quality for that particular consumer process. Domestic supply requires the most stringent standards and highest water quality. In the European Union this is governed by two directives, one for surface waters and one for groundwaters (Kiely, 1997). These cover over 100 different chemical and microbial parameters. The 1974 Safe Drinking Water Act and 1989 Surface Water Treatment Rules set standards at a national level in the United States and similar legislation exists throughout the world, largely driven by the World Health Organization's water quality criteria. In contrast, use of waterways for navigation or industrial cooling can be met with waters of the poorest quality. However, to manage the freshwater ecosystem for multiple consumer processes, water quality needs to be maintained at the highest level demanded by the most stringent user. Chapman (1992) gives a detailed overview of water quality issues and standards and Kiely (1997) discusses water and waste water treatment processes used to meet these standards.

But maintaining chemical water quality cannot by itself safeguard biological integrity. A range of factors such as loss of habitats, bioaccumulation of pollutants at low concentrations, manipulation of surface and groundwaters, nutrient enrichment from diffuse agricultural sources, atmospheric deposition of pollutants (such as acid rain), and introduction of exotic species can all have strong negative effects. We will explore some of these in the next few sections.

The consequences of water regulation

Streams and rivers provide the important natural resources of water and potential energy. One way of ensuring reliable sources of both is to dam upland rivers. Dams create reservoirs of water for domestic supply, irrigation and industry, harness its energy to allow the generation of hydroelectric power, and can potentially solve the problem of flooding of downstream settled floodplains by regulating the natural patterns of flow. Most of the large northern rivers of the world in particular are affected by flow regulation for one or more of these uses. New and often controversial dams continue to be built elsewhere. Perhaps the most controversial is the massive Three Gorges dam on the Yangtze river in China, which is due for completion in 2009.

Upstream effects of dams

When a barrier is put across a river, the ecological conditions change dramatically for some distance upstream as the aquatic system essentially switches from a river to a lake. Deposition of fine sediments on to the original river substrate can result from the reduction of flow rate behind the dam. This can have dramatic consequences, as seen in the destruction of populations of the giant freshwater mussel for several kilometres upstream of the Roseires dam on the Blue Nile (Hammerton, 1972). The gradual decomposition of drowned terrestrial vegetation by bacteria both releases nutrients but also decreases oxygen levels, possibly leading to deoxygenation of bottom waters. The production of suspended inorganic iron and manganese hydroxides or dissolved hydrogen sulphide can result from such conditions. The reduction of current, the retention of suspended organic matter, and release of nutrients produce the right conditions for dramatic increases in primary production of the waterbody. Following filling of the Sennar and Roseires dams on the Blue Nile, for example, there was a 10- to 200-fold increase in phytoplankton over a 650 km upstream stretch of the river (Hammerton, 1972).

Dams also cut linkages between upstream and downstream which can have serious consequences for fish migration by creating barriers to species that breed in headwater streams. This has been particularly important for salmonids. The introduction of fish ladders, which break the ascent past a dam to a manageable series of stepped pools, can help, but they are no panacea. As a last resort it may be necessary for the fisheries authority to catch salmon below the dam and physically transport the fish upstream. Although this practice helps the overall fish production, it is unsatisfactory and indeed costly. Another way to maintain a fishery in a regulated river is to undertake an introduction programme of hatchery-reared fish. Large numbers may be released upstream of the dam, but problems still arise during downstream migration when the smolts (young salmon) are trying to return to sea. Modification of the design or operating procedures of dams and hydroelectric power (HEP) stations are required or the alternative is again physical transportation, this time downstream. Hatcheries in Sweden and Finland rear salmon smolts that are released at the river mouths to compensate for the losses caused by HEP exploitation. Of course, this does not benefit the river, but helps to sustain the salmon fishery in the Baltic Sea.

The changes in rivers upstream of dams also heralds the unwelcome appearance of pest and nuisance species. The introduced water fern *Salvinia molesta* is one such species that has rapidly colonized many African rivers upstream of dams. It severely impedes navigation and fishing and affects water quality largely through indirect deoxygenation beneath the weed cover. Pest insects are also favoured under the new environmental conditions, such as the biting blackfly (Simuliidae) whose adults can carry river blindness (onchocerciasis) in Africa and tropical Latin America.

Downstream effects of dams

Downstream of dams, the river tends to lose much of its dynamic nature as flow patterns are mediated and more regular, although they can also become more extreme. A number of other physical changes also take place.

Flow patterns

Where water is abstracted from a dammed river, then clearly overall river discharge downstream of the dam will be reduced. This can be very dramatic, as in the Nile, when following closure of the Aswan dam in 1964, annual flow decreased to 10% of the previous discharge (Hargrave, 1991). The Colorado river in the United States has seen just as dramatic a reduction over time (Fig. 9.1) and a similar situation has occurred for rivers draining into the Aral Sea (see Fig. 2.3, p. 24). Flow regimes below the dams are also altered, but the new regime depends on the use of the reservoir. Flood-mitigation dams store peak discharges that would normally overflow the channel downstream. Reservoirs used for domestic

Fig. 9.1 The impact of water abstraction from the Colorado river in the United States. The histogram shows the volume of water remaining after abstraction demands are satisfied and illustrates the gradual reduction of river flow over time as abstraction has increased. (Redrawn from Newson, 1994.)

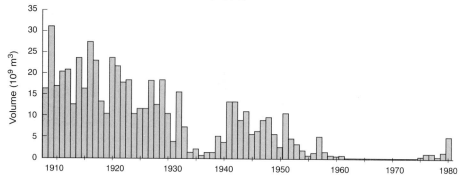

abstraction are built to attempt to even out supply over the year, again by storing water during high flows and augmenting supply downstream during periods of low flow. Reservoirs used for irrigation supply and HEP also store water during high runoff periods for release when demands are highest. In rivers regulated for HEP, typically the seasonal and diel dynamics of flow below the dam reflect patterns of electricity demand. Thus in Sweden, flow regimes are altered with a reduced spring flood and elevated winter discharge compared to 'normal'. HEP production that responds to peak electricity demand also imposes an 'on-off' pattern on the natural flow regime as turbines are brought on line to satisfy peak electricity demands. This often leads to high daytime/weekday flows and low night-time/weekend flows.

A combination of regulation and abstraction can thus reduce discharge below a dam to a fraction of the natural flow and in some areas with extended dry seasons, river channels below dams can be completely dry for part of the year. These changes can be seen in Fig. 9.2, where in regulated but unreduced flow systems, there are larger short-term variations and flow reductions than in unregulated rivers but lower monthly variation, evening out the natural spring flood following snow melt. In regulated but reduced flow systems, there are long periods of low and stable flow, interspersed by short periods of vastly increased and highly variable flow (purge flows).

Temperature, sediment loads, and other factors

As we saw in Chapter 3, temperature is important in freshwater systems, and the location of reservoirs on river channels can significantly alter temperature regimes. In summer if the outflow is from surface waters of the reservoir, the downstream system can be warmer than in unregulated rivers, and can often have high oxygen levels (a result of the high plankton activity). On the other hand, outflows from deeper waters may be low in oxygen (see above) and certainly relatively colder, especially if the reservoir is thermally stratified. The general pattern for impounded rivers in the United Kingdom is for a decrease in the

Fig. 9.2 Hydrographs for selected sites (rivers (a) Vindel, (b) Ljungan, (c) Faxalven, (d) Giman, (e) Langan, and (f) Skellefte) that are subjected to different degrees of regulation and abstraction to show the effects on the flow regime. (From Englund and Malmqvist, 1996.)

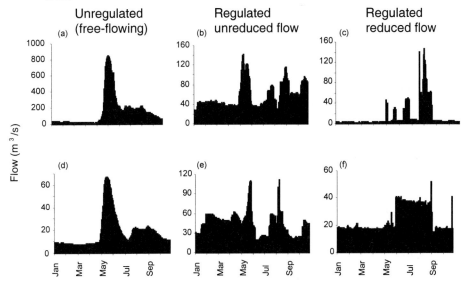

amplitude of monthly mean temperatures and a lag in the seasonal cycle of temperature change compared to unregulated rivers (Crisp, 1987). One of the most detailed studies on the effects of impoundment on thermal regimes has been carried out by Webb and Walling (1993) over 10 years on the River Haddeo below Wimbleball dam in southern England. The overall effects were an increase in mean water temperature (on average by 0.5° C), elimination of freezing conditions and reduction in the degree of variation between temperature extremes (by between 0.1–3.7° C) in comparison to a nearby unregulated river. The most marked influence on the seasonal cycle was the delay in the autumnal decline, and temperatures between September and December could be more than 4° C warmer than in an unregulated river. The magnitude of diel variation was also halved compared to an unregulated river. The effects on the biota can be quite dramatic, as we will see later. What was also important from this study, was that the effects were still evident 5 km downstream of the dam, and that there was considerable variation from year to year, as the ranges above indicate.

As we mentioned earlier, much of the sediment load carried by the river is deposited behind the dam, and downstream levels can be significantly reduced. In glacial streams, such as in the Swiss Alps, suspended sediment peaks can exceed 2000 mg l^{-1}, but below dams, they typically fall to <100 mg l^{-1} and even <20 mg l^{-1} further downstream (Petts and Bickerton, 1994). However, during 'purge' flows, when huge volumes of water are released, dramatic sediment pulses of between 20 000 and 120 000 mg l^{-1} are generated which can have devastating effects. Not only is the amount of sediment altered by impoundment, but the nature of the suspended organic matter changes also, from largely allochthonous detritus to autochthonous plankton (phytoplankton and zooplankton from the reservoir) which can persist for long distances in large rivers.

A number of other changes that result from damming should also be mentioned as they can impact on the biology of the regulated river. For example, the downstream channel morphology can be altered. Impounded glacial streams change from cold, turbid, and torrential braided channels to narrower, single-thread meandering channels below dams (Gurnell, 1983). Water regulation with flow reduction in northern Swedish rivers leads to a 50% increase in distances between rapids (Malmqvist and Englund, 1996). Temporal fluctuations in depth which often accompany water regulation can lead to difficulties in the establishment of riparian flora of the downstream river and littoral vegetation of the upstream reservoir. In many parts of the world, there is a diverse and broad riparian zone that is maintained by annual flood disturbances. Under strong river regulation, this zone shrinks and the surrounding forest expands towards the river margins (Nilsson, 1996).

Finally, it is worth mentioning that the downstream effects are not just confined to the river system. The regulation of water decreases or eliminates regular inundation and deposition of nutrient-rich sediments on the floodplain, breaking the lateral links between channel and land in the lower reaches of the river. This can have profound effects on both aquatic and terrestrial ecosystems. But even more serious and on a larger scale, are the potential effects on coastal marine systems. This is clearly shown by the tremendous impact of the Aswan dam on the southeastern region of the Mediterranean Sea near the Nile Delta. Sediments previously transported downstream had counteracted the erosion of the delta by the sea and had provided nutrients to the marine system. The massive reduction in flow reaching the Mediterranean since construction of the dam has resulted in a gradual erosion of the Nile Delta, and secondly in a decrease in productivity of coastal waters and subsequent decline in important fisheries (Hargrave, 1991). Even more dramatic is the possibility that the reduced freshwater input into the Mediterranean could result in the loss of the freshwater barrier across the northern end of the Suez Canal to the Red Sea. Such a loss could lead to movement of species, in one direction or another, between the two seas, with potentially huge cascade effects. This illustrates an important link between freshwater and marine ecosystems.

Biological effects of damming

As we have seen, the physical effects of the regulation of flow on the river system can be dramatic, and it will come as no surprise that the effects of these perturbations will be equally dramatic on the biota. Petts (1984) has reviewed the whole subject quite thoroughly, so here we will simply provide a few examples to illustrate both the general patterns of response, but also the fact that such responses can be species-specific.

At worst, river regulation can lead to the extinction of species from the water course, as in the case of the turtle *Emys orbicularis* in the regulated upper Rhine (Thienemann, 1950). In contrast, certain taxa can be favoured downstream of dams, and a characteristic feature of impoundment outlets, just as for lake outlets, is the high population density of filter-feeding invertebrates due to improved food conditions associated with planktonic wash-out. Other significant community level changes can also occur following regulation. The effects of the Grand Dixence hydroelectric scheme in the Swiss Alps provide an example (Petts and Bickerton, 1994). Normally, glacial rivers are dominated by chironomids (see Chapter 4 and p. 199), and they tend to be turbid, cold (<4° C), with physically unstable channels. In the regulated rivers, immediately below the water intakes of the Grand Dixence, the streams are intermittent, flowing only during system purges and high floods, and are devoid of animals over approximately 1.5 km. Further downstream, the water abstraction scheme isolates glacial melt from the river, which is converted to a warmer, clearer and more stable channel, which in turn leads to increased diversity of invertebrates and an extended distribution of species to higher altitudes than normal.

A recent large-scale study in northern Sweden has investigated the impacts of river regulation with and without additional flow reduction due to abstraction. The general approach has been to examine species richness and abundance in rapid zones of unregulated rivers and from these data to predict the number of species and abundances that should occur in the regulated rivers. The deviation between observed and predicted values was then used as an indicator of the effect of flow regulation. For bryophytes, regulation and reduced flow led to a reduction of 22% in species richness and in regulated rivers without flow reduction a loss of 26%. Overall abundance of moss was unaffected but the abundances of some individual species did change (Englund *et al.*, 1997a). In particular, two *Fontinalis* species had lower abundance at sites with reduced flow, whereas two small species *Blindia acuta* and *Schistidium agassizii*, had higher abundance than normal at regulated but unreduced sites (Fig. 9.3a). In other studies the general pattern under conditions of reduced flow variation is for an increase in mosses and algae downstream of dams. The more stable conditions created by regulation can allow strong competitors to monopolize space (Moss, 1998).

From what we know about the influence of moss on macroinvertebrates (see pp. 42–4) such changes should lead to increases in invertebrate densities and production, as well as affecting retention of organic particles. In the Swedish sites, the picture was more complex. Species richness of invertebrates decreased by up to 38% (mean 7.5%) in regulated sites with reduced flow. There were no obvious effects in regulated but unreduced flow sites (Englund and Malmqvist, 1996). When broken down to functional feeding groups, it was apparent that the abundances of collectors and predators were reduced in both types of regulated rivers, but grazers declined only at sites with reduced flow (Fig. 9.3b). Shredders and filter-feeders were largely unaffected although in the latter group this resulted from a balance between a decrease in net-spinning caddis and an increase in simuliids, probably resulting from reduced predation and competition (Zhang, *et al.*, in press). The magnitude of flow variation seemed to be a very important factor here, particularly the maximum increase from one day to the next (i.e. the occurrence of single extreme events are critical). Turning to particular taxonomic groups, mayflies were generally more common in unregulated sites but individual species responded differently to distinctive regulation-related factors such as peaking flow regimes, reduced discharges, and increased constancy (Malmqvist and Englund, 1996). Net-spinning caddis can be influenced in different ways depending on the nature of regulation. Densities of hydropsychids can increase in relation to stable flow regimes, increased availability of high quality suspended food particles, and favourable temperature regimes below dams. On the other

Fig. 9.3 The effect of flow regulation and flow reduction on: (a) the abundance of five common bryophytes; (b) the species richness and abundance of macroinvertebrate functional feeding groups; (c) the abundance of four common net-spinning caddis species. The effects were calculated as the difference between observed numbers and those predicted from a model based on data from unregulated sites (the 0 line). Error bars represent 95% confidence intervals. (From Englund *et al.*, 1997*a*. Reproduced with kind permission of Elsevier Science; Englund and Malmqvist, 1996; and Englund *et al.*, 1997*b*, respectively.)

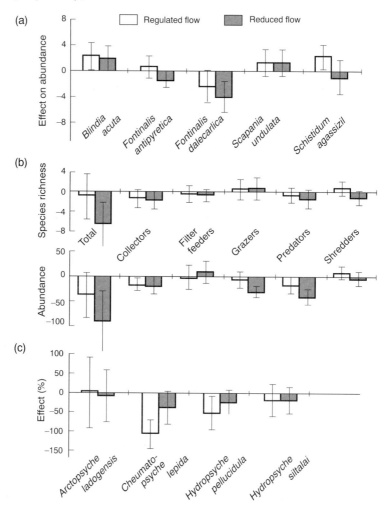

hand, reduced densities have been associated with violently fluctuating flow or release of bottom waters from the reservoir. In the Swedish study, abundance declined in both types of regulated rivers, but species richness declined only in those with reduced flow (Fig. 9.3c). Again individual species responded differently and timing of zero flow in relation to the life cycle was critical (Englund *et al.*, 1997*b*).

As well as changes to the flow regime, the temperature changes discussed above will influence the downstream biota below dams. Based on literature information on the biology of five insect species, Webb and Walling (1993) predicted what the likely influences of the temperature changes below Wimbleball dam might be. Somewhat surprisingly, the impact on invertebrates would probably be relatively small but quite variable from one year to the next and would depend a lot on when eggs were laid. For trout however, the effects were likely to be quite significant. Incubation time of eggs was predicted to be shorter and growth of fry faster in the regulated stream than in an unregulated one. In fact, 0+ fish were predicted to be up to 30% heavier at the end of their first year.

Overall, the effects of dams and water regulation are rather negative, but in the past, environmental concerns have always played second fiddle to economic benefits. However, perhaps attitudes are changing a little as objections to new developments grow stronger and there was a recent report that a dam on the Clyde River in Newport, Vermont had become the first to be removed on purely environmental grounds (Chatterjee, 1997).

Drainage and enhanced flows

In addition to water regulation schemes, the floodplains of most temperate rivers, both in Europe and the United States, have been greatly altered, and considerable sections of the river channels have been deepened, straightened, confined with embankments, and lined with concrete. Bankside vegetation and aquatic vegetation and debris are often also removed. Drainage of the land has been increased by digging smooth-walled ditches or drains, particularly during preparation for afforestation or agriculture. The major objective of much of this engineering work is to prevent over-bank flows and flooding of the surrounding land or to drain it; in other words to increase the capacity of the channel to carry more water more quickly. The effect is to shorten the response time from rainfall in the catchment to peak flow—the volume of runoff may be similar to that before such channelization or arterial drainage, but it leaves the land much faster. This is particularly important in urban areas, where storm drains remove rainfall. Former natural channels are often culverted underground or so completely constrained between concrete banks and beds that they are effectively open drains (Newson, 1994). Sewerage and storm drainage are usually separated but in some countries the latter is an integral part of the functioning of the former. In such situations when storms exceed a certain threshold size, the sewers spill their contents to the nearest water course causing a pollution incident.

The changes to the physical characteristics of the river channel have a huge range of effects on the lotic ecosystem. First, there is a marked reduction in habitat diversity, including the loss of riffles and pools and of overhead and instream cover. Loss of riparian vegetation reduces allochthonous inputs and the loss of the instream snags, removal of boulders, etc. by dredging, reduces the retentive ability of the system, So what little organic matter is available is not retained so effectively. Hydrographs are sharper during storm events. Pre-afforestation drainage, for example, can cause a reduction by as much as 50% to time to peak flow (Institute of Hydrology, 1984–7). This is accompanied by increased velocities during storms, especially in confined channels, leading to disturbances of the stream bed of greater than normal magnitudes. Channelization and arterial drainage, not suprisingly, lead to a decline in the diversity of communities, damage to natural fisheries (Hellawell, 1986), and often population crashes of semi-aquatic mammals such as the otter. The initial impacts tend to be more dramatic than longer-term ones if the altered channel is allowed to naturalize as a result of colonization by plants and animals. For example, even after a 5- to 7-fold decrease in abundance of fauna caused by dredging, one system recovered after a year (Crisp and Gledhill, 1970). But if the environment is catastrophically altered, or continually dredged, it will not return to anything like its natural state.

Although the modifications are designed to reduce flooding, under severe weather conditions flood-control procedures combined with human modification and degradation of catchment areas can lead to extreme flooding and sedimentation of abnormally long duration. The spectacular flooding episodes in the Mississippi and Missouri river basins in the United States during the summer of 1993 and spring of 1995, are clear examples of this. In effect, so much water entered these channelized and confined rivers that the embankments could not cope and broke down. These were not new phenomena. The US Congress created the Mississippi River Commission in 1879 to try and prevent such floods, but in 1882, a hundred-year flood broke the levees in 280 places (McPhee, 1989).

Flow rates can be increased not only by channelization and dredging but also through inter-basin transfer. As we mentioned in the earlier section, water demand often exceeds supply and one way to cope is to transfer water from one catchment to another. Some projects build canals, while others use natural stream channels to carry water to the recipient systems. Davies et al. (1992) reviewed such diverse projects in Africa, Australia, and United States, but we basically know relatively little about the effects on the carrier or recipient systems. One study did examine the impacts of short-term trial flows in Sister Grove Creek in Texas, which was being tested as a carrier stream for water from Lake Texoma to Lake Lavin, both man-made reservoirs. Not only did water flow increase in the creek but conductivity almost doubled with the input of transfer water. At some stations examined, fish assemblages differed markedly before and after trial flows but within the time-frame of the study, the effects were relatively minor for the fish fauna of the carrier stream as a whole (Matthews et al., 1996). Imagine, however, what might have happened in Russia had the extraordinary plans publicized a few years ago gone ahead to divert some of the great north-flowing Siberian rivers to the south for irrigation purposes. It is likely that inter-basin transfers will increase in the future, so clearly more work is needed to identify and ameliorate any possible detrimental effects.

Water pollution

Any change in the natural water quality implies pollution. Some natural events, such as hurricanes, mud flows, and torrential rainfall, can lead to local deterioration in water quality but most serious, longer-term and larger-scale water quality problems arise as a result of human activities. Pollution of the aquatic environment means the introduction by man, directly or indirectly, of substances or energy (heat) that result in deleterious effects. These may include harm to biological resources, hazards to human health, hindrance to instream aquatic activities, such as fishing, and impairment of water quality with respect to a desired consumer process, such as agriculture, industry, amenity, or domestic supply (Chapman, 1992). A pollutant, in turn, can be defined as 'a substance that occurs in the environment, at least in part, as a result of human activities, and which has a deleterious effect on the environment' (Moriarty, 1990). Pollution and water quality degradation can thus interfere with vital and legitimate water uses from local to international scales and, just as importantly, damage the nature and functioning of the natural ecosystem.

Pollution can be usefully divided into two categories: those that affect the physical environment in which organisms live and those that are directly toxic to the organisms themselves (Table 9.3). Some pollution incidents, such as accidental chemical spillage, act as true disturbances whereas others, such as excess nutrients leading to eutrophication, cause a longer-term directed environmental change. The resulting impacts and possibility of recovering to the previous state will be clearly different.

Water pollution has been the subject of a large number of books from the seminal text of Hynes (1960) to more recent texts such as Hellawell (1986), Mason (1991), Chapman (1992), and Haslam (1995), to name but a few. They consider both the nature and effects of river pollution as well as methods of monitoring pollution levels. We will not attempt a comprehensive coverage here but simply discuss a few of the more important issues and effects on the biology of streams and rivers.

Table 9.3 Categories of diffuse (d) and point source (p) pollutants that are either toxic or affect the physical environment in lotic ecosystems.

Toxic effects	Physical effects
Acids and alkalis (d,p)	Detergents (p)
Anions (e.g. sulphides, sulphates, cyanide) (p)	Domestic sewage and farm manures (p)
Metals (e.g. mercury, lead, aluminium) (p)	Food processing wastes (p)
Oil and oil dispersants (p)	Heat (p)
Organichlorines (e.g. pesticides and polychlorinated biphenols) (d,p)	Nutrients (d)
Organic toxic wastes (e.g. formaldehydes and phenols) (p)	
Radionuclides (p)	

Point sources

Point sources of pollutants refer to specific outfalls such as continuous discharges from sewage treatment works or industrial concerns, or where there is a known single point of entry, such as mine drainage or accidental spillages. These can be large-scale once-off events such as the dramatic toxic chemical spill into the River Rhine arising from the accident at the Sandoz Plant in Switzerland on 1 November 1986. This resulted in massive inputs of pesticides, solvents, and dyes (Capel et al., 1988). There were highly publicized fish kills, and a slug of highly polluted water that travelled downstream and led to the closure of all abstraction points in The Netherlands as the polluted water made its way down the river to the North Sea. Point sources can also be small scale, affecting just a few hundreds of metres to a few kilometres of stream reach. Dilution, chemical changes, and incorporation into sediments help reduce concentrations downstream. Recovery over time at the site of input and over space downstream will tend to track the reduction in concentration of the toxin and will also be influenced by the nature of the chemical itself (Yount and Niemi, 1990). Recovery times from chemical spills range from nearly instantaneous to greater than 10 years, but most studies indicate fairly rapid recovery (a few months to couple of years, Niemi et al., 1990). The effect of such toxic pollutants on the biota depends, of course, on the concentration, but also on the formulation of the chemical. Most heavy metals are only absorbed by organisms if they are in a methylated form, and only certain 'species' of metals with particular charges are toxic. Aluminium for example is toxic in the labile monomeric form, which only occurs in acidified streams of certain low pH levels. In addition, the persistence or half-life of the toxic chemical is important (the time to 50% of the compound disappearing or being changed to a non-toxic form).

The most serious pollutants to the ecosystem are those which are highly persistent. These can *bioaccumulate* in organisms and become *biomagnified* within the ecosystem. Bioaccumulation occurs due to the similarity between toxic compounds like heavy metals (such as zinc and copper) and essential trace elements that form part of the diet. These persistent chemicals may be dilute in the environment yet accumulate in various tissues of the organism and are not readily excreted. The toxic burden of organisms at lower trophic levels may not be so high as to cause serious problems, but the chemical can biomagnify up through the food chain as predators consume many prey and hence the concentration of the chemical increases, especially in top predators. The toxic pollutant may reach concentrations in the tissues that prove to be lethal or it may have sub-lethal effects at the genetic, biochemical, physiological, or behavioural levels which can have population effects. One of the more recent and controversial discoveries, for example, is the presence of what appear to be endocrine disrupters in sewage effluents that can mimic oestrogens and can lead to the feminization of a proportion of male fish in the population.

As tissue levels of many toxic pollutants relate to environmental levels, the organisms themselves can be used as bioindicators to monitor pollution. Benthic algae and bryophytes are good indicators of metal pollution (Melhaus *et al.*, 1978; Mouvet, 1985). Biomonitoring for trace metals using amphipod crustaceans has also been utilized (Amyot *et al.*, 1996). Changes in macroinvertebrate communities can be used to monitor metal pollution, because taxa vary in their sensitivity to exposure to metals. Herbivores and detritivores are generally more sensitive to copper than predators, and mayflies (especially heptageniids) and some stoneflies tend to be more sensitive than caddisflies and chironomids (Kiffney and Clements, 1994). Thus, in sites affected by acid mine drainage, there is usually a decrease in mayflies and communities tend to be dominated by caddis.

The inputs of sewage and industrial effluents on the other hand can be continuous, resulting in the establishment of a longitudinal succession of physical conditions and biota downstream of the outfall. This can be seen quite clearly for organic pollutants arising from sewage effluent discharge where the effluent makes up a considerable proportion of the stream volume. The diagrammatic representation of these downstream changes first illustrated in 1960 by Hynes is still

Fig. 9.4 A diagrammatic representation of the longitudinal zonation established downstream of the outfall of a continuous organic effluent discharge: (a) and (b) are physical and chemical changes; (c) changes in microorganisms and plants; (d) changes in larger organisms. (After Hynes, 1960.)

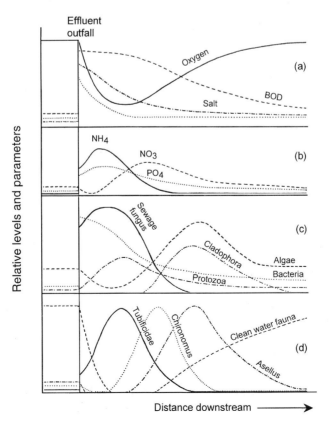

valid (Fig. 9.4). The main effect is a change to the physical environment, particularly the oxygen content, which 'sags' some way downstream of the outfall due to the activities of aerobic microbes breaking down the organic matter (a relatively slow process, hence the low point of oxygen concentration downstream of the outfall). The extent of the oxygen sag depends on the biological oxygen demand (BOD) of the effluent (the amount of oxygen consumed by a known volume of effluent over 5 days in the dark at $20°C$), the water temperature, the dilution of the effluents, the total organic load of the river, extent of re-aeration, the oxygen concentration, and the numbers and types of microbes. Severe organic pollution can lead to the total deoxygenation of a stretch of river. Nitrification of ammonium (NH_4) also occurs. In response to the physical features a longitudinal zonation or succession of microbes, algae, and animals is produced, with the most pollution-tolerant species nearest the outfall and gradual recovery of the pollution-sensitive, clean water, fauna further downstream as the physico-chemical environment recovers. These relationships between pollution levels and the stream or river community have been utilized in the development of a range of biotic indices, particularly successful for organic pollution, which are used in most of the developed countries to monitor water pollution (see Washington, 1984; Rosenberg and Resh, 1993; Giller *et al.*, 1997).

Diffuse sources

Control of point source pollution is at least practical, but pollutants that enter streams and rivers from diffuse sources are exceptionally difficult to deal with.

Eutrophication

Some of the most important pollutants are inorganic plant nutrients that arise from groundwater and surface runoff draining intensively managed agricultural land (from fertilizers and animal waste), in rainfall, or from catchments undergoing land use change (such as afforestation or deforestation) (see p. 49). Inputs of nitrates and phosphates have been shown to enhance primary production and cause the gradual eutrophication of many rivers, especially lowland rivers. Such eutrophication can also result from cumulative point sources of organic matter which are broken down to inorganic nutrients. But whatever the cause, the net result is a directed and continued change in physico-chemical conditions and in the biota. This tends to be quite long term, as seen in the River Seine in France, where one of the longest records of water quality shows that nitrate, ammonium and chloride concentrations have increased continuously since 1890, with a marked acceleration in the 1950s (Naves *et al.*, 1990). Increased plant nutrients can lead to extreme macrophyte growth, including *Ranunculus* and the large filamentous alga *Cladophora*, to large blooms of phytoplankton, or in the tropics to huge populations of the water hyacinth *Eichhornia crassipes*. The large increase in organic detritus generated by the enhanced primary production in turn leads to sedimentation and reduced dissolved oxygen levels. Invertebrate and fish assemblages are affected by these changes (particularly the reduced oxygen levels) and hence the whole food web can be altered over time. Invertebrate diversity may initially increase during the early stages of eutrophication (where primary production in streams can be boosted) but certainly in more eutrophic systems diversity is reduced. Similarly, salmonids and similar groups of fish that live in well-oxygenated waters will decline to be replaced by the more tolerant cyprinids. The changes we described earlier (Fig. 8.2, p. 197) in the tributaries of the River Rhine over the last eighty or so years are largely a result of gradual eutrophication. River restoration of the Rhine has involved a decrease in ammonium, phosphates and toxic metals since the peak in the 1960s and 1970s due to the introduction of sewage treatment works, the ban or reduction in phosphate-based detergents in Germany and Switzerland, and the decrease in industrial effluents. Yet nitrates continue to rise due to intensive agriculture (Meybeck, 1996).

Eutrophication can cause problems for the use of water resources, especially where river water is abstracted. High algal densities can block filters in water treatment/purification plants, high nitrate levels can pose serious health risks especially to young infants, and toxins produced by cyanobacteria have caused severe illness and even death to humans and livestock as well as wildlife.

Acidification

Eutrophication is generally a problem of the populated lowlands, but in the more remote upland regions, particularly for catchments lying on poorly weathered rocks and thin soils on poorly buffered geologies, acidification can be a problem (see pp. 47–8 and Table 3.6). This has been a major focus for political and scientific activity largely because of its transboundary nature, and even though the foundations of our understanding of acid deposition were set in the last century, its effects on soils, forests, and fisheries were not appreciated until the 1960s.

The primary cause is atmospheric pollution from the combustion of fossil fuels by power-generating plants and motor vehicles and from industrial processes all producing oxides of sulphur and nitrogen as well as from agricultural production of ammonia. These pollutants undergo chemical change in the atmosphere in the presence of water vapour leading to the production of acids (nitric and sulphuric) and hence acid rain (see Campbell and Lee, 1996 for a detailed discussion of these processes). Acid rain can reach a pH as low as 2.1, but the effect on running water systems depends on the nature of the catchment geology, soils, and vegetation as we discussed on pp. 45–6. Suffice to say at this point that catchments with a poorly buffered geology are sensitive to acidification and acid rain can reduce the pH of the streams and rivers, while others, with well-buffered geologies, are not affected. The presence of coniferous afforestation on sensitive catchments can exacerbate the problem (see Table 3.5). The effect has been most dramatic in those sensitive areas receiving atmospheric pollution, such as in Scandanavia, Scotland and Wales in the United Kingdom, and Canada.

The influence of acidification on surface waters in general has received considerable attention not only because of changes to water quality but also due to changes to the ecology of the system. Acidification has been shown to impact on

Fig. 9.5 The percentage frequency of macroinvertebrate family richness at 25 sites on moorland and afforested catchments illustrating the effect of acidification of afforested streams in sensitive regions of Wales, United Kingdom. (After Ormerod *et al.*, 1987*a*.)

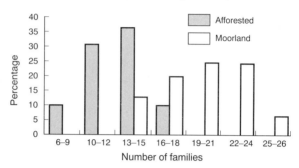

organisms from all trophic levels, including algae, macrophytes, micro- and macroinvertebrates, fish, amphibians, and riparian birds and there is a very extensive literature available. The effects are due to a combination of acidity (directly through physiological stress or indirectly through changes to food supply, habitat provision, or predation) and to the toxic (lethal or sub-lethal) effect of elevated aluminium leached from the surrounding soil (see p. 48). Seasonal variations in water chemistry and episodic pulse events are very important in this context. Under high flow conditions, particularly in winter, aluminium levels are generally at their highest, while pH and hardness levels are at their lowest. For example, in a Welsh stream on a sensitive afforested catchment, pH dropped from 6 to 4 and aluminium concentration increased by 1 mg l^{-1} over just 11 hours during a particular storm event (Gee and Stoner, 1989). As we saw on p. 54, the biota differs among sites which vary in pH and obviously acidification of a system will cause changes in line with these differences. Mean species richness and total species pools decrease with decreasing pH, and several plant and invertebrate species and families are absent from sites of low pH while others seem to be more tolerant. A clear example of the kind of impact on invertebrates is shown in Fig. 9.5. Changes in the geographic distribution of fish due to acidification are well described and characterized again by reduced diversity, and eels may be the only fish present in headwater streams with a pH <4.5. Most studies have dealt with the impact of aluminium exposure following acidification, not only to fish but also to benthic invertebrates and periphyton. In sensitive animals this effect may be due to accumulation of aluminium ions in ion-regulating organs, perhaps affecting osmoregulation (Vuori, 1996). Physical irritation of gills of fish and mayflies due to precipation of aluminium hydroxide may also affect respiration.

Prevention of acidification is difficult as the source of the problem is usually distant from the areas affected. Nevertheless, international co-operation has led to agreements by the polluting countries to reduce sulphur and nitrous oxide emission through, for example, the use of flu gas scrubbers (for desulphurization) on power stations, and of catalytic converters on vehicles. Otherwise, the only other avenue open is to 'cure' acidification on site through the use of liming of catchments or waters. The success has been equivocal—it seems to work for lakes as the carbonate is retained in the system but not so well for streams, which tend to flush out the added carbonate, and in many cases, liming itself acts as a significant disturbance. Liming the catchment though can have a longer term benefit.

Organochlorines

Some chemicals also enter rivers and streams from diffuse sources and of these the most serious are the organochlorines, such as pecticides like DDT and dieldrin and polychlorinated biphenyls (PCBs). PCBs in particular are transported over wide areas by winds and are washed into waterbodies with precipitation, or enter from landfill sites and sewage effluent. Like other organochlorines, they are highly persistent. In the Hudson river, New York state, levels of PCBs from a variety of sources amounted to over 1350 tonnes in the late 1970s (Clesceri, 1980). Most was actually held in the sediments and less than 0.1% was present in the biota, yet levels in three species of commercial fish exceeded those thought safe for human consumption and the large shellfish industry had to be closed. Sediment-based PCBs are taken up by riverine zooplankton and planktivorous fish, as well as bottom-living fish like eels (Larsson, 1984). Benthic invertebrates also bio-accumulate PCBs. Concentrations thus get biomagnified into top predators. Even in the relatively unpolluted environment of Ireland, quite significant levels of PCBs have been found in certain locations in dippers (O'Halloran *et al.*, 1993) and otters (Mason and O'Sullivan, 1993). The effects tend to be sub-lethal but particularly influence reproductive processes. Some authors even suggest that this has been a major cause of the decline of otters in Northern Europe (Mason, 1991).

The extent of pollution

The extent of pollution in running waters varies considerably on a global scale. Worst case scenarios have traditionally been found in countries which have a heavy industrial base but low levels of water management, and poor legal controls on discharges and water treatment facilities, such as parts of Eastern Europe where toxic pollution and organic waste levels are generally high. Areas of very high populations in developing countries can suffer from excessive organic pollution of rivers. But even the more developed countries with extensive water management schemes and rigorous legal frameworks for control of effluents and land use practices are not immune from pollution, largely due to the diffuse inputs

Table 9.4   Results of the water quality survey of the 2900 km baseline of Irish rivers.

Class		1971	1981	1986	1990
A	Unpolluted	2400(83)	2250(78)	2000(69)	1900(65)
B	Slightly polluted	150 (5)	324(11)	580(20)	570(20)
C	Moderately polluted	150 (5)	206 (7)	240 (8)	380(13)
D	Seriously polluted	200 (7)	120 (4)	80 (3)	50 (2)

Classes A to D refer to quality categories assigned on the basis of biotic indices developed by the Environmental Research Unit (now the EPA). Values are kilometres of river with percentages of surveyed rivers in parentheses. (From ERU Water Quality in Ireland, 1987–90 report.)

and extensive use made of rivers (see earlier), especially in lowland reaches. As an example, Table 9.4 presents the results of a large-scale survey of 2900 km of Irish rivers carried out over the period from 1971 to 1990. The general pattern over time, as it has been for most developed countries, is for a decrease in the extent of serious river pollution as a result of the implementation of legal controls but an increase in the extent of waterways suffering from slight to moderate pollution, hence a decrease in the proportion of waterways unpolluted. This is a cause of some concern world-wide, not only for human health, but also for the maintenance of diversity and ecosystem function in our natural streams and rivers.

The effects of tourism and sport fishing

As we mentioned a little earlier, freshwaters are often a focus for leisure activities. Local bankside activities such as angling, birdwatching, and picnicking usually have an insignificant direct effect on the invertebrate life in streams and rivers. Problems may arise, however, under certain circumstances. For instance, negative impacts can occur as a result of habitat change in the vicinity, from building works in or near the water, from pollution, or following the introduction or use of infected equipment (as seen in the transmission of the crayfish plague fungus from one system to another). Vertebrates, however, are probably more easily disturbed than benthic organisms and populations of breeding birds especially can suffer from intruding anglers and birdwatchers. At popular sites, the activities of anglers and hunters can give rise to pollution from lead shot and fishing weights which have both been identified as a major cause of lead poisoning in water fowl such as swans, which ingest grit to help digestive processes in the gizzard (e.g. O'Halloran et al., 1988). Instream activities, such as boating, particularly involving large or fast craft, can also have serious effects. The Norfolk Broads in England, for example, have suffered from the dramatic increase in pleasure craft leading to erosion of river banks from water turbulence, increase in sediment loads, destruction of macrophyte beds, and disturbance of semi-aquatic wildlife.

Manipulation of natural fish stocks has been and still is popular to 'improve' the local fishery, often by removing the natural species and replacing them with salmonids or other sport fish, as mentioned earlier. Eradicating the natural fish stock is often accomplished through the application of a toxin called rotenone, which is relatively harmless to humans and breaks down rapidly in nature. Since fish predation is potentially an important process in lotic system (see pp. 182–7 and 202–4), the altered fish community structure following rotenone (or similar) treatment may cascade down to lower trophic levels. Similarly, the introduction of piscivorous sport fish can also lead to trophic cascades. Intense fishing pressure by itself can also change the abundance and size structure of the fish community which in turn is likely to influence the abundances of different prey organisms. Unfortunately, there have been relatively few studies of such indirect effects on streams, and we cannot be certain of the consequences.

A related and indeed quite drastic manipulation of natural populations has been carried out to control lampreys. The land-locked sea lamprey (*Petromyzon marinus*)

Fig. 9.6 The mean number of taxa (±1 standard deviation) in different freshwater habitats in Tenerife, the Canary Islands, showing the importance of lotic habitats in the overall diversity of freshwater macroinvertebrates of the island. (From Malmqvist *et al.*, 1995.)

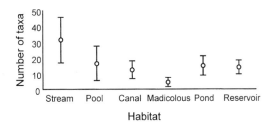

is thought to have invaded the Great Lakes in the United States and Canada when the Welland canal (bypassing the Niagara Falls) was built in the mid-1800s. Now more than 200 tributaries in the Great Lakes area are treated with a lamprey toxin on a regular basis at a yearly cost of nearly $100 million dollars, since it is believed that the sea lamprey causes damage to the fishery in the lakes. The specific toxin, TFM, is supposed to have little effects on other organisms, although some studies have reported strong mortality in leeches and worms. Even if direct mortality is low, TFM application has been observed to cause substantial drift of certain taxa such as amphipods (Dermott and Spence, 1984).

From a more applied standpoint, the tourism industry indirectly threatens natural freshwater resources. As an example, the number of tourists in Tenerife in the Canary Islands approximately doubled in a 10-year period to reach 2.5 million in 1988. Along with the residents' 7-fold population increase since the turn of the century, forest degradation and increased agriculture, an overall negative water balance has arisen. That is, the demand for water exceeds the supply from precipitation. Partly to service the tourism, the expanding production of crops, primarily bananas, potatoes, and greenhouse products, is a terrific drain on water resources and agriculture is responsible for 70% of the consumption of freshwater in Tenerife. A serious consequence is that streams dry up and in fact few permanent streams remain today. It is unfortunate that it is the running waters, which are the most species-rich of all freshwater habitats on the island (Fig. 9.6), that suffer most from the dewatering process. Some species can survive in irrigation channels but many species seem to lack the capacity to switch to artificial waterways. It is plausible that similar negative impacts on streams and their biota could be found on other 'islands in the sun' or even mainland areas in other subtropical and tropical parts of the world.

The introduction of exotic species

Expanding on one of the themes we raised in the previous section, introduction of species to areas previously outside their geographic range can be deliberate, as in sport fish and decapods, or can be accidental as in most invertebrates and aquatic weeds.

When exotics invade communities of species that have co-evolved over long periods in the absence of the invader, the balance between the native species may become seriously disrupted. This can take place through competition, predation, hybridization, or through the transfer of parasites and diseases. Island systems are particularly vulnerable to exotic invaders. In New Zealand, for example, only 26 of the 46 freshwater fish species are native, all others have been introduced. Island faunas are usually species-poor but may have a large proportion of unique (endemic) species and the ecological literature abounds with examples of extinctions of terrestrial species following the introduction of exotics. Nevertheless, our knowledge about exotic introductions to island streams is rudimentary. Continental systems can also be affected. For example, in the United States, only 6 exotic freshwater fish species were known in the 1920s. Sixty years later, the number of established species had increased 6-fold (Allan and Flecker, 1993); in addition, 50 further species had been recorded. Of the established species, 12 were introduced via government agencies and the rest were escaped or released pet species. As many as one-tenth of all introductions of exotic fish species may be accidental. For instance, small cyprinids can easily slip through with the introduction of target species.

To these exotic introductions one can add the numerous translocations within countries. Again, most of the information relates to the very extensive manipulations of fish populations. The problem is that translocations upset the genetic adaptations of local populations to the environmental conditions that have evolved over long periods of time. These translocations have been initiated mainly for improving recreational and commercial fishery but have also resulted from accidental releases from fish farms and restocking of populations. In this latter case, the problem of so-called 'genetic pollution' of natural genetic stock is of concern, particularly with salmonids.

Another reason for introducing species is their conceived importance in biological control. A striking example is the introduction of mosquitofish (*Gambusia affinis*) and guppy (*Poecilia reticulata*) to many parts of the world as a part of mosquito control programmes. Similarly, tilapia and carp have been introduced in many places for weed control (often exotic weeds!). No doubt, these introductions have frequently been successful, in that they have strongly reduced the abundances of invertebrates/ weeds, but their impact on the overall system has not been properly evaluated.

Some commercially important invertebrates, notably decapod crustaceans, may have been deliberately introduced to many systems but in general, the introduction of exotic invertebrates is almost always unintentional, and often brought about via fish introduction but also with ship ballast water. The accidental introduction of the water hyacinth into rivers and lakes in the Nile system has been a particularly unfortunate occurrence both for use of water resources and for the natural ecosystems (see earlier).

The consequences of exotic introductions for natural stream and river communities have rarely been studied. However, Ross (1991) analysed 31 cases where exotic or transplanted fish had been introduced to stream communities and the

Fig. 9.7 The abundance of kokanee salmon, bald eagles, and opossum shrimps (*Mysis relicta*) in Flathead lake showing the plummeting populations of salmon and eagles after the introduction of the opossum shrimp. Salmon and eagle data are absolute counts, opossum shrimp data mean densities (m² ± 95% confidence limits). (Redrawn after Spencer *et al.*, 1991.)

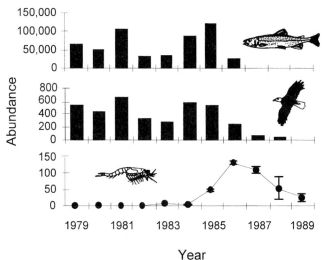

consequences were depressing: in 24 of these communities, native species had declined or had been eliminated. The introduction of opossum shrimps (*Mysis relicta*) as fish food in Montana, USA, is one such example (Spencer *et al.*, 1991). It led to the collapse of the kokanee salmon (also introduced), which in turn negatively affected its predators, including bald eagles and grizzly bears, exploiting the salmon during the spawning in the lake's tributaries (Fig. 9.7.). Apparently, the opossum shrimps consumed the kokanees' primary zooplankton food organisms, but without taking over their role in the diet of the salmon. One of the best-documented series of invasions has been in the lower Rhine in The Netherlands, where a series of exotic bivalves and crustaceans have been invading progressively upstream as general quality of the river water has changed and become slightly more saline through pollution (van den Brink, 1994). The invasions have resulted in significant impacts on native benthic species but in contrast to the Montana example, the invading crustaceans have at least become important components of the diet of predatory fish (perch and eels) (Kelleher *et al.*, in press).

With the increasing mobility of man, exotic introductions are likely to develop into a continually growing problem. Species introductions often fail, but ironically the processes they change often tend to be irreversible. It is hoped that these experiences will result in greater care before any species is intentionally introduced in the future.

The protection of species and habitats

It has been estimated that 20% of the world's freshwater fish species are either extinct or seriously declining (Wilson, 1992). A large portion of these may be species confined to running waters. Many fish species and local races have disappeared as a consequence of human activities, such as by damming as we discussed earlier in this chapter. Corresponding knowledge about invertebrates and plants is much more limited, although there are some examples, such as the net-spinning caddisfly *Hydropsyche tobiasu*, which existed in the Rhine until the 1920s but has not been encountered since.

Probably the single most serious threat to unique species of animals and plants in running water systems comes from human-related habitat degradation. As an example, the habitat degradation of Asian rivers has been caused primarily by deforestation and overgrazing (Dudgeon 1992). Clearing of forests is undertaken to increase the extent of arable land and for fuel wood. The resulting flooding and erosion in turn increase sediment loads with all their adverse consequences for the life in the rivers. Primary production is reduced and floodplain habitats are changed through siltation. Silt also destroys habitats preferred by many invertebrates, when spaces under and between larger substrate particles are filled in, reducing interstitial habitats and predation refuges for invertebrates as well as fish spawning beds (see Chapter 3, pp. 41–4). The main problems in Europe and North America relate to river regulation, channelization and drainage schemes, and clearance of riparian zones. Many countries have come to realize the problems that such activities have generated and they have initiated remedial programmes of river restoration in various areas. This is most commonly directed specifically at improving habitat for fisheries, including addition of woody debris, re-establishment of riffle–pool sequences and creation of instream and bankside cover. These of course carry additional benefits for the rest of the biota. River restoration is gradually developing its own methodology and theoretical framework drawing from geomorphology, hydrology, engineering, and ecology. Rather than attempting to give a brief overview of this complex and important topic in the limited space we have here, we would recommend readers consult the edited volumes of Petts and Calow (1996) and Laenen and Dunnette (1997).

More than 100 countries have declared through 'The convention on biological diversity' that they will work for the conservation of biological diversity and the sustainable use of its components. Enforced in December 1993, it is one of the most far-reaching environmental conventions ever developed. The commitment by the nations involved is substantial and will require an aggressive policy to protect biodiversity. It is as powerful for freshwater organisms as for terrestrial and marine ones. The question is, however, whether the community is willing to carry through its content not only for the obvious species but also for various freshwater insect species of minor significance to all except the taxonomic specialists?

Why is it so important to retain a high diversity? After all, while some species are abundant or 'keystone species' most species are rare and are likely to have only a modest role in various ecosystem processes. The strongest argument being put forward to justify the preservation of biodiversity in general is the assumed importance of a diverse system to ensure against large ecosystem changes and to maintain efficiency of ecosystem processes (Chapin *et al.*, 1995). For example, in a natural community, every species has its own unique optimum with regard to temperature, and therefore as the argument goes, the effects of climatic disturbances, for example, on system processes will be less the more diverse the biological community is. Over time (on a scale ranging from decades to centuries) it may indeed be possible to show that few species are redundant in this sense. In addition, there is the ethical standpoint in that man has no moral right to cause the extinction of another species. Other arguments include the potential role of as yet unknown chemical substances present in rare species that can become of medical importance or provide some other resource or ecological service. By allowing species to go extinct today we will deprive ourselves of such assets for all time.

As far as lotic organisms are concerned, our knowledge about the significance of a high biodiversity is minimal. Given that the arguments presented above about ecosystem stability and function are correct, and there is evidence accruing from terrestrial systems that suggests they are, there is good reason to intensify efforts to protect aquatic species and their habitats. Moreover, there is an obvious need to increase our knowledge of the effects of species richness on lotic ecosystem processes. Some processes that we might expect to be influenced by biodiversity include breakdown of litter and other organic matter, reoxygenation of water, grazing, predation and control of pest populations. We also need to know more about the organization of lotic communities. Only through a better knowledge of what species there are and how they interact will it be possible to implement efficient conservation measures. However, since time is short and the rate of extinction fast (especially in tropical regions), a principle of caution should be employed where representative streams and rivers are protected against destruction.

It is obvious that stream-living species cannot be protected other than through protection of their habitats. There are several possible strategies to accomplish this. An obvious one would be to preserve sites which are known to accommodate rare or endangered species. But this is not enough as we have come to realize that running waters are open systems and that they are influenced by their upstream sections and surrounding catchments, including those that are disturbed by man. This means we cannot simply look only at the scale of the site of interest alone, but that we must increase the scale of approach and include the whole catchment upstream. This problem of stream sites being such extended habitats led Ladle (1991) to rank running waters as 'a conservationist's nightmare'!

Another strategy would be to preserve selectively large river systems under the assumption that such systems are more species-rich than smaller ones, and that they accommodate those species also found in smaller and less diverse systems in the same region. These assumptions might, though, be incorrect in detail. However, if the protection includes all tributaries and source areas in the catchment, it could be a good strategy. One should also try to maximize the number of different habitat types to ensure that every specialist species is being protected. Samways (1994) suggested not only should as many and as varied a range of biotopes and landscapes be set aside, but also as large sites as possible should be safeguarded.

National parks have been established world-wide. More rarely, but of particular interest in the context of this book, is the strategy to protect rivers as 'national rivers', an approach which has been put into operation in Sweden, which presently has four such rivers. Here, it was deemed necessary that these last four major free-flowing rivers should be protected against damming for hydroelectric power, a threat that is expected to increase as nuclear power plants are being closed down. Where our knowledge is reasonably good, it would be possible to identify a number of 'type' rivers of special interest for conservation. These should be selected to be representative but also for their quality in terms of species richness and for harbouring threatened species. Often the knowledge about the biodiversity of natural systems is inadequate and what is worse, we are only beginning to understand what factors govern species richness in running water systems.

In arid regions of the world, as we discussed ealier (pp. 216–22), the pressure on freshwater is often enormous, reflecting the paucity of this vital resource. For the biota, this situation is especially serious and dewatering of rivers will obviously have detrimental repercussions often to a point beyond return. Only in the source areas, and only when they are situated relatively high up in mountain areas, may undisturbed stream fragments remain. Such mountain streams often have many unique species that require a conservation management plan. However, there are many problems, and such areas have rarely been investigated with regard to plant and animal life, and many may probably have not even been discovered!

For some threatened birds and mammals, spectacular efforts have been made to keep individuals (rather than populations) in captivity for the purpose of keeping the species alive, and perhaps actually increasing their number, while the cause of the 'near extinction' is being removed. For practically any lotic species this strategy would be a virtually impossible mission. Therefore, it all boils down to a matter of preserving the habitats in which these organisms live. From a practical point of view, it often hardly seems legitimate to protect aquatic ecosystems, and thus remove the basis for human existence, for the benefit of a few species of aquatic bugs! This suggests that it is clearly necessary that actions to preserve biodiversity must be accompanied by social and other activities in cohesive and sustainable plans on a regional or national level. An important component of this problem has to do with education. E.O. Wilson (1992) argues: 'the better an ecosystem is known, the less likely it will be destroyed', and Baba Dioum, as quoted by Wilson summarized this point of view in a classic phrase: 'In the end, we will conserve only what we love, we will love only what we understand, we will understand only what we are taught'. We hope that this book has helped in some small way to this end.

Studies in running waters

As can be gathered from the range of experimental, observational, and survey work described in this book, there is huge scope for biological and ecological studies in streams and rivers. While for some localities access may be a problem during the winter when streams are frozen or during the summer/dry season when temporary streams may dry up, in most other lotic habitats studies are possible at any time of the year. This is one of the advantages of running waters as research systems—there are always animals and plants present.

What we have tried to do in the sections below is give a brief outline of the kind of approaches that may lead to interesting and more detailed studies. Naturally, we have had to be selective, and the bias towards invertebrates reflects both our own experience and the fact that these are the easiest groups to work with and to sample. The exact methodologies can be gleaned from the references cited in the appropriate sections of the main text, and we have deliberately steered away from studies that need sophisticated equipment. We hope these will give a flavour of the kind of work that is readily possible.

Water flow in streams

Add fluorescine to a stream and observe how fast the dye spreads downstream in the centre of the channel. Very little dye will be seen along the margins in the beginning of the experiments. Later, when the dye has been washed away in the central parts, it will have reached the margins and bays. This experiment can be repeated at a finer scale by adding the fluorescine from a syringe very close the surface of a rock and observing the spread of the dye through a viewing box (a glass-bottomed box or dish). Note how dye is retained longer within the viscous sublayer close to the surface of the rock. It is also possible to study from where in the water column the food of a suspension feeders, like a net-spinning caddis larva, is derived.

The influence of macroinvertebrates on leaf breakdown rates

There are a number of experiments that can be conducted using the detritivore–detritus interaction. Place replicate litterbags constructed from netting of two different mesh sizes (e.g. 5 mm and 0.5 mm) and stocked with dried and pre-weighed leaves of one tree species (e.g. alder) in a stream and anchor them. Litterbags with coarse meshes will allow macroinvertebrates to colonize the enclosed leaf packs whereas leaves in fine-mesh bags will be affected only by microorganisms and small invertebrates. Expose the bags for 2–5 weeks and compare dry weight losses.

Preferences and the effect of conditioning can be examined in the field or laboratory. Litterbags can be made up with leaves of different tree species (e.g. oak, beech, alder, ash) in the same way as above and weight losses compared. Leaves can be conditioned by exposure in the stream in fine-meshed bags for a couple of weeks, then exposed in coarse mesh bags and compared with unconditioned leaves. Alternatively, standard leaf discs can be presented to amphipods or stoneflies held in containers in cold rooms ($<12°$ C) and consumption compared and preferences identified.

Longitudinal changes in benthic community structure

Invertebrate and algal communities change longitudinally in response to changes in physicochemical factors. This can be examined in a number of situations. For example, take quantitative benthic samples at different distances downstream below a lake outlet. Identify the animals and classify them with respect to functional feeding group. Compare the downstream changes in number, biomass, and functional group composition. By examining the nature of the drift using drift samplers, and the periphyton by scraping stones some explanation for the changes may be found.

Pollution outfalls also lead to longitudinal sequences of species. By sampling upstream and at successive distances downstream of a pollution outfall, such as from a sewage works, the degree of perturbation and the extent downstream influence can be assessed by comparing the invertebrate assemblages among sample sites. Application of diversity and biotic indices can give an indication of the degree of pollution and rate of recovery with distance from the outfall. These data can be compared with results from water analysis (e.g. for oxygen, nitrates, total phosphorus, chloride, pH, suspended solids, conductivity, etc,).

Longitudinal patterns of the relative abundance of various functional groups can also be investigated along stream lengths (on the scale of kilometres) and with altitude and findings compared with the predictions of the river continuum concept.

Patchiness of the stream benthos

Macroinvertebrate populations are usually aggregated, but the degree of aggregation varies amongst taxa and with the heterogeneity of the stream itself. By taking many replicate quantitative samples (e.g. with a standard Surber or Hess sampler) from randomly selected points, and measuring a range of factors at these points (e.g. depth, current velocity, amount of detritus in the sample, substrate type, degree of shade, etc.) some relationships can be derived between physical factors and density. Variance to mean ratio tests are a simple way of comparing aggregation among taxa of different functional feeding group.

Diel patterns of invertebrate drift

Place replicate drift nets in a stream with fish. Record the catches over 1–3 hours during the daytime and during the night, or more frequently if nets clog. Record current velocity in the drift net mouth at the start and the end of the experiment to provide data on the volume of water passing through the net. Compare drift densities (numbers per unit volume) between night and day. If possible, run a parallel experiment in a fishless stream (or use two streams with significantly different fish densities) to show differences in drift behaviour in the presence and absence of fish.

Drift densities versus benthic densities

Take replicate night drift samples in a riffle stream section (see above). On the next day, take quantitative and replicate benthic samples in the riffle area upstream of the nets. Identify and count macroinvertebrates and compare the two sample sets in terms of relative abundances. Which taxa are most drift-prone? Are there any differences between sizes of individuals in drift and benthos?

The collector's curve. How species richness increases with increasing numbers of samples

This kind of study explores the relationship between species richness and area and is one way to objectively identify the local community of species. Take several (10 or more) quantitative benthic samples. Pick, sort, identify, and count the macroinvertebrates. Plot the number of animals (x) and the number of identified taxa (y) of the first sample. For the next sample plot the cumulative number of individuals and species from the two samples and so on. The curve will level off and asymptotically approach the species number in the stream section. Different streams will show different slopes to the asymptote and different numbers of samples (hence area) at the asymptote.

A similar approach can be used to examine the macrophyte community in a river. Instead of replicate benthic samples, replicate contiguous stream lengths are examined and macrophyte species recorded. Plot the cumulative number of taxa against stream length investigated. Sharp changes in stream morphology often lead to sharp changes in the slope of the species accumulation curve.

The study of blackfly feeding rates

Blackfly larvae are indiscriminate feeders of small particles and the food does not mix in the gut. These facts make it possible to estimate the feeding rate of these suspension feeders. Locate an aggregation of blackfly larvae. Administer a charcoal slurry from a container with a hose upstream of the aggregation and time the start of the experiment and keep adding the slurry for about 1 minute. Wait a further 30 minutes and collect the larvae and kill them in alcohol. The gut contents between the oesophagus and the black band indicates the amount of particles ingested. Variation among individuals in relation to position in the aggregation, the size of the individual, or the flow rate of water is worth investigating.

Patterns in predator and prey sizes

Larvae of certain stoneflies are predators and engulf their food whole. This makes it possible to not only quantify their diet in terms of numbers and kind of food items consumed, but also to readily observe the size of the prey. Collect stoneflies, such as perlids, perlodids or chloroperlids, or polycentropid caddis and preserve them in alcohol. In the laboratory, remove the guts under a dissecting microscope and identify and measure prey size. Compare graphically the size of the predator and that of a common prey taxon (e.g. chironomids). Does prey size increase with predator size or is there merely an expansion in the range of prey sizes with increasing size of predator?

Similar approaches can be adopted to investigate the change in diet of stoneflies or caddis (cased and caseless) with age. Holding predators in cold water ($<12°\,C$) in the laboratory in individual containers makes it possible to examine functional responses to changes in prey density. Vary the nature of the substrate and examine the effect this has on the shape of the response.

Algal–grazer interactions

Grazing caddis larvae, such as the cased glossosomatids, can be readily studied in the laboratory if they are provided with oxygenated, cold water. The influence of food patch size is interesting in terms of feeding strategies and distributions of the grazers. Collect similar-sized pebbles or small stones from the stream, scrub half clean and leave half with their periphyton coating. Place the caddis in an arena with the pebbles arranged in various patterns and clumped together in various ways to make patches of different sizes with high and low food levels. Monitor the movement of the caddis over time and their distribution amongst the patches and on the individual pebbles. The time spent in patches of different size and food levels can be compared.

Influence of water chemistry on stream communities

pH and alkalinity have a strong influence on the nature and diversity of macro-invertebrate and algal communities. Using geological maps, identify river systems that lie on different geologies and compare communities in the different river systems. Measurements of water chemistry (e.g. pH, alkalinity, nitrate, conductivity, suspended solids) should be taken at base flow and high water and assessment of the substrate, flow, bankside vegetation, and catchment land use should also be made.

Similar approaches can be used to examine the influence of various types of land use, such as forestry and agriculture, on communities. On a smaller scale, compare reaches of the same stream that are shaded or open and examine differences amongst animals and plants in abundances, biomass, species richness, and functional groups.

Vertebrate diets and relationships to habitat

The diet of predatory vertebrates like the dipper and otter can be investigated through an examination of the faeces. Dippers deposit faeces on rocks at the waters edge, and otters leave their 'spraints' in prominent positions on the bankside. Faecal deposits can be collected, dried and prey parts removed (sometimes after treatment with potassium hydroxide or similar chemicals) and compared with a reference collection. Mouthparts are the main items recovered from dipper faeces and hard body parts such as insect elytra, crustacean carapaces, and fish bones or vertebrae are found in otter faeces.

The distribution of these signs can be related to various habitat features such as nature of bankside cover, depth and flow, surrounding landscape, provisions of nest or holt sites, etc.

Further reading

General texts

Allan's (1995) book gives a readable and up-to-date account of stream ecology. Cushing, Cummins, and Minshall's (1995) volume in the *Ecosystems of the world* series on streams and rivers holds a wealth of information and is very readable. Hynes' (1970) book is a classic and still has a lot of useful material, while Moss (1998) is a more general freshwater text, but has a lot of good information, particularly on large rivers.

Types of habitats

Cushing *et al.* (1995) again offers a lot on various lotic habitats of the world. For more detailed treatment of some of the types of lotic habitat, we would suggest the following references: Ferrington (1995) and Williams and Danks (1992) for springs; Murvosh and Hogue (1991) for torrential habitats; Milner and Petts (1994) for high-latitude rivers; Clifford (1966) and Fisher *et al.* (1982) for intermittant and arid rivers; Richardson and Mackay (1991) for lake outlet streams; and Welcomme (1979) for floodplain rivers.

Physiochemical factors

Every freshwater biologist should read Hynes' (1975) *The stream and its valley*, which highlights the important link between the lotic system and its catchment. A summary of the effects of various physical factors on life history characteristics of insects is given by Sweeney (1984), and there are a number of other useful chapters on other aspects in the same edited book by Resh and Rosenberg (1984). Likens and Bormann (1995) have revised their book on the biogeochemistry of the famous Hubbard Brook experimental catchment. A good shorter review of how natural and anthropogenic environmental changes influence ecosystem processes is given by Hornung and Reynolds (1995). Turning to flow, Stazner *et al.* (1988) has provided a very thorough review, and Vogel's (1994) book on living in a fluid environment is well worth investigating. A good introduction to hydrology and hydraulics for biologists can be found in Gordon *et al.* (1992). Finally, *The rivers handbook*, Part 1 (Calow and Petts, 1992) is worth consulting.

Animals and plants

Thorp and Covich (1991) is currently the best book on the general biology of freshwater invertebrates, covering a full range of topical areas from behaviour to reproduction for all groups. Petts and Calow (1996) covers a wider range of organizations including microbes and algae, as well as fish, but in lesser detail. For specific groups, we would recommend the following references.

For micobes and for aquatic hyphomycetes, see Maltby (1992) and Bärlocher (1992), respectively. Merritt and Cummins (1996) is useful as both an introductory text and general key to the insects of North America. Nilsson (1996/1997) provides a taxonomic handbook for aquatic insects of northern Europe, and good identification keys for specific groups in the British Isles are available from the Freshwater Biological Association. Texts on specific insect groups are available, such as Hickin (1967) for caddis, Armitage *et al.* (1995) for Chironomidae, Crosskey (1990) for blackflies, and detailed reviews on a number of other groups can be found in various issues of the *Annual Review of Entomology*. Turning to vertebrates, we would recommend Elliott's (1994) book on the brown trout and Chanin's (1985) book on otters.

Adaptations

Various chapters in Resh and Rosenberg (1984) discuss adaptations in insects, and Ward's (1992*a*) book on insect ecology is also useful. Thorp and Covich (1991) again offers much information on all invertebrate groups, and Hynes (1970) has a lot of interesting material. The references suggested above for various groups should also be consulted.

Ecosystem processes

An excellent summary of stream organic matter budgets from 35 streams around the world has been edited by Webster and Meyer in a recent issue of the *Journal of North American Benthological Society* (**16**, 1997). Webster and Benfield (1986) have reviewed the breakdown of vascular plant in streams, and Benke *et al.* (1988) have examined energy flow in lotic systems. The role of macroinvertebrates in stream ecosystems has been reviewed by Wallace and Webster (1996). Wetzel and Ward (1992) discusses methods of measuring primary production, and Benke *et al.* (1988) gives references to methods for measuring secondary production.

Species interaction and community structure

Kerfoot and Sih's (1987) edited volume covers all aspects of predation in aquatic communities, and Cooper *et al.* (1990) is a benchmark paper on the effects of predation. McAuliffe (1984*a*) and Kohler (1992) are among the most cited papers on competition. The more recent Kohler and Wiley (1997) paper on the role of the grazing caddis *Glossossoma* and its parasite will likely become equally well cited.

Hart (1983) gives a good review of resource partitioning in streams. Wooster and Sih (1995) review responses of prey to predators. The work on new glacial streams communities by Milner (1994) is interesting, and Hildrew's (1996a) review of food webs in streams offers a useful overview. Powers and Matthews (1983), Wallace *et al.* (1997), and Hart (1992) provide good insights into trophic cascade effects, and Vinson and Hawkins (1998) explore species diversity patterns.

Applied issues

A special issue of *Environmental Management* (**14**, (5), 1990) is dedicated to the nature and effects of disturbance and subsequent recovery in lotic systems and is well worth consulting. Chapman (1992) is a useful source of information on regulations, standards, and monitoring of water quality. Gleick (1993) and Cohen (1995) highlight the problems relating to water resources, and Allan and Flecker (1993) provide a good review of biodiversity issues in running waters. A number of other general texts were referred to in Chapter 9.

References

Adams, J. and Greenwood, P. (1983). Why are males bigger than females in pre-copula pairs of *Gammarus pulex*. *Behavioural Ecology and Sociobiology*, **13**, 239–41.

Admiraal, W. and van Zanten, B. (1988). Impact of biological activity on detritus transported in the lower river Rhine: an exercise in ecosystem analysis. *Freshwater Biology*, **20**, 215–25.

Allan, J. D. (1978). Trout predation and the size composition of stream drift. *Limnology and Oceanography*, **23**, 1231–7.

Allan, J.D. (1982). The effects of reduction in trout density on the invertebrate community of a mountain stream. *Ecology*, **63**, 1444–55.

Allan, J.D. (1995). *Stream ecology, structure and function of running waters*. Chapman and Hall, London.

Allan, J.D. and Flecker, A.S. (1993). Biodiversity conservation in running waters. *BioScience*, **43**, 32–43.

Allen, K.R. (1951). The Horokiwi stream. A study of a trout population. *New Zealand Marine Department Fisheries Bulletin*, **10**, 1–238.

Amyot, M., Pinel-Alloul, B., Campbell, P.G.C. and Désy, J.C. (1996). Total metal burdens in the freshwater amphipod *Gammarus fasciatus*: contribution of various body parts and influence of gut contents. *Freshwater Biology*, **35**, 363–73.

Andersen, N.H. and Wissema, R.W. (1987). Recovery of the Trichoptera fauna near Mt. St. Helens five years after the 1980 eruption. In *Proceedings of the 5th International Symposium on Trichoptera* (ed. M. Bournaud and H. Tachet), pp. 367–73. Dr W. Junk Publishers, Dordrecht, The Netherlands.

Anderwald, P.H., Konar, M. and Humpesch, U.H. (1991). Continuous drift samples of macroinvertebrates in a large river, the Danube in Austria. *Freshwater Biology*, **25**, 461–76.

Anholt, B.R. (1995). Density dependence resolves the stream drift paradox. *Ecology*, **76**, 2235–39.

Armitage, P.D. (1995). Behaviour and ecology of adults. In *The Chironomidae. The biology and ecology of non-biting midges* (ed. P. Armitage, P.S. Cranston and L.C.V. Pinder), pp.194–224. Chapman and Hall, London.

Armitage, P.D. (1996). Prediction of biological responses. In *River biota diversity and dynamics* (ed. G. Petts and P. Calow), pp. 231–52. Blackwell, Oxford.

Armitage, P., Cranston, P.S. and Pinder, L.C.V. (ed.) (1995). *The Chironomidae. The biology and ecology of non-biting midges*. Chapman and Hall, London.

Arnold, S.J. (1983). Morphology, performance and fitness. *American Zoologist*, **23**, 347–61.

Baker, J.A. and Ross, S.T. (1981). Spatial and temporal resource utilization by southeastern cyprinids. *Copeia*, 178–89.

Baltanás, A. (1992). On the use of some methods for estimation of species richness. *Oikos*, **65**, 484–92.

Banarescu, P. (1990). *Zoogeography of fresh waters. General distribution and dispersal of freshwater animals*, Vol. 1. Aula-Verlag, Wiesbaden.

Bärlocher, F. (1985). The role of fungi in the nutrition of stream invertebrates. *Botanical Journal of the Linnaean Society*, **91**, 83–94.

Bärlocher, F. (ed.) (1992). *The ecology of aquatic hyphomycetes*. Ecological Studies, 94. Springer-Verlag, Berlin.

Barr, W.B. (1984). Prolegs and attachment of *Simulium vittatum* (sibling 1S-7) (Diptera: Simuliidae) larvae. *Canadian Journal of Zoology*, **62**, 1355–62.

Bayley, P.B. and Li, H.W. (1996). Riverine Fishes. In *River biota diversity and dynamics* (ed. G. Petts and P. Calow), pp. 92–122. Blackwell, Oxford.

Bengston, S.-A. (1972). Breeding ecology of the harlequin duck *Histrionicus histrionicus* (L.) in Iceland. *Ornis Scandia*, **3**, 1–19.

Benke, A.C. (1984). Secondary production of aquatic insects. In *The ecology of aquatic insects* (ed. V.H. Resh and D.M. Rosenberg), pp. 289–322. Praeger, New York.

Benke, A.C., Gillespie, D.M., Parrish, F.K., Van Arsdall, T.C., Hunter, R.J. and Henry, R.L. (1979). *Biological basis for assessing impacts of channel modifications: invertebrate production, drift, and fish feeding in a southeastern blackwater river*. Environmental Resources Center Publication No. ERC 06–79. Georgia Institute of Technology, Atlanta.

Benke, A.C., Hall, C.A.S., Hawkins, C.P., Lowe-McConnell, R.H., Stanford, J.A., Suberkropp, K. *et al.* (1988). Bioenergetic considerations in the analysis of stream ecosystems. *Journal of the North American Benthological Society*, **7**, (4), 480–502.

Benson, L.J. and Pearson, R.G. (1987). The role of drift and effect of season on macroinvertebrate colonization of implanted substrata in a tropical Australian stream. *Freshwater Biology*, **18**, 109–16.

Berg, M.B. (1995). Larval food and feeding behaviour. In *The Chironomidae* (ed. P. Armitage, P.S. Cranston and L.C.V. Pinder), pp. 136–168. Chapman and Hall, London.

Berner, E.K. and Berner, R.A. (1987). *The global water cycle*. Prentice-Hall, Englewood Cliffs, New Jersey.

Billen, G., Décamps, H., Garnier, J., Boët, P., Meybeck, M. and Servais, P. (1995). Atlantic river systems of Europe (France, Belgium, The Netherlands). In *Ecosystems of the World 22. River and stream ecosystems* (ed. C.E. Cushing, K.W. Cummins and G.W. Minshall), pp. 389–418. Elsevier, Amsterdam.

Bird, G.A. and Hynes, H.B.N. (1981). Movements of immature insects in a lotic habitat. *Hydrobiologia*, **77**, 103–12.

Bishop, J.E. and Hynes, H.B.N. (1969). Downstream drift of the invertebrate fauna in a stream ecosystem. *Archiv für Hydrobiologie*, **66**, 56–9.

Bisson, P. A. and Sedell, J. R. (1984). Salmonid populations in streams in clearcut vs old-growth forests of western Washington. In *Fish and wildlife relationships in old growth forests*, Proceedings of a symposium (ed. W. Meehan, T. Merrell and T. Hanley), pp. 121–129. American Institute of Fishery Research Biologists.

Biswas, S.P. (1996). Global water scarcity: issues and implications with special reference to India. *Internationale Vereinigung für theoretische und angewandte Limnologie*, **26**, 115–21.

Blake, M.A. and Hart, P.J.B. (1993). The behavioural responses of juvenile signal crayfish, *Pacifastacus leniusculus*, to stimuli from perch and eels. *Freshwater Biology*, **29**, (1), 89–97.

Bogatov, V., Sirotsky, S. and Yuriev, D. (1995). The ecosystem of the Amur river. In *Ecosystems of the world 22. River and stream ecosystems* (ed. C.E. Cushing, K.W. Cummins and G.W. Minshall), pp. 601–13. Elsevier, Amsterdam.

Borchardt, D. (1993). Effects of flow and refugia on drift loss of benthic macroinvertebrates: implications for habitat restoration in lowland streams. *Freshwater Biology*, **29**, 221–7.

Bott, T.L. and Kaplan, L.A. (1985). Bacterial biomass, metabolic state and activity in stream sediments: relation to environmental variables and multiple assay comparisons. *Applied and Environmental Microbiology*, **50**, 508–22.

Bott, T.L., Kaplan, L.A. and Kuserk, F.T. (1984). Benthic bacterial biomass supported by streamwater dissolved organic matter. *Microbial Ecology*, **10**, 335–44.

Boulten, A., Spangaro, G. and Lake, P. (1988). Macroinvertebrate distribution and recolonisation on stones subjected to varying degrees of disturbance: an experimental approach. *Archiv für Hydrobiologie*, **113**, 551–76.

Bournaud, M. (1975). Eléments d'observation sur la cinématique, la dynamique et l'énergétique de la locomotion dans le courant chez une larve de Trichoptère à fourreau. *Hydrobiologia*, **46**, 489–513.

Bowden, W.B., Finlay, J.C. and Maloney, P.E. (1994). Long-term effects of PO₄ fertilization on the distribution of bryophytes in an arctic river. *Freshwater Biology*, **32**, 445–54.

Bowlby, J.N. and Roff, J.C. (1986). Trophic structure in southern Ontario streams. *Ecology*, **67**, 1670–9.

Bowman, J.J. and Bracken, J.J. (1993). Effect of run-off from afforested and non-afforested catchments on the survival of brown trout *Salmo trutta* L. in two acid-sensitive rivers in Wicklow, Ireland. *Biology and Environment. Proceedings of the Royal Irish Academy*, **93B**, 143–52.

Brewin, P.A. and Ormerod, S.J. (1994). Macroinvertebrate drift in streams of the Nepalese Himalaya. *Freshwater Biology*, **32**, 573–84.

Briand, F. (1985). Structural singularities of freshwater food webs. *Internationalen Vereinigung für theoretische und angewandte Limnologie*, **22**, 3356–64.

Briand, F. and Cohen, J.E. (1987). Environmental correlates of food chain length. *Science*, **238**, 956–60.

Bridcut, E.E. and Giller, P.S. (1993). Diet variability and foraging strategies in brown trout (*Salmo trutta*): an analysis from subpopulations to individuals. *Canadian Journal of Fisheries and Aquatic Science*, **52**, 2543–52.

Brinck, P. (1949). Studies on Swedish stoneflies. *Opuscula Entomologica*, (suppl. 11), 1–250.

Brinkhurst, R.O. and Gelder, S.R. (1991). Annelids. In *Ecology and classification of North American invertebrates* (ed. J. Thorp and A. Covich), pp. 401–36. Academic Press, San Diego.

Brittain, J.E. (1982). Biology of mayflies. *Annual Review of Entomology*, **27**, 119–47.

Brönmark, C. (1985). Interactions between macrophytes, epiphytes, and herbivores: an experimental approach. *Oikos*, **45**, 26–30.

Brönmark, C. and Hansson, L.-A. (1998). *The biology of lakes and ponds*. Oxford University Press.

Brönmark, C. and Malmqvist, B. (1984). Spatial and temporal patterns in lake outlet benthos. *Internationale Vereinigung für theoretische und angewandte Limnologie*, **22**, 1986–91.

Brönmark, C., Herrmann, J., Malmqvist, B., Otto, C. and Sjöström, P. (1984*a*). Animal community structure as a function of stream size. *Hydrobiologia*, **112**, 73–9.

Brönmark, C., Malmqvist, B. and Otto, C. (1984*b*). Anti-predator adaptations in a neustonic insect (*Velia caprai*). *Oecologia*, **61**, 189–91.

Brown, A.V. and Matthews, W.J. (1995). Stream ecosystems of the central United States. In *Ecosystems of the World 22. River and stream ecosystems* (ed. C.E. Cushing, K.W. Cummins, and G.W. Mindshall), pp. 89–116. Elsevier, Amsterdam.

Brown, K.M. (1991). Mollusca: Gastropoda. In *Ecology and classification of North American freshwater invertebrates* (ed. J.H. Thorp and A.P. Covich), pp. 285–314. Academic Press, San Diego.

Brundin, L.Z. (1988). Phylogenetic biogeography. In *Analytical biogeography, an integrated approach to the study of animal and plant distributions* (ed. A.A. Myers and P.S. Giller), pp. 343–69. Chapman and Hall, London.

Bunn, S.E. and Hughes, J.M. (1997). Dispersal and recruitment in streams: evidence from genetic studies. *Journal of the North American Benthological Society*, **16**, 338–346.

Burgis, M. J. and Morris, P. (1987). *The natural history of lakes*. Cambridge University Press.

Butler, M.G. (1984). Life histories of aquatic insects. In *The ecology of aquatic insects* (ed. V.H. Resh and D.M. Rosenberg), pp. 24–55. Praeger, New York.

Byers, G.W. (1996). Tipulidae. In *An introduction to the aquatic insects of North America*, (3rd edn) (ed. R.W. Merritt and K.W. Cummins), pp. 549–70. Kendall/Hunt, Dubuque, IA

Calow, P. and Petts, G. (1992). *The rivers handbook*, Part 1. Blackwell Science, Oxford.

Cambell, R.N.B. (1985). Comparison of the drift of live and dead *Baëtis* nymphs in a weakening water current. *Hydrobiologia*, **126**, 229–36.

Campbell, G.W. and Lee, D.S. (1996). Atmospheric deposition of sulphur and nitrogen species in the U.K. *Freshwater Biology*, **36**, 151–67.

Canhoto, C. and Graça, M.A.S. (1995). Food value of introduced eucalypt leaves for a Mediterranean stream detritivore: *Tipula lateralis*. *Freshwater Biology*, **34**, 209–14.

Capel, P.D., Giger, W., Reichert, P. and Wanner, O. (1988). Accidental input of pesticides into the Rhine River. *Environmental Science and Technology*, **22**, 992–7.

Cargill, A.S., Cummins, K.W., Hanson, B.J. and Lowry, R.R. (1985). The role of lipids, fungi and temperature on the nutrition of a shredder caddisfly, *Clistoronia magnifica* (Trichoptera: Limnephilidae). *Freshwater Invertebrate Biology*, **4**, 64–78.

Cellot, B. (1989). Macroinvertebrate movements in a large European river. *Freshwater Biology*, **22**, 45–55.

Cellot, B. (1996). Influence of side-arms on aquatic macroinvertebrate drift in the main channel of a large river. *Freshwater Biology*, **35**, 149–64.

Chamier, A.C. (1987). Effect of pH on microbial degradation of leaf litter in seven streams of the English Lake District. *Oecologia*, **71**, 491–500.

Chance, J.M. and Craig, D.A.. (1986). Hydrodynamics and behaviour of Simuliidae larvae (Diptera). *Canadian Journal of Zoology*, **64**, 1295–309.

Chanin, P. (1985). *The natural history of otters*. Christopher Helm, London.

Chapin III, F.S., Lubchenco, J. and Reynolds, H.L. (1995). Biodiversity effects on patterns and processes of communities and ecosystems. In *Global biodiversity assessment* (ed. V.H. Heywood), pp. 289–301. Cambridge University Press.

Chapman, D. (ed.) (1992). *Water quality assessments*. Chapman and Hall, London.

Charnov, E.L. (1976). Optimal foraging: the marginal value theorem. *Theoretical Population Biology*, **9**, 129–36.

Chatterjee, P. (1997). Dam busting. *New Scientist*, **154**, 17 May, 34–7.

Christensen, L.B. (1988). Undersøgelser af naturlige og kunstige gydepladser for laksefisk. *Hedeselskabets Forskningsvirksomhed Beretning*, **39**, 1–110.

Clesceri, L.S. (1980). PCBs in the Hudson River. In *Introduction to environmental toxicology* (ed. F.E. Guthrie and J.J. Perry), pp. 227–35. Blackwell, Oxford.

Clifford, H.F. (1982). Life cycles of mayflies (Ephemeroptera), with special reference to voltinism. *Quaestiones Entomologicae*, **18**, 15–90.

Clifford, H.F. (1966). The ecology of invertebrates in an intermittent stream. *Investigations of Indiana Lakes and Streams*, **7**, 57–98.

Clinton, S.M., Grimm, N.B. and Fisher, S.G. (1996). Response of a hyporheic invertebrate assemblage to drying disturbance in a desert stream. *Journal of the North American Benthological Society*, **15**, 700–12.

Cloe, W.W. and Garman, G.C. (1996). The energetic importance of terrestrial arthropod inputs to three warm-water streams. *Freshwater Biology*, **36**, (1), 105–14.

Cohen, J. (1995). *How many people can the earth support?* W.W. Norton, New York.

Collier, K.J. and Winterbourn, M.J. (1987). Faunal and chemical dynamics of some acid and alkaline New Zealand streams. *Freshwater Biology*, **18**, 227–40.

Connors, M.E. and Naiman, R.J. (1984). Particulate allochtonous inputs: relationships with stream size in an undisturbed watershed. *Canadian Journal of Fisheries and Aquatic Science*, **41**, 1473–84

Cooper, S.D. (1984). The effect of trout on water striders in stream pools. *Oecologia*, **63**, 376–9.

Cooper, S.D., Walde, S.J., and Peckarsky, B.L., (1990). Prey exchange rates and the impact of predators on prey populations in streams. *Ecology*, **71**, 1503–14.

Corbet, P.A. 1983). *A biology of dragonflies*. E.W. Classey, Faringdon.

Corkum, L.D. (1990). Intrabiome distributional patterns of lotic macro-invertebrate assemblages. *Canadian Journal of Fisheries and Aquatic Science*, **47**, 2147–57.

Corkum, L.D. (1991). Spatial patterns of macroinvertebrate distribution along rivers in eastern decidious forest and grassland biomes. *Journal of the North American Benthological Society*, **10**, 358–71.

Corkum, L.D. and Currie, D. (1987). Distributional patterns of immature Simuliidae (Diptera) in Northwestern North America. *Freshwater Biology*, **17**, 201–21.

Covich, A.P. (1988). Geographical and historical comparisons of neotropical streams: biotic diversity and detrital processing in highly variable habitats. *Journal of the North American Benthological Society*, **7**, 361–86.

Covich, A.P. (1996). Stream biodiversity and ecosystem processes. *Bulletin of the North American Benthological Society*, **13**, 294–303.

Covich, A.P. and Thorp, J.H. (1991). Crustacea: Introduction and Peracarida. In *Ecology and classification of North American freshwater invertebrates* (ed. J.H. Thorp and A.P. Covich), pp. 665–89. Academic Press, San Diego.

Crisp, D. and Gledhill, T. (1970). A quantitative description of the recovery of the bottom fauna in a muddy reach in a mill stream in Southern England after draining and dredging. *Archiv für Hydrobiologie*, **67**, 502–41.

Crisp, D.T. (1987). Thermal 'resetting' of streams by reservoir releases with special reference to effects on salmonid fishes. In *Regulated streams advances in ecology* (ed. J.F. Craig and J.B. Kemper), pp. 163–82. Plenum Press, New York.

Crosskey, R.W. (1990). *The natural history of blackflies.* Wiley, Chichester.

Crowl, T.A. and Covich, A.P. (1990). Predator-induced life history shifts in a freshwater snail. *Science*, **247**, 949–51.

Cuffney, T.F., Wallace, B.J. and Lugthart, C.J. (1990). Experimental evidence quantifying the role of benthic invertebrates in organic matter dynamics of headwater streams. *Freshwater Biology*, **23**, 281–99.

Cummins, K.W. (1962). An evaluation of some techniques for the collection and analysis of benthic samples with special emphasis on lotic waters. *American Midland Naturalist*, **67**, 477–504.

Cummins, K.W. (1973). Trophic relations of aquatic insects. *Annual Review of Entomology*, **18**, 183–205.

Cummins, K.W. (1974). Structure and function of stream ecosystems. *BioScience*, **24**, 631–41.

Cummins, K.W. and Merritt, R.W. (1996). General morphology of aquatic insects. In *An introduction to the aquatic insects of North America* (ed. R.W. Merritt and K.W. Cummins), pp. 5–11. Kendall/Hunt, Dubuque, IA.

Cummins, K.W., Petersen, R.C., Howard, F.O., Wuychech, J.C. and Holt, V.I. (1973). The utilization of leaf litter by stream detritivores. *Ecology*, **54**, 336–45.

Cummins, K.W., Sedell, J.R., Swanson, F.J., Minshall, G.W., Fisher, S.G., Cushing, C.E. *et al.* (1983). Organic matter budgets for stream ecosystems: problems in their evaluation. In *Stream ecology* (ed. J.R. Barnes and G.W. Minshall), pp. 299–353. Plenum Press, New York.

Cummins, K.W., Minshall, G.W., Cushing, C.E. and Petersen, R.C. (1984). Stream ecosystem theory. *Internationale Vereinigung für theoretische und angewandte Limnologie*, **22**, 1818–27.

Cummins, K.W., Cushing, C.E. and Minshall, G.W. (1995). Introduction: an overview of stream ecosystems. In *Ecosystems of the world 22. River and stream ecosystems.* (ed. C.E. Cushing, K.W. Cummins and G.W. Minshall), pp. 1–8. Elsevier, Amsterdam.

Cunningham, W.P. and Saigo, B.W. (1990). *Environmental science.* Wm. C. Brown, Dubuque, IA.

Cushing, C.E., Cummins, K.W., and Minshall, G.W. (ed.) (1995). *Ecosystems of the world 22. River and stream ecosystems.* Elsevier, Amsterdam.

Dahl, J. and Greenberg, L. (1996). Impact on stream benthic prey by benthic vs drift feeding predators: a meta-analysis. *Oikos,* **77**, 177–81.

Davies, B.R., O'Keeffe, J.H. and Snaddon, C.D. (1995). River and stream ecosystems in southern Africa: predictably unpredictable. In *Ecosystems of the World 22. River and stream ecosystems* (ed. C.E. Cushing, K.W. Cummins and G.W. Minshall), pp. 117–187. Elsevier, Amsterdam.

Davies, B.R., Thoms, M. and Meador, M. (1992). An assessment of the ecological impact of inter-basin water transfers, and their threats to a river basin integrity and conservation. *Aquatic Conservation: marine and freshwater ecosystems,* **2**, 325–49.

Davies, R.W. (1991). Annelida: leeches, polychaetes and acanthobdellids. In *Ecology and classification of North American freshwater invertebrates* (ed. J.H. Thorp and A.P. Covich), pp. 437–79. Academic Press, San Diego.

de Becker, E., Billen, G. and Servais, P. (1984). Evaluation de la contamination des eaux des surface en nutriments (N, P, K) par drainage des sols agricoles en Belgique. *Revue Agriculture,* **37**, 117–36.

Décamps, H. and Tabacchi, E. (1994). Species richness in vegetation along river margins. In *Aquatic ecology: scale pattern and process,* 34th Symposium of the British Ecological Society (ed. P.S. Giller, A.G. Hildrew and D.G. Rafaelli), pp. 1–20. Blackwell, Oxford.

Delucchi, C.M. and Peckarsky, B.L. (1989). Life history patterns of insects in an intermittent and a permanent stream. *Journal of the North American Benthological Society,* **8**, 308–21.

den Boer, P.J. (1968). Spreading of risk and stabilisation of animal numbers. *Acta Biotheoretica,* **18**, 165–94.

Dermott, R.M. and Spence, H.J. (1984). Changes in populations and drift of stream invertebrates following lampricide treatment. *Canadian Journal of Fisheries and Aquatic Science,* **41**, 1695–701.

Dietrich, M. and Anderson, N.H. (1995). Life cycles and food habits of mayflies and stoneflies from temporary streams in western Oregon. *Freshwater Biology,* **34**, 47–60.

Disney, R.H.L. (1972). Larval Hydroptilidae (Trichoptera) that prey upon Simuliidae (Diptera) in Cameroon. *Entomologist's Monthly Magazine,* **108**, 84.

Dobson, M. and Hildrew, A.G. (1992). A test of resource limitation among shredding detritivores in low order streams in southern England. *Journal of Animal Ecology,* **61**, 69–78.

Dole-Olivier, M.J. and Marmonier, P. (1992). Effects of spates on the vertical distribution of the interstitial community. *Hydrobiologia,* **230**, 49–61.

Downes, B.J. and Lake, P.S. (1991). Different colonization patterns of two closely related stream insects (*Austrosimulium* spp.) following disturbance. *Freshwater Biology*, **26**, 295–306.

Dudgeon, D. (1992). Endangered ecosystems: a review of the conservation status of tropical Asian rivers. *Hydrobiologia*, **248**, 167–91.

Dudgeon, D. (1995). The ecology of rivers and streams in tropical Asia. In *Ecosystems of the world 22. River and stream ecosystems* (ed. C.E. Cushing, K.W. Cummins and G.W. Minshall), pp. 615–57. Elsevier, Amsterdam.

Dudley, T.L., Cooper, S.D. and Hemphill, N. (1986). Effects of macroalgae on a stream invertebrate community. *Journal of the North American Benthological Society*, **5**, 93–106.

Dudley, T.L., D'Antonio, C.M. and Cooper, S.D. (1990). Mechanisms and consequences of interspecific competition between two stream insects. *Journal of Animal Ecology*, **59**, 849–66.

Edington, J.M. (1968). Habitat preferences in net-spinning caddis larvae with special reference to the influence of water velocity. *Journal of Animal Ecology*, **37**, 675–92.

Edington, J.M., Edington, M.A. and Dorman, J.A. (1984). Habitat partitioning amongst hydrophyschid larvae of a Malaysian stream. Fourth international symposium on Trichoptera. *Entomologica*, **30**, 123–9.

Edmunds Jr., G.F. (1972). Biogeography and evolution of Ephemeroptera. *Annual Review of Entomology*, **17**, 21–42.

Edwards, R.T. and Meyer, J.L. (1987). Bacteria as a food source for black fly larvae in a blackwater river. *Journal of the North American Benthological Society*, **6**, 241–50.

Eichenberger, E. and Schlatter, A. (1978). Effect of herbivorous insects on the production of benthic algal vegetation in outdoor channels. *Internationale Vereinigung für theoretische und angewandte Limnologie*. **20**, 1806–10.

Elliott, J.M. (1971*a*). Upstream movements of benthic invertebrates in a Lake District stream. *Journal of Animal Ecology*, **40**, 235–52.

Elliott, J.M. (1971*b*). The distances travelled by drifting invertebrates in a Lake District stream. *Oceologia*, **6**, 191–220.

Elliott, J.M. (1975). The growth rate of brown trout (*Salmo trutta* L.) fed on maximum rations. *Journal of Animal Ecology*, **44**, 805–21.

Elliott, J.M. (1982). The life cycle and spatial distribution of the aquatic parasitoid *Agriotypus armatus* (Hymenoptera: Agriotypidae) and its caddis host *Silo pallipes* (Trichoptera: Goeridae). *Journal of Animal Ecology*, **51**, 923–41.

Elliott, J.M. (1983). The response of the aquatic parasitoid *Agriotypus armatus* (Hymenoptera: Agriotypidae) to the spatial distribution and density of its caddis host *Silo pallipes* (Trichoptera: Goeridae). *Journal of Animal Ecology*, **52**, 315–30.

Elliott, J.M. (1987). The distances travelled by downstream-moving trout fry, *Salmo trutta*, in a Lake District stream. *Freshwater Biology*, **17**, 491–9.

Elliott, J.M. (1994). *Quantitative ecology and the brown trout*. Oxford University Press.

Elliott, J.M. (1995). Egg hatching and ecological partitioning in carnivorous stoneflies (Plecoptera). *Comptes Rendus de l'Académie des Sciences, Paris, Sciences de la Vie, Biologie et Pathologie Animale*, **318**, 237–43.

Englund, G. (1991*a*). Asymmetric resource competition in a filter-feeding stream insect (*Hydropsyche siltalai*: Trichoptera). *Freshwater Biology*, **26**, 425–32.

Englund, G., (1991*b*). Effects of disturbance on stream moss and invertebrate community structure. *Journal of the North American Benthological Society*, **10**, 143–53.

Englund, G. and Malmqvist, B. (1996). Effects of flow regulation, habitat area and isolation on the macroinvertebrate fauna of rapids in north Swedish rivers. *Regulated Rivers*, **12**, 433–45.

Englund, G. and Olsson, T.I. (1990). Fighting and assessment in the net-spinning caddis larva *Arctopsyche ladogensis*: a test of the sequential assessment game. *Animal Behaviour*, **39**, 55–62.

Englund, G., Jonsson, B-G. and Malmqvist, B. (1997*a*). Effects of flow regulation on bryophytes in north Swedish rivers. *Biological Conservation*, **79**, 79–86.

Englund, G., Malmqvist, B. and Zhang, Y. (1997*b*). Using predictive models to estimate effects of flow regulation on net-spinning caddis larvae in north Swedish rivers. *Freshwater Biology*, **37**, 687–97.

Englund, G., Sarnelle, O. and Cooper, S.D. The importance of data selection criteria: meta-analysis of stream predation experiments. *Ecology* (in press).

Erlandsson, A. and Giller, P.S. (1992). Distribution and feeding behaviour of field populations of the water cricket *Velia caprai* (Hemiptera). *Freshwater Biology*, **28**, 231–36.

Erman, N.E. (1986). Movements of self-marked caddisfly larvae, *Chyranda centralis* (Trichoptera: Limnephilidae), in a sierran spring stream, California, USA. *Freshwater Biology*, **16**, 455–64

Erman, N.A. and Erman, D.C. (1995). Spring permanence, Trichoptera species richness, and the role of drought. *Journal of the Kansas Entomological Society*, **68**, (suppl.), 50–64.

Evans, P.G.H. (1988). *The natural history of whales and dolphins*. Christopher Helm, London.

Farrell, E. P. and Boyle, G. M. (1991). *Monitoring a forest ecosystem in a region of low level anthropogenic emissions: Ballyhooly Project*. Final Report, EC Programme on the Protection of the Community's Forests Against Atmospheric Pollution (Project No. 8860IR001), Brussels.

Ferrington, L.C. (ed.) (1995). Biodiversity of aquatic insects and other invertebrates in springs. *Journal of the Kansas Entomological Society*. Special Publication 1, **68**, (2), 1–165.

Findley, S., Meyer, J. and Smith, P.J. (1986). Contribution of fungal biomass to the diet of a freshwater isopod (*Lirceus* sp). Freshwater Biology, **16**, 377–85.

Fisher, S.G. (1983). Succession in streams. In *Stream ecology* (ed. J.R. Barnes and G.W. Minshall), pp. 7–27. Plenum Press, New York.

Fisher, S.G. (1990). Recovery processes in lotic ecosystems: Limits of successional theory. *Environmental Management*, **14**, 725–36.

Fisher, S.G. (1994). Pattern, process and scale in freshwater systems: some unifying thoughts. In *Aquatic ecology: scale pattern and process*, 34th Symposium of the British Ecological Society (ed. P.S. Giller, A.G. Hildrew and D.G. Rafaelli), pp. 575–91. Blackwell, Oxford.

Fisher, S.G. (1995). Stream ecosystems of the western United States. In *Ecosystems of the world 22. River and stream ecosystems* (ed. C.E. Cushing, K.W. Cummins and G.W. Minshall), pp. 61–87. Elsevier, Amsterdam.

Fisher, S.G. and Likens, G.E. (1973). Energy flow in Bear Brook, New Hampshire: an integrative approach to stream ecosystem metabolism. *Ecological Monographs*, **43**, 421–39.

Fisher, S.G., Gray, L.J., Grimm, N.B. and Busch, D.E. (1982). Temporal succession in a desert stream ecosystem following flash flooding. *Ecological Monographs*, **52**, 93–110.

Fjellheim, A. (1980). Differences in drifting of larval stages of *Ryacophila nubila* (Trichoptera). *Holarctic Ecology*, **3**, 99–103.

Flannagan, J.F., Townsend, B.E. and de March, B.G. (1980). Acute and long term effects of methoxychlor larviciding on the aquatic invertebrates of the Athabasca River, Alberta. In *Control of blackflies in the Athabasca River*. Technical Report. (ed. W.O. Haufe and G.C. Croome), pp. 151–8. Alberta Environment, Edmonton, Canada.

Flecker, A.S. (1992). Fish predation and the evolution of invertebrate drift periodicity: evidence from neotropical streams. *Ecology*, **73**, 438–48.

Forrester, G.E. (1994). Influences of predatory fish on the drift dispersal and local density of stream insects. *Ecology*, **75**, 1208–18.

Freilich, J.E. (1991). Movement patterns and ecology of *Pteronarcys* nymphs (Plecoptera): observations of marked individuals in a Rocky Mountain stream. *Freshwater Biology*, **25**, 379–94.

Frey, D.G. (1977). Biological integrity of water—an historical approach. In *The integrity of water*. Proceedings of a symposium (ed. R.K. Ballentine and L.J. Guarraia), pp. 127–40. US Environmental Protection Agency, Washington, DC.

Frissell, C.A., Liss, W.J., Warren, C.E. and Hurley, M.D. (1986). A hierarchial framework for stream habitat classification: viewing streams in a watershed context. *Environmental Management*, **10**, 199–214.

Frost, T.M. (1991). Porifera. In *Ecology and classification of North American freshwater invertebrates* (ed. J.H. Thorp and A.P. Covich), pp. 95–124. Academic Press, San Diego.

Gaines, W.L., Cushing, C.E. and Smith, S.D. (1989). Trophic relations and functional group composition of benthic insects in three cold desert streams. *The Southwestern Naturalist*, **34**, 478–82.

Gee, A.S. and Stoner, J.H. (1989). A review of the causes and effects of acidification of surface waters in Wales and potential mitigation techniques. *Archives Environmental Contamination and Toxicology*, **18**, 121–30.

Georgian, T. and Wallace, J.B. (1983). Seasonal production dynamics in a guild of periphyton-grazing insects in a southern Appalachian stream. *Ecology*, **64**, 1236–48.

Giller, P.S. (1984). *Community structure and the niche*. Chapman and Hall, London.

Giller, P.S. (1986). The natural diet of the Notonectidae: field trials using electrophoresis. *Ecological Entomology*, **11**, 163–172.

Giller, P.S. (1996a). Floods and droughts: the effects of variations in water flow on streams and rivers. In *Disturbance and recovery of ecological systems* (ed. P.S. Giller and A.A. Myers), pp. 1–19. Royal Irish Academy, Dublin.

Giller, P.S. (1996*b*). The diversity of soil communities, the 'poor man's tropical rainforest'. *Biodiversity and Conservation*, **5**, 135–68.

Giller, P.S. and Cambell, R.N.B. (1989). Colonisation patterns of mayfly nymphs (Ephemeroptera) on implanted substrate trays of different size. *Hydrobiologia*, **178**, 59–71.

Giller, P.S. and Sangpradub, N. (1993). Predatory foraging behaviour and activity patterns of larvae of two species of limnephilid cased caddis. *Oikos*, **67**, 351–7.

Giller, P.S. and Twomey, H. (1993). Benthic macroinvertebrate community organisation in two contrasting rivers—between-site differences and seasonal patterns. *Biology and Environment. Proceedings of the Royal Irish Academy*, **93B**, 115–26.

Giller, P.S., Sangpradub, N. and Twomey, H. (1991). Catastrophic flooding and macroinvertebrate community structure. *Internationale Vereinigung für Theoretische und Angewandte Limnologie*, **24**, 1724–9

Giller, P.S., O'Halloran, J., Hernan, R., Roche, N., Clenaghan, C., Evans, J. *et al.* (1993). An integrated study of forested catchments in Ireland. *Irish Forestry*, **50**, 70–88.

Giller, P.S., Myers, A.A. and O'Halloran, J. (1997). Ecological systems, disturbances and pollution. In *Environmental engineering* (ed. G. Kiely), pp. 231–62. McGraw-Hill, London.

Gíslason, G.M. (1994). River management in cold regions: a case study of the River Laxá, North Iceland. *The rivers handbook. Hydrological and ecological principles*, Vol. 2 (ed. P. Calow and G.E. Petts), pp. 464–83. Blackwell, Oxford.

Gleick, P.H. (ed.) (1993). *Water in crisis. A guide to the world's fresh water resources.* Oxford University Press, New York.

Glozier, N.E. and Culp, J.M. (1989). Experimental investigations of diel vertical movements by lotic mayflies over substrate surfaces. *Freshwater Biology*, **21**, pp. 253–60.

Godbout, L. and Hynes, H.B.N. (1982). The three dimensional distribution of the fauna in a single riffle in a stream in Ontario. *Hydrobiologia*, **97**, 87–96.

Gordon, N.D., McMahon, T.A. and Finlayson, B.L. (1992). *Stream hydrology: an introduction for ecologists.* Wiley, Chichester.

Gore, J.A. (1982). Benthic invertebrate colonization: source distance effects on community composition. *Hydrobiologia*, **94**, 183–93.

Gray, J.R. and Edington, J.M. (1969). Effect of woodland clearance on stream temperature. *Journal of the Fisheries Research Board of Canada*, **26**, 399–403.

Gray, L.J. and Fisher, S.G. (1981). Postflood recolonization pathways of macroinvertebrates in a lowland Sonoran Desert stream. *American Midland Naturalist*, **106**, 249–57.

Gregory, S.V. (1983). Plant-herbivore interactions in stream systems. In *Stream ecology. Application and testing of general ecological theory* (ed. J.R. Barnes and G.W. Minshall), pp. 157–89. Plenum Press, New York.

Grimm, N.B. (1994). Disturbance, succession and ecosystem processes in streams: a case study from the desert. In *Aquatic ecology: scale pattern and process*, 34th

Symposium of the British Ecological Society (ed. P.S. Giller, A.G. Hildrew and D.G. Rafaelli), pp. 93–112. Blackwell, Oxford.

Grubaugh, J.W., Wallace, J.B., and Houston, E.S. (1996). Longitudinal changes of macroinvertebrate communities along an Appalachian stream continuum. *Canadian Journal of Fisheries and Aquatic Sciences*, **53**, 896–909.

Gurnell, A.M. (1983). Downstream channel adjustments in response to water abstraction for hydro-electric power generation from Alpine glacial melt-water streams. *The Geographical Journal*, **149**, 342–54.

Haay, W.R., Butler, R.S. and Hartfield, P.D. (1995). An extraordinary reproductive strategy in freshwater bivalves: prey mimicry to facilitate larval dispersal. *Freshwater Biology*, **34**, 471–6.

Haeckel, J.W., Meijering, M.P.D. and Rusetzki, H. (1973). *Gammarus fossarum* Koch als Fallaubzersetzer in Waldbächen. *Freshwater Biology*, **3**, 241–9.

Hammerton, D. (1972). The Nile River—a case history. In *River ecology and man* (ed. R.T. Oglesby, C.A. Carlson and J.A. McCann), pp. 171–214. Academic Press, New York.

Hansen, R.A., Hart, D.D. and Merz, R.A. (1991). Flow mediates predator-prey interactions between triclad flatworms and larval black flies. *Oikos*, **60**, 187–96.

Hargrave, B.T. (1991). Ecology of deep-water zones. In *Fundamentals of aquatic ecology*, (2nd edn) (ed. R.S.K. Barnes and K.H. Mann), pp. 77–90. Blackwell, Oxford.

Hart, D.D. (1978). Diversity in stream insects: regulation by rock size and microspatial complexity. *Internationale Vereinigung für theoretische und angewandte Limnologie Verhandlungen*, **20**, 1376–81.

Hart, D.D. (1983). The importance of competitive interactions within stream populations and communities. In *Stream ecology* (ed. J.R. Barnes and G.W. Minshall), pp. 99–136. Plenum Press, New York.

Hart, D.D. (1985). Causes and consequences of territoriality in a grazing stream insect. *Ecology*, **66**, 404–14.

Hart, D.D. (1986). The adaptive significance of territoriality in filter-feeding larval blackflies (Diptera: Simuliidae). *Oikos*, **46**, 88–92.

Hart, D.D. (1992). Community organization in streams: the importance of species interactions, physical factors, and chance. *Oecologia*, **91**, 220–8.

Hart, D.D. and Horwitz, R.J. (1991). Habitat diversity and the species-area relationship: alternative models and tests. In *Habitat structure. The physical arrangement of objects in space* (ed. S.S. Bell, E.D. McCoy and A.R. Mushinsky), pp. 47–68. Chapman and Hall, London.

Hart, D.D., Merz, R.A., Genovese, S.J. and Clark, B.D. (1991). Feeding posture of suspension-feeding larval blackflies: the conflicting demands of drag and food acquisition. *Oecologia*, **85**, 457–63.

Harvey, B.C. and Marti, C.D. (1993). The impact of dipper, *Cinclus mexicanus*, predation on stream benthos. *Oikos*, **68**, 431–6.

Haslam, S.M. (1990). *River pollution: an ecological perspective*. Wiley, Chichester.

Hasselrot, R.T. (1993). Insights into a Psychomiid life. Towards the understanding of the ecology of the caddisfly *Tinodes waeneri* L. (Trichoptera, Psychomyiidae). PhD thesis, Uppsala University.

Hawkins, C.P. and Furnish, J.K. (1987). Are snails important competitors in stream ecosystems? *Oikos*, **49**, 209–70.

Heard, S.B. and Richardson, J.S. (1995). Shredder-collector facilitation in stream detrital food webs: is there enough evidence? *Oikos*, **72**, 359–66.

Hellawell, J.M. (1986). *Biological indicators of freshwater pollution and environmental management. Pollution monitoring series*. Elsevier, London.

Heltshe, J.F. and Forrester, N.E. (1983). Estimating species richness using the jackknife procedure. *Biometrics*, **39**, 1–11.

Hemphill, N. (1988). Competition between two stream dwelling filter-feeders, *Hydropsyche oslari* and *Simulium virgatum. Oecologia*, **77**, 73–80.

Hemphill, N. (1991). Disturbance and variation in competition between two stream insects. *Ecology*, **72**, 864–72.

Hemphill, N. and Cooper, S.D. (1983). The effect of physical disturbance on the relative abundances of two filter-feeding insects in a small stream. *Oecologia*, **58**, 378–82.

Hesthagen, T. (1990). Home range of juvenile Atlantic salmon, *Salmo salar*, and brown trout, *Salmo trutta*, in a Norwegian stream. *Freshwater Biology*, **24**, 63–7.

Hickin, N.E. (1967). *Caddis larvae. Larvae of the British Trichopetra*. Hutchinson, London.

Higler, L.W.G. (1975). Reactions of some caddis larvae (Trichoptera) to different types of substrate in an experimental stream. *Freshwater Biology*, **5**, 151–8.

Hildrew, A.G. (1996a). Food webs and species interactions. In *River biota, diversity and dynamics* (ed. G. Petts and P. Calow), pp. 123–44. Blackwell, Oxford.

Hildrew, A.G. (1996b). Whole river ecology: spatial scale and heterogeneity in the ecology of running waters. *Archiv für Hydrobiologie*, **10**(suppl. 11, Large rivers), 324–43.

Hildrew, A.G. and Edington, J.M. (1979). Factors affecting the coexistence of hydropsychid caddis larvae (Trichoptera) in the same river system. *Journal of Animal Ecology*, **48**, 557–76.

Hildrew, A.G. and Giller, P.S. (1994). Patchiness, species interactions and disturbance in the stream benthos. In *Aquatic Ecology: scale pattern and process*, 34th Symposium of the British Ecological Society (ed. P.S. Giller, A.G. Hildrew and D.G. Rafaelli), pp. 21–62. Blackwell, Oxford.

Hildrew, A.G. and Townsend, C.R. (1977). The influence of substrate on the functional response of *Plectrocnemia conspersa* (Curtis) larvae (Trichoptera: Polycentropodidae). *Oecologia*, **31**, 21–26.

Hildrew, A.G. and Townsend, C.R. (1980). Aggregation, interference and foraging by larvae of *Plectrocnemia conspersa* (Trichoptera: Polycentropodidae). *Animal Behaviour*, **28**, 553–60.

Hildrew, A.G. and Townsend, C.R. (1987). Organization in freshwater benthic communities. In *Organization of communities: past and present* (ed. J.H.R. Gee and P.S. Giller), pp. 347–71. Blackwell, Oxford.

Hildrew, A.G. and Wagner, R. (1992). The briefly colonial life of hatchlings of the net-spinning caddisfly *Plectrocnemia conspersa. Journal of the North American Benthological Society*, **11**, 60–8.

Hildrew, A.G., Townsend, C.R. and Francis, J. (1984). Community structure in some southern English streams: the influence of species interactions. *Freshwater Biology*, **14**, 297–310.

Hildrew, A.G., Townsend, C.R. and Hasham, A. (1985). The predatory Chironomidae of an iron-rich stream: feeding ecology and food web structure. *Ecological Entomology*, **10**, 403–13.

Hildrew, A.G., Raffaelli, D.G. and Giller, P.S. (1994). Introduction. In *Aquatic ecology: scale pattern and process*, 34th Symposium of the British Ecological Society (ed. P.S. Giller, A.G. Hildrew and D.G. Rafaelli), pp. ix–xiii. Blackwell, Oxford.

Holdich, D.M. and Reeve, I.D. (1991). Distribution of freshwater crayfish in the British Isles, with particular reference to crayfish plague, alien introductions and water quality. *Aquatic Conservation: Marine and Freshwater Ecosystems*, **1**, 139–58.

Hornung, M. and Reynolds, B. (1995). The effects of natural and anthropogenic environmental changes on ecosystem processes at the catchment scale. *Trends in Ecology and Evolution*, **10**, 443–9.

Hornung, M., Le-Grice, S., Brown, N. and Norris, D. (1990). The role of geology and soils in controlling surface water acidity in Wales. In *Acid waters in Wales* (ed. R.W. Edwards *et al.*), pp. 55–66. Kluwer, Dordrecht.

Howard-Williams, C., Vincent, C.L., Broady, P.A. and Vincent, W.F. (1986). Antarctic stream ecosystems: variability in environmental properties and algal community structure. *Internationale Revue der Gesamte Hydrobiologie*, **71**, 511–44.

Huet, M. (1954). Biologie, profils en long et en travers des eaux courantes. *Bulletin Français Piscicine*, **175**, 41–53.

Hughes, J.M., Bunn, S.E., Hurwood, D. and Kingston, M. (1995). Genetic differentiation of populations of *Paratya australiensis* (Decapoda: Atyidae) in rainforest streams in south-east Queensland. *Journal of the North American Benthological Society*, **14**, 158–73.

Hugueny, B. (1989). West African rivers as biogeographic islands: species richness of fish communities. *Oecologia*, **79**, 236–43.

Hullar, M.A. and Vestal, J.R. (1989). The effects of nutrient limitation and stream discharge on the epilithic microbial community in an oligotrophic Arctic stream. *Hydrobiologia*, **172**, 19–26.

Humpesch, U.H. (1981). Effect of temperature on larval growth of *Ecdyonurus dispar* (Ephemeroptera: Heptageniidae) from two English lakes. *Freshwater Biology*, **11**, 441–57.

Huryn, A.D. (1990). Growth and voltinism of lotic midge larvae: Patterns across an Appalachian Mountain base. *Limnology and Oceanography*, **35**, 339–51.

Huryn, A.D. and Wallace, J.B. (1987). Production and litter processing by crayfish in an Appalachian mountain stream. *Freshwater Biology*, **18**, 277–286.

Hutchinson, G.E. (1981). Thoughts on aquatic insects. *BioScience*, **31**, 495–500.

Hynes, H.B. (1960). *The biology of polluted waters.* Liverpool University Press.

Hynes, H.B.N. (1970). *The ecology of running waters.* Liverpool University Press.

Hynes, H.B. (1975). The stream and its valley. *Internationale Vereinigung für theoretische und angewandte Limnologie*, **19**, 1–15.

Ingold, C.T. (1975). *Guide to aquatic hyphomycetes.* Freshwater Biological Association, Publication No. 30. Ambleside, Cumbria, UK.

Institute of Hydrology (1984–87). *Research report 1984–1987*. Natural Environment Research Council, UK.

Irons III, J. G., Oswood, M.W., Stout, R.J. and Pringle, C.M. (1994). Latitudinal patterns in leaf litter breakdown: is temperature really important? *Freshwater Biology*, **32**, 401–11.

Jackson, S. and Davis, W. (1994). Meeting the goal of biological integrity in water-resource programs in the US Environmental Protection Agency. *Journal of the North American Benthological Society*, **13**, 592–7.

Jacobi, G.Z. and Cary, S.J. (1996). Winter stoneflies (Plecoptera) in seasonal habitats in New Mexico, USA. *Journal of the North American Benthological Society*, **15**, 690–9.

Jacobsen, D. and Sand-Jensen, K. (1992). Herbivory of invertebrates on submerged macrophytes from Danish freshwaters. *Freshwater Biology*, **28**, 301–8.

Jacobsen, D. and Sand-Jensen, K. (1994). Invertebrate herbivory on the submerged macrophyte *Potamogeton perfoliatus* in a Danish stream. *Freshwater Biology*, **31**, 43–52.

Jacobsen, D. and Sand-Jensen, K. (1995). Variability of invertebrate herbivory on the submerged macrophyte *Potamogeton perfoliatus* in a Danish stream. *Freshwater Biology*, **34**, 357–65.

Jacobsen, D., Schultz, R. and Encalada, A. (1997). Structure and diversity of stream invertebrate assemblages: the influence of temperature with altitude and latitude. *Freshwater Biology*, **38**, 247–61.

Jansson, A. and Vuoristo, T. (1979). Significance of stridulation in larval Hydropsychidae (Trichoptera). *Behaviour*, **71**, 167–86.

Jeffries, M.J. and Lawton, J.H. (1985). Predator-prey ratios in communities of freshwater invertebrates: the role of enemy free space. *Freshwater Biology*, **15**, 105–12.

Johnson, P.D., Brown, K.M. and Covell, C.V. (1994). A comparison of the macroinvertebrate assemblage in Doe Run Creek, Kentucky: 1960 and 1990. *Journal of the North American Benthological Society*, **13**, 496–510.

Johnson, S.L. and Covich, A.P. (1997). Scales of observation of riparian forests and distribution of suspended detritus in a prairie river. *Freshwater Biology*, **37**, 163–75.

Kat, P.W. (1984). Parasitism and the Unionacea (Bivalvia). *Biological Review*, **59**, 189–207.

Kaushik, N.K. and Hynes, H.B.N. (1971). The fate of autumn-shed leaves that fall into streams. *Archiv für Hydrobiologie*, **68**, 465–515.

Kelleher, B. *et al.* Effects of exotic amphipod invasions on fish diet in the lower Rhine. *Archiv für Hydrobiologie* (in press).

Keller, R. (1984). The world's fresh water: yesterday, today, tomorrow. *Applied Geography and Development*, **24**, 7–23.

Kennedy, G.J.A. and Strange, C.D. (1986). The effects of intra- and inter-specific competition on the distribution of stocked juvenile Atlantic salmon, *Salmo salar* L., in relation to depth and gradient in an upland trout, *Salmo trutta* L., stream. *Journal of Fish Biology*, **29**, 199–214.

Kerfoot, W.C. and Sih, A. (1987). *Predation: Direct and Indirect Impacts on Aquatic Communities*. University Press of New England, Hanover, NH.

Kiely, G. (ed.) (1997). *Environmental engineering*. McGraw-Hill, London.

Kiffney, P.M. and Clements, W.H. (1994). Effects of heavy metals on a macroinvertebrate assemblage from a Rocky Mountain stream in experimental microcosms. *Journal of the North American Benthological Society*, **13,** 511–23.

Kiffney, P.M., Little, E.E. and Clements, W.H. (1997). Influence of ultraviolet-B radiation on the drift response of stream invertebrates. *Freshwater Biology*, **37,** 485–92.

Koetsier III, P., McArthur, J.V. and Leff, L.G. (1997). Spatial and temporal response of stream bacteria to sources of dissolved organic carbon in a blackwater stream system. *Freshwater Biology*, **37,** 79–89.

Kohler, S.L. (1985). Identification of stream drift mechanisms: an experimental and observational approach. *Ecology*, **66,** 1749–61.

Kohler, S.L. (1992). Competition and the structure of a benthic stream community. *Ecological Monographs*, **62,** 165–88.

Kohler, S.L. and Wiley, M.J. (1997). Pathogen outbreaks reveal large-scale effects of competition in stream communities. *Ecology*, **78,** 2164–76.

Kolasa, J. (1991). Flatworms: Turbellaria and Nemertea. In *Ecology and classification of North American freshwater invertebrates* (ed. J.H. Thorp and A.P. Covich), pp. 145–71. Academic Press, San Diego.

Kullberg, A. (1988). The case, mouthparts, silk and silk formation of *Rheotanytarsus muscicola* Kieffer (Chironomidae: Tanytarsini). *Aquatic Insects*, **10,** 249–55.

Kullberg, A. and Petersen, R.C. (1987). Dissolved organic carbon, seston and macroinvertebrate drift in an acidified and limed humic system. *Freshwater Biology*, **17,** 553–64.

Ladle, M. (1991). Running waters: a conservationist's nightmare. In *The scientific management of temperate communities for conservation*, 31st symposium of the British Ecological Society (ed. I.F. Spellberg, F.B. Goldsmith and M.G. Morris), pp. 384–93. Blackwell, Oxford.

Laenen, A. and Dunnette, D. A. (1997) (ed.). *River quality, dynamics and restoration*. CRC Lewis, Boca Raton, USA.

Lake, P.S. (1995). Of flood and droughts: river and stream ecosystems of Australia. In *Ecosystems of the world 22. River and stream ecosystems*. (ed. C.E. Cushing, K.W. Cummins and G.W. Minshall), pp. 659–94. Elsevier, Amsterdam.

Lake, P.S. and Doeg, T.J. (1985). Macroinvertebrate colonization of stones in two upland southern Australian streams. *Hydrobiologia*, **126,** 199–211.

Lamberti, G.A. and Resh, V.H. (1987). Seasonal patterns of suspended bacteria and algae in two northern California streams. *Archiv für Hydrobiologie*, **110,** 45–57.

Lamberti, G. A. and Steinman, D. (1997). A comparison of primary production in ecosystems. *Journal of the North American Benthological Society*, **16,** 95–103.

Lancaster, J. (1996). Scaling the effects of predation and disturbance in a patchy environment. *Oecologia*, **107,** 321–31.

Lancaster, J. and Hildrew, A.G. (1993*a*). Characterizing in-stream flow refugia. *Canadian Journal of Fisheries and Aquatic Sciences*, **50,** 1663–75.

Lancaster, J. and Hildrew, A.G. (1993*b*). Flow refugia and the microdistribution of lotic macroinvertebrates. *Journal of the North American Benthological Society*, **12,** 385–93.

Lancaster, J. and Robinson, A.L. (1995). Microcrustacean prey and macro-invertebrate predators in a stream food web. *Freshwater Biology*, **34**, (1), 123–34.

Lancaster, J., Hildrew, A.G. and Gjerlov, C. (1996). Invertebrate drift and longitudinal transport processes in streams. *Canadian Journal of Fisheries and Aquatic Sciences*, **53**, 572–82.

Larsson, P. (1984). Uptake of sediment-released PCBs by the eel *Anguilla anguilla*, in static model systems. Ecological Bulletin. **36**, 62–7.

Leopold, L.B. (1962). Rivers. *American Scientist*, 511–37.

Leopold, L.B., Woolman, M.G. and Miller, J.F. (1964). *Fluvial processes in geomorphology*. Freeman, San Francisco.

LeSage, L. and Harrison, A.D. (1980). The biology of *Cricotopus* (Chironomidae: Orthocladiinae) in an algal enriched stream. 1. Normal biology. *Archiv für Hydrobiologie*, **57**(suppl.), 375–418.

Lewis Jnr., W.M., Hamilton, S.K. and Saunders III, J.F. (1995). Rivers of northern South America. In *Ecosystems of the world 22. River and stream ecosystems* (ed. C.E. Cushing, K.W. Cummins and G.W. Minshall), pp. 219–56. Elsevier, Amsterdam.

Lillehammer, A. (1988). Stoneflies (Plecoptera) of Fennoscandia and Denmark. *Fauna Entomologica Scandia*, **21**, 1–165.

Lillehammer, A., Brittain, J.E., Saltveit, S.J. and Nielsen, P.S. (1989). Egg development, nymphal growth and life cycle, strategies in Plecoptera, *Holarctic Ecology*, **12**, 173–86.

Likens, G.E., and Bormann, F.H. (1995). *Biogeochemistry of a forested ecosystem*, (2nd edn). Springer-Verlag, New York.

Lock, M.A., Wallace, R.L., Costerton, J.W., Ventullo, R.M. and Charlton, S.E. (1984). River epilithon: toward a structural-functional model. *Oikos*, **42**, 10–22.

Loudon, C. and Alstad, D.N. (1990). Theoretical mechanisms of particle capture: predictions for hydropsychid caddisfly distributional ecology. *American Naturalist*, **135**, 360–81.

Lowe-McConnell, R.H. (1970). Ecological studies on tropical freshwater food fishes. In *Proceedings of the regional meeting of inland water biologists in southeast Asia*, pp. 91–103. Unesco Field Science Office for southeast Asia, Djakarta, Indonesia.

Lowe-McConnell, R.H. (1987). *Ecological studies of tropical fish communities*. Cambridge University Press, New York.

Macan, T.T. (1976). *A revised key to the British water bugs (Hemiptera-Heteroptera) with notes on their ecology*. Freshwater Biological Association, Scientific Publication, No. 16. Ambleside, Cumbria, UK.

Mackay, R.J. (1995). River and stream ecosystems of Canada. *Ecosystems of the world 22. River and stream ecosystems* (ed. C.E. Cushing, K.W. Cummins and G.W. Minshall), pp. 33–60. Elsevier, Amsterdam.

Mackey, A. P., Ham, S. F., Cooling, D. A. and Berrie, A. D. (1982). An ecological survey of a limestone stream, the River Coln, Gloucestershire, England, in comparison with some chalk streams. *Archiv für Hydrobiologie*, **64**(suppl.), 307–340.

Maitland, P.S. (1990). *Biology of freshwater* (2nd edn). Blackie and Son, Glasgow.

Malas, D. and Wallace, J.B. (1977). Strategies for coexistence in three species of net-spinning caddisflies (Trichoptera) in second-order southern Appalachian streams. *Canadian Journal of Zoology*, **55**, 1829–40.

Malmqvist, B. (1988). Downstream drift in Madeiran levadas: tests of hypotheses relating to the influence of predators of the drift of insects. *Aquatic Insects*, **10**, 141–52.

Malmqvist, B. (1991). Stonefly functional responses: Influence of substrate heterogeneity and predator interaction. *Internationale Vereinigung für theoretische und angewandte Limnologie*, **24**, 2895–900.

Malmqvist, B. (1992). Stream grazer responses to predator odour: an experimental study. *Nordic Journal of Freshwater Research*, **67,** 27–34.

Malmqvist, B. (1993). Interactions in stream leaf packs: effects of a stonefly predator on detritivores and organic matter processing. *Oikos*, **66**, 454–62.

Malmqvist, B. (1994). Preimaginal blackflies (Diptera: simuliidae) and their predators in a central Scandinavian lake outlet stream. *Annals Zoologici Fennici*, **31**, 245–55.

Malmqvist, B. (1996). The ibis fly, *Atherix ibis* (Diptera: Athericidae), in Sweden: the distribution and status of a red-listed fly species. *Entomologisk Tidskrift*, **117**, 23–8.

Malmqvist, B. and Englund, G. (1996). Effects of hydropower-induced flow perturbations on mayfly (Ephemeroptera) richness and abundance in north Swedish river rapids. *Hydrobiologia*, **341**, 145–58.

Malmqvist, B. and Eriksson, Å. (1995). Benthic insects in Swedish lake outlet streams: patterns in species richness and assemblage structure. *Freshwater Biology*, **34**, 285–96.

Malmqvist, B. and Sackmann, G. (1996). Changing risk of predation for a filter-feeding insect along a current velocity gradient. *Oecologia*, **108**, 450–8.

Malmqvist, B. and Sjöström, P. (1980). Prey size and feeding patterns in *Dinocras cephalotes* (Plecoptera). *Oikos*, **35**, 311–16.

Malmqvist, B. and Sjöström, P. (1987). Stream drift as a consequence of predator disturbance—field and laboratory experiments. *Oecologia*, **74**, 396–403.

Malmqvist, B., Rundle, S., Brönmark, C. and Erlandsson, A. (1991*a*). Invertebrate colonization of a new, man-made stream in southern Sweden. *Freshwater Biology*, **26**, 307-*24*.

Malmqvist, B., Sjöström, P. and Frick, K. (1991*b*). The diet of two species of *Isoperla* (Plecoptera: Perlodidae) in relation to season, site and sympatry. *Hydrobiologia*, **213**, 191–203.

Malmqvist, B., Nilsson, A.N. and Baez, M. (1995). Tenerife's freshwater fauna: status and threats (Canary Islands, Spain). *Aquatic Conservation*, **5**, 1–24.

Malmqvist, B., Meisch, C. and Nilsson, A.N. (1997). Distribution patterns of freshwater Ostracoda (Crustacea) in the Canary Islands with regards to habitat use and biogeography. *Hydrobiologia*, **347**, 159–70.

Maltby, L. (1992). Heterotrophic microbes. In *Rivers handbook*. Vol. 1 (ed. P. Calow and G.E. Petts), pp. 165–94. Blackwell, London.

Mann, K.H., Britton, R.H., Kowalczewski, A., Lack, T.J., Mathews, C.P. and McDonald, I. (1972). Productivity and energy flow at all trophic levels in the R.

Thames, England. In *Proceedings of the IBP-UNESCO symposium on productivity problems of freshwaters*, Kazimierz Dolny, 7–12 May, 1970 (ed. Z. Kajak and A. Hillbricht-Ilkovska), pp. 579–96. PWN, Polish Scientific Publishers, Warsaw.

Mann, R.H.K. and Penczak, T. (1986). Fish production in rivers: a review. *Polskie Archiwum Hydrobiologii*, **33**, 233–47.

Marchant, R. and Yule, C.M. (1996). A method for estimating larval life spans of aseasonal aquatic insects from streams on Bougainville Island, Papua New Guinea. *Freshwater Biology*, **35**, 101–7.

Marden, J.H. and Kramer, M.G. (1995). Locomotor performance of insects with rudimentary wings. *Nature*, **337**, 332–4.

Martin, I.D. and Mackay, R.J. (1982). Interpreting the diet of *Rhyacophila* larvae (Trichoptera) from gut analysis: An evaluation of techniques. *Canadian Journal of Zoology*, **60**, 783–9.

Marvanová, L. and Müller-Haeckel, A. (1980). Water-borne spores in foam in a subarctic stream system in Sweden. *Sydowia, Annales Mycologici Series 11*, **33**, 210–20.

Mason, C.F. (1991). *Biology of freshwater pollution*, (2nd edn). Longman, Harlow, UK.

Mason, C.F. and O'Sullivan, W.M. (1993). Further observations on PCB and organochlorine residues in Irish otters *Lutra lutra*. *Biology and Environment, Proceedings of the Royal Irish Academy*, **93B**, 187–8.

Matthews, W.J., Schorr, M.S. and Meador, M.R. (1996). Effects of experimentally enhanced flows on fishes of a small Texas (USA) stream: assessing the impact of interbasin transfer. *Freshwater Biology*, **35**, 349–62.

Maude, S.H. and Williams, D.D. (1983). Behavior of crayfish in water currents: hydrodynamics of eight species with reference to their distribution patterns in southern Ontario. *Canadian Journal of Fisheries and Aquatic Science*, **40**, 68–77.

McCahon, C.P., Maund, S.J., and Poulton, M.J. (1991). The effect of the acanthocephalan parasite (*Pomphorhynchus laevis*) on the drift of its intermediate host. *Freshwater Biology*, **25**, 507–13.

McAuliffe, J.R. (1984*a*). Competition for space, disturbance, and the structure of a benthic stream community. *Ecology*, **65**, 894–908.

McAuliffe, J.R. (1984*b*). Resource depression by a stream herbivore: effects on distributions and abundances of other grazers. *Oikos*, **42**, 327–33.

McCarthy, T.V. (1986). Biogeographic aspects of Ireland's invertebrate fauna. In *Proceedings of the postglacial colonisation conference* (ed. D.P. Sheenan, R. Devoy and P. Woodman), pp. 67-84. Occasional publications of the Irish Biogeographical Society, Dublin.

McIntire, C.D. (1973). Periphyton dynamics in laboratory streams: a simulation model and its implications. *Ecological Monographs*, **43**, 399–420.

McIntosh, A.R. and Peckarsky, B.L. (1996). Differential behavioural responses of mayflies from streams with and without fish to trout odour. *Freshwater Biology*, **35**, 141–8.

McIntosh, A.R. and Townsend, C.R. (1995). Impacts of an introduced predatory fish on mayfly grazing in New Zealand streams. *Limnology and Oceanography*, **40**, 1508–12.

McMahon, R.F. (1991). Mollusca: Bivalvia. In *Ecology and classification of North American freshwater invertebrates* (ed. J.H. Thorp and A.P. Covich), pp. 37–93. Academic Press, San Diego.

McPhee, J. (1989). *The control of nature*. Farrar, Straus, and Giroux, New York.

Melhaus, A., Seip, K.L. and Seip, H.M. (1978). A preliminary study of the use of benthic algae as biological indicators of heavy metal pollution in Sorfjorden, Norway. *Environmental Pollution*, **15**, 101–7.

Menge, B.A. (1976). Organization of the New England rocky intertidal community: role of predation, competition, and environmental heterogeneity. *Ecological Monographs*, **46**, 355-93.

Merritt, R.W. and Cummins, K.W. (Eds) (1996). *An introduction to the aquatic insects of North America* (3rd edn). Kendall/Hunt Publishing Company, Iowa.

Merritt, R.W., Cummins, K.W. and Burton, T.M. (1984). The role of aquatic insects in the processing and cycling of nutrients. In *The ecology of aquatic insects* (ed. V.H. Resh and D.M. Rosenberg), pp. 134–63. Praeger, New York.

Meybeck, M. (1996). River water quality. Global ranges, time and space variabilities, proposal for some redefinitions. *Internationale Vereinigung für theoretische und angewandte Limnologie*, **26**, 81–96,

Miller, J.C. (1987). Evidence for the use of non-detrital dissolved organic matter by microheterotrophs on plant detritus in a woodland stream. *Freshwater Biology*, **18**, 483–94.

Miller, M.C., DeOliveira, P. and Gibeau, G.G. (1992). Epilithic diatom community response to years of PO_4 fertilization: Kuparuk River, Alaska (68 N Lat). *Hydrobiologia*, **240**, 103–19.

Milliman, J.D. (1990). Fluvial sediment in coastal seas: flux and fate. *Nature Resources*, **26**, 2–22.

Milliman, J.D. and Meade, R.H. (1983). World-wide delivery of river sediment to the oceans. *Journal of Geology*, **91**, 1–21.

Milner, A.M. (1994). Colonization and succession of invertebrate communities in a new stream in Glacier Bay National Park, Alaska. *Freshwater Biology*, **32**, 387–400.

Milner, A.M. and Petts, G.E. (1994). Glacial rivers: physical habitat and ecology. *Freshwater Biology*, **32**, 295–307.

Minshall, G.W. (1984). Aquatic insect-substratum relationships. In *The ecology of aquatic insects* (ed. V.H. Resh and D.M. Rosenberg), pp. 358–400. Praeger, New York.

Minshall, G.W. (1988). Stream ecosystem theory: a global perspective. *Journal of the North American Benthological Society*, **7**, 263–88.

Minshall, G.W. and Petersen Jr., R.C. (1985). Towards a theory of macroinvertebrate community structure in stream ecosystems. *Archiv für Hydrobiologie*, **104**, 49–76.

Molloy, D.P. (1987). The ecology of blackfly parasites. In. *Blackflies. Ecology, population management, and annotated world list* (ed. K.C. Kim and R.W. Merritt), pp. 315–26. Pennsylvania State University, University Park.

Molloy, J.M. (1992). Diatom communities along stream longitudinal gradients. *Freshwater Biology*, **28**, 59–69.

Moriarty, F. (1990). *Ecotoxicology: a study of pollutants in ecosystems*, (2nd edn). Academic Press, London.

Moss, B. (1998). *Ecology of fresh waters*, (3rd edn). Blackwell Science, Oxford.

Moss, D., Furse, M., Wright, J. and Armitage, P. (1987). The prediction of macroinvertebrate fauna of unpolluted running water sites in Great Britain using environmental data. *Freshwater Biology*, **17**, 41–52.

Mouvet, C. (1985). The use of aquatic bryophytes to monitor heavy metal pollution of freshwaters as illustrated by case studies. *Internationale Vereinigung für theoretische und angewandte Limnologie*, **22**, 2420–5.

Moyle, P.B. and Senanayake, R. (1984). Resource partitioning amongst the fishes of the rainforest streams of Sri Lanka. *Journal of Zoology, London*, **202**, 195–224.

Müller, K. (1954). Investigations of the organic drift in North Swedish streams. Institute of Freshwater Research, Drottningholm. Report, **34**, 133–48.

Müller, K. (1974). Stream drift as a chronobiological phenomenon in running water ecosystems. *Annual Review of Ecology and Systematics*, **5**, 309–23.

Müller, K. (1982). The colonization cycle of freshwater insects. *Oecologia*, **52**, 202–7.

Müller-Haeckel, A. (1973). Experimente zum Bewegungsverhalten von einzelligen Fliesswasseralgen. *Hydrobiologia*, **41**, 221–46.

Mulholland, P.J. and Lenat, D.R. (1992). Streams of the southeastern piedmont, Atlantic drainage. In *Biodiversity of the southeastern United States: aquatic communities* (ed. C. Hackney, S. Marshall Adams and W. Martin), pp. 193–232. Wiley, New York.

Muotka, T. and Penttinen, A. (1994). Detecting small-scale spatial patterns in lotic predator-prey relationships: statistical methods and a case study. *Canadian Journal of Fisheries and Aquatic Science*, **51**, 2210–18.

Muotka, T. and Virtanen, R. (1995). Stream as habitat templet for bryophytes: distribution along gradients in disturbance and substratum heterogenerity. *Freshwater Biology*, **33**, 141–9.

Murvosh, C.M. and Hogue, C.L. (1991). The torrential insect fauna of North America. *Bulletin of the North American Benthological Society*, **8**, 322–7.

Naiman, R.J. (1983). The annual pattern and spatial distribution of aquatic oxygen metabolism in boreal forest watershed. *Ecological Monographs*, **53**, 73–94.

Naiman, R.J., Johnston, C.A. and Kelley, J.C. (1986). Alteration of North American streams by beaver. *BioScience*, **38**, 753–62.

Naiman, R.J., Melillo, J.M., Lock, M.A. and Ford, T.E. (1987). Longitudinal patterns of ecosystem processes and community structure in a subarctic river continuum. *Ecology*, **68**, 1139–56.

Naiman, R.J., Décamps, H., Pastor, J. and Johnston, C.A. (1988). The potential importance of boundaries to fluvial ecosystems. *Journal of the North American Benthological Society*, **7**, 289–306.

Natarajan, A.V. (1989). Environmental impact of Ganga Basin development on gene-pool and fisheries of the Ganga River system. *Canadian Special Publications of Fisheries and Aquatic Science*, **106**, 545–60.

Naves, J., Bousquet, G., Leroy, P., Hubert, P. and Vilagines, R. (1990). Evolution de la qualité de l'eau de la Seine à Ivry-sur-Seine (France) de 1887 à 1986. In *Application des modèles mathématiques à l'evolution des modifications de la qualité de l'eau: 35–44.* ENIT, Tunis, 7–12 May.

Newbold, J.D. (1992). Cycles and spirals of nutrients. In *Rivers handbook*, Vol. 1 (ed. P. Calow and G.E. Petts), pp. 379–408. Blackwell, London.

Newbold, J.D., Elwood, J.W., O'Neill, R.V. and Sheldon, A.L. (1983). Phosphorus dynamics in a woodland stream ecosystem: a study of nutrient spiralling. *Ecology*, **64**, 1249–65.

Newson, M. (1994). *Hydrology and the river environment.* Clarendon Press, Oxford.

Niemi, G.J., DeVore, P., Detenbeck, N., Taylor, D., Lima, A., Pastor, J. *et al.* (1990). Overview of case studies on recovery of aquatic systems from disturbance. *Environmental Management*, **14**, 571–87.

Nilsson, A.S. (ed.) (1996/1997). *Aquatic insects of North Europe. A taxonomic handbook*, Parts 1 and 2. Apollo Books, Stenstrup.

Nilsson, C. (1996). Remediating river margin vegetation along fragmented and regulated rivers in the north: What is possible? *Regulated Rivers*, **12**, 415–31.

Nilsson, C. and Jansson, R. (1995). Floristic differences between riparian corridors of regulated and free-flowing boreal rivers. *Regulated rivers: research and managment*, **11**, 55–66.

Nilsson, C., Nilsson, E., Johansson, M.E., Dynesius, M., Grelsson, G., Xiong, S. *et al.* (1993). Processes structuring riparian vegetation. In *Current topics in botanical research*, Vol.1 (ed. J. Menon), pp. 419–31. Council of Scientific Research Integration, Trivandrum.

Odum, H.T. (1957). Trophic structure and productivity of Silver Springs. *Ecological Monographs*, **27**, 55–112.

O'Halloran, J., Myers, A.A. and Duggan, P.F. (1988). Blood lead levels and free red blood cell protoporphyrin as a measure of lead exposure in Mute swans. *Environmental Pollution*, **52**, 19–38.

O'Halloran, J., Ormerod, S.J., Smiddy, P. and O'Mahony, B. (1993). Organochlorines and mercury content of dipper eggs in south west Ireland. *Biology and Environment, Proceedings of the Royal Irish Academy*, **93**, 25–31.

O'Halloran, J., Giller, P.S., Clenaghan C., Wallace, J. and Koolen, R. (1996). Plantation forestry in river catchments: disturbance and recovery. In *Disturbance and recovery of ecological systems* (ed. P.S. Giller and A.A. Myers), pp. 68–83. Royal Irish Academy, Dublin.

Olsson, T.I. (1981). Overwintering of benthic invertebrates in ice and frozen sediments in a north Swedish river. *Holarctic Ecology*, **4**, 161–6.

Ormerod, S.J. and Tyler, S.J. (1991). Exploitation of prey by a river bird, the dipper *Cinclus cinclus* (L.), along acidic and circumneutral streams in upland Wales. *Freshwater Biology*, **25**, 105–16.

Ormerod, S.J., Tyler, S.J. and Lewis, J.M.S. (1985). Is the breeding distribution of dippers influenced by stream acidity? *Bird Study*, **32**, 33–9.

Ormerod, S.J., Boole, P., McCahon, C.P., Wetherly, N.S., Pascoe, D. and Edwards, R.W. (1987*a*). Short term experimental acidification of a Welsh stream: comparing the biological effects of hydrogen ions and aluminium. *Freshwater Biology*, **17**, 341–56.

Ormerod, S.J., Wade, K.R. and Gee, A.S. (1987*b*). Macro-floral assemblages in upland Welsh streams in relation to acidity, and their importance to invertebrates. *Freshwater Biology*, **18**, 545–57.

Oswood, M. W. (1976). Comparative life histories of the *Hydropsyche* in a Montana lake outlet. *American Midland Naturalist*, **96**, 493–97.

Oswood, M.W., Irons III, J.G. and Milner, A. (1995). River and stream ecosystems of Alaska. In *Ecosystems of the world 22. River and stream ecosystems* (ed. C.E. Cushing, K.W. Cummins and G.W. Minshall), pp. 9–32. Elsevier, Amsterdam.

Ottino, P. (1997). Studies on otters in the Araglin Valley, southern Ireland. Unpublished Msc thesis, National University of Ireland.

Otto, C. (1984). Adaptive head coloration in case-making caddis larvae. *Freshwater Biology*, **14**, 317–21.

Otto, C. and Svensson, B. (1976). Consequences of removal of pupae for a population of *Potamophylax cingulatus* (Trichoptera) in a south Swedish stream. *Oikos*, **27**, 40–3.

Otto, C. and Svensson, B.S. (1980). The significance of case material selection for the survival of caddis larvae. *Journal of Animal Ecology*, **49**, 855–65.

Otto, C. and Svensson, B.S. (1981). How do macrophytes growing in or close to water reduce their consumption by aquatic herbivores? *Hydrobiologia*, **78**, 107–12.

Page, L.M. and Schemske, D.W. (1978). The effect of interspecific competition on the distribution and size of darters of the subgenus *Catonotus* (Percidae: *Etheostoma*). *Copeia*, 406–12.

Palmer, M.A. (1992). Incorporating lotic meiofauna into our understanding of faunal transport processes. *Limnology and Oceanography*, **37**, 329–41.

Palmer, M.A., Bely, A.E. and Berg, K.E. (1992). Response of invertebrates to lotic disturbance: a test of the hyporheic refuge hypothesis. *Oecologia*, **89**, 182–94.

Palmer, M.A., Allan, J.D. and Butman, C.A. (1996). Dispersal as a regional process affecting the local dynamics of marine and stream benthic invertebrates. *Trends in Ecology and Evolution*, **11**, 322–6.

Patrick, R. (1964). A discussion of the result of the Catherwood expedition to the Peruvian headwaters of the Amazon. *Internationale Vereinigung für theoretische und angewandte Limnologie*, **15**, 1084–90.

Pearson, R.G. and Jones, N.V. (1987). Short-term movements of chalk-stream invertebrates. *Freshwater Biology*, **18**, 559–568.

Peckarsky, B.L. (1983*a*). Biotic interactions or abiotic limitations? A model of lotic community structure. In *Dynamics of lotic ecosystems* (ed. T.D. Fontaine and S.M. Bartell), pp. 303–23. Ann Arbor Science Publishers, Ann Arbor.

Peckarsky, B.L. (1983*b*). Use of behavioral experiments to test ecological theory in streams. In *Stream ecology* (ed. J.R. Barnes and G.W. Minshall), pp.79–97. Plenum Press, New York.

Peckarsky, B.L. (1986). Colonization of natural substrates by stream benthos. *Canadian Journal of Fisheries and Aquatic Sciences*, **43**, 700–9.

Peckarsky, B.L. and Penton, M.A. (1988). Why do *Ephemerella* nymphs scorpion posture: a 'ghost of predation past'? *Oikos*, **53**, 185–93.

Peckarsky, B.L. and Wilcox, R.S. (1989). Stonefly nymphs use hydrodynamic cues to discriminate between prey. *Oecologia*, **79**, 265–70.

Peckarsky, B.L., Cowan, C.A., Penton, M.A. and Anderson, C. (1993). Sublethal consequences of stream-dwelling predatory stoneflies on mayfly growth and fecundity. *Ecology*, **74**, 1836–46.

Pennak, R.W. (1989). *Fresh-water invertebrates of the United States. Protozoa to Mollusca*, (3rd edn). Wiley, New York.

Petersen, L.B.M. and Petersen, R.C. (1983). Anomalies in hydropsychid capture nets from polluted streams. *Freshwater Biology*, **13**, 185–91.

Petersen, R.C. (1986). In situ particle generation in a southern Swedish stream. *Limnology and Oceanography*, **31**, 423–37.

Peterson, R.C. and Cummins, K.W. (1974). Leaf processing in a woodland stream. *Freshwater Biology*, **4**, 343–68.

Petersen, R.C., Gíslason Jr., G.M. and Petersen, L.B-M. (1995). Rivers of the Nordic countries. In *Ecosystems of the World 22. River and stream ecosystems* (ed. C.E. Cushing, K.W. Cummins and G.W. Minshall), pp. 5295–341. Elsevier, Amsterdam.

Peterson, B., Fry, B., Deegan, L. and Hershey, A. (1993). The trophic significance of epilithic algal production in a fertilized tundra river ecosystem. *Limnology and Oceanography*, **38**, 872–8.

Petts, G.E. (1984). *Impounded rivers*. Wiley, Chichester.

Petts, G.E. and Bickerton, M.A. (1994). Influence of water abstraction on the macroinvertebrate community gradient within a glacial stream system: La Borgne d'Arolla, Valais, Switzerland. *Freshwater Biology*, **32**, (2), 375–86.

Petts, G. and Calow, P. (ed.) (1996). *River biota: diversity and dynamics*. Blackwell, Oxford.

Pinder, L.V. (1985). Studies on Chironomidae in experimental recirculating stream systems. 1. *Orthocladius (Euorthocladius) calvus* Sp. nov. *Freshwater Biology*, **15**, 235–41.

Pinder, L.C.V. (1986). Biology of freshwater Chironomidae. *Annual Review of Entomology*, **31**, 1–23.

Platts, W.S., Megahan, W.F. and Minshall, G.W. (1983). *Methods for evaluating stream, riparian, and biotic conditions*. General Technical Report INT-138, USDA Forest Service, Intermountain Forest and Range Experimental Station, Ogden, UT.

Poff, N.A., Voelz, N.J., Ward, J.V. and Lee, R.E. (1990). Algal colonization under four experimentally controlled current regimes in a high mountain stream. *Journal of the North American Benthological Society*, **9**, 303–8.

Poff, N.L. and Ward, J.V. (1989). Implications of streamflow variability and predictability for lotic community structure: a regional analysis of streamflow patterns. *Canadian Journal of Fisheries and Aquatic Science*, **46**, 1805–18.

Poff, N.L. and Ward, J.V. (1990). Physical habitat template of lotic systems: recovery in the context of historical pattern of spatiotemporal heterogeneity. *Environmental Management*, **14**, 629–45.

Poinar, G.O. (1991). Nematoda and Nematomorpha. In *Ecology and classification of*

North American freshwater invertebrates (ed. J.H. Thorp and A.P. Covich), pp. 249–83. Academic Press, San Diego.

Power, M.E. (1990). Effects of fish in river food webs. *Science*, **250**, 811–14.

Power, M.E. and Matthews, W.J. (1983). Algae-grazing minnows (*Campostoma anomalum*), piscivorous bass (*Micropterus spp.*), and the distribution of attached algae in a small prairie-margin stream. *Oecologia*, **60**, 328–32.

Power, M.E., Matthews, W.J. and Stewart, A.J. (1985). Grazing minnows, piscivorous bass, and stream algae: dynamics of a strong interaction. *Ecology*, **66**, 1448–56.

Power, M.E., Stout, R.J., Cushing, C.E., Harper, P.P., Hauer, F.R., Matthews, W.J. *et al.* (1988). Biotic and abiotic controls in river and stream communities. *Journal of the North American Benthological Society*, **7**, 456–79.

Power, M.E., Parker, M.S. and Wootton, J.T. (1996). Disturbance and food chain length in rivers. In *Food webs. Integration of patterns and dynamics* (ed. G.A. Polis and K.O. Winemiller), pp. 286–97. Chapman and Hall, New York.

Pringle, C.M., Blake, G.A., Covich, A.P. Buzby, K.M. and Finlay, A. (1993). Effects of omnivorous shrimp in a montane tropical stream: sediment removal, disturbance of sessile invertebrates and enhancement of understory algal biomass. *Oecologia*, **93**, 1–11.

Pritchard, G. (1983). Biology of Tipulidae. *Annual Review of Entomology*, **28**, 1–22.

Pritchard, G. (1992). Insects in thermal springs. In *Arthropods of springs, with particular reference to Canada* (ed. D.D. Williams and H.V. Danks), pp. 89–106. *Memoirs of the Entomological Society of Canada*, **155**.

Quammen, D. (1996). *The song of the dodo: island biogeography in an age of extinctions.* Scribner, New York.

Quinn, J.M. and Hickey, C.W. (1994). Hydraulic parameters and benthic invertebrate distributions in two gravel bed New Zealand rivers. *Freshwater Biology*, **32**, 489–500.

Rabinowitz, D. (1981). Seven forms of rarity. In *The biological aspects of rare plant conservation* (ed. H. Synge), pp. 205–17. Wiley, Chichester.

Rader, R.B. and Ward, J.V. (1987). Resource utilization, overlap and temporal dynamics in a guild of mountain stream insects. *Freshwater Biology*, **18**, 521–8.

Radke, R.L. and Kinzie, R.A. (1996). Evidence of a marine larval stage in endemic Hawaiian stream gobies from isolated high-elevation locations. *Transactions of the American Fisheries Society*, **125**, 613–21.

Reice, S.R. (1980). The role of substratum in benthic macroinvertebrate microdistribution and litter decomposition in a woodland stream. *Internationale Vereinigung für theoretische und angewandte Limnologie*, **20**, 1396–400.

Reice, S.R. (1991). Effects of detritus loading and fish predation on leafpack breakdown and benthic macroinvertebrates in a woodland stream. *Journal of the North American Benthological Society*, **10**, 42–56.

Reynolds, C.S. (1994). The role of fluid motion in the dynamics of phytoplankton in lakes and rivers. In *Aquatic ecology: scale pattern and process*, 34th Symposium of the British Ecological Society (ed. P.S. Giller, A.G. Hildrew and D.G. Rafaelli), pp. 141–87. Blackwell, Oxford.

Reynolds, C.S., Carling, P.A. and Beven, K.J. (1991). Flow in river channels: new insight into hydraulic retention. *Archiv für Hydrobiologie*, **121**, 171–9.

Richardson, J.S. (1991). Seasonal food limitation of detritivores in a montane stream: an experimental test. *Ecology*, **72**, 873–87.

Richardson, J.S. and Mackay, R.J. (1991). Lake outlets and the distribution of filter feeders: an assessment of hypotheses. *Oikos*, **62**, 370–80.

Ricklefs, R.E. and Miles, D.B. (1994). Ecological and evolutionary inferences from morphology: an ecological perspective. In *Ecological morphology. Integrative organismal biology*. (ed. P.C. Wainwright and S.M. Reilly), pp. 13–41. University of Chicago Press.

Rosenberg, D. and Resh, V. H. (1993). *Freshwater biomonitoring and benthic macroinvertebrates*. Chapman and Hall, New York.

Rosenzweig, M.L. (1995). *Species diversity in space and time*. Cambridge University Press.

Rosenfeld, J. and Roff, J.C. (1991). Primary production and potential availability of autochthonous carbon in southern Ontario streams. *Hydrobiologia*, **224**, 99–109.

Ross, S.T. (1991). Mechanisms structuring stream fish assemblages: are there lessons from introduced species? *Environmental Biology of Fish*, **30**, 359–68.

Rounick, J.S., Winterbourn, M.J. and Lyon, G.L. (1982). Differential utilization of allochthonous and autochthonous inputs by aquatic invertebrates in some New Zealand streams: a stable carbon isotope study. *Oikos*, **39**, 191–8.

Rundle, S.D. and Hildrew, A.G. (1990). The distribution of micro-arthropods in some southern English chalk-streams: the influence of physiochemistry. *Freshwater Biology*, **23**, 411–32.

Sabater, F., Guasch, H., Marti, E., Armengol, J. and Sabater, S. (1995). The Ter: a Mediterranean river case-study in Spain. In *Ecosystems of the world 22. River and stream ecosystems* (ed. C.E. Cushing, K.W. Cummins and G.W. Minshall), pp. 419–38. Elsevier, Amsterdam.

Sæther, O.A. and Willasen, E. (1987). Four new species of *Diamesa* Meigen, 1835 (Diptera: Chironomidae) from the glaciers of Nepal. *Entomologica Scandinavica*, **29** (suppl.), 189–203.

Samways, M.J. (1994). *Insect conservation biology*. Chapman and Hall, London.

Sattler, W. (1963). Über den Körperbau und Ethologie der Larve und Puppe von *Macronema* Pict. (Hydropsychidae), ein als Larve sich von 'Mikro-Drift' ernährendes Trichopter aus dem Amazongebiet. *Archiv für Hydrobiologie*, **59**, 26–60.

Schlosser, I.J. (1991). Stream fish ecology: a landscape perspective. *BioScience*, **41**, 704–12.

Schoener, T.W. (1974). Resource partitioning in ecological communities. *Science*, **2**, 369–404.

Schreiber, E.S.G. (1995). Long-term patterns of invertebrate stream drift in an Australian temperate stream. *Freshwater Biology*, **33**, 13–25.

Séchan, Y. (1980). Durée du developement des stades préimaginaux de *Simulium sirbanum* Vajime and Dunbar, 1975 à la limite nord de son aire de répartition en Afrique occidentale. *Cahiers ORSTOM, Entomologie médicale et Parasitologie*, **18**, 59–60.

Shannon, J.P., Blinn, D.W. and Stevens, L.E. (1994). Trophic interactions and benthic animal community structure in the Colorado River, Arizona, USA. *Freshwater Biology*, **32**, 213–20.

Sheldon, A.L. (1972). Comparative ecology of *Arcynopteryx* and *Diura* in a California stream. *Archiv für Hydrobiologie*, **69**, 521–46.

Sherman, B.J. and Pinney, H.K. (1971). Benthic algal communities of the Metolius River. *Journal of Phycology*, **7**, 269–73.

Short, R.A. and Maslin, P. (1977). Processing of leaf litter by a stream detritivore: Effect on nutrient availability to collectors. *Ecology*, **58**, 935–8.

Short, R.A., Canton, S.P. and Ward, J.V. (1980). Detrital processing and associated macroinvertebrates in a Colorado mountain stream. *Ecology*, **61**, 727–32.

Sih, A. and Wooster, D.E. (1994). Prey behavior, prey dispersal, and predator impacts on stream prey. *Ecology*, **75**, 1199–207.

Simon, B.M. and Jones, J.G. (1992). Some observations on the absence of bacteria from acid waters in northwest England. *Freshwater Forum*, **2**, 200–11.

Sinclair, B.J. and Marshall, S.A. (1986). The madicolous fauna in southern Ontario. *Proceedings of the Entomological Society of Ontario*, **117**, 9–14.

Sinsabaugh, R.L., Golladay, S.W. and Linkins, A.E. (1991). Comparison of epilithic and epixylic biofilm development in a boreal river. *Freshwater Biology*, **25**, 179–87.

Sinsabaugh, R.L., Weiland, T. and Linkins, A.E. (1992). Enzymic and molecular analysis of microbial communities associated with lotic particulate organic matter. *Freshwater Biology*, **28**, 393–404.

Sioli, H. (1964). General features of the limnology of Amazonia. *Internationale Vereinigung für theoretische und angewandte Limnologie*, **15**, 1053–8.

Sioli, H. (1975). Tropical river: the Amazon. In *River ecology* (ed. B.A. Whitton.), pp. 461–88. University of California Press, Berkeley.

Sjöström, P. (1985a). Territoriality in nymphs of *Dinocras cephalotes* (Plecoptera). *Oikos*, **45**, 353–7.

Sjöström, P. (1985b). Hunting behaviour of the perlid stonefly nymph, *Dinocras cephalotes* (Plecoptera) under different light conditions. *Animal Behaviour*, **33**, 534–40.

Sleigh, M.A., Baldock, B.M. and Baker, J.H. (1992). Protozoan communities in chalk streams. *Hydrobiologia*, **248**, 53–64.

Smith, B.P. (1988). Host-parasite interaction and impact of larval water mites on insects. *Annual Review of Entomology*, **33**, 487–507.

Smith, I. and Lyle, A. (1978). *Distibution of freshwaters in Great Britain*. Institute of Terrestrial Ecology, Edinburgh.

Smith, I.M. and Cook, D.R. (1991). Water mites. In *Ecology and classification of North American freshwater invertebrates* (ed. J.H. Thorp and A.P. Covich), pp. 523–92. Academic Press, San Diego.

Smith, R.F.J. (1992). Alarm signals in fishes. *Reviews in Fish Biology and Fisheries*, **2**, 33–63.

Smith-Cuffney, F.L. and Wallace, J.B. (1987). The influence of microhabitat on availability of drifting invertebrate prey to a net-spinning caddisfly. *Freshwater Biology*, **17**, 91–8.

Smock, L.E., Gladden, J.E., Riekenburg, J.L., Smith, L.C. and Black, C.R. (1992). Lotic macroinvertebrate production in three dimensions: channel surface, hyporheic and floodplain environments. *Ecology*, **73**, 876–886.

Soluk, D.A. (1993). Multiple predator effects: predicting combined functional response of stream fish and invertebrate predators. *Ecology*, **74**, 219–25.

Soluk, D.A. and Richardson, J.S. (1997). The role of stoneflies in enhancing growth of trout: a test of the importance of predator-predator facilitation within a stream community. *Oikos*, **80**, 214–9.

Southwood, T.R.E. (1977). Habitat, the templet for ecological strategies? *Journal of Animal Ecology*, **46**, 337–65.

Spencer, C.N., McClelland, B.R. and Stanford, J.A. (1991). Shrimp stocking, salmon collapse, and eagle displacement. *BioScience*, **41**, 14–21.

Stanford, J.A. and Ward, J.V. (1988). The hyporheic habitat of river ecosystems. *Nature*, **335**, 64–6.

Stanford, J.A. *et al.* (1996). A general protocol for restoration of regulated rivers. *Regulated Rivers*, **12**, 391–413.

Statzner, B. and Borchardt, D. (1994). Longitudinal patterns and processes along streams: modelling ecological responses to physical gradients. In *Aquatic ecology: scale, pattern and process*, 34th Symposium of the British Ecological Society (ed. P.S. Giller, A.G. Hildrew and D.G. Raffaelli), pp.113–40. Blackwell, Oxford.

Statzner, B. and Higler, B. (1985). Questions and comments on the river continuum concept. *Canadian Journal of Fisheries and Aquatic Sciences*, **42**, 1038–44.

Statzner, B. and Higler, B. (1986). Stream hydraulics as a major determinant of benthic invertebrate zonation patterns. *Freshwater Biology*, **16**, 127–39.

Statzner, B. and Holm, T.F. (1982). Morphological adaptions of benthic invertebrates to stream flow—an old question studied by means of a new technique (laser doppler anemometry). *Oecologia*, **53**, 290–2.

Statzner, B. and Holm, T.F. (1989). Morphological adaptation of shape to flow: microcurrents around lotic macroinvertebrates with know Reynolds numbers at quasi-natural flow conditions. *Oecologia*, **78**, 145–57.

Statzner, B. and Kohmann, F. (1995). River and stream ecosystems in Austria, Germany, and Switzerland. In *Ecosystems of the World 22. River and stream ecosystems* (ed. C.E. Cushing, K.W. Cummins and G.W. Minshall), pp. 439–78. Elsevier, Amsterdam.

Statzner, B., Gore, J.A. and Resh, V.H. (1988). Hydraulic stream ecology: observed patterns and potential applications. *Journal of the North American Benthological Society*, **7**, 307–60.

Strahler, A.N. (1952). Dynamic basis of geomorphology. *Geological Society of America Bulletin*, **63**, 1117–42.

Strayer, D. (1983). The effects of surface geology and stream size on freshwater mussel (Bivalvia, Unionidae) distribution in south-eastern Michigan, USA. *Freshwater Biology*, **13**, 253–64.

Strayer, D.L. and Smith, L.C. (1996). Relationships between zebra mussels (*Dreissena polymorpha*) and unionid clams during the early stages of the zebra mussel invasion of the Hudson River. *Freshwater Biology*, **36**, 771–9.

Stewart, K.W. and Stark, B.P. (1988). *Nymphs of North American stonefly genera* (*Plecoptera*), Vol. 12. Thomas Say Foundation, Denton.

Stoneburner, D.L. and Smock, L.A. (1979). Seasonal fluctuations of macro-invertebrate drift in a South Carolina piedmont stream. *Hydrobiologia*, **63**, 49–56.

Suberkropp, K. and Klug, M.J. (1980). The maceration of deciduous leaf litter by aquatic hyphomycetes. *Canadian Journal of Botany*, **58**, 1025–31.

Suren, A.M. (1994). Macroinvertebrate communities of streams in western Nepal: effects of altitude and land use. *Freshwater Biology*, **32**, 323–36.

Sweeney, B.W. (1984). Factors influencing life-history patterns of aquatic insects. In *The Ecology of aquatic insects* (ed. V.H. Resh and D.M. Rosenberg), pp. 56–100. Praeger, New York.

Sweeney, B.W. and Vannote, R.L. (1982). Population synchrony in mayflies: a predator satiation hypothesis. *Evolution*, **36**, 810–21.

Tank J.L. and Winterbourn, M.J. (1995). Biofilm development and invertebrate colonization of wood in four New Zealand streams of contrasting pH. *Freshwater Biology*, **34**, 303–15.

Taylor, W.D. and Sanders, R.W. (1991). Protozoa. In *Ecology and classification of North American freshwater invertebrates* (ed. J.H. Thorp and A.P. Covich), pp. 37–93, Academic Press, San Diego.

Tavares-Cromar, A.F. and Williams, D.D. (1996). The importance of temporal resolution in food web analysis: evidence from a detritus-based stream. *Ecological Monographs*, **66**, 91–113.

Tesch, F-W. (1977). *Biology and management of anguillid eels*. Chapman and Hall, London.

Thienemann, A. (1950). Verbreitungsgeschichte der Süsswassertierwelt Europas. *Die Binnengewässer*, Stuttgart, **18**, 1–809.

Thorp, J.H. and Covich., A.P. (ed.) (1991). *Ecology and classification of North American freshwater invertebrates*. Academic Press, San Diego.

Thorpe, W.H. (1950). Plastron respiration in aquatic insects. *Biological Reviews*, **25**, 334–90.

Thorup, J. (1966). Substrate type and its value as a basis for the delimitation of bottom fauna communities in running waters. Special publications of the Pymaluning Laboratory, University of Pittsburgh, **4**, 59–74.

Thrush Jr., W.J. (1979). The effects of area and surface complexity on the struc-ture and formation of stream benthic communities. Unpublished MSc thesis. Virginia Polytechnic Institute and State University, Blacksburg, VA.

Thurmen, E.M. (1985). *Organic geochemistry of natural waters*. Martin Nijhoff/Dr. W. Junk Publishers, Dordrecht.

Tikkanen, P., Muotka, T. and Huhta, A. (1996). Fishless-stream mayflies ex-press behavioural flexibility in response to predatory fish. *Animal Behaviour*, **51**, 1391–9.

Tikkanen, P., Muotka, T. and Juntunen, A. (1997). The roles of active predator choice and prey vulnerability in determining the diet of predatory stonefly (Plecoptera) nymphs. *Journal of Animal Ecology*, **66**, 36–48.

Tokeshi, M. (1994). Community ecology and patchy freshwater habitats. In

Aquatic ecology: scale, pattern and process, 34th Symposium of the British Ecological Society (ed. P.S. Giller, A.G. Hildrew and D.G. Raffaelli), pp. 63–91. Blackwell, Oxford.

Tolkamp, H.H. (1980). *Organism-substrate relationships in lowland streams*. Agricultural Research Report, 907. Agricultural University, Wageningen, The Netherlands.

Townsend, C.R. and Hildrew, A.G. (1976). Field experiments on the drifting, colonization and continuous redistribution of stream benthos. *Journal of Animal Ecology*, **45**, 759–72.

Townsend, C.R. and Hildrew, A.G. (1979). Form and function of the prey catching net of *Plectrocnemia conspersa* larvae (Trichoptera). *Oikos*, **33**, 412–18.

Townsend, C.R., Hildrew, A.G. and Francis, J. (1983). Community structure in some southern English streams: the influence of physicochemical factors, *Freshwater Biology*, **13**, 521–44.

Townsend, C.R., Hildrew, A.G. and Schofield, K. (1987). Persistence of stream invertebrate communities in relation to environmental variability. *Journal of Animal Ecology*, **56**, 597–613.

Tunney, H., Carlton, O.T. and Magette, W.L. (1996). Trends in phosphorus fertiliser use, soil reserves, animal manures and managment strategies to reduce loss to water. In *Disturbance and recovery of ecological systems* (ed. P.S. Giller and A.A. Myers), pp. 155–62. Royal Irish Academy, Dublin.

Twomey, H. and Giller, P.S. (1991). The effects of catastrophic flooding on the benthos and fish of a tributary of the River Araglin, Co. Cork. In *Irish rivers: biology and management* (ed. M.W. Steer), pp. 59–81. Royal Irish Academy, Dublin.

Tyler, S.J. and Ormerod, S.J. (1994). *The dippers*. Poyser, London.

Ulfstrand, S. (1968). Bentic animal communities in Lapland streams. *Oikos*, **10** (suppl.), 1–120.

Ulfstrand, S., Nilsson, L.M. and Stergar, A. (1974). Composition and diversity of benthic species collectives colonizing implanted substrates in a south Swedish stream. *Entomologica Scandinavica*, **5**, 115–22.

UNESCO (1978). *World water balance and water resources of the earth*. UNESCO Press, Paris.

Vaillant, F. (1956). Recherches sur la faune madicole (hygropétrique s.l.) de France, de Corse et d'Afrique du Nord. *Mémoires Musée Natural Histoire National Paris, N.S.A.*, **11**, 1–258.

van den Brink, F.W. (1994). *Impact of hydrology on floodplain lake ecosystems and the lower Rhine and Meuse*. CIP-Gegevens Koninklijke Bibliotheek, The Hague.

van den Brink, F.W., van der Velde, G. and Chzemier, W.G. (1990). The faunistic composition of the freshwater section of the River Rhine in the Netherlands: present state and changes since 1900. In *Biologie des Rheins*, Vol. 1 (ed. R Kinzelbach and G. Friedrich), pp. 191–216. Gustav Fisher Verlag, Stuttgart.

van der Kamp, G. (1995). The hydrogeology of springs in relation to the bio-diversity of spring fauna: a review. *Journal of the Kansas Entomological Society*, **68** (suppl.), 4–17.

Vannote, R.L., Minshall, G.W. , Cummins, K.W. , Sedell, J.R. and Cushing, C.E.

(1980). The river continuum concept. *Canadian Journal of Fisheries and Aquatic Science*, **37**, 130–7.

Vepsäläinen, K. and Nummelin, M. (1985). Female territoriality in the waterstriders *Gerris najas* and *G. cinereus*. *Annales Zoologici Fennici*, **22**, 433–9.

Vinson, M.R. and Hawkins, C.P. (1998). Biodiversity of stream insects: variation at local, basin, and regional scales. *Annual Review of Entomology*, **43**, 271–93.

Vogel, S. (1994). *Life in moving fluids. The physical biology of flow.* Princeton University Press, New Jersey.

Vuori, K.-M. (1996). Acid-induced acute toxicity of aluminium to three species of filter feeding caddis larvae (Trichoptera, Arctopsychidae and Hydropsychidae). *Freshwater Biology*, **35**, 179–87.

Wallace, J.B. and Anderson, N.H. (1996). Habitat, life history and behavioral adaptations of aquatic insects. In *An introduction to the aquatic insects of North America* (ed. R.W. Merritt and K.W. Cummins), pp. 41–73. Kendall/Hunt, Dubuque, IA.

Wallace, J.B. *et al.* (1997). Multiple trophic levels of a forest stream linked to terrestrial water inputs. *Science*, **277**, 102–4.

Wallace, J.B., Webster, J.R. and Cuffney, T.F. (1982). Stream detritus dynamics: regulation by invertebrate consumers. *Oecologia*, **53**, 197–200.

Wallace, J.B., Webster, J.R. and Lowe, R.L. (1992). High-gradient streams of the Appalachians. In *Biodiversity of Southeastern United States aquatic communities* (ed. C.T. Hackney, S.M. Adams and W.A. Martin), pp. 133–91. Wiley, New York.

Wallace, J.B., Grubaugh, J.W. and Whiles, M.R. (1996). Biotic indices and stream ecosystem processes: results from an experimental study. *Ecological Applications*, **6**, 140–51.

Wallace, R.L. and Snell, T.W. (1991). Rotifera. In *Ecology and classification of North American freshwater invertebrates* (ed. J.H. Thorp and A.P. Covich), pp. 187–248. Academic Press, San Diego.

Wallace, J.B., Webster, J.R. and Woodall, W.R. (1977). The role of filter feeders in flowing waters. *Archiv für Hydrobiologie*, **79**, 506–32.

Ward, J.V. (1985). Thermal characteristics of running waters. *Hydrobiologia*, **125**, 31–46.

Ward, J.V. (1986). Altitudinal zonation in a Rocky Mountain stream. *Archiv für Hydrobiologie*, **2**, 133–99.

Ward, J.V. (1989). The four-dimensional nature of lotic ecosystems. *Journal of the North American Benthological Society*, **8**, 2–8.

Ward, J.V. (1992*a*). *Aquatic insect ecology.* 1. Biology and habitat. Wiley, New York.

Ward, J.V. (1992*b*). River Ecosystems. *Encyclopedia of Earth System Science*, 4. Academic Press.

Washington, H.G. (1984). Diversity, biotic and similarity indices, a review with special relevance to aquatic ecosystems. *Water Research*, **18**, 653–94.

Waters, T.F. (1972). The drift of stream insects. *Annual Review of Entomology*, **17**, 253–72.

Watson, D.J. and Balon, E.K. (1984). Ecomorphological analysis of fish taxocenes in rain-forest streams of northern Borneo. *Journal of Fish Biology*, **25**, 371–84.

Watson, J.A.L., Theischinger, G. and Abbey, H.M. (1991). *The Australian dragon-*

flies. A guide to the identification, distributions and habitats of Australian Odonata. CSIRO, Canberra.

Webb, B.W. and Walling, D.E. (1993). Temporal variability in the impact of river regulation on thermal regime and some biological implications. *Freshwater Biology*, **29**, 167–82.

Webster, J. (1981). Biology and ecology of aquatic hyphomycetes. In *The fungal community. Its organisation and role in the ecosystem* (ed. P. Wicklow and G. Carroll), pp 681–91. Marcel Dekker, New York.

Webster, J.R. and Benfield, E.F. (1986). Vascular plant breakdown in freshwater ecosystems. *Annual Review of Ecology and Systematics*, **17**, 567–94.

Webster, J.R. and Meyer, J.L. (1997). Stream organic matter budgets—introduction. *Journal of the North American Benthological Society*, **16**, 3–43.

Webster, J.R., Wallace, J.B. and Benfield, E.F. (1995). Organic processes in streams of the eastern United States. In *Ecosystems of the world 22. River and stream ecosystems*. (ed. C.E. Cushing, K.W. Cummins and G.W. Minshall), pp. 117–87. Elsevier, Amsterdam.

Weissenberger, J., Spatz, H.-Ch., Emanns, A. and Schwoerbel, J. (1991). Measurement of lift and drag forces in the mN range experienced by benthic arthropods at flow volocities below 1.2 m s^{-1}. *Freshwater Biology*, **25**, 21–31.

Welcomme, R.L. (1979). *Fisheries ecology of floodplain rivers*. Longman, London.

Welcomme, R.L. (1985). *River fisheries*. FAO Fisheries Technical Paper No. 262. Food and Agriculture Organization, Rome.

Westlake, D.F. and Ladle, M. (1995). River and stream ecosystems of Great Britain. In *Ecosystems of the world 22. River and stream ecosystems* (ed. C.E. Cushing, K.W. Cummins and G.W. Minshall), pp. 343–88. Elsevier, Amsterdam.

Wetzel, R. (1983). *Limnology*, (2nd edn). Saunders, New York.

Wetzel, R.G. and Ward, A.K. (1992). Primary production. In *Rivers handbook*, Vol. 1 (ed. P. Calow and G.E. Petts), pp. 354–69. Blackwell, London.

White, D.S. and Brigham, W.U. (1996). Aquatic Coleoptera. In *An introduction to the aquatic insects of North America*. 3rd Edition. (ed. R.W. Merritt and K.W. Cummins), pp. 399–473. Kendall/Hunt, Dubuque, IA.

Wiggins, G.B. (1973). A contribution to the biology of caddisflies (Trichoptera) in temporary pools. *Life Sciences Contributions of Royal Ontario Museum*, **88**, 1–28.

Wilcox, R.S. (1972). Communication by surface waves. Mating behavior of a water strider (Gerridae). *Journal of Comparative Physiology*, **80**, 255–66.

Wilcox, R.W. and Ruckdeschel, T. (1982). Food threshold territoriality in a water strider (*Gerris remigis*). *Behavioural and Ecological Sociobiology*, **11**, 85–90.

Wiley, M.J. and Kohler, S.L. (1980). Positioning changes of mayfly nymphs due to behavioral regulation of oxygen consumption. *Canadian Journal of Zoology*, **58**, 618–22.

Wiley, M.J. and Kohler, S.L. (1981). An assessment of biological interactions in a epilithic stream community using time-lapse cinematography. *Hydrobiologia*, **78**, 183–88.

Wiley, M.J. and Kohler, S.L. (1984). Behavioural adaptations of aquatic insects. In *The ecology of aquatic insect*, (ed. V.H. Resh and D.M. Rosenberg), pp. 101–33. Praeger, New York.

Wiley, M.J. and Warren, G.L. (1992). Territory abandonment, theft, and recycling by a lotic grazer—a foraging strategy for hard times. *Oikos*, **63**, 495–505.

Williams, D.D. and Danks, H.V. (ed.) (1992). *Arthropods of springs, with particular reference to Canada. Memoirs of the Entomological Society of Canada*, **155**, 1–217.

Williams, D.D., Williams, N. and Hogg, I. (1995). Life history plasticity of *Nemoura trisinosa* (Plecoptera: Nemouridae) along a permanent-temporary water habitat gradient. *Freshwater Biology*, **34**, 155–63.

Willoughby, L. and Mappin, R. (1988). The distribution of *Ephemerella ignita* (Ephemeroptera) in streams: the role of pH and food resources. *Freshwater Biology*, **19**, 145–56.

Wilson, D.S., Leighton, M. and Leighton, D. (1979). Interference competition in a tropical ripple bug (Hemiptera: Veliidae). *Biotropica*, **10**, 302–6.

Wilson, E.O. (1992). *The diversity of life*. Belknap Harvard, Cambridge, MA.

Wilzbach, M.A., Cummins, K.W. and Knapp, R. (1988). Towards a functional classification of stream invertebrate drift. *Internationale Vereinigung für theoretische und angewandte Limnologie*, **23**, 1244–64.

Winterbottom, J.H., Orton, S.E. and Hildrew, A.G. (1997). Field experiments on the mobility of benthic invertebrates in a southern English stream. *Freshwater Biology*, **38**, 37–47.

Winterbourn, M.J. (1995). Rivers and streams of New Zealand. In *Ecosystems of the world 22. River and stream ecosystems* (ed. C.E. Cushing, K.W. Cummins and G.W. Minshall), pp. 695–716. Elsevier, Amsterdam.

Winterbourn, M.J. and Townsend, C.R. (1991). Streams and rivers: one-way flow systems. In *Fundamentals of aquatic ecology* (ed. R.S.K. Barnes and K.H. Mann), pp. 230–42. Blackwell, Oxford.

Winterbourn, M.J., Cowie, B. and Rounick, J.S. (1984). Food resources and ingestion patterns of insects along a West Coast, South Island river system. *New Zealand Journal of Marine and Freshwater Research*, **15**, 321–28.

Winterbourn, M.J., Hildrew, A.G. and Box, A. (1985). Structure and grazing of stone surface organic layers in some acid streams of southern England. *Freshwater Biology*, **15**, 363–74.

Wolda, H. (1987). Seasonality and the community. In *Organisation of communities past and present* (ed. J. Gee and P. Giller), pp. 69–98. Blackwell, Oxford.

Wooster, D. (1994). Predator impacts on stream benthic prey. *Oecologia*, **99**, 7–15.

Wooster, D. and Sih, A. (1995). A review of the drift and activity responses of stream prey to predator presence. *Oikos*, **73**, 3–8.

Wotton, R.S. (1988). Very high secondary production at a lake outlet. *Freshwater Biology*, **20**, 341–6.

Wotton, R.S. (1996). Colloids, bubbles, and aggregates—a perspective on their role in suspension feeding. *Journal of the North American Benthological Society*, **15**, 127–35.

Wotton, R.S., Joicey, C. and Malmqvist, B. (1996). Spiralling of particles by suspension feeders in a small lake-outlet stream. *Canadian Journal of Zoology*, **74**, 758–61.

Wotton, R.S., Malmqvist, B., Muotka, T. and Larsson, K. (1998). Fecal pellets from a dense aggregation of suspension feeders: and example of ecosystem engineering in a stream. *Limnology and Oceanography*, **43**

WRI (World Resource Institute) (1992). *World resources 1992*. WRI, Washington, DC.

Yodzis, P. (1989). *Introduction to theoretical ecology*. Harper and Row, New York.

Yount, J.D. and Niemi, G.J. (1990). Recovery of lotic communities and eco-systems from disturbance—a narrative review of case studies. *Environmental Management*, **14**, 547–69.

Zaret, T.M. and Rand, A.S. (1971). Competition in tropical stream fishes: support for the competitive exclusion principle. *Ecology*, **52**, 336–42.

Zhang, Y. and Malmqvist, B. (1996). Relationships between labral fan morph-ology and habitat in North Swedish blackfly larvae (Diptera: Simuliïdae). *Biological Journal of the Linnean Society*, **59**, 261–80.

Zhang, Y., Malmqvist, B. and Englund, G. (1998) Ecological processes affecting community structure of blackfly larvae: a regional study. *Journal of Applied Ecology* (in press).

Ziegler, D.D. and Stewart, K.W. (1977). Drumming behavior of eleven Nearctic stonefly (Plecoptera) species. *Annals of the Entomological Society of America*, **70**, 495–505.

Index